DIARY of an OD MAN

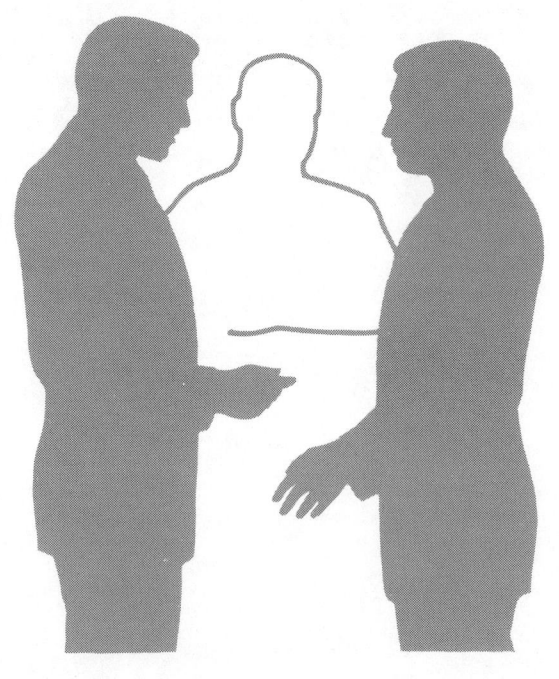

DIARY of an OD MAN

Dr. Robert R. Blake
Dr. Jane Srygley Mouton

 Gulf Publishing Company, Book Division, Houston, Texas

Diary of an OD Man
Copyright© 1976 by Gulf Publishing Company, Houston, Texas. All rights reserved. This book, or parts thereof, may not be reproduced in any form without permission of the publisher.

**Library of Congress
Catalog Card Number
75-18202
ISBN 0-87201-169-0**

Contents

Preface ix

1 Organization Development
  Begins at Lakeside 1

2 The Union Throws Down
  the Gauntlet 13

3 After Listening, What? 22

4 The First Bargaining
  Session 30

5 The Crane Crisis 38

6 Attacking Problems on Two Fronts:
  Bargaining and Development 45

7 A Time for Review and
  Target Setting 53

8 Headquarters Intervenes 63

9 Bargaining and OD Under External
  Conditions 78

10 The Great Headquarters
   Reorganization 87

11 Contract Complications and
   Management Mentalities 95

12 In and Around Both Camps 111

13 Give and Take 120

14 Win—Lose Relationships Within
   Top Teams 128

15	Plans and Predictions Which Shape Outcomes	135
16	Decentralization: Myth or Reality	145
17	The Prospects Worsen	150
18	Grappling With Internal and External Problems	162
19	The Union Comes on Strong	173
20	Promoting Progress Amid Storm Warnings	185
21	Onward to the Summit	196
22	The Summit Needn't be the Ceiling	207
23	More Bargaining	213
24	Let's Impress Headquarters	224
25	Limbo and Ferment	228
26	Smoke	243
27	My Mini-Lecture to Headquarters	249
28	Pickup from the Down Side	255
29	A New Year Begins	265
30	Switchback to a Settlement	278
31	Pecking and Packaging	291
32	Dan on the Carpet	302
33	Change Becomes Official	315
34	Transition and OD Theory	326
35	The End of an Era	337
36	The End is a New Beginning	346
	Afterword	355

Preface

This diary describes organization development activities aimed toward organization excellence. The setting is a large manufacturing plant which employed about 800 managers and several thousand wage people.

The diary deals with problems which have plagued industrial society for decades and which are becoming increasingly significant as free enterprise organizations come under greater challenge for both productivity and social responsibility. It offers suggestions for how changes needed to reduce or solve some of these problems may be brought about.

How Was It Written?

I joined the Lakeside plant as an internal OD man and remained there for almost three years. It was my purpose to intervene with individuals and groups whenever I detected something that was contradictory to sound behavioral science principles. In this way, it was presumed managers and workers alike would become more aware of what they were doing; and of alternatives for doing better; sounder decisions would be made and better implementation would result.

Steady progress toward corporate excellence was the goal.

Each night on returning to my apartment, I dictated the important happenings and personal interventions of that day. I also reviewed the principles on which my interventions were based. I frequently made predictions as to what the consequences of my interventions might be. Later, I recorded what actually unfolded. These dictations were sent to Jane Srygley Mouton who, as a "neutral" outsider, listened to them and evaluated what was going on. During this period I was on leave of absence from The University of Texas where Jane remained a professor. Periodically I returned and we would review together what I had been doing and she would suggest alternative possibilities of interventions for my consideration during the next period. Since there were no precedents for how to do OD-types of interventions, this opportunity of continuous consultation with a colleague hastened the emergence of OD and the techniques of intervention which are now somewhat typical of OD men. Though the story is a Blake diary, it was truly a Blake/Mouton undertaking.

Persons, places, and products have been changed by using different names. Otherwise, the text is a blow-by-blow account of what happened as seen through our eyes. Approval to report this work was one of the conditions in accepting the assignment.

It is necessary to know something about the cast of characters and organizations to sense the flow of the diary. These are:

ERA: World headquarters
EPOCH: Headquarters of the domestic U.S. company
Lakeside: A manufacturing plant in the Midwest manned by approximately 800 managers and several thousand wage people
Quinn Morton: Plant manager
Van Gray: The general superintendent
Wes Stratton: The personnel manager
IEW: A wage union at Lakeside
Dan Ives: The IEW union president

Although the total number of characters approaches fifty, these are the most predominant. Quinn, Van, Wes, Dan, and some eight other "foreground" characters are engaged in alternately painful, exciting, humorous, and poignant aspects of a search for higher-quality resolutions of barriers to corporate excellence.

The diary begins on July 1 and goes through an eight-month period. The actual duration of my work at Lakeside was longer, but most of the significant OD activities are recorded here.

The story has a naturally unfolding plot, continued tension, and a difficult-to-predict denouement. Three themes run through it. One is management's attempt to convert a win-lose battle with the union into a problem-solving orientation that would satisfy both the company's need for efficiency and the wage earners' needs for security. Another is the effort to increase the quality of collaboration and cooperation among managers as they went about solving long- and short-range management problems which arose from market pressures, product quality, new technology, and raw materials availabilities. The third is concerned with how pressures imposed upon Lakeside by its headquarters often constituted "silent" forces that kept management continuously vacillating between one course of action which was "best" in terms of local circumstances and another which was congruent with wide corporate interests.

From a personal point of view, this diary records the unfolding of the idea of an internal OD man. It fills in details needed to understand the history of OD and what may become an important way of strengthening human institutions.

Our appreciation is expressed to Freddie Little Groveton McCann, who worked on the original manuscript, and R.C. Tillam, who transformed the documentation into the present story form.

Robert R. Blake
Jane Srygley Mouton

January, 1976

DIARY of an OD MAN

1
Organization Development Begins at Lakeside

Quinn Morton, top manager of Lakeside, a big manufacturing plant, came to a behavioral science seminar where I was an instructor. He wasn't in my group so I didn't get to know him personally at the time. Yet, because I took a lot of responsibility for lectures during general sessions, he got to know something about my thinking.

The last Thursday evening after dinner, he and I began talking about the week's learning. He said he was impressed with some of the issues we had focused on because they represented the kinds of dilemmas he was trying to deal with day after day.

As we continued talking, an idea began to take shape. He finally put it into words. He said, "Look, Bob, would you be interested in coming to Lakeside for two or three years to help us put these principles into practice and so increase our effectiveness as an organization? Our goal would be to see how good you can make a company when you really go all out to make it *excellent*."

That was the kind of a challenge that doesn't come to a university professor every day. I was convinced that behavioral science principles had significant implications, not only for increasing productivity, but also for increasing the gratification that people receive from their work. I said, "Quinn, I'd like to think that one over. It's too big a question for a 'yes' or 'no' right off the top of my head. I'd like to talk with my family and my colleagues, and then I'll be back in touch with you by the middle of next week."

I did this, and the Lakeside project came into being. Two stages of development were involved. First, several hundred managerial personnel went to seminars to learn key theories of behavioral science regarding individual, group, and intergroup factors influencing action in problem solving. The idea was that before people could really think constructively in terms of organization excellence they ought to examine and understand fundamental ideas of conflict, teamwork, candor, and so on.

The second stage of the project was for me to move physically into the company with a view to getting the principles that had been learned in the seminars applied to the operational problem-solving life of Lakeside. For about two months I did an initial study of the organization and interviewed many of the people I had gotten to know during the training program. The absence of precedents for this situation marked the beginning of OD.

From the very outset, I had specified conditions under which I would join the organization. It was agreed that if I joined, I would in no way involve myself in personnel evaluation. I wanted no part in trying to influence reconstruction of the power system in terms of "which people should be placed in what roles." I had a clear reason, based on systematic behavioral science criteria, for adopting this approach. This was that, to a substantial degree, the problems of an organization are not to be found "inside" people, but are more closely related to organization-wide assumptions as to how people should relate with one another, and to attitudes existing between groups. Therefore, my contribution would be to help people directly in their relationships with one another; to help reform interpersonal attitudes within groups; and to help resolve problems between groups. I also indicated I wanted no company car, office, telephone, or any other symbols that might imply I was occupying a position within Lakeside's organizational format.

I joined the organization under these circumstances. For some time, initially, it was difficult for Quinn to adjust to my presence without forever asking me with whom I was working and on what problems I was engaged. Frequently he quizzed me on these points, but on each occasion I referred him back to our earlier agreement. I said I appreciated his need to monitor my performance, but on the other hand he should appreciate *my* problem of ensuring that the confidences and secrets presently being entrusted to me would continue to be made available. This would be the case only if I maintained the conditions of non-reporting that we had previously agreed upon. Eventually he came to accept this.

By taking this approach, I was able to become active in any part of the organization to which I could attach myself. Wherever I could gain access, I was free to do whatever I wanted. First, I became a member of a special one-day-a-week meeting in the Engineering Department. Then, as labor contract bargaining got underway, I regularly attended the preparatory conferences where the management team members were briefed on the technical points involved in upcoming sessions. I sat in at management's post-bargaining evaluation meetings as well. In all of these situations my only basis for participation was in terms of questioning or commenting upon attitudes, assumptions, and process problems. My journal of ongoing events picks up from here.

Current Battle Lines at Lakeside

The situation at Lakeside on July 1 is one where the management-union battle between efficiency and security emphases, respectively, is dangerously close to the jugular of institutional survival. Managers say that Lakeside's profit margin is much too narrow. Without increased efficiency, the plant may go under. Owing to management's past efforts to gain greater profit via extensive layoffs, "craft consolidation"[1] for greater work-scheduling flexibility, and the automation of tasks formerly done by people, the threat to the security and dignity of workers is close to an all-time high. Union demands, which sometimes run head-on into management's pressures for profitable production, are more extensive than ever. Unless there can be a positive resolution of this state of warfare, the plant may not be able to justify its existence. Will Lakeside lose out because of its current labor-management deadlock and be forced to close its doors and bow out in favor of other units which, at this stage in the game, retain a competitive advantage?

Some background description of Lakeside and its troubles may help to put the total problem in perspective. Why, indeed, is there such a malignant situation here? The problem can be stated from three standpoints: (a) as seen by management; (b) as seen by the union and the work force; and (c) as seen by headquarters.

Management's Perspective: Pressures for Profit

Management sees a series of problems with the key issue being how to become increasingly efficient in order to look better in the eyes of Headquarters. To stay in business, Lakeside must contribute a profit. Efficiency[2] is the answer. There are several reasons why Lakeside is having more difficulty than other plants in meeting efficiency criteria.

One is Lakeside's location in a high-cost real estate area where taxes skim a significant margin off the profit. High taxes have forced many organizations to shift their locations, an option that may be open to Lakeside. Additionally, competing production centers, located at distant points, are closer to the sources of raw materials. Consequently, these locations enjoy a distinct competitive advantage because heavy transportation expenses are not included in their production costs. They can process products, ship the more lucrative lines to distant points, and still retain a competitive advantage. Less remunerative lines can be distributed locally from the point of production to reduce transportation expense.[3]

The profit squeeze at Lakeside is also related to the cost of labor in this particular area of the Midwest as compared to other parts of the country where labor costs are less. To obtain labor, the company must compete for the same people as, for example, the construction trade. Because "construction" cannot be shipped from a distant point but must be done on the spot, workers in that industry tend to be employed in the Lakeside area at the rates they demand, or else there is no construction. This is a fact of the local labor market Lakeside has to live with. It has to meet the costs stemming from interindustry market competition to retain its work force.

An additional consideration is that Lakeside is a long established unit of an old blue-chip organization. To help keep a stable work force, an excellent benefit program has been built up. People here tend to be "in for life;" they do not want to leave. This is true for managerial personnel as well as for the work force. It is a good place to work. People feel pride when they say, "I work for Lakeside." But now the expenses of high fringe benefits are said to have eroded Lakeside's profit picture relative to other comparable plants.

From management's perspective, then, Lakeside's profit margin is wafer-thin. If things get much worse, Headquarters might decide it would be unwise to continue the heavy investment in Lakeside, in view of the insufficient rate of return.[4]

Labor's Perspective: Arbitrary Actions and Threats to Membership

From the standpoint of management, then, everything points compellingly to the need to become more profitable. During the post-war years, management has tried to move in these directions. It has had heavy layoffs, invoked conditions of work flexibility against the wishes of the skilled-labor force, and in many other ways had made strenuous efforts to stay out of the accountant's red ink. As a result, wage personnel have become angry and insecure. Layoffs, craft consolidation, pushing for production, and many of the other things necessary to retain efficiency can strike at the very heart of employees' security and turn their thoughts and emotions toward a union for protection.

The industrial worker, traditionally, is not thought of by management as a whole man, but as a hand to run the machine. A man's services are purchased for what management thinks they will contribute to the efficient use of equipment and materials. When his services are no longer seen as contributing to efficiency—for example, when he is getting old and slow, or when newly introduced technical processes no longer require his presence—he is let go.

Under these circumstances *seniority* and its prerogatives which spell security will seem highly valuable to him. When workmen start thinking about security they soon begin asking, "How can we be sure we can keep our jobs?" If a man's job isn't safe after years of service, what security does he have? The seniority provision is a security "must" in most workers' minds. It's something to hang onto if things don't go well. It can protect you more the older you get. To wage earners, these are important considerations.

The way that people try to achieve security and personal dignity, when they can't get these directly as individuals, is by joining together. A union is formed to procure and maintain security and dignity. To accomplish such objectives, the workers' representatives will singlemindedly press toward them, sometimes with scant regard for management's emphases on efficiency, productivity, and profit. To preserve security in an era of technological change and economic fluctuations, employees want a seniority system which ensures that the first man in is the last man to be laid off. In addition, they want the senior man to be the first to be elevated to a new post. But if seniority rules are strict and rigid, the company is sometimes obligated to use people who lack know-how to do vital things. To management, this is an extremely inefficient way to do business, though in the minds of wage people, gaining a livelihood takes precedence. A couple of hundred years ago, the major innovation was to replace hands with machines. Now giant strides are being made toward replacing heads with machines.

Over the years, management of Lakeside has had the coveted opportunity of working with an independent union, the IEW. The situation is enviable because, to the degree it knew how, this union has been responsive to the immediate pressures acting on management. However, when layoffs, work flexibility, and productivity pressures came along in quick succession, the mounting anxieties and resentments of its membership were just enough to trigger the union into aggressive action. It felt it needed additional power. One way to gain this was to consider and perhaps threaten affiliation with an international union. To have an independent union looking toward international affiliation is quite threatening to Lakeside management. In this way, the IEW confronted the management with a challenge, and widened and deepened their intergroup chasm. Accusations, counter-accusations, criticisms, counter-criticisms, threats, and counter-threats have been everyday dynamics of the relationship.

In the recent past, a union election took place in which Lakeside management exercised substantial influence by going over the heads of the incumbent union officers to propagandize union members directly. To some managers this seemed a natural extension of what, during contract negotiations, is called "bargaining with the people." They gave maximum informal and other support to help a particular slate of candidates defeat incumbent union officials who favored international affiliation. In spite of management's leanings, the incumbents won.

The Shadow of Headquarters

The immediate context and focal point of conflict is the bargaining room in which the management bargaining committee meets with IEW delegates. Leading the union contingent are three of the reelected international sympathizers. There are, however, other significant attitudes that need to be clearly seen and evaluated as factors in the intergroup conflict. The EPIC headquarters casts a shadow over the entire situation. Unless one is far enough away from the local scene, historically and geographically, the shadow is difficult to assess.

The historical experience of EPIC as a headquarters corporation with a number of production centers, including Lakeside, has played an important part in defining current attitudes. The dominant theme is one of intense corporate pride, both in product accomplishment and in terms of human relations.

EPIC is proud of its past growth and its contributions to the nation's economy in terms of efficiency and productivity. It has gained eminence, not only in day-by-day operations but also by reason of its performance in national emergencies. Such was true during World War II when it received government merit awards for outstanding services. EPIC also has a distinguished track record for developing a wide range of profitable products produced at a volume sufficient to make them widely available to the nation's consumers. There has been substantial progress in technological advancement, stemming from new products that EPIC has introduced and the new processes it has engineered. By and large, it is pleased with its long-term accomplishments in terms of products, profits, and innovations.

This company also has another and more recent source of pride. Back in the 1920's, EPIC suffered a traumatic strike in which blood was spilled and lives lost. Here was an industrial conflict which erupted into physical warfare and deeply disturbed the company. In EPIC's history this one incident, perhaps more than any other, helped to foster a corporate conscience with heightened awareness of people. The question formulated at that time remains as a background consideration in managing the company today. It is, "How do we relate to our people so that they feel pride and pleasure in being EPIC employees?"

Thus, EPIC's conscience supports the belief that there is a better-than-traditional way for a management to relate to its work force. Through years of trial and error—and eventually through planned effort—there emerged the idea of the *independent* organization of wage people collaborating with a *decentralized* management for joint investigation, study, analysis, and solution of problems of common concern. This concept of local problem solving has been nurtured, fostered, and matured in most of the company's far-flung units. The ideal and sometimes typical picture is of independent unions and decentralized managements working together harmoniously, and constructively. This positive state of affairs leads Headquarters executives to feel that they have found a way to solve problems in a mutually acceptable manner; one which brings the greatest satisfaction and security to all.

It is satisfying to Headquarters' decision makers to work with a production center characterized not only by effectiveness and productivity with profit but also evidences of good labor-management relations. But at the plant level this is not an easy combination to achieve. It would be easier to push singlemindedly for efficiency or singlemindedly to promote employee satisfaction. Yet in periodic personal reviews, a measure of "the effective EPIC manager" is to be able to accomplish both in an integrated way.

However, an outsider notices something else. Efficiency and good relations are not a "seamless web" at Lakeside. A frequent practice is to manage according to the "pendulum theory." This is based on the notion that efficiency and satisfaction can't be obtained at the same time; there can only be one or the other. A campaign for efficiency is conducted until, eventually, it is obtained. Then, if that campaign has produced too much disturbance, managers swing to the other side and concentrate on the problems generated during the efficiency-drive period. This time, productivity may suffer while harmony is promoted. After employee feelings of indignity and insecurity have been relieved, managers take another notch in their belts and shoot for greater efficiency again. In time, this second swing toward the efficiency pointer will be completed, and its side effects of reducing dignity and security must be attended to again. So the pendulum swings back and forth, from "hard" to "soft," in a never-ending alternation.

This way of managing is disquieting to Headquarters officials. They don't like it because the operation is not simultaneously smooth, coordinated, and effective in all of its dimensions. Nonetheless, many of EPIC's production centers have been swinging from hard to soft to hard again in the last five years; a period during which there have been tremendous pressures to improve efficiency, which in turn have provoked dissension and a concentration of counter-pressures from the unions. In several EPIC operating units, satisfactory states of efficiency have been achieved, and now strenuous efforts for restoring dignity and security and good labor relations are underway. Lakeside is one of these.

In some of these operating segments, it would appear that the problem has been solved. Efficiency is being maintained and even increased while good labor relations are under cultivation. Contrasting with the smiling profiles of successful segments are those sadder EPIC units which seem unable to achieve a combination, even in such an oscillating fashion as would be described by the pendulum theory. These units—of which Lakeside is the most conspicuous—are under searching examination by EPIC.

"Why is it," EPIC officers ask, "that Lakeside seems unable to accomplish both objectives?" The inevitable, unasked, but implicit question is, "What is wrong with the *management* which has a record of several years' unresolved employee unrest? Could it be that while they are smart businessmen—as they obviously must be in terms of efficiency they achieve—they are also insensitive, unresponsive and even resistant to the legitimate needs of people? Are Lakeside executives truly unable to integrate our two necessary criteria of effective management?"

The future is not too hopeful for managers who are unable to accomplish this two-headed objective. Why? Because who in Headquarters wants to entrust a position of high responsibility to a manager who is unable to merge efficiency with good labor relations? Probably no one! Therefore, and as of now, the fundamental top-management motivation within Lakeside is to achieve good labor relations, not primarily to produce better lives for work people, but to be favorably evaluated by Headquarters management. This is an overriding pressure upon every top manager at Lakeside.

Management Efforts: Laying the Groundwork for Diplomacy

Signals of serious strife with the union had not gone unnoticed by management, however. About two years ago, responsible managers became acutely aware of the precariousness of their positions, brought on by the stepped up pressures for profit. Although substantial efficiency gains had been made, the signs of continuing labor strife, bickering, conflict and threat foreshadowed an eventual strike, which could ruin Lakeside as a business entity. While the union continued to prepare for war, management was beginning to orient itself toward achieving a statesmanlike posture.

As management began seeking to change its historic relationship with the union, it recognized that there were grave mutual problems of communication, participation, identification, and so on. Managers who wanted to improve these called on a group of behavioral scientists which included myself, in the hope that their approach would establish constructive relations between management and the union.

In coming into the situation, the behavioral scientists made an effort to create circumstances under which they could have access to the entire organization, not just management. The rationale was that an organization is better conceptualized as a single unit rather than as two or more subgroups with battle lines drawn. Management agreed to this and invited the union to participate in these behavioral science seminars. The union officers immediately rejected the request as just another example of management's efforts to "brainwash" them and the union membership.

So, instead of tackling the organization as a whole, the behavioral scientists initially worked with management. In the seminars they created miniature experimental battle situations between groups of managers to make it possible for them to recognize the consequences of a win-lose fight. They also examined the conditions under which cooperation and collaboration between groups can be produced out of an opening situation of competition and fighting. Against the conflict-laden experiences of many Lakeside managers, this particular field of behavioral science was interesting. It was practical. It made sense. Managers listened and were impressed. They began wanting to establish conditions of cooperation with the union even though, for some, the old fight urge was still deep. During the seminars and in later interviewing I noticed that attitudinally, many of them inhabited two worlds. The ostensibly humane attitudes of people who have received formal education sometimes only mask deep feelings of resentment. There are managerial people who truly despise the work force. Such feelings are particularly prevalent among those engineers, supervisors and foremen who have at some time risen above the level of the "blue-collar stiff."

The most striking result of exposing management to the learning theory of the dynamics of intergroup warfare on one hand and intergroup collaboration on the other was that management found itself split by anomalous feelings. Part of it wanted to search for constructive problem-solving relations with the union. The other part wanted to continue the ancient feud under the latest impetus of righteous indignation stimulated by "selfish, negative, and nasty" union attitudes encountered when management had tried to work with the wage people in a more understanding manner.

Upon completing the laboratory-seminars, management took the crucial last step prior to bargaining. A series of conferences were held at "Green Acres." Participants were the top 100 or so members of management who represented all levels of supervision except first and second line foremen. The purpose of these meetings was to develop shared convictions and concrete proposals for actions in response to the question, "How can we create better relations between union and management?"

By this time, I had accepted Quinn's invitation to join the Lakeside organization as its "organization development" (OD) man.

There were three such sessions, reaching down into the organization through the regional supervisory level, which is five steps from the top. The first Green Acres session included four hierarchy levels from Quinn, the general manager, down to the division heads. Quinn and two of his key men also attended the other sessions. The second one included some more division heads but was mostly made up of unit supervisors. In EPIC, below the level of the unit supervisor is the regional supervisor, and below this is the foreman.

In arranging each Green Acres conference, I put people into three cross-section groups. Quinn sat in one group. Van Gray, the operations superintendent, was in another and Wes Stratton, the personnel chief, in a third. The groups struggled with the problem of how to improve union-management relations. Their proceedings were fascinating to listen to, because a fairly substantial number of the managers considered this key question a hopeless one to answer. "There is no way to bring about any improvement with the thugs, thieves and crooks presently running the union. How can you cooperate and collaborate with such a rat pack?" In effect, this was a cathartic release where attitudes of antagonism and hostility needed to be vented to unblock men's minds for more objective problem solving.

Then as the problem was debated and scrutinized from many points of view, a new concept began to appear. Consciousness dawned that one can never look forward to improve union-management relations unless this deepseated attitude—namely, that the union is composed of thugs, thieves and crooks—is erased or at least given an experimental adjournment in the minds of management. Now it was said, "Regardless of what the union officers are personality-wise and what their history has been, the only conceivable way to resolve this conflict is by treating the union officers as officers and according them the dignity and respect due those who are duly elected. It is not our place to judge the people who have been chosen by their membership. Our role is to meet with them and search for whatever conditions of cooperation and collaboration are possible."

Many other recommendations began to emerge, but the outstanding one was, "Treat the union and its officers with dignity and respect." It was fascinating to watch members of management do such a complete "reversal of field." And this occurred in the course of an eight-hour debate.

The conclusion just reported was much stronger during the first two sessions than among participants in the third seminar, almost all of whom were regional supervisors. These latter were outspokenly critical of top management; saying, in effect, "Our views are important because we're down where the job gets done. We have told you and told you and told you what it is we think you should do, and we want to see action. Give us feedback on your actions, and then we will know how to react." They also tied their conclusions regarding subsequent sessions for foremen and wage people to the condition that management provide the feedback requested. By that stage summer was coming on. I was on my way to the other commitments, and so we never conducted sessions for those last two levels in the organization.

I noticed interesting contrasts in the behavior of Quinn during and after the Green Acres conference. Earlier, during the sessions, he was continuously flip-flopping. One day his argument would be, "We must cooperate, but how can we?" The next day it would be, "We must create conditions under which these rascals can be seen, by the people who elected them, in the true phosphorescent light of their putridity so that when the wage people come to ballot again they'll do a better job." Quinn's behavior vacillated like a weather vane, pointing to the left one day, pointing to the right the next day, but never pointing forward in a positive sense.

After the Green Acres conference, however, he was of a single mind. He had worked through his antagonisms and hostility. He had shifted his thinking to the position that there is no way to go but forward, and that there is no group to go forward with except the union delegation. It was this unlocking of attitudes and emotions, more than any other thing, which freed Lakeside management, enabling it to start creating sounder conditions of collaboration. The point here is that management had to first develop a uniform attitude at the emotional level.

The Union Girds for War: Creating a Paper Bomb

The union officers had no such mixture of feelings about management. Their attitudes were clear and straightforward. Officers were still smoldering over management's shenanigans prior to the recent IEW election. They glowered as they recalled the events of two years ago when, after a bitter siege, management had "won" in significant areas of contract negotiations and had achieved a breathing spell for itself. They were aware that management was in training for the next contract confrontation. While management was shaping up at Green Acres, the union closed ranks and examined its own past behavior in an effort not to repeat past mistakes which had caused rejection of their proposals.

One mistake the union felt it had made early in the game was to bargain under definitions and interpretations proposed by management. After management had been able to put the situation in a certain context, the union frequently had been unable to dislodge them from their positions. As a result, the union had lately spent much time composing a comprehensive draft contract upon which they intended to base the next round of bargaining.

Dan Ives, the president, expressed the prevailing attitude of his group when he said, "None of the old legal stuff in this contract. None of those whereases, and wherefores, and wherewiths. This is going to be written so that my 12 year old boy can understand it."

This proposal contained many positions that management would find difficult if not impossible to accept. Among other things, it called for a 35-hour week with 40 hours' pay, doubling vacation time, and joint determination of job content. It contained demands which, if accepted by management, would put Lakeside out of business by eliminating its profit.

By this time, the union felt stronger than ever before. It was tough. It was disciplined. It was motivated and eager. It knew what it wanted, and it was ready to bargain, bicker, argue, angle, push, pull and whatever else was necessary to win this upcoming battle. By now, pamphlets had replaced the 1920's bullets, but they aimed at the same target areas. Union officials were saying, "We'll show those people. They'll bargain from *our* terms or there won't be any bargaining. If they don't give in this time there will be real war. We have the support to do it and if we can't win alone, we'll affiliate with the International."

References

1. The technical imperatives which underlie union-management negotiations on "craft consolidation" are described in Seligman, B.B. *Most Notorious Victory: Man in an Age of Automation.* New York: The Free Press, 1966, Chapter 4. See also: Buckingham, W.S. *Automation: Its Impact on Business and People.* New York:

Harper, 1961. The findings of inter-disciplinary researches into the impact of technological change upon American values are presented in Baier, K. and Rescher, N. *Values and the Future.* New York: The Free Press, 1968.

2. *Efficiency* is formally defined as "an optimum relationship between input and output." See: Horngren, C.T. *Accounting for Management Control* (2nd Ed.). Englewood Cliffs, N.J.: Prentice-Hall, Inc., 1970, pp. 270-271.

3. An analytic approach to plant location is described in Buffa, E.S. *Modern Production Management* (3rd Ed.). New York: John Wiley & Sons, Inc., 1969, Chapter 10.

4. The "abandonment decision" is discussed from a financial-management point of view in Van Horne, J.C. *Financial Management and Policy.* Englewood Cliffs, N.J.: Prentice-Hall, Inc., 1968, pp. 99-100. Alternatives from a top management point of view are indicated in Blake, R.R. & Mouton, J.S. *How to Assess the Strengths and Weaknesses of a Business Enterprise,* volume 6, "Corporate Leadership." Austin, Texas: Scientific Methods, Inc., 1972, p. 86.

2

The Union Throws Down the Gauntlet

On August 1, the union delivered its contract demands to management. IEW was ready for a fight. Managers knew how to fight too, but their historic perspective had been refocused by the behavioral science training experience. They said they were prepared to take a collaborative problem-solving attitude toward the union.

I was present at the meeting when management received the union document. Quickly they scanned and studied it. In economic terms, what would it cost? Probably an additional three million dollars a year! This is a substantial percentage of the total operating budget and would put Lakeside deeper into the red than the layoff action a few years previously.

In a dramatic discussion by top management, several members of the bargaining committee led the initial reaction into a win-lose posture. They threw their hands up, saying, "This proves what an impossible union we have to deal with."

"Even you," they said turning to me, "will recognize the absurdity of trying to work with this union group."

Aggressive attitudes began to emerge in statements such as, "Let's have a meeting with them, take this document, and throw it in their faces. We'll face the consequences, but we can't work with this impossible union. It is completely irresponsible, asking for things no one can give." There was a shared sense of adrenal readiness for conflict, and so they went on to discuss arena arrangements for meeting with the union.

"Where should we meet?" was the first question.

"Let's meet here in the administration building. The union doesn't like to come over here, they don't feel comfortable in this setting. Let's call up and tell them the meeting's to be in this building. That'll frustrate 'em."

"When shall we meet?" was the next issue.

"Let's schedule it for 10:00 in the morning, so as to complete it at 2:00 p.m. Then, these bums will start the day in their work clothes. They will have to change into decent clothing, so to speak, before we meet. We'll break for lunch early so we can talk more about how to shove the document back down their throats. Then they'll have to trot to the cafeteria and back again; and at 2:00 p.m. when we've finished up with them, they'll have to go back to the line, change back to work clothes, and put in another two hours' work before the day is over."

"What shall we do?" was the question that rounded out the picture.

"When we invite the union to this meeting, let's not tell them what we want to talk about. Instead, we'll say that all we can do is just explore with them the impossibility of this document and hand it back."

These were the initial reactions. To me, it was a clear case of "going into orbit," which typically starts when you are getting so excited and feel so threatened that you take off for the emotional stratosphere rather than recognizing that there are opportunities beneath the surface problems galling you.

At this point I came in with a critical intervention which challenged their impulsive actions and attitudes. "Wait a minute," I said. "Let's examine what's going on and what the consequences would be of shoving the document 'back down their throats.' What would that produce? It would abort negotiations and mean the reopening—perhaps on a public level—of hostilities. What would that gain? Could management, having taken this action, ever look toward future consensus with IEW on a mutually agreeable contract, or would it be that present lines of communication would be so obliterated that no future collaboration could be anticipated for the next several years?"

Since management had already learned at laboratory-seminars the deeper lessons of intergroup warfare, as compared with cooperation, these remarks were enough to shatter the impulse for precipitous action and reset management's orientation. I continued to confront the bargaining committee with the discrepancy between their intentions as formulated during the conference program and their reactions under this present test of convictions.

"Look. You are doing exactly what you said you wouldn't. You are reacting to this situation with feelings and emotions rather than thought and logic. You're going into orbit. The moment you take off, you're as good as dead. You have no evidence that the union is rigidly committed to the proposals outlined here. They could be regarded as points of departure, just as reasonably as they could be seen as final positions. It depends upon how you think about them. If you view them as final positions, they may well be impossible. But if you think of them as initial positions, they comprise a stance that may be modified through negotiation. They're asking for more than they expect to receive, but what's wrong with that for openers? Just because the union has a win-lose orientation you should by no means conclude that it can't be moved to a problem-solving orientation. Hold on. Don't act impulsively. If you do, there is no recourse but warfare."

There was an intense and excited session from that point on. According to some, here was an outsider calling on them to be reasonable in a situation where they were facing nothing but unreason. On the other hand, certain members of the management bargaining committee, particularly Carl O'Brien, saw a ray of hope. I think Carl, the head of Chemical Products, started to interpret the situation in the sense of "Cast your bread upon the waters . . ." rather than, "An eye for an eye and a tooth for a tooth." He began to limber up his brain and think, "Is there such a possibility?"

As he showed a bit of reason, others including Wes Stratton began to respond with a glimmer of hope too. Wes felt he had good personal relations with the union as a group and as individuals. He saw the possibility of constructive collaboration, if only the management committee were smart enough to find the conditions for shifting union thinking from win-lose to problem solving. Then others began to depart from their initial convictions that problem solving was impossible. The negative attitudes of hopelessness began to dissipate.

Finally, the decision was made: to establish a spirit of cooperation rather than planning how to get the opponent on the defensive to knock him out.

"Look, Wes, why don't you get with the union chief and find out where they would like to meet?" I suggested to get the action started. This was kicked around awhile, after which people began saying, "Well, okay. Let's find out where they would like to meet, and when, and what they want to talk about."

So Wes went to the union president and said, "Dan, let's open negotiations. Where would you like to meet? We could meet in the administration building, in the personnel department conference room, or somewhere outside."

Dan said, "Oh, let's meet in the personnel department."

"When would you like to meet?"

"What about after lunch? We could get cleaned up at the noon break and put on our city clothes, and then we wouldn't have to change back again later."

"What do you want to talk about, Dan?"

"Oh, I don't know. Maybe we had better get together to talk about what we need to talk about before we set up an agenda. Let's spend the first meeting setting an agenda."

The time, place, and circumstances were agreed upon, instead of being dictated by one side. In contrast to management's initial reaction, a different set of attitudes directed this approach. Seeds of problem solving had been sown.

Union and management got together on August 7. After a brief exchange of pleasantries, the plunge toward the proposal was taken. The first decision made was innocuous but important. Perhaps the sensible thing to do would be for the union to read the proposal to management and to explain it, line by line. Management would listen and not interrupt except to clarify its understanding of the content. This was an unheard of thing to attempt, but the suggestion was agreed to nonetheless. For the first time in at least a decade, both sides were making a real effort to talk and to listen with understanding.

When the union started reading and explaining its proposals, it turned out that the words used in the document were in many respects different from the intentions behind those words. Also, the union was perceiving some realistic problems which management had not understood to exist. Management was surprised. There were some sound intentions behind some bad words, and it had been these words that had produced the initial misunderstandings by management.

When the reading got into the economic area of the document, management stopped asking questions to clarify intent and started asking questions to probe for justification or the lack of it. Van Gray queried, "What possible reasons can you have for asking for this?" Immediately tension and a win-lose atmosphere could be felt. Both groups almost took off into orbit! Van quickly pulled back so that the reading could continue at the level of understanding the document's contents and what these involved, rather than demanding justification. This was a crucial learning experience, and prompted the following theory-based commentary.

The Influence of Psychological Assumptions in Human Relations

At this point in the management-union contacts there are two critical, interrelated sets of prevalent assumptions regarding relationships with people (*qua* people) that I am trying actively to "put under arrest" in the minds of the managers as they interact with the union. I say "actively arrest" because both of these assumptions are deeply ingrained in our traditional ways of thinking. To counteract what might be disastrous effects—if these principles continue operating silently—I had to keep awareness of them constantly in the forefront of my critical thinking today as I worked with management members to bring similar awareness on their part. Only by this never-ending effort to override the automatic behavior of the past years could a change in relationships even be a remote possibility.

The Psychodynamic Fallacy

The first widespread psychological assumption is the psychodynamic determination of behavior.[1] This assumption, that personality is the *sole* cause of behavior, places severe limitations on solving problems that arise between people. The reason is that a person who has achieved a normal level of maturity and effectiveness in everyday living—such as driving a car, paying his taxes, and living in a house with a family—has all the primary raw skills for being an effective person. Whether he *is* an effective person often is due to interpersonal or group influences, rather than to some dominant personality theme.

Under some circumstances a person will be cooperative, friendly, problem-solving, lovable—a good Joe. But the same person under different interpersonal pressures will become a manipulator, play his cards close to his chest, be hostile, aggressive, threatening and destructive. The same person can behave in vastly dissimilar ways at different times and under different conditions.

The everyday assumption is that what a person reveals over a period of time in a particular setting is his "*basic personality*." This means that after you see him "act" in a certain way in one situation, you can expect him to be relatively the same, time after time, because that is the way he *is*. The counter proposition is that what is superficially seen as constant behavior is not an inevitable function of personality but may be due largely to static circumstances. At home, perhaps, Jekyll is seen as Jekyll; at the office, he is identified as Hyde. If in the home or at the office the situation has not changed, the stabilized conditions "cause" the same behavior to appear again and again. Yet—as in Jekyll's postulated home life—if conditions that facilitate cooperation are surrounding him, an entirely different person is seen, in contrast to the office "Hyde." Quite probably, at the office he is part of a competitive, back-biting group, which maintains a fragile unity only by dedicating itself to winning at all costs against some external "enemy."

The assumption that psychodynamic considerations strongly dictate personal behavior underlies management's general picture of human action. From the standpoint of management, union people are perennially hostile to and unsympathetic with the real corporate problems. In terms of past experience, these are the behaviors that union officers have characteristically exhibited in response to management's fiats and kiss-offs. In a conference they appear by turns to be piranha-opportunistic, antagonistic, ear-muffed, dumb, and generally hopeless. When negotiations bog down, according to management, it's because of union people's "poison" personalities.

Viewed in their homes, however, these same union officers tend to be good husbands and adequate fathers; in short, typical people; some even outstandingly kind, warm and loving. So the same person can be described in two ways: hostile and aggressive, warm and friendly, depending on the people to whom he is responding.

When observers only look "inside" a person, they miss a significant point. They blunder by seeing certain consistencies and interpreting them as being factors characteristic of the person. But if you change the conditions, most people change their behavior.

In the situation at Lakeside, management has become somewhat aware at Green Acres of how the "personality fallacy" operates, but in today's meeting that fallacy *did* begin operating, unnoticed by them. So, when gross generalizations were made about union officials in terms of their past behavior, my strategy was to intervene and suggest that checks could be made to find out whether this person "universally" conformed to that description or whether he might not be responding to relatively constant forces in a series of similar situations. Management's "going into orbit" remarks such as, "They are unreasonable, blind, unthinking persons," were of a gross personality-labeling nature. Through my interventions which argued for a more thorough, thoughtful evaluation, I was able to forestall the knee-jerk behavior that otherwise would have followed.

The Self-Fulfilling Prophecy and the Heisenberg Principle

The second set of assumptions regarding relationships is covered by two basic principles which tend to go together as two sides of a coin. One is called the "self-fulfilling prophecy," and the other is the Heisenberg principle.

The self-fulfilling prophecy[2] is a prophecy made by oneself which in experience is fulfilled; not because it is an accurate prediction of the inevitable, but because the person who makes the prophecy alters his own actions in such a way as to *cause* his expectations to be met. For example, if person A "knows" that person B is hostile, then A shifts his behavior—usually in an aggressive or defensive or withdrawing manner—to anticipate and deal with the presumed hostility. By A's adjusting his behavior in any of these ways, person B is quite likely to react in a hostile manner. A's conclusion is, "See, just as I figured, B is a hostile cuss." A's prophecy is fulfilled. What A fails to recognize, however, is that his own behavior greatly influenced the fulfillment. Groups, even more than individuals, engage in self-fulfilling prophecies.

The Heisenberg Principle[3] works this way. Person A, in gearing his own behavior for anticipating hostility rather than warmth or cooperation, fails to recognize that the signals he puts out dictate, to a significant degree, the kinds of signals he evokes from B. The Heisenberg Principle in effect says that the observer is a critical factor in the observation process. In psychological application the observer, A in this case, is unaware of how his own behavior influences the behavior of B. He cannot recognize his influence on the situation; the Principle implies that the observer is unaware of the contribution that his own behavior makes in determining what it is that he sees in others. The self-fulfilling prophecy means that what one puts out as a silent signal dictates, in part, what the other person does. Associating these two concepts in action therefore means fulfillment of one's prophecies or predictions regarding the other person.

*Application of Assumptions during
Management's "Orbit Session"*

The initial reactions by management in today's "orbit session" illustrate the combined operations of the psychodynamic fallacy, self-fulfilling prophecy, and the Heisenberg Principle. Later, when confronted by me, the management committee was able to think forward, in hypothetical terms, toward consequences—in effect, predicting the outcome of these initial reactions. The reasoning went this way:

"If we as the bargaining committee 'know' that the union is out to milk us for all it can get, then we will react in a defensive way and thwart them from gaining anything substantial. Throwing the union proposal right back in their faces would do this. Our actions under these conditions would prove to the union that it has to be tough to deal with us because we resist coming to terms with human requirements that are integral to Lakeside. Our initial attitude will generate signals which will be 'read' by the union. Reading these signals will cause IEW to react in such a way as to force us to put out more and stronger signals of the same kind, which, in turn, will result in more of the same antagonistic union behavior. By this time our management prophecy will be fulfilled, not only in outline but in detail. The union indeed will be out to milk us for all it can get. We will have proven by our initial prophecy that it is impossible to deal with this union."

The antidote to the entire psychodynamic/self-fulfilling prophecy/Heisenberg entrapment was as described earlier. In the "orbit session," I intervened to get the management committee's attitudes examined by the participants, so they could test the validity of the principles described. Then, rather than broadcasting signals of antagonism and animosity, management sent signals of cooperation, understanding, and respect, by asking for and arranging meeting time, place, and agenda which were consistent with union requirements as well as their own.

How did the union react to these signals? First, of course, still sniffing the smoke of previous warfare, the union was suspicious. Nonetheless, management was committed to its new approach and it continued to put out signals of collaboration. Then after a while, the union began to reexamine its position. "Maybe Quinn and his cohorts are people we can deal with after all." So the union became somewhat more attentive and responsive to what it was hearing. Results: the signals the union was beginning to transmit were different than those that had been death-rayed to management in the past. Management was validating its hypothesis too. By trying to cooperate, cooperation was being evoked. Management and the union had taken the first step in liberating themselves from the psychodynamic fallacy.

A Critical Chat with the Union Chief

One day during the proposal reading, but prior to the beginning of the bargaining and problem solving, I happened to meet Dan Ives on a sidewalk. It was a cold day and I had my hands stuck in the pockets of my coat. I said, "Hi there, Dan, how are things going?"

"Terrible."

"What's the matter?"

He started by saying, "You'd have to have four sets of eyes to watch these thieves," referring to the management committee. His attitudes were negative and destructive. On and on he went.

I listened a bit more and finally decided to take a critical step to try to disrupt the conventionality of *his* thinking. I pulled my hand out of my pocket, plunged by forefinger into his chest as hard as I knew how without being impolite, and said, "Look, Dan, I'll tell you my conviction. Management now wants to enter into a problem-solving relationship with your union. You could miss the biggest opportunity of your life if you have your hearing aid turned down and can't catch the message that management is trying to send. It would be pathetic for you, pathetic for your people, and pathetic for management if you miss the point now! This is a crucial opportunity. Listen with both ears. Keep your eyes focused. If you have to have other sets of eyes in the back of your head and alongside your ears, keep them open too, but don't be looking for so many clues to misbehavior that you fail to see other clues that point to proper behavior. That is all I have to say."

His immediate reaction was, "Look, we're ready to meet these guys halfway. If they really want to bargain, we want to bargain also. But if they want warfare, we'll give them warfare." He did not promise one way or the other, but he did indicate he was ready to explore the possibilities of collaboration and cooperation.

References

1. Freud, S. *The Ego and the Id.* London: Hogarth, 1927.

2. Lawless, D.J. *Effective Management: Social Psychological Approach.* Englewood Cliffs, N.J.: Prentice-Hall, Inc., 1972, pp. 146-147, provides an example of the "self-fulfilling prophecy" operating in management-worker interaction.

3. In its original version, the Heisenberg (or "Uncertainty" or "Indeterminacy") Principle states that it is impossible to specify or determine simultaneously both the position and velocity of a particle with full accuracy. Rather, the more accuracy in one, the increasing uncertainty in the other. See: Heisenberg, W. *The Physical Principles of the Quantum Theory.* Chicago: University of Chicago Press, 1930. Besides its pertinence to atomic physics, for example, the Principle has implications for the basic philosophical issue of the degree—if any—to which nature is deterministic. See also: London, I.D. "Psychology and Heisenberg's Principle of Indeterminacy,"

Psychological Review, 52, 3, 1945, pp. 162-168. London, while stressing that "indeterminacy in psychology becomes too handy and ready a refuge for inability to formulate one's problems in such terms as to admit of refinement in measurement" (p. 164), nonetheless bases part of his argument against the Heisenberg Principle's applicability for psychology on the assertion that "a chemist or biologist, for instance, prepares and modifies his specimens in advance before proceeding to experimental analysis; a psychologist cannot do otherwise" (p. 167).

3

After Listening, What?

It took five weeks or so to read the union proposal. Now it was mid-September. Management had learned a lot just by listening according to ground rules of: "Let's not get mad. Let's not jump down their throats. Let's ask questions to clarify intentions, but not questions that demand justification." By the time that the management bargainers had listened through 50 pages, they were well informed of union viewpoints. But they were still sure there would be a hopeless situation when it came right down to making decisions.

The listening period was over now. The union was sitting pat, awaiting management's answers. "To what, if anything, will management say 'yes,' and in what ways will it crack down and say 'no'? Does 'no' mean the opening of warfare? If so, are we in good shape to give 'em hell?" These were the questions in the minds of the union officers. Management, on the other hand, recognized that even though the two groups were far apart on many issues, concrete problems were resolvable if a cooperative atmosphere could be created and sustained.

But if management wants to solve problems while the union still wants to win, the question becomes, "Can management approach the union under conditions that will produce a relationship where *everyone* can win; or will it fall back into the Maginot line defense posture waiting for the next attack?" If it does the latter, problem-solving possibilities will be lost.

Presently the management bargaining committee sees a sliver of light shining through a small crack in an otherwise dark room. During the past few weeks they have noticed that as they persevered to listen, and restricted themselves to asking only genuine clarification questions, some members of the union group began to listen too. So management has started to see an ever-so-slight possibility for producing a climate of cooperation. If it can continue to withhold its immediate and impulsive negative reactions; and if, instead, it can explore, assess, evaluate, and examine, both sides might be able to reach a position of mutual understanding and respect.

On September 14, the bargaining committee is scheduled to meet at Lake Michigan Lodge to explore some of the problems confronting it as the search for conditions of cooperation continues. First in order are the problems of relationship within the bargaining committee itself. There have been wide differences in points of view as to whether any possibility of cooperation with the union exists. In earlier sessions some members wanted to fight immediately, while others counseled taking preparatory steps to ensure management builds the strength to win. Still others have wanted to approach the situation from a problem-solving point of view. Working through these various attitudes to approach unanimity seems a formidable task.

Beyond internal conflict within the committee are relations between it and the management "constituency" it represents. Not having explored the problems of collaboration in the same intensive and detailed way as the committee, these other segments are in a far less cooperative mood than some committee members. Even if the bargaining committee can pull its own members together and work successfully with the union, how can it communicate that it is not being "soft"? If the committee cannot adequately communicate the tenor of its efforts to the rest of management, alienation might develop between it and the larger group. "How best to plan for continued communication and understanding between ourselves and the rest of management?" is the issue here.

Another question is, "What will the plant manager think of us?" Additional problems arise in coordinating performance between individual committee members and Quinn. How can a bargaining committee of high ranking organization members spend the demanding amounts of time in working through problems with the union, while simultaneously doing their everyday jobs? Quinn obviously must attend to the total functioning of Lakeside, not merely its union-management relations and progress on the next labor contract. Also, since the plant manager is not a full-time member of the bargaining committee, he is not as well acquainted with the atmosphere and details of bargaining as are these committee members. This, too, widens the gap.

Next comes, "What procedures can we rely on for working with the union?" Though the procedural aspect may seem mechanical, alternative procedures can result in markedly different outcomes. For example, should the bargaining committee talk through to agreement on one aspect of the contract, and then take up a new point to discuss, leaving "the big write-up" until negotiations are completed; or should it try to document, point by point, its agreements with the union when these are reached?

Prediction

After thinking about these and other aspects of the evening of September 13, I feel that tomorrow will be a crucial day. It could be a day when the basic methodology of problem solving is crystallized by management. It surely will be a day when fundamental decisions can make the difference between being successful in solving problems with the union or regressing into industrial warfare. The stakes seem high. The only way that I can see for Lakeside or any other organization to remain profitable is to solve problems. If the problems with the wage personnel are not solved, management will face more acrimony, greater demands, and finally utter discouragement. It will stop searching for a way out. If that happens, Lakeside could head into a terminal tailspin.

Furthermore, if efforts to produce a cooperative environment fail, then those members of management who want to be "tough and hard" will have found justification for their point of view—that the union is an impossible group to deal with. Thus, if warfare does result, the scope for future cooperation will have been exhausted.

The future emerging from tomorrow can be looked at from either one of two points of view. Point of view A is that it is futile to seek conditions of cooperation because such overtures simply will not be responded to by "the other side." Point of view B is that failure to approach problems in a constructive manner means the inevitable end of any peace-with-progress hopes. These are some of the major reasons why September 14 is a crucial day. Not that the 14th will determine everything for all time, but it *will* shape the posture that will be tried on the 15th, 16th, or 17th and in October and in January, and so on.

My prediction is that the management bargaining committee will find consensus for a determined push toward cooperation. If it tries and fails, it will not immediately "throw in the sponge," but will try again and keep on trying until finally the union responds to the legitimate and compelling demands of cooperation. If this happens, the result can only go one way: a period of labor-management statesmanship will follow, replacing the period of intergroup warfare of the past ten years. Then behavioral science concepts will have established their relevance for dealing constructively with one of the most critical cleavages in industry.

Entering into Negotiation

I am dictating these notes late in the evening of September 14. The bargaining committee has completed its session at Lake Michigan Lodge. After a day of intensive interaction, the course they will try to pursue with the IEW is clear. Let's look at each of the areas of concern they have examined and the paths that have crystallized.

Major Areas of Concern

First of all, significant cleavages that exist between the bargaining group were examined again and again through the day. A major bone of contention was, and still is, differences between the "line" manufacturing point of view and that of the personnel department "staff" group.[1] The line people, mostly engineers, see themselves—and want to be seen by others—as businessmen "charged with the responsibility of making a profit." Since the entire organization is also judged by Headquarters in terms of its employee relations, the operating departments want good human relations but not at the expense of efficiency.

In contrast, the personnel department is seen by line managers as being so far in the "employees' corner" as to be quite resistant to business-logic decisions that line people must necessarily make for the pursuit of profit, considered *per se*. But the personnel executives see themselves as no different from the line managers in their own orientation toward profit. They argue, however, that sound personnel administration and employee relations are not frills. Rather, these contribute significantly, albeit indirectly, to overall profitability. The staff people resent the line's allegations of "softness." As a result, misunderstanding, distrust, and suspicion have characterized everyday interaction between the operating departments and members of the personnel department.

This issue was brought to the surface early this morning. It was frequently returned to during the course of the day-long discussion. In my view, the problems was not solved, but there was progress toward understanding and clarification. I asked the operating managers and supervisors to tell the personnel people how they saw them. Operating managers said that the personnel staff "sit in judgment on complaints about operational decisions," rather than providing a staff service which enables the line to do a better job. Next, I suggested that personnel people open up. They did so. The line people were told with relative frankness that their heavy and sometimes exclusive emphasis on profit is not truly profitable; that it is even bad from a long-term point of view because it leads to unnecessary conflict that subsequently requires excessive "repair" time to be spent maintaining even minimally adequate interpersonal relations. The staff executive viewpoint is that people ought to be able to go about their work productively without expending so much effort to clear up misunderstandings that could have been foreseen and avoided, "given a little applied humanitarianism."

This problem area merits further investigation. Perhaps it never will be entirely resolved, but getting the feeling into the open for discussion today represents real progress.

The major portion of the discussion concerned the bargaining committee's relations with the rest of management. Again, my strategy was to aid each "side" to clarify its attitudes and test assumptions for their soundness and validity toward unifying management's posture toward the union. Members of the committee clearly perceived the dilemma. Its problem-solving approach leads to the possibility of conflict on both flanks: with the rest of management on one side and with the more intransigent union officers on the other. The approach to reducing the bargaining team's potential "representatives versus constituency" problem will be through more intensive efforts at communicating to the rest of Lakeside management their intentions in the light of surrounding "social facts" such as current team-union climate and feeling. Several procedures were agreed on.

Management's bargaining team has formal responsibility for communicating with the rest of management. Historically such communication has been both oral (e.g., during department meetings), and written (through newsletters to management). Before the last IEW election, however, so-called "newsletters to management" were used intensively to communicate over the heads of the union directly to the wage people. In effect, the newsletters subtly coached first-line supervisors and foremen in "how to knock" incumbent union officers and attempted to persuade wage people to vote for the management-favored opposition candidates. But the Dan Ives group was re-elected! Now the union profoundly distrusts the management bargaining team's motives for issuing newsletters. It has told management this in explicit and colorful language. In today's discussion, team members concluded that, for the present at least, management has no obligation to report on negotiations directly to the wage people and that, indeed, it would violate an appropriate condition of relationship with the union if it did. The reason for this is simple enough. The union represents the wage people. As such, it alone has the responsibility for communicating its own actions to its own people. A decision was made to explore the possibility of letters to the homes of the supervisors to keep them up to date, but in so doing, to preclude any accusation of going "over the heads" of the union.

Next, extensive discussion took place regarding the "fish bowl" situation of the management bargaining team. Its behavior serves as the signal to the rest of management as to what management's intentions are. If management talks one way as a bargaining group and other ways in its departmental relations, then the whole of management is confused. After considerable exploration of this knotty problem, they decided on a long-term effort to aid each member, particularly the line members, to speak a single point of view in talks with their subordinate groups about ongoing negotiations. The general notion is that if the bargaining committee doesn't talk consistently in terms of problem solving and doesn't communicate an air of confidence in its pioneering approach, then the rest of management inevitably will respond to old win-lose signals.

Rather than generalizing about the attitudinal or atmospheric aspects of communications, specific suggestions were made by me with respect to communicating feelings and emotions. I stressed that committee members can help other managers by communicating the "experimental" quality of their present and future interactions with the union, and also by communicating to other managers their need for sympathetic appreciation of the dilemma they face in seeking to produce collaboration out of a background of competition.

Another important matter discussed was relations between Quinn, the general manager, and themselves. Here the committee is under another set of pressures. Certain of its members are production department heads. Time consumed in bargaining is unavailable for operations. Quinn is as much interested in day-by-day operational efficiency as in resolving labor-management conflict.

How should the committee members deal with this one? Should they delegate authority for managing operations to assistant department heads or should they try to do both jobs simultaneously? If they turn things over to the assistant department heads, this makes each senior man uneasy and it exposes him to queries from Quinn which he is unable to answer because he is uninformed on operations details. On the other hand, if operational authorities are not delegated to assistant department heads, what happens? No time is left for thinking through the background problems associated with the concrete issues that need to be studied and investigated as the bargaining proceeds. In fact, little time is even available for getting together with the union.

An added aspect is, "How long will it take to negotiate a new contract?" The general manager has informally suggested it might be worthwhile for the group to think in terms of completing contract negotiations in three or four months. From the standpoint of the bargaining team, however, this is a questionable proposition because it is impossible to foresee difficulties that might confront them. Three or four months would be ideal, but is it realistic? If a time goal is not established, then the future length of negotiations is indeterminate. If a deadline date is set, negotiators feel "under the gun," and might push too hard or approach problems in a shallow manner, or both, only to come up with flimsy proposals rather than thorough resolutions.

Here again, today's consensus by the bargaining committee seems sensible. The approach can be expressed as, "Let's be tentative about this one. Let's go ahead to see how we progress, looking toward some closing time in the future, but not projecting one that would be brittle and mechanical."

A further period of discussion involved how to go about recording agreements with the union. Would it be best simply to debate one topic to agreement and then go on to other matters before coming to final conclusions of the entire contract? Or, whenever agreements are reached, would it be best to write them down as a record of mutual understanding? It was decided to raise this problem perhaps at the next bargaining meeting. This would be a natural way of getting into problem-solving interaction with the union. Many other matters were discussed, but the ones just mentioned have been the central issues debated today at Lake Michigan Lodge.

I would characterize the attitude of management at this stage as being committed to the proposition that constructive work *can* be done in a genuine search for mutually acceptable solutions to disturbing problems. Its position is that by being open, honest, and free in expression, by sharing anxieties and concern, by exposing their senses of threat and distrust, it should be possible for two reasonably intelligent groups to find common ground. However, it can't be said that this position is fervently supported by everyone on the team. Therefore, it is apropos to characterize individual members as they impress me at present.

Carl O'Brien, who heads the Chemical Products Department, believes in exemplifying Christian ethics. He wants to do the "right" thing. As he correctly admits, he, as well as others, doesn't know how to go about it, but he is convinced that the effort is worth a try. He wants to go the problem-solving route.

Hal Harvey really doesn't yet have the point. Hal, incidentally, is third in the Lakeside pecking order, as head of Engineering. He still wants to play the cards close to his chest; he is distrustful, suspicious, and highly oriented toward the anvil of efficiency and to hammering out what needs to be done to be profitable, even if it produces sparks and brush fires as side effects.

Wes Stratton and his Personnel Department sidekick, Mac Anthony, possess the most person-centered attitudes of all. They are not only ready, they are eager to bring a human relations orientation to the productivity-profit quest. Their goal is to move, to develop a problem-solving atmosphere, to come up with unique, creative solutions; to experiment, to devise, to implement. One of their aims is to get the union and management negotiating teams to study the *needs* of the total bargaining committee from both management's side and the union's side; then try to find mutually acceptable ways to approach problems to meet the legitimate and accepted *needs* of both groups.[2] Wes and Mac constitute vital influences for problem solving. As such, Hal seems to feel threatened by them.

Van Gray, the operations superintendent and chairman of management's bargaining team, is somewhat in between. Like Wes and Mac, he sees no alternative except to try to solve problems, but as Quinn's second-in-command, he is under even more efficiency motivation pressure than Hal. More than any other member of the group, he feels obligated to find a happy balance between efficiency and employee security. That is, he'd like a full measure of both but will settle for half-and-half. He wants to do the "right thing," which, presently, is to problem solve.

He doesn't feel secure in the sense that he can confidently predict the outcome, but he wants to "go." He wants the bargaining team to stick together, to try to do an honest job of communicating to other members of management, to avoid communications that, if aimed into the wage ranks, would return a union-influenced "boomerang made of dynamite" effect. He wants management's representatives to listen and to seek to understand. He also positions himself in the role of an intermediary between line and staff, trying to keep the two in balance rather than permitting an extreme swing in either direction. He is respected by all.

Prediction

From my background point of view, I feel that the present initiatives will be successful. For Lakeside, the consequences of further failure are almost too terrifying to conceive. Failure means a breakdown of negotiations, probably followed by international unionization, a strike, supply disruptions, financial losses, and perhaps a permanent close-down of the plant by EPIC headquarters. Failure also means collapse of the ethical plane on which the management bargaining team is venturing; it would represent their personal failure to relate with another group in a dignified and mature manner. It would mean that men had sought to act in an ethical manner, but had insufficient skills or fortitude, or both, to be successful.

References

1. As Gross, B.M. comments, ". . . various members of an organization may have 'functional,' 'technical,' or 'professional' authority over other members who are subordinate to them only on certain types of problems or with respect to the enforcement of certain rules. Typical cases are found in the authority of . . . 'staff' specialist over administrators in the 'line' or the 'field.' " *The Managing of Organizations,* volume I. New York: The Free Press, 1964, p. 377. For examples of problems associated with these arrangements, see: Dalton, M. "Conflicts Between Staff and Line Managerial Officers," *American Sociological Review, XV,* 3, June 1950, pp. 342-350; Toussaint, M.N. "Line-staff Conflict—Its Causes and Cure," *Personnel, 39,* 3, May-June 1962, pp. 8-20.

2. For an account of labor-management consensus-seeking, see: National Planning Association, *Fundamentals of Labor Peace,* case study 14. Washington, NPA, 1953.

4

The First Bargaining Session

Initial Steps Are Taken

September 15, the first day of problem solving with the union, has drawn to a close. Management's approach seems to have been successful. Two principal bargaining issues were discussed. One was resolved, the other tabled. As usual I did not attend the bargaining session itself, but rather met with the bargaining committee in its preparatory meeting this morning and will also sit in at the post-session critique early tomorrow.

New Hires and Union Membership

The issue that was solved takes up part of the first page of the union's 50-page contract proposal. The descriptive term for it is "union shop, with membership maintenance.[1] The union's draft stipulates that new hires are obligated to join the union after a month's employment, with the option of terminating the relationship at the end of one year. The issue here does not appear especially crucial, as the same clause has been in earlier contracts, even though it was not included in the last one. But the union's page one placement of this issue does indicate its significance to them. At all events, this first agreement between the negotiators means that a "union shop with membership maintenance" clause will be included in the next contract.

Union Use of Bulletin Boards

The other main issue discussed was in regard to union use of bulletin boards owned and maintained by the company. This one eventually was tabled with the hope of resolution at the next meeting. The two positions which could not be immediately reconciled were these. Management claims it is inappropriate for unions to use bulletin boards to "attack" it. The union, on the other hand, claims that managerial actions sometimes give the IEW no choice *but* to attack so as to bring into the open behavior that is an affront to human decency as well as being inconsistent with contractual rights to command workers, not to mention gaining their respect.

In my view, the crux of the issue is in the undefined term "*attack*." What does it mean? Management has not taken the stance of wishing to obstruct communications which help the union convey its point of view. That is why bulletin boards were made available in the first place. Does pointing out and categorizing management's behavior which is off limits in terms of the contract or otherwise unacceptable from a wage earner's viewpoint constitute an "attack?" Maybe or maybe not—but how can you know? Presently there is no criterion for determining whether a given statement constitutes a concrete description of an event or a vicious attack. Management legitimately wants to guard against defamation, character assassination, vicious innuendos and all the other things that incite emotions but fail to clarify and resolve a problem. The union, though, claims its interests are parallel to EPIC's in the area of seeking more effective management. It only wants to be accurate and explicit in pointing out policy-puncturing peccadilloes.

Will it be possible for management and the union to find some meaningful mutual definition of "attack"? Now that the issue has been tabled, various pros and cons of bulletin board use will be discussed by the bargaining committee in preparation for the next bargaining session scheduled for September 17.

Procedural Agreements

Another significant step toward agreement was taken today. The decision was a procedural one which the management committee had put to the union for discussion and agreement. Having reached agreement on the union shop/membership maintenance item, the procedural followup step was for one representative of the union and one of management to get together in an informal session, outside of the regular meeting, to write down the consensus reached. The objective here was to prevent issues already talked through to agreement to continue "on probation," as it were, because the language documenting the agreement had not been established.

Documenting interim agreements is a sound procedure, for otherwise too many of the varied connotations and interpretations associated with verbal understandings will be forgotten or changed. Then it becomes much more difficult to resolve later disagreements. If the fine points still needing examination are worked out when people can recall the emotions, implications, and intentions surrounding the generalized verbal agreement, it should be relatively easy to iron out the technical wrinkles. The union-management bargaining conference now plans to bring verbal agreements to full written understanding as soon as possible.

My feeling tonight is that problem-solving contact with the union has been established. The tone of the session was low key. The union listened, and understood what it heard. It caucused, then returned to the bargaining table in an agreeable mood. This represents a great accomplishment.

The present state of progress is that having listened to the union explain—for five weeks—the intentions behind its proposals, many of these have been certified by management as legitimate, meaningful, and understandable. If granted, they would provide genuine breakthroughs toward what the union is seeking; namely, to be a strong representative body that brings initiative to problem solving with management and which in turn can "deliver" its members' commitment to work and to collaborate constructively under the contract terms. Other requests—like 40 hours' pay for 35 hours' work—appear irreconcilable at present, but they too might be "routine" in the future.

Today then was Day 1 of problem-solving contact. This is not dancing, this is work. Yet is the Lakeside organization, as a whole, prepared for this way of working? What is it doing to create a more favorable climate that will permit the new approach to blossom and eventually become a way of life?

At one level, the organization is "ready." During training sessions, we posed a problem which all participants were required to solve through individual study and analysis followed by team discussion toward consensus. This was, "How can we improve relations between the union and management?" The solutions evolved in this manner were remarkable. No group in the entire seminar membership of about 250 people ever came up with the idea that a successful way to improve union-management relations is to "fight." When analyzed in the cool atmosphere of laboratory training conditions, the answer seemed obvious. Yet the real issue at this time is one of followup: to rehabilitate Lakeside from the effects of years of win-lose, day-to-day interactions and keep collaboration in focus as the objective. In the feverish environment of minute-by-minute efficiency-seeking operations, though, it is hard *not* to solve a problem by push, drive, tell, force, impulse, or prod. It is difficult to sit back and to think through, to interact with associates, and to try to understand the other person's point of view when you need to get the job done in minutes. At an intellectual level, then, Lakeside managers are in fairly uniform agreement. They *think* the way to go is to establish conditions of problem solving with the union. But in the heat of production requirements, problem solving frequently is *felt* to be a "weak" approach to getting the job done. OD strategy is involved here in breaking the self-defeating cycles of the past in which ramrodding the employees provoked counter-reactions that made the net situation worse than the previous one.

So then the question becomes, "What has management done to initiate a deliberate and diligent effort toward problem solving?" The answer is obvious and somewhat disappointing. Management has, in a sense, taken the pledge to "go on the wagon." It has said, "No more fighting. From now on we will travel the straight and narrow path." In committee meetings, the pledge has been taken repeatedly. Back in the plant, however, day after day the pledge gets violated. Lakeside history, engineering logic, and time pressures all say, "Push, drive, pressure, oversee, direct, dictate." A few days' laboratory experience says, "Think, participate, communicate, collaborate, and seek creative consensus as you and your colleagues look for solutions." Tradition runs strong and a production-oriented, hard-driving culture is silently exerting pressures which are second nature and hard to break.

Management Bargaining Committee Critique Session

At the "critique" of the September 15 bargaining, which was conducted early on the 16th, a number of issues were thrashed out. Primary focus was on broad process aspects of the bargaining sessions as well as those sessions' impact on Lakeside's management and wage people.

One significant aspect I focused on was the interaction between bargaining committee members during yesterday's session. The critique centered on examining first what had actually occurred and then considering whether alternative ways of relating might be more effective.

What did happen yesterday was that Van Gray, the committee chairman, did nearly all of the talking. He voiced management's attitudes and he expressed reactions to the union bargainers when they had points of view that varied with managerial ones.

This morning when critique comments were invited, other members of the bargaining committee said they had been reluctant to speak during yesterday's debates since doing so might have put them into conflict with their own leader. We found, too, that Van, as soloist, had been overburdened by trying to follow procedural and process considerations simultaneously. He was too busy thinking through the *content* of what was being said and about what he wanted to say next in reply.[2] A third consideration is that, both as operations superintendent and committee chairman, he is the senior man present. Yet in terms of knowledge of *specific content,* he doesn't necessarily have the same breadth and depth as others have within their individual specialisms. Jack Smith, head of Engineering's maintenance division, for example, is intimate with the problems of keeping plant facilities in working order. Van, a graduate engineer himself, knows the generalities and some specifics of plant maintenance, but from the rather different standpoint of coordinating production and keeping a number of programs on schedule. Wes, head of the Personnel Department, is knowledgeable from the employee relations viewpoint, and so on for the other members, each of whom represents a different department or division.

All in all, it was found that this pattern of interaction, with the head of the committee doing all the talking, is an unsatisfactory use of the skills of management's *total* bargaining membership.

One alteration in the pattern was agreed upon during this critique session. Van will take the initiating role either to suggest discussion topics and their sequence, or to respond to union suggestions in this area. If they say, for example, "We would like to pursue the bulletin board issue," and Van agrees, then the member of management who is best acquainted with that problem and, therefore, most appropriately the person to speak on that issue, will hold forth. Afterwards Van will supplement or clarify or summarize or do whatever else is indicated from a procedural and process point of view.

There are three advantages in this method. The first is that it provides an opportunity for Van to function as chairman; to watch for procedural and process problems which he is in a unique position to help relieve or correct. The second advantage is that the most competent and informed person is able to present management's points of view. The third advantage is that if things go in a negative direction, or if correction of some inappropriate statement is needed, the committee chairman, being highest in rank, is the appropriate person to evaluate and take action.

By comparison, a situation in which the chairman might make incorrect points and then be put back on the track by one of his own subordinates as the union officers watch and listen, doesn't seem attractive to anyone because it violates organization hierarchy and conditions of respect necessary in this kind of a situation. Neither does Van want to make a blunder under circumstances where other team members, who could bring relevant knowledge to the problem, are bound by protocol to remain mute.

The same logic explains why he, not the general manager, heads the bargaining team. While Van can be overruled by Quinn, the opposite is not true. If Quinn headed the bargaining team, and if negotiations got into an impasse, there would be no one of higher rank in Lakeside to call the shots or otherwise reshape the situation.

Another consideration probed today was committee members' developing awareness of the tremendous amount of time that is likely to be consumed before any satisfactory contract can be drawn up and signed. These bargaining committee members are among the top ranking people of the Lakeside organization. Each has a heavy responsibility for effective operations as well as for bargaining.

The kind of problem-solving approach now being applied to bargaining requires much discussion. Yet it is not only the actual time spent in bargaining sessions, but also the personal preparation and evaluation of background materials which erode the work-day. With much of their time consumed in this way, members of the committee are having difficulty maintaining day-by-day contact with the operations or staff functions for which they are responsible. Yet, in terms of reporting at Quinn's top-management "stewardship" meetings, they are the ones who are officially obligated to know the "spit and polish" detail of each nut and bolt. Their internal conflicts can be stated as, "How does one find the time for bargaining and still maintain day-by-day executive responsibilities?"

They say it is impossible. I believe it is. It is my impression that a fundamental decision will have to be taken soon. Its effect will be that, for some time into the future, assistant department heads become the functioning department heads while the department heads themselves take responsibility for moving the bargaining forward to a mutually acceptable union-management contract that will structure future years of productive collaboration. In respect to management development at Lakeside, the obvious advantage here is that it will provide the assistant department heads a unique opportunity to experience increased responsibility they otherwise would only bear for short intervals, such as when the boss is sick or on vacation.[2] Generally, too, this decision should preclude the consequences of having overworked and frenzied managers juggling conflicting responsibilities of bargaining and operations.

A final proposal was to try to improve communications between the bargaining committee and the line organization.

Crucial Issues Affecting "Total Lakeside"

Now that negotiations between management and the union are underway, I want to step back from the narrow perspective of the person-to-person interaction so as to examine some of the crucial Lakeside issues which affect the current situation.

One significant feature is that not a single person in the organization is solely assigned to a job of seeing to it that concrete steps are taken toward enlightened union-management relations. There are people responsible for every operational activity. There is an Operations Superintendent responsible for overall production, but nowhere is there a person seriously dedicated and formally committed by continuous assignment to improving relations between the work force and management. This remains a crying need. If Quinn would put into one man's hands the overall responsibility for nursing into existence a mature, strong, collaborative relationship between management and the work force throughout the entire organization, the goal could be accomplished. Presently there are scattered individual commitments to a "blue sky" goal and spasmodic, sporadic attempts to achieve it, but not the unified, comprehensive effort which must be one person's responsibility for spearheading. That is, there ought to be an incompany OD Coordinator in place to work in this area, consult with me and stay at it after I'm gone.

Once such a comprehensive program has been initiated it should spread. Paying heed to EPIC ideals and evaluative criteria, each manager might take as his goal to have sound problem-solving relations with union representatives and his wage people. As yet, this goal is only dimly visible to the most enlightened manager. Nonetheless, under my terms of reference the goal must be to generate within Lakeside the most cohesive, organizationally identified,[4] humanely responsible group of people that is possible, given their present skills and understandings. A farther future could be even better.

Probably the most crucial issue is the inability of people to separate their *personal* needs from the needs of the situation.[5] If only they could, they would then take a cooler problem-solving approach to issues. They would be able to receive hostility and react with respect; to take barbs but to return gracious, understanding reactions. This is the toughest switch of all; it takes real strength. The instinctive way to react to a jab is to throw your mitts up and fight back. That is the common definition of a man in a man's world. You measure a man by his readiness to give as "good" as he gets—so the saying goes. What are its consequences? Blow—counterblow, stab—counterstab, push—counterpush, slug—slug back, stomp—crush. These are the primitive measures of a man. They run so deep it is hard for strong men to see a more mature way of behaving.

In the light of problem solving, rather than in the red glare of win-lose contest, the critical question is, "When you meet someone in the posture of a pugilist, can you see behind the fist to his deeper needs of retaining his self-respect which he is trying to fulfill by defending himself?" You can *kill* a man by reacting his way. You can *create* a man by reacting in a more mature manner. The question is, in a figurative sense, "How can one react to a fist other than *with* a fist?"

In my view, the thing to do is *ask*, "Why do you want to fight?" By asking this question, you put your finger on the emotional pulse of the other person. It is hard to fight someone who recognizes your real motivation and who wants to deal with the problem at the level where it bothers you. The difficulty in all of this is that failure to respond fist-for-fist is often interpreted by red-blooded men as a sign of weakness. To deal with the emotion that produces the clenched fist is the true measure of a man's strength; but few seem to realize this. Rather, they make the mistake of assuming that the measure of a man is his readiness to retaliate.

The question of whether or not the management team can continue to hold back from the fight orientation will be answered in time.

References

1. For a description of various forms of "union security" under law, see: Beal, E.F. and Wickersham, E.D. *The Practice of Collective Bargaining* (3rd Ed.). Homewood,

Ill.: Richard D. Irwin, Inc., 1967, p. 242; Linke, W.R. "The Complexities of Labor Relations Law." In Moore, R.F. (ed.), *Law for Executives*. New York: American Management Association, Inc., 1968, p. 161.

2. For a description and discussion of "process," see: Gross, B.M. *The Managing of Organizations*, volume I. New York: The Free Press, 1964, pp. 248-252. The difference between "process" and "content" is explained by Strauss, G., and Sayles, L.R., *Personnel: The Human Problems of Management*. Englewood Cliffs, N.J.: Prentice-Hall, 1960, p. 242.

3. For a concise "management development" discussion and bibliography, see: Kindall, A.F. *Personnel Administration: Principles and Cases*, (3rd Ed.). Homewood, Ill.: Richard D. Irwin, Inc., 1969, pp. 127-130.

4. "Identified" in the sense of having adopted the EPIC ideals because these are perceived as being associated with satisfying on-the-job conditions and relationships. In contrast, Freud suggests that "identification" can occur when the ego (postulated as the conscious part of individual personality) sees itself as similar to some other person; or envies and wishes to participate in the other's success, authority, or attributes; or because another person threatens the ego with aggression and the ego seeks to conquer its fear. See Brown, R. *Social Psychology*. New York: The Free Press, 1965, pp. 374-376.

5. As far back as 1925, Mary Parker Follett suggested that a solution would be "to depersonalize the giving of orders, to unite all concerned in a study of the situation, to discover the law of the situation and obey that." See: Metcalf, H.C. and Urwick, L.F. (eds.). "The Giving of Orders." *Dynamic Administration: The Collected Papers of Mary Parker Follett*. New York: Harper & Brothers, 1940, pp. 58-64.

5

The Crane Crisis

Lakeside faces a break in the progress of the bargaining due to an operational matter which touches on raw nerves and chronic sources of conflict between union and management. The present unpleasantness focuses on the use or non-use of a crane. I will describe this sequence of interactions centering on the crane as a complete episode, rather than as it occurred day by day, since it serves as an example of union-management relations during a transition period from fighting to collaboration. As will be seen, this incident is but one of many operational problems likely to occur during contract bargaining or other types of negotiations and thereby influence them. It serves to exemplify why considerations of day-by-day operational problems cannot be isolated from other problems.

The crane, which is to be used to lift massive structures at the new chemical unit, came into the gate today, September 16. The specific problem is that this crane can't be rented without employing its operator, who holds membership in the Union of Operating Engineers. In effect, work that can be done by IEW people is being given to an international union. To the independent union, this means work is being taken away from its own members.

Management's Actions

From the management point of view, however, the issue is quite simple and straightforward. In the past, management has rented other cranes and operators. Each time, the operator has come into the plant, has not worked, but has watched the operations. An IEW man has sat at the crane's controls and actually done the lift work involved. Management now feels this procedure must not continue. "To continue would be to condone *featherbedding*. It would be immoral and weak on our part to permit that to happen."

This stance has been taken on past occasions too, and the equipment hirers have gone as far away as Chicago to find a crane without an Operating Engineer aboard. Management has decided not to do that again, since the expense is doubled when a crane is brought in from such a distance. It takes approximately one day to bring it from Chicago and another day to return it. The crane is paid for at the regular rate during periods of movement since the portal-to-portal principle applies.

Union Protest

When the crane came in today, the union immediately put up a stiff protest. Dan phoned Wes, they had an unproductive talk and finally the union president hung up in the personnel chief's face. This typifies the state of aerimony and misunderstanding over the chronic crane issue.

The union has a flying wedge that management has not foreseen. A crane has to be rigged, but the operator of the crane does not rig it. Lakeside's riggers are IEW members. If the union wishes to fight, this circumstance provides sufficient ammunition to become a threat to management. According to *international* union rules, it is illegal for an Operating Engineer to work a crane that is not rigged by the international union to which non-Lakeside riggers belong. Therefore, all that the president of the IEW has to do is call up the Union of Iron Workers nearby and point out that an Operating Engineer is working a crane that was rigged by non-international riggers. The Ironworkers will picket the plant and the Operating Engineer responsible for working the crane will not cross the picket line. The result is that management will be blocked from carrying out the lift operation and will lose great sums of money every day the dispute continues. If the independent union is provoked into such action, it will have Lakeside management over a barrel.

The interesting question is, "What impact will this have on the developing contract negotiations?" The personnel chief and the union president are meeting day by day, either in the bargaining room or elsewhere, to discuss the next contract. Will the union use this crane incident as a basis for grieving rather than bargaining tomorrow? Will the meeting agenda be overturned so that a gripe session replaces it? Or, even worse, will the union men only continue to bargain on the wage contract if management backs down on the crane matter and agrees to go along with the union's stipulations? This might push the immediate bargaining situation over a precipice, if the union feels itself to be eyeball to eyeball with management where it will either have to back down and be defeated or demonstrate its capacity to deal strongly with the bosses.

Crane Crisis Crunch

Today is September 17, the day after the crane arrived. The crisis began at the crack of dawn and continued until the lights of the plant could be seen vividly against the black of night. The crane problem has been plaguing production all week.

In today's bargaining session, the union again brought up the crane matter. It was decided at the inception of the session that the matter of the crane was not a "bargainable issue" in terms of a contract. Rather, it was an issue that should be discussed as a separate matter in a different context. A session was scheduled for 8:30 a.m. between Van, Wes and others directly associated with the problem from a management point of view, and five or so members from the union including the IEW president.

Union Threatens Management

Dan started the discussion with a tirade. He ripped and tore. He accused and implied, inferred and insulted. He did a consummate job of needling at the emotional level. He roared and wrangled. Then the personnel chief took the bull by the horns and tried to pin its shoulders to the mat. He wrenched and smashed and hit. It was verbally bloody.

After Dan and Wes had exhausted their rhetorics, things settled down somewhat; not that people became more reasonable, but they seemed less emotional. By now they were into a cold nerves-of-steel power hassle. Threats were thrown in the same free way as on the previous day, when Dan had said he would have the Ironworkers picketing the plant by 3:00 p.m. The threat still had sufficient reality to be of considerable disturbance to management.

In spite of the fact that for several days management has vowed, member-by-member, that it would not back down on this one, after a while you could see them beginning to turn, tuck tail, and run for cover. Management began looking for "peace with honor." "Honor" in this sense is measured by living up to its vows to avoid featherbedding while at the same time meeting the legitimate request of the Lakeside labor force that work should not be denied them.

Union Supplies a Way Out for Management

Toward the end of this hectic session, Dan made a casual remark to the effect that the union had investigated crane rentals and had found no difficulty in locating a supplier who would provide a crane without an operator. Management pricked its ears and protested that it had been unable to find such a supplier. The union said that not only were there suppliers nearby, but that the job could be done more cheaply by IEW people and that the cost of the unmanned crane would be in line with the cost of the present crane.

Searching for a basis of resolution, Van Gray made the following proposal to the union. "Look Dan, as we all know, there's a crane in place right now, ready to lift. In that sense the die is cast; we're already committed for *this* week's crane unless you want us to back the thing out and hire another one. Now, Dan, here's our offer. If you can satisfy us that a local supplier can provide a crane at a comparable cost, so that on the *next* big lift which is scheduled March or April, we have a crane that can be operated by Lakeside people with no hired gun from outside, then we'll accommodate you *this* time. We'll leave the Operating Engineer in the cab today as an observer, *not* as an operator. We'll use a local man to actually do the lift. In this way, no work will be taken away from an IEW man, and we only will be condoning featherbedding this final time."

"Agreed," said the union, "We can do it."

Part of management was not convinced. Hal Harvey, the Engineering boss, said, "Show us the evidence that you can do it." Management still had time to haggle because the lift job was not scheduled until 2:30 p.m., and by now it was only 11:00 a.m. So they began to prod into the union information about where to get a crane next time. Nonetheless, the IEW's data checked out as sound enough, and the deal seemed ready to close.

Management Representatives Confront Their Constituency

Prior to making its final commitment, management knew it had to consider the following problem. Having been appointed as representatives, Van, Wes and the others had promised their colleagues they would not back down on this crane issue, regardless of what occurred. So Van said to the union, "We would like an hour and a half between now and 12:30 to talk this matter through with the management people who are most directly involved. We'll give you the final word on this by 12:30." The union left, apparently satisfied that justice would be done.

Hal Harvey then told his assistant department head, Earl Higgins, to get together with the division heads and unit supervisors who were intimately involved in the problem. Earl did so, and painted in the background of the picture in broad strokes, pointing to the difficulties created by the lift operator and the desire of management to solve the problem in a way that supported the independent union. Then, he described the union-management deal that was ready for ratification.

According to Earl, he met a wave of opposition. "Absolutely not!" was the reaction. "This is yielding to pressure. This is bowing to coercion. Have we no guts? If you yield on this one, we'll give up on promoting efficiency, because every time we do, you fellows squeak out and don't support us."

Earl got on the horn to Hal and Van. "The boys say no, flat no." A flurry of excitement followed.

Finally, Van, as operations superintendent, said, "Look, this lift can't be delayed. We can't get internal agreement among ourselves, so someone has to call the signal. We can't have one set of signals from one spot and another set from elsewhere and anticipate any coordinated action. Right? Now, the signal is, Hal, that at 12:30 you tell Earl and I'll tell Dan that we'll go ahead with our plan as agreed."

"Okay, if that's the way you want it."

"That's the way I want it."

But well before the union returned at 12:30 a new anxiety arose. The hired crane was of 60-ton capacity and it was to be used for a lift job. In fact, four cranes were involved, but three were company owned and smaller. The new anxiety was, "Do we have a man competent and qualified to operate the 60-tonner?" Hal got Earl Higgins, who was now back in the room, to check on this point.

Earl phoned the foreman in charge of the job. "Pete, we've decided to put one of our own men on this job and have the Operating Engineer in the cab, but not to take the job away from the Lakeside man. Can you supply a fellow to do it?"

Pete said, "I'll check, I don't know." Pete checked and time passed. Suspense was as thick as a London fog where everyone's groping but no one knows where anyone else is.

The phone rang. Pete was back on the line. "We have only one man I would even consider putting on this job. He hasn't operated a crane of this size in over two years, and besides, he is unfamiliar with the type of crane you've hired."

"That does it, then," said Van. "We can't use him on a job of this magnitude. We can't afford the risk. The lift is being done in a cramped space. If it were out in the middle of a fifteen acre lot, maybe we could go ahead. In this cramped location, though, one mistake could cost a million. There is no Lakesider I'm willing to trust with the job."

Now management was in a pickle again. One part of management had practically given the union a "Let us go forward together" answer. Van had felt constrained to intervene and resolve an internal management dispute. That meant another segment of management had been backed down and felt rejected. Now, on technical grounds, Van had reversed field in a fashion that could not be reconciled with his earlier decision. The union has gone away feeling that satisfaction was assured, but now it can't reap the fruits of the agreement because there is not one wage man available who seems competent to do the job.

Management Fails to Satisfy the Union

It was 12:30 p.m. Preparation for the lift was underway. What was to be done? The union was back in the room. The operations superintendent spoke.

"Well, fellows, it's this way. We're ready to go along with you, but we don't have anyone down there who's regarded by the foreman as having the skill qualifications to operate the big crane under the risks involved. We just can't meet you on this one. We're sorry, we tried our best. We just can't do it."

"Okay. This means war," retorted the union president.

"No," said management, "this shouldn't mean war. This means failure. We tried. We wanted to go along. We wanted to meet you. We are unable to because of technical skill and experience factors."

Then the union officers started to dig in. "What *are* the qualifications you demand for this kind of job? How do you *know* you don't have an adequately qualified person?" Of course, here, management was embarrassed because there were no well-defined or clearly stated criteria to identify those who can and can't do this kind of job.

Dan stomped out of the room, disgusted and rejected, but defiant. Three other union officers hung around. One of them finally opened up. He said, "I'm really disappointed that you were unable to help, but I know you tried. For myself, I'm not going to go along with Dan. If he calls in the Ironworkers he is going to have to do it on his own initiative." A second officer repeated the same sentiments. So did the third.

Dissension in the Union

The union president was on his own now, out on a limb. He had lost the solid support that up to now he had been receiving from his colleagues. Why? Because management's representatives had genuinely sought to solve this problem in an acceptable manner. The other union people sensed management's intentions and responded, even though the performance fell short of ideal. Dan had failed to appreciate the legitimate and sincere intentions guiding management's efforts to solve this problem.

Earl Higgins said to the union officers who remained, "Look, we have this next lift coming along. Let's start working on it next week, to make arrangements on an amicable basis before it divides and splits us even more."

But the union officials were turning gloomy. They said, "If we run into these kinds of problems again and again, there is little use in trying. How do we know that you'll have qualified an operator by next March, when you're still on dead center now in September? It just isn't worth it. We'll just have to work out the problem some other way." So here is another example of good effort gone awry; failure produced in spite of a college try to be collaborative.

Finale

The lift job is over. It went smoothly. The unit that had to be lifted is now securely in place. It was a brilliant job of engineering which took about two and one-half hours. From the union standpoint, the opportunity to veto the operation has passed. Has a background for future cooperation been established? Possibly so, but more possibly not.

People get discouraged under these circumstances. Once they try and fail, the readiness to try again is reduced. It becomes a creeping failure fester. These pathetic periods of imbalance and confusion are disturbing and threatening to management, to the union, and to the work force. Progress is difficult. One impasse after another seems to arise.

This union and this management seem oddly magnetized toward each other; one being able to create deadlock situations that totally frustrate the other and provoke hostile reactions rather than cooperative responses. It is as though two fighters were in a ring intending to spar to see which could win the most points, but then one foolishly strikes low. The other gets mad. They start shoving and swiping and jabbing and cutting and bloodying until they are totally involved in blind, destructive conflict.

There is another pathetic element in all of this which can be illustrated by what happened later in the day. We went out to the lift location where 30 or 40 people were involved. One crane operator belonged to the Union of Operating Engineers. The rest, all local people, were pulling together in a beautiful job of teamwork with complete attention focused on the problem of the lift. Watching the people, you might conclude that the union-management issue being debated with such emotionality and illfeeling was of little concern to them. They had a challenging job to do.

You got the feeling that the real pathos in this situation is that so many of the issues are ideological, theoretical, and matters of principle. So few seem concerned with the work itself, the conditions of being secure, or realistic considerations of dignity. Is it the battle of the politicians, as distinct from the problems of the people?

6

Attacking Problems on Two Fronts: Bargaining and Development

This week's crane incident served to define one of the key procedural issues of present bargaining. This was, "Can either union or management legitimately bring operational matters into the bargaining session for resolution there?" If so, either side could bypass routine "grievance"[1] channels. This issue was dealt with and the union-management conferees agreed that they would, whenever necessary, adjourn bargaining so that various members could engage in separate grievance sessions to resolve major operations-related problems. We have seen how this occurred over the past two days.

Small though it was, this procedural thing could be an important step toward developing a clear-cut objective for the bargaining conference: to deal with matters of contract revision rather than with problems of operational detail. If the point can be firmly established, the result should be quite a gain for both management and union.

On the afternoon of September 17, as soon as the crane problem had been squared away, the committee met to resume its work. Then bargaining got down to the issue of management's desire to restrict the union's present privilege of placing whatever it wishes on the 50 bulletin boards around the plant. Since September 15, when the issue was first discussed, neither side's position has shifted markedly. The word "attack" continues to be the stumbling block to finding a satisfactory basis for resolution.

The union was forthright in maintaining its desire to continue posting minutes of grievance sessions and other materials that might be regarded more as propaganda than fact. Their delegates insisted that propaganda is one of the few tools available for arousing wage people's emotions and support in favor of the essentially valid positions the union wants to pursue.

Then an interesting switch took place. They got into examining the kinds of materials that management puts in its *own* bulletins that are routed to managers, engineers, supervisors and foremen, and which also can be read by anyone else who might stop by a bulletin board. During discussion, the union made the point that it was willing to put itself under the same rules of communicative propriety as management. This proposal seemed entirely reasonable from management's point of view, till after the session when committee members had the opportunity to examine some of the materials published over the past few years. Then, management felt that perhaps it would be unwise to commit itself to living under the same restraints it was asking of the union.

In any event, a clause to appear in the contract regarding notices placed on bulletin boards could be that neither union nor management will intentionally attack individuals or groups. If management is willing to buy this, the union will accept it.

One other truly imperative issue came to the fore during today's interaction. This issue is vital for it concerns whether or not the union can participate in defining job content. If it can, it has achieved what unionists call "codetermination."

Management wants full authority to define the limits, scope, and depth of a wage man's activities. It wants no restraints on its freedom to do so. Management feels that in operating a sound business, it is justified in setting or altering a man's assignment without union involvement.

The union, on the other hand, sees job content as one area in which a man's legitimate rights can be violated. He can be given assignments totally inappropriate to his background, experience and skill. So-called "restructuring" of a job may amount to victimization. Sometimes it is a conveyor-belt to termination. Dan Ives made an impassioned speech, asserting that without codetermination there would be no contract agreement. Management's position is equally rigid, insisting on having the sole and final authority to determine a man's work. Negotiations on this issue will be initiated next week.

Interestingly enough, management has been pressured again by the union to speed up bargaining, to move faster, and to spend more time on it. This afternoon, the union challenged the meetings schedule. Management finally agreed to three sessions next week; two half-day sessions and one full-day session.

An external event which has been impinging on the wage aspects of bargaining is that one of the EPIC's major competitors, which has three plants comparable to Lakeside, today offered a five percent general increase covering all three. Two of them have independent unions and at the other, an international is bargaining agent. The word is that the international will not accept the five percent, but rather will strike to test how much more might be gained under the pressure of threat. It is thought tonight that the two independents will respond favorably to the increase offered.

A General Wage Increase

Ever present in the undercurrents of bargaining is the expectation of a general wage increase. This matter has not yet been brought up in the bargaining sessions at Lakeside, but every now and then some rumbles indicate that the time is drawing near when the issue will erupt. It is fascinating to study the matter of wages, rates, and pay scales, and to ask what is the basis for a man's pay. Is it his worth as measured by some traceable contribution to profit? Or may it be traditional that some lines of work receive more money than others because they are regarded as more honorable or more essential? Or is it the pressure of bargaining and the threat of strike that determines a man's wages? All of these are factors, but the real basis for wage setting in the EPIC companies is in *area competition* comparisons. For example, a number of plants in the Lakeside area pay certain rates for laborers, pipe fitters, plumbers, masons, and so on. Data regarding these pay scales—minimums, maximums, average and modal values, and so on—are regularly collected and made available to other local plants. Consequently, every interested unit knows whether its wage and salary scales are below the area average, on a par with the prevailing rate, or above it. This can be done specifically for each craft or skill. Since comparative data are available, employers never talk about what the *man* is worth, what the *activity* is worth, or what a man's *contribution* to the development of the company is worth. Rather, the question is "Is our company in or out of line?"

This question tends to be asked if the plant management is concerned that it is paying either more or less than its competitors. If it is paying more, the easy answer is that labor costs are higher than they should be. If it is paying less, the study of comparative rates may only serve to confirm why some capable people have been leaving the organization. In this case, the plant may have to offer above-average rates to fill key vacancies quickly. This and its ensuing response-ripples are among the factors that will influence the next period's wage pattern. In these and possibly other ways, competition with other companies determines what a company pays, not necessarily a man's worth.

In any competitive operation, performance statistics are computed for comparison against other production centers. In wage matters, use of one's own unit's competitors as basis for comparison may be right in some respects, but not in others.

For example, in the engineering department at Lakeside, some people do maintenance work, and others do construction. Within the region, many other production and service facilities such as garages, factories and so on, also employ maintenance people. Similarly the local construction industry, as well as Lakeside, employs people who have skills and craft capabilities. Thus a man who engages in these types of work at Lakeside compares himself with his acquaintances who may be working in an entirely unrelated maintenance or production activity elsewhere in the district. For him, the comparison is man to man, or—if he looks farther afield—neighborhood to neighborhood. But for the company, the basis for comparison is plant to plant.

This difference in the reference unit as a comparison basis means that wage people feel they are being evaluated on an impersonal basis wherever they go, since they do more or less the same thing. When inequalities become apparent to the man, he sees them only as differences between relatively "good" and relatively "bad" places to work.

Inside his own organization each man intuitively compares himself with his work partners. Here his basis for evaluating a just return for his performance is the amount of effort he sees himself putting out in comparison with others.

Wage and salary administration is a complex field in which many conflicting considerations arise.[2] Perhaps the single greatest weakness in using comparison statistics as a basis for setting a wage structure is that it fails to respect individual differences in effort. Under "equal qualification along with seniority" a man is not motivated to put out more than perfunctory effort. Regardless of how much or how little he puts out, as long as it is not below some managerial tolerance, no financial distinction exists between himself and his fellow workers.

A result is that a norm quickly arises which constitutes a "fair day's work." The norm itself may relate partly to pay, partly to attitudes toward the foreman or one another, but *not* to one's personal capacity to produce.[3]

As I can observe, a university setting operates in the same manner in that one university uses others of similar size and reputation for comparative purposes. Unwisely, it doesn't consider what a particular faculty member can make in industry. For example, a professor may be evaluating whether a continued academic career or a new industrial career is the better prospect for him. Thus, his basis for comparison may vary completely with the basis used by the university in its salary offers to him. The same is true in religious institutions where a minister's rate of pay is determined by what other churches are paying rather than what the same man might earn in a more commercial type of activity.

It is because of this tendency for organizations to use other units similar to themselves as a basis for comparison, and for employees, in contrast, to compare themselves with other people doing similar activities, that chronic tensions generate around the matter of financial incentives. Using money as a motivator would become much more realistic if it were based on individual effort and contribution, rather than on comparison.

A tremendous amount of jockeying is going on over a general wage increase. There has not been one for a long time, and each major company in the industry is trying to find a level—whether three, five, or whatever percent—as an offering basis. Obviously these competing companies cannot formulate an agreed strategy because this would violate Federal law.[4] Not only does Lakeside management anticipate pressure by IEW for a general wage increase but it is already under the pressure of movements throughout the industry to strike the best level at the best time. This is a fascinating process of bidding. The company that offers five percent today will not, in my view, be successful in establishing a level for the industry. The amount is likely to be substantially more than five percent before the game is over.

Between September 21-23 there were three bargaining sessions, one on Monday morning, another on Tuesday afternoon, and the third all day on Wednesday. Negotiations hung up on only one point, which was the issue of codetermination of job content. It was decided to table this problem and plow on to other outstanding issues on which accord might be more readily achieved.

Management's Bargainers Report Back

Tonight, September 28, around 5:00 p.m., the management bargaining committee met with Quinn to survey areas where the bargainers are proposing changing past practices. On several occasions Quinn was surprised by the extent to which members of the committee had moved toward understanding and agreeing with labor's point of view. The general consensus is that "give and take" readiness has been established and that—barring unforeseen circumstances—it may eventually be possible for management and the IEW union to come to a meeting of the minds. Three months ago, such a prediction would have been totally disbelieved and laughed off the table.

Tomorrow's bargaining is scheduled for the afternoon. As of today, I feel that the task I originally faced has been completed. This is not to say that a contract is likely to be signed in the near future. But recent events have shown that the methodology of avoiding win-lose traps and engaging in a problem-solving process based orientation is entirely feasible even against a past background of bitter intergroup warfare and strife.

Two months ago, members of management were suspicious, distrustful, even vitriolic toward labor's representatives. Today they joined with the union officers and sang "Happy Birthday" to one of the latter. This happened in the middle of some intense bargaining on a technical matter involving definitions of "work day" and "work week."

The bargaining is tough-minded, yet the degree of trust between the two groups seems continuously to be on the increase. Management has released no propaganda bulletins and the union has refrained from launching any attacks on management. At Lakeside this is the first time the union has engaged in bargaining without trying to inflame the work force. Management has communicated to supervisors through a letter sent to their homes. It describes the status of negotiations. The union recently issued a handout concerned with problems of membership participation in union affairs and also announced a general meeting for the night of September 30. At this meeting there will be a report on the status of negotiations.

The reason IEW has taken this course is that it wants to communicate the *atmosphere* of present negotiations as well as their content. Union officers feel the membership will thereby better understand current intentions and ultimate goals while the officers will gain increased support when the membership realizes that its elected representatives are trying to bargain in good faith in an atmosphere newly characterized by statesmanship.

It has been unequivocally established both in my mind and in those of Lakeside's top management that it is possible to bargain successfully with the IEW. It also has been established in the minds of the union members that this management has become concerned with solving the interrelated problems of wage people, of the union, and of the Lakeside plant in general. Negotiations could still eventually come to an impasse, but I think it has already been demonstrated that the two groups can become more insightful about one another's tensions and needs. As this occurs, they shift into a confronting yet amicable problem-solving relationship which they should be able to continue.

Today, in the post-negotiation meeting, the committee members revealed for the first time what their attitudes had been when I told them the only practical way to proceed was to search for problem-solving conditions. It turns out that no member of management—neither those sitting at the bargaining session, nor at the top of the organization, nor at any other position for that matter—believed it was possible to establish problem-solving conditions with the union. Their general convictions were that Blake was insane; that he was just unresponsive to the intricacies and distraught and disturbed relations existing between the union and themselves. They said, furthermore, that although they had begun proceeding in this direction, it was not because they were convinced this was a good way to go. Rather, it was because they could see no alternative way to go other than terminating negotiations immediately, which would verify the union propaganda that management was arbitrary and impossible to work with.

So the management bargaining committee went into intergroup problem solving with the half-hearted and semi-hopeful conviction that it should show "good faith." The moment they began credibly to manifest good faith, they were responded to in a like manner. The rest is "history" up until the present circumstances. It is remarkable to see men—who for years had been locked in controversy, conflict, derision and all of the other things that cause groups to remain separated and hostile—pulling together in the search for solutions to common problems and joining together in a song of "Happy Birthday" to one of their number.

Development Report

A new departure today was the planning of a new series of managerial development meetings starting with top management. Today also, I discussed with Quinn the possibility of repeating the organization-wide critique sessions.

At Quinn's "stewardship" meeting, to be held tomorrow, I will report on my activities at Lakeside. There are three major points I want to cover. One is concerned with my talks with and observations of the union. Another relates to my in-plant activities not concerned with union-management relations. A third is to deal with the problem of psychological tests and their shortcomings. I intend to tackle each topic only in the context of what, to me, are more relevant matters. My goal is to trace the course of development at Lakeside over the nine months that I have been here, and to address the general manager's staff group on some crucial action steps they could well consider taking during the period ahead.

The "reporting problem" in this upcoming session is that many of my contacts are private and are based on mutual trust. I know many secrets only because people trust me and feel I will not communicate their confidences to any other person or group. Therefore, I have a personal stake in protecting the anonymity of individuals and situations. My goal in this session is one of basic inquiry into future actions, rather than tracking the mechanics of the past. At my suggestion, Quinn now intends to initiate a second round of organization-wide critique sessions as a basis for assessing our present position and seeing where we should aim in the period ahead. This represents a big opportunity.

References

1. For a general description of grievance procedure operating through the respective management and union organizational hierarchies and within the collective bargaining relationship itself, see: Dunlop, J.T. and Healy, J.J. *Collective Bargaining: Principles and Cases.* Homewood, Ill.: Richard D. Irwin, Inc., 1955, pp. 43-44, 48-49, and 78-81.

2. See: Dunn, J.D. and Rachel, F.M. *Wage and Salary Administration.* New York: McGraw-Hill Book Company, Inc., 1971.

3. See, for example, the descriptions of informal output norms within the "Bank Wiring Observation Room." In Homans, G.C. *The Human Group.* New York: Harcourt, Brace & Co., 1950, pp. 60-64.

4. While it is certainly permissible for two or more employers, or an employers' association, to discuss or even coordinate their negotiating strategies vis-á-vis one or

more unions, there are areas in which such actions might be suspect as violating federal and/or state antitrust laws; for example, when these appear to be "in restraint of trade"; and particularly when unions, through contract agreements, thereby become parties to several large companies' collusive bidding arrangements. Additionally, one employer's "refusal to bargain until its competitors have done so" is illegal. See: Hills, C.A. (ed.). *Antitrust Adviser.* New York: McGraw-Hill Book Company, 1971, Chapter 14.

7

A Time for Review and Target Setting

The top man in an organization has the opportunity to create the tone, atmosphere, color and tempo of the organization. On a day-by-day basis, he does this by his actions, pronouncements, edicts, and queries. If he wishes, he can emphasize productivity to the near exclusion of morale and other interpersonal considerations. Or, at the other extreme, he can concentrate on improving human relations, possibly to the detriment of high productivity. Any top man exerts substantial influence simply by virtue of his personal predispositions.

There are, of course, some definite limiting circumstances. If profit margins are too low, the manager is under pressure to increase productivity. If labor relations are bad, he is under pressure to improve them. If both are in good shape, he can run a smooth, effective operation. If both production and human relationships are in bad shape, his job is likely to be endangered. Although these are circumstances which to some extent are beyond a manager's personal control—particularly in a decentralized plant, which, like Lakeside, has to accept certain guidelines from headquarters—the personal touch of the manager is still a critical ingredient.

When a manager or a top man puts on the pressure, it is usually applied to those immediately beneath him. They in turn apply the pressure to their immediate subordinates, and so on down the line. Applying production pressure through a line organization is relatively easy. The quest for better human relations is usually more elusive because methods of monitoring production are more adequate, concrete, and easily applied than the methods for measuring human relations.

So, in a production center, pressure from the top is transmitted down the line through the various levels until it reaches the foreman, who actually applies these pressures in his dealings with the work force. Most foremen are practical men elevated from the wage ranks because they were good workers, not because they were skilled as personnel administrators. Thus, whenever the top man applies *production* pressures, these are immediately understandable to the foreman.

But it is more difficult to apply top-to-bottom pressures that say "Improve human relations!" One reason is that intermediate echelons in the hierarchy must transmit to the foreman whatever emphasis the top man places on human relations. Although the foreman isn't in direct contact with the top man, he has an image of what the top man is like. He remembers productivity actions that have been sought in the past, and compares them with this new message which by contrast is unspecific. What he knows the top man to have said on previous occasions and what his immediate supervisor is now passing down are often seen by the foreman as contradictory statements. The top man's pronouncements regarding better human relations sound like platitudes, words to soothe the multitude, opiates. He can't believe he is supposed to translate them into actions. They smack more of goodwill offerings spoken by the top man at a three-martini luncheon. Why should he, the foreman, change his entire approach just because of one out-of-character statement by the brass? And even if he were willing to, how *could* he?

Since production is more heavily emphasized and more easily measured than human relations, foremen are valued more or less by their contributions to production. They, in turn, supervise and make judgments about subordinates in much the same way, disregarding human relations except in extreme cases. Then, if he sees the situation as a "one or the other" dilemma, the foreman is likely to do one of two things. He either lets up altogether, without trying either for production or human relations; or he swings from one to the other in a pendulum type way, pressing for production today, and pushing for good human relations tomorrow. Each of these options produces worker discontent and executive frustration. In particular, after a period of pressure for production, it is difficult to shift the system so that it will generate conditions that lead to better human relations.

Strengthening Human Relations at Lakeside

Up to now, at Lakeside, it has been possible for me, slowly but surely, to exert positive influence toward effective human relations. Beginning with the general manager and his top group, these influences are spreading down to department heads, particularly those engaged in bargaining. The bargaining table is an excellent followup to laboratory training. It enables managers to discover their assumptions which appear in the work setting. They are also able to contrast their similar efficiency goals with one another's more or less mediocre skills in understanding people. As a result, management's bargaining team has undergone an extensive educational experience during the past three months. In contrast to the slow but perceptible change in skill and in attitude at the top of the organization, what do the next-to-bottom people—the foremen—say? Something like, "Laboratory training had an impact on me, a good one, but its effects are wearing off. I know that even though Quinn has been heard to say he wants good human relations, my supervisor really wants production and will sacrifice humanity to get it. So, do I go against my supervisor and try to work in a way that could lessen productivity until my people get a handle on what I learned was worthwhile in on-the-job human relations? No, I can't risk that, so I'll have to keep the pressure on. A steady level of day-by-day results is what my supervisor wants and that's what I'm going to give him."

I have now worked out a proposal for activating the human side of foremen. This should start with Quinn enunciating clearly and distinctly to the entire organization a goals-setting development program which is intended to spread throughout management, beginning with the foremen. The first step is one in which foremen sit down either with their supervisors or with training consultants and develop a specific program to improve relationships with their subordinates. Such a program is specific, giving names and the related concrete actions intended, and whether these are to be implemented in group or individual-interview situations. Every foreman should have completed this task within two months. Next, each supervisor of foremen will be made responsible for two things: for carrying out the same type of task in respect to the foremen who report to him; and for reviewing and helping each foreman with his individual plans for improving work relations. The supervisor at the next level is responsible for doing the same, and so on, up to the top man.

All of these programs of improvement are to be written down and copies sent to each successively higher level, and eventually, in summary form, to the general manager. The statement should specify concrete individual and group goals, with accomplishment targeted according to schedules between January 1 and December 31 of next year.

To get a program of this type off the ground, Quinn ought to convene the entire plant's supervisory group—possibly in three different shift sections—and directly state to them his convictions and expectations for accomplishment in the relationships area. In addition, he should express how he wants to see the organization move toward accomplishing these objectives. For example, and in terms of specific individual goals, each supervisor could be made accountable for reporting at quarterly intervals the extent to which he has made progress in accomplishing his stated objectives, and revising those which have been identified as unsound.

A Session with the General Manager

I met with Quinn this morning, September 29, at 8:45. To understand our discussion it is necessary to appreciate that the three days of bargaining last week had a fundamental impact both on the bargaining committee and on Quinn himself. These three days, possibly more than any events of the past six months, clearly demonstrated to management that the union's intentions are sound and honorable. It does want to clear up the morass of chronic problems and find constructive solutions. Even yesterday, my first day back at Lakeside after a week away, I had not sensed the full intensity of the change that has now permeated top management.

Quinn and I explored the matter of bottom-to-top goal setting as a method of improving the human side of the organization. His reactions were favorable. As we talked, a new issue emerged. This concerned the Green Acres series of conferences that took place last February and March.

One of the immediate consequences of Green Acres can be characterized in the following way. Before then, Quinn was taking a rather on-and-off, hot-and-cold attitude toward the union. One day his attitude would be, "We must cooperate and establish sound working relations." The next day, his attitude would be that the union is a hopeless group, and that its officers are too bad a bunch to even attempt cooperative relationships. After Green Acres, Quinn's attitude solidified. His views from that point forward, with a few minor exceptions, have been consistent with the conference's recommendations, namely, "We must treat the union with dignity and respect. We must react to their officers as office-holders rather than as personalities."

Because of this clarification of direction and sense of certainty, Quinn's evaluation of the union has become more favorable. In fact, his only unhappiness is that the initial conferences' effects have not permeated farther down the organization. As we talked this morning, the idea emerged that considering the events of the last six months, maybe we should return to Green Acres to inquire whether the decisions made then were wise, and if so, what the next steps of action should be; and if not, which way we should move now.

The idea behind this recommendation was that after a six-month interval, management should examine how Lakeside is moving toward both its production objectives and toward fulfilling its commitment to establish more effective human relations. As Quinn and I debated this proposal, it became clear that the Green Acres format was a better approach for accomplishing objectives than the more formalistic program which I had suggested at the beginning of our meeting.

Tomorrow afternoon at the general manager's staff meeting, my report on my past year's activities will be presented. I intend to sketch the critical events as I have seen them. Since it was more Quinn's idea than mine to "return to Green Acres," I hope that after I have confronted the organization with the dilemma as I now see it, he will trigger discussion of a second Green Acres series. If he does this, and others agree, then the pattern is again established for the future, and we will try to press through a number of sessions before the end of November.

The goal will be to deal with the rest of the organization by forming groups consisting of supervisors at the same level as those who participated in the four previous sessions. My general reaction is that we have again struck on a new theme—or reaffirmed an old theme—which has great organizational validity and soundness. The organization critique constitutes a useful way for an organization to study itself and plot its directions of development, not from arbitrary top-level edicts but through convictions derived from participative diagnosis of the situation. Each organization member can contribute to this by personal involvement in attitude assessment and problem solving.

Reporting to the Management Staff Group

The management group met today, September 30, to hear the report of my activities to date at Lakeside. It seemed it might be valuable to recapitulate the background of the projects during the last nine months, so I began my report with a historical review.

To understand the progress in the bargaining committee, it is necessary to look back at the last election of the wage union officers, and the months leading up to it. The election was a complicated one in many respects. Two independent unions were vying for the right to represent all Lakeside workers. An NLRB election[19] was held to determine which group should constitute Lakeside's authorized independent union. One of the groups was known as "independent-independents" while the other, headed by Dan Ives, was labeled "international-independents." This was because the international-independents were presumed to be sympathetic to ICEW, the international union which was eager to get into Lakeside, and to have its active support.

The election fight was bitter. Management's not-so-tacit endorsement of the independent-independents was visible in many attitudes, expressions, and actions throughout the campaigning period. When the election took place, though, the international-independents won. This placed management in an unattractive position because the faction which it had rejected was now within an inch of becoming the Lakeside workers' official bargaining agent.

A few days thereafter there was a run-off election, under NLRB rules, to determine whether the international itself or the newly elected IEW independent group would be the actual unit to represent Lakeside's wage employees.

Between the two elections, Quinn had gone on television to emphasize that the people who were voting for the Ives-headed IEW group were not necessarily voting for later affiliation with the ICEW. After the election, in which the independent union came in ahead of ICEW by a thin margin, a long period of uneasy truce—masking seething resentments on both sides—began. During this period IEW started to develop the contract proposal which has been so much in the forefront of recent negotiations.

Shortly after the second election, I was invited to Lakeside to consider coming into the organization, either on a permanent basis or on some kind of interim appointment, to aid management's bargaining team to achieve a more stable, productive and collaborative relationship with the IEW, as well as between the entire management group and the wage force. I did not take the job immediately, but set up a six weeks period to study the possibility. During January and February I had about forty interviews with many people I had met in laboratory-seminars. In addition, I had intensively studied the rival unions' pamphlets and Lakeside's controversial "Newsletters to Management" to see what insights into union-management history they could give me. During March and April, a further step resulted from the four Green Acres sessions. It was also during this period that a psychological consultant's evaluation project was itself evaluated and came to a close.

During May, the major activities were focused on problems of psychological testing, too numerous to mention here beyond saying that engineers, as much as any single group, have a bad understanding of the limitations of psychological testing and the narrow improvement in executive selection/promotion procedures possible from them. It was also during this period that I had my first talks with Dan Ives and Dick Kelly, the two power figures of the IEW. We had numerous discussions through July regarding the appropriateness of training laboratories for their members. Finally we had to table the idea that training of this kind for wage people was feasible at this time.

During July, bargaining with the salary union got under way. It was characterized by considerable discussion regarding how to establish a problem-solving relationship within the salary bargaining committee. This was successfully accomplished, and negotiations are proceeding at the present time. The beginnings of wage bargaining were also initiated during July.

In that month, pressures were applied by people in management's ranks who earlier had tried to exert background influence in the union elections. Now they had a program to stimulate wage people to run for elective offices which would be voted upon in September. For management to actively influence people to be candidates, would be, I felt, intervention and manipulation of a devious political character. Lakeside management took the problem under study and developed the attitude that management should avoid playing politics, either in identifying candidates or helping to turn out the vote. So far, though, the election, so fervently demanded in July to take place in September, has not been formally scheduled.

August and September brought a heavy increase in wage and salary bargaining, committee meetings, and a further concern with psychological testing. It was during September that I became strongly involved in analyzing conditions that had generated numerous grievances. In addition to these activities over the several months, I attended regular meetings in several production departments as well as the management committee meetings, where the state of the business is evaluated and reviewed; and the general manager's staff meeting, where the report that I am describing here was made. A continuing activity has been working with Wes Stratton and others in the personnel department.

Significant Interventions

I regard three of my interventions in particular as the most successful in terms of being highly relevant to what is going on now. The first one, already described, is the initiation of Green Acres organization critique sessions. These were highly significant, for they defined the path on which the organization is still traveling. Another event was the famous session when the management bargaining committee first received the union's proposals. This was when I challenged them to recognize that they were "going into orbit" and that such behavior only would prove to the union officers and to wage personnel alike that here was an arbitrary hostile group which was unresponsive to employees' legitimate needs for security and dignity. The third intervention I see as having been an important breakthrough in these months was my heart-to-heart, finger-into-the-chest conversation with Dan Ives, where I argued that he could make the worst mistake of his life if he failed to recognize the problem-solving motivation currently existing within management. Each of these three interventions has led in one way or another to the union-management negotiations which are now taking place under quite favorable circumstances. It is a flat prediction that without any of these three critical events, relations with the IEW and the salary union would be bogged down at the present time.

Points of Failure

There are several activities I felt would have contributed significantly but did not. I regard these as failures in my efforts. One of these was the proposed but as yet unaccepted three-day laboratory to enable the top thirteen managers of Lakeside to explore their interpersonal relationships and problems of working toward organization goals.

The second point of failure is that I have had relatively little access to foremen. I regard foremen relationships with wage people as the next most crucial area requiring improvements. In the analogy of football, foremen constitute the "line." A person like myself, cast in the consulting role, can spend his entire energies consulting with the backfield of top management, but if the backfield has no line to help it move forward, touchdowns will be few and far between.

My third area of failure was that I have had no access to wage people, except through contacts with union officers. Fourthly, followups on the recommendations that came out of the Green Acres sessions had not been as successful as I had hoped they would be.

Considerable discussion took place regarding these points of failure as Quinn's staff group members debated them. Calvert Carroll echoed some of my sentiments. Cal was the number two man of Lakeside until a few months ago, when he suffered a coronary. He is now back on a part-time basis, handling a training assignment. Cal said that he, too, found it difficult to get access to unit supervisors and foremen. His voice, added to mine, aroused substantial concern among the top group, which had now learned that lower-ranking members of the organization are under such trigger pressure for production that they don't find it convenient to leave the work place for even a 30-minute conference.

Finally, I stated what is, in my judgment, the present dilemma confronting Lakeside. I can expect no enduring success from the laboratory-seminars and the Green Acres conferences, or even from the present wage and salary union negotiations, if Lakeside management is unable to improve relationships between the foremen and the work force. These are relationships which, on a day-by-day basis, mold attitudes and feelings which either create cohesion or crack it; which generate good morale or disrupt it. No amount of work on any production or special-interest group level will suffice for dealing with Lakeside's most critical problem: the relationship between a foreman and his men. This point of view immediately took hold, and we devoted another two hours to investigating how to crack the problem wide open.

One of the issues debated during this exploration period was the EPIC policy slogan: "Our responsibility is to operate in a sound business manner, consistent with good human relations." It dates back to the "great inquest" EPIC conducted on itself after a blood-spattering strike incident in the 1920s. I have heard the slogan repeated so often around Lakeside that it has become nearly unbearable. Today I brought this out into the open.

I said, "This phrase is very much like a Rorschach ink blot. It means all things to all people. It can be interpreted by anyone to justify his behavior, even indeed to justify acting in the same old way rather than changing." As an example, I described the situation in another EPIC subsidiary, American Chemical Company, where one day's human relations training each month is required for every foreman. In that company, this is regarded as running the business in a sound manner consistent with good human relations. I also provided another example from the same organization: that if it comes to a choice as to who is right—a foreman or a wage earner—the standing rule is that it's the wage earner. This, as seen by American Chemical, is consistent with good human relations. The Lakeside organization doesn't have even this degree of definition to guide its search for what is meant by "sound business operation consistent with good human relations."

Human Relations Training

Early this morning, October 1, I phoned the general manager and said, "Quinn, let's go a little slower in instigating a human relations program, so we can be sure that the plan we formulate is sound, thorough, and adequate." He agreed, but only with reluctance, because he wants to move quickly in the direction we discussed before I reported to the management staff group. I said that it may take between now and the end of this month to formulate a plan significant enough to merit the effort that it would entail. He was disappointed, but said, "If necessary, okay."

Wes and I were due to start working on the problem that afternoon, so we had lunch together. As we began talking about ways the organization could spearhead a comprehensive development program that would result in rejuvenating and revitalizing the climate at Lakeside, Wes picked up my theme of giving foremen clearly defined responsibilities for improving relations with wage people.

Then we began to explore what would be the implications if the top brass of Lakeside, who number fifty-two people in all—general manager, operations superintendent, department heads, assistant department heads, and division heads—would establish a clear mandate for human relations. Such a mandate could include two parts; the first being a task definition to encourage the top level group to engage in a continuing and thorough analytic review and revision of human relations policies. Second, the same group would formulate a mandate to the remainder of the organization to receive and implement these updated policies during the next year.

Then we evolved the idea that since American Chemical can spend one day per month in training, why can't Lakeside? In other words, why not formulate a more comprehensive mandate, by which the top management group would engage in a continuous examination of policy in the process of training *itself* in human policy development; while at the same time, other echelons of the organization would spend one day per month studying ways to implement policy to bring about desired results. It all seemed so natural that it took, maybe, twenty minutes to formulate the basic plan.

We did some embroidering on these ideas, of course. One day per month seemed too infrequent, so we began to break the day up into two half days per month. Then we crystallized the final plan. We would propose that the top fifty-two people at Lakeside divide into two equal groups and go into application laboratory sessions at Lincoln Lodge. There they would explore our ideas and determine whether or not these indicated a wise way to go. If it were, they would establish the mandate, both for themselves and for their subordinates, specifying those who should implement it. An additional part of the mandate would be that each person is responsible, in whatever groupings emerge, for making at least one day a month available for human relations training, analysis, evaluation, planning, and so on.

It was about 1:30 by now, and Quinn and Hal Harvey were finishing their lunch at a table behind us. We called them over. They sat down. Wes ran the idea out in about four minutes. They said, "This is it. Let's go. We're ready to commit the top management group to examining this proposal. If they're satisfied with it or can improve upon it, we'll commit the entire organization."

What could happen to a massive, complex, highly competitive industry if it were to allocate two hours a week—or four hours every two weeks, or eight hours every month—specifically oriented toward studying and formulating how to improve human relations? The result can be forecast. It would be fantastic. Over a year, seven hundred managerial personnel would confront themselves in a behavioral mirror at least every two weeks to ask, "What am I doing in the human relations area to improve the operation of this organization?" If every man were to ask that question openly in the presence of his peers twenty-four times in one year and spend the time digging out what he could do better, the results could be of truly historic proportions.

One further idea emerged: namely, what *is* our goal in the human relations field? In previous remarks, I have mentioned that a business organization customarily assesses itself in comparative terms, using, as evaluative benchmarks, performance and other data concerning its competitors. Since comparisons are the basis for judgment, why not confront Lakeside with the idea that its goal is to develop the *best* human relations—not merely among local organizations or other EPIC plants, but of anywhere? Why shouldn't Lakeside shoot for the stars and try to create the best human relations in this country? So there is the idea in three parts: (1) a mandate to the planning and implementing components of the organization to take responsibility for its human relations; (2) make at least a day a month available for accomplishing this objective; and (3) to hitch the objective to the stars and to shoot for an organization in which the human relations situation is the ideal one for this country. All of this sounds fantastic, but nonetheless, it is possible.

References

1. For details of NLRB procedures, see: Linke, W.R. "The Complexities of Labor Relations Law." In Moore, R.F. (ed.), *Law for Executives*. New York: American Management Association, Inc., 1968, pp. 150-152; Beal, E.F. and Wickersham, E.D. *The Practice of Collective Bargaining* (3rd Ed.). Homewood, Ill.: Richard D. Irwin, Inc., 1967, pp. 146-150.

8

Headquarters Intervenes

October 6 began routinely. Management's bargaining with the IEW union has been going fairly smoothly. Plans are being worked on for the series of management conferences at Lincoln Lodge to establish next year's human relations goals and to set up training schedules to help attain them. The idea of conducting extensive action research to evaluate the extent to which these goals are achieved seems acceptable to Lakeside management, and preliminary plans for doing so are being drafted. Discussions during the morning focused on several aspects of the project. A number of agreements were achieved fairly quickly regarding ways to administer yesterday's decision.

Around one o'clock I went to lunch with Edwards, an assistant department head. As we went through the cafeteria line, Mac Anthony of the personnel department left a table where Quinn and others were seated, and came by, I thought, to say hello and pass on some information to me.

However, he said, "Could you join us for lunch?"

I said I could, but would prefer not to because I was eating with Edwards. I queried, "Is there some reason why I should?"

"Yes, there is."

"What?"

"We're in a jam."

"A bad one?"

"Yes."

By this time, Edwards had found a table. I went over and explained, "Look, Ed, I've been asked to sit and chat with the boys over there, and since it's kind of a command performance, I feel I'd better go."

"OK," he replied, "but keep your hand on your pocket."

So I joined the table with the senior officers. Everyone was seated tightly together, and I could tell that the conversation was intense. All of them had finished their lunch. I started mine.

Someone said, "Let him finish before you tell him."

Someone else said, "No, tell him now."

I said, "Tell me whenever you want," and bit into my sandwich.

Quinn got up and came to where I was. He began to tell me the nature of the problem under debate. Before I describe it, however, it is best to drop back to a point earlier in the history of union-management bargaining at Lakeside.

After the nearly six-week period during which the union read through its contract proposals, and management listened keenly, albeit uneasily and hesitantly, bargaining was finally launched on September 15. One of the early items discussed was the "union shop with membership maintenance" clause. The *union shop* aspect of the issue was whether a new employee should be required—within one month after taking employment—to join the union as a condition of continued employment. *Membership maintenance* requires all employees who are union members to remain "in good standing" (with regard to paying union dues) for the term of the labor agreement. Although newly joined members may, at the end of one year's membership, withdraw from the union, another subclause in the proposal provides that the employer will, at the union's request, discharge an employee who has failed to maintain his membership in good standing.

Management's argument usually had been that such conditions are unacceptable; that a man is employed because of his competence to do a job, and that membership in some group should not be necessary for continuing as an employee.

The union's contention, however, was that a man operates under contracted work conditions agreed to by the union after long, difficult and expensive negotiations. Since the man's rights are protected and any grievance he may have is acted upon by the union, whether or not he is a member, the union argued that a man should be required to become a union member to express himself on his work conditions. Furthermore, the union argument went, near-universal membership aids the union to be a more representative bargaining unit, and thus it should not be denied the right to require membership.

This whole question of some kind of "union security" clause in the labor contract has been debated for years. There are convincing arguments on both sides. In the final analysis, the side that is uppermost when a "controversy coin" finally stops spinning and falls, depends on subjective or ideological convictions more than on logical considerations.

When negotiations began, Lakeside management considered its own position on the issue, but listened intently to the reasons why the union felt that this form of security, which is permissible under labor law, would help it. With minor reservations, management agreed to a union shop/membership maintenance clause. Its change of mind on this point represented a major accomplishment for the union. Officers felt gratified that now an important prerequisite for increasing their union's internal strength as representative of the people had been met. Management felt pleased because, in order to do a realistic bargaining job, they prefer to sit across the table from a union which is more representative of the people it purports to serve than the present IEW seemed to be. On September 15, I also had been favorably impressed by the new procedural step whereby the interim verbal agreement had been passed to a two-member union-management subcommittee for immediate drafting into written language.

Now, then, back to the lunch table. Quinn said, "I've just had a call from EPIC. They're dead set against any union-shop proposition. What it comes down to now is that we have to retract our agreement on that clause, which was nailed down more than two weeks ago."

I inquired, "How are you going to retract?"

Quinn explained, "I am going to say that I was uneasy about the agreement at the time it was made, on a tentative basis, by our representatives. Since then, I have thought about it and finally have come to the conclusion that it was the wrong thing to do and that I want to reverse the previous position." In effect, since Quinn is not the head of management's bargaining team, this piece of fiction—that the general manager is now, after two weeks' cerebration, annulling the tentative agreement made by his bargaining agents—might at least be credible to the union. But what else would it be?

The other six or seven people at the table sat frozen, waiting for my reaction. While I had been busy on other matters, they had started debating, perhaps at 11:00 a.m.

I said, "Quinn, if you go to the union at two o'clock and do this, you will appear arbitrary, unreasonable, inconsistent, and lacking in integrity. Over the past few weeks, they've begun to trust management a little; now you're going to wreck all that. Surely you know what's at stake here. Do you have to take action right away?"

"EPIC wants me to."

"Can't you get some breathing space for further consideration? Perhaps you could go in after the coffee break and do something more positive."

He agreed, "Well, OK." Then he turned to those at the table who were on the bargaining committee and said, "Why don't you fellows go ahead and get started. I'll let you know at coffee time." To Wes and myself, he said, "How about the three of us going to my office to discuss it further?" Hal Harvey came along too.

The discussion picked up again. By this time, Quinn had convinced himself that he had been wrong from the start to give assent to the union's "security" clause. We explored that. I said I thought he was punishing himself and reacting with emotion rather than logic. Perhaps he had erred in not clearing with EPIC the position he was going to adopt. That by no means implied that a decision made over two weeks ago, and already communicated to managers and supervisors through an informal bulletin sent to their homes, was wrong and needed to be turned upside down simply because the distant headquarters group was reacting unfavorably. We debated and debated and debated.

Finally, I drew a horizontal line across the blackboard. The line was long enough to represent many conceivable ways in which the problem might be handled. At its left-hand end I put, *Resist the pressure, say no to EPIC.* On the extreme right, I put, *Capitulate to EPIC, but tell the union that the shift in your thinking on this matter was not influenced by any outside source; rather, it's your own decision for which you take full responsibility.* In the middle I put, *Go to the union, lay the cards on the table, expose every relevant fact, explain your predicament, request help.* Then over on the left-hand side, next to the "resist" alternative, I put, *Challenge headquarters, try to exert influence toward changing its position so as to accord with yours.* Between the middle position and the right-hand extreme, I put, *Say to the union, "New facts and attitudes have come to our attention. We are forced to reconsider the agreement that we came to some time ago. Rather than going into the surrounding factors that cause our difficulties, I want to explain the issue as it is seen now from our viewpoint, and then explore whether you and ourselves can find a common ground of mutual help."*

Other positions along this continuum were identified as the afternoon wore on and three o'clock came and went. However, Quinn, Hal, and Wes seemed inclined toward the position on the extreme right which was, "Don't implicate headquarters; the good manager never reveals what pressures have influenced him. He has to appear strong and decisive, capable of imposing his own solutions."

Furthermore, EPIC headquarters had said distinctly, "We don't care how you do this as long as you accomplish the retraction and don't implicate us." As this debate continued, we began to explore why headquarters might have taken such a position. Something didn't ring true. Sure, EPIC resists change, but is it so militantly committed to preserving tradition? Why was it adamantly refusing to even explain its reasons for trampling the agreement underfoot? Quinn felt that EPIC was doing this to punish Lakeside for agreeing to something it had not cleared with headquarters.

Then a new idea emerged. Wes placed a long distance call to a friendly and trustworthy information source in ERA, the new super-headquarters above EPIC. During the call, which took perhaps 45 minutes, we continued to debate the potential impact of any action on (1) the future of negotiations with the union, and (2) other segments of the Lakeside organization, such as management and supervisors.

The information from the call shed some light on why EPIC had been so eager for Lakeside to repudiate its union-security clause agreement. ERA, the new pinnacle unit of the organization, had recently been superimposed upon EPIC headquarters and the rest of the existing structure. A number of

ERA officers already had been chosen and their appointments announced. One of the unfilled vacancies was that of Vice President of Production. There were two people in EPIC probably being considered as candidates. One of them had made the retraction call to Quinn.

Furthermore, it was known that senior people now in ERA had previously taken a vigorous, adamant position against union security clauses in labor contracts. No EPIC plant had such a clause, although Lakeside did have one once. Since some big wheels at ERA had this attitude, it was only logical to assume they might question the wisdom of selecting a vice president from EPIC who would allow Lakeside to agree to a union shop with membership maintenance.

These considerations began to explain the intense concern of EPIC in getting Lakeside's commitment retracted. Quinn then called Irv Irwin in EPIC, who had been so insistent about the immediate retraction. Quinn made the following points during his conversation with Irv. "Look, your pressure is going to push us into making a second error to correct the first—if that, indeed, *was* an error. The consequences of the second error may be much more tragic than the consequences of the first. It could mean that bargaining will be terminated as of the time I make my big announcement. How would it look to ERA if, by compelling us to retract our agreement, you made our relations with the union much worse and maybe left us wide open to International unionization, or triggered off a strike?"

The dilemma had turned 180 degrees now. To act in such a way as to compound the error could reflect even more negatively on potential candidates for the Vice President of Production slot. The logic of these implications made good sense to Irv. Time pressure was reduced from "immediately" to "as soon as possible." But the accompanying verb was still "retract." Now Quinn centered on, "How much time do we have, and how strongly opposed to our position are those persons in ERA and EPIC?" Quinn learned that EPIC personnel are cross with him for several reasons. One is that they got word of the union-security agreement in Lakeside, not from Quinn, but from ERA. They had never been cut in. EPIC was put in an embarassing position relative to ERA, and apparently did feel the desire to punish Lakeside and establish clearly the lines of control.

After an afternoon of intense debate, the problem remained hung, suspended and ticking. Neither Quinn nor his advisors were daring enough to resist the command from above. They were going to retract, one way or another.

The remaining question was whether the retraction announcement would be on the extreme right side of alternatives spelled out on the blackboard, or more in terms of approaches described in the middle. That is, would Lakeside management take sole responsibility for reversing itself, or would it reveal the strings from above that, when jerked, cause it to jump and somersault? Most probably, some position between the center and the right.

My prediction is that if management were to take the intermediate position, putting all the facts on the table, two results would occur. One would be that though the pill was bitter and hard to swallow, the union would not break off negotiations. Indeed, it is conceivable that the union would accept a tabling of its "security" proposal, particularly if management were to say that it would make an effort to shift EPIC's and ERA's attitudes and thinking. The other prediction is that if Lakeside were to take sole responsibility, then the management team would be viewed as arbitrary, unreasonable, shifting, untrustworthy and unacceptable as a bargaining counterpart. Under these conditions, negotiations very well might be terminated by the union with the statement, "You gave your hand of agreement. Now, like unprincipled slobs, you have shifted your position. We will return to bargaining when you return to your senses. Let us know when this happens." Then the union would get up, walk out, and go off to work on an international affiliation, or even to prepare for more direct fight actions.

Here then, is a magnificent four-layer intergroup problem. On the bottom is the union. Next is the Lakeside management bargaining unit, up from them is EPIC, the intermediate headquarters, and on top is ERA, the new super-headquarters. All of the last-mentioned three are jockeying among themselves. Lakeside management wants to avoid something that would embarrass those who are its immediate superiors in EPIC. Management in EPIC wants to avoid both embarrassment to itself and outside perception of its arbitrariness. So, in effect, it says, "Let Quinn take the consequences of reneging on what we see as a mistaken decision." From another point of view, ERA super-headquarters wants complete assurance of the "right thinking" of anyone in EPIC who might be promoted to Vice President of Production.

Under these circumstances, who takes the brunt of the political intrigues? Down below is the IEW union composed of people trying to do a job for a very small psychological reward, and no monetary remuneration, which is the shock absorber for all the pressure and chaos upstairs. This kind of thing has been going on for two decades. If it were not for the fear that the IEW union would join forces with an international I have no doubt that management would not have given a second thought to retracting its agreement. In effect, management would have said, "If you don't like it, lump it."

This leads me to speculate that really there is a five-group struggle over these issues. The fifth group is the big and strong international union, ICEW, which is waiting at the gate. Depending on how management handles the retraction, it may open the gate and swing it wide; or, if management has the intelligence not to be cunning, and exposes its problems in an honest, forthright way, it could be that the gate will be forever locked.

Mapping the Retraction Morass

Today, October 7, was the second day of the crisis which is expected to come to a head in the morning when Quinn meets with the union and retracts management's previous agreement. Today Quinn, Van, Hal, Wes and myself convened at 2:00 p.m. and worked until 5:30 p.m, We reviewed the entire situation from many angles. One thing that can be said is that while Lakeside management sometimes may not put the appropriate weight upon various aspects of an issue, it certainly examines future actions and the anticipated consequences in a most intensive and detailed manner.

The big issue was, "Who should make the actual retraction statement?" Should it be a whole-team operation with each member giving part of the justification? Or should it be a solo performance, and if so, who was the most appropriate spokesman: Wes, Van, or Quinn?

In favor of Wes's doing it is the fact that he is personnel chief, and since the union shop/membership maintenance matter directly affects Personnel Department procedures, Wes may have more comprehension of the overall problem than anyone else. He dislikes the union-security clause, and can argue against it with genuine conviction. However, Van continuously pointed out the unreality of Wes's position, since this particular clause is currently in 75% of the contracts around the country.[1]

A second possibility was that the retraction should be made by Van because as chairman of management's bargaining committee, he customarily introduces procedural questions and subject-matter issues. Therefore, it would be appropriate for him to handle this issue.

A third possibility was Quinn. He is Lakeside's general manager, but not a member of the bargaining committee. The advantage of his doing it, then, is that speaking for the entire production center his voice will carry more force. As an outside authority, he probably would be listened to more soberly, albeit with great somberness. When all of these considerations were weighed it was decided that the spokesman would be Quinn.

The next topic in the discussion concerned the content of the announcement. This raised some most intricate problems. The major issue was where and how to attribute *why* management is doing a sudden about-face. Three possibilities existed. One would be to say, "As our bargaining team reviewed the various positions it subscribed to, it became more and more concerned regarding the inappropriateness of this particular agreement, and finally decided against it."

A second possibility was to blame Quinn. The story would be that he, having a background of wider experience and responsibility, examined the union-security problem from a different point of view, and concluded that, for good and sufficient reasons, he was obligated to cancel the tentative agreement.

The third possibility was to identify the cause where it actually exists: in EPIC headquarters under the urgings of ERA super-headquarters. The shining advantage of doing this is that it tells the truth.

I noticed, as the discussion went on, that the first two alternatives—which involved outright lying—were attractive to these men because of a superordinate managerial ethic: namely, that you never expose your own boss to criticism by subordinates or outside parties. This ethic states that the up-front individual assumes personal responsibility for getting through any predicament imposed from above. There is no such thing as passing the buck or dodging the issue. A manager ought to be a *man,* and as a man he should bear the brunt of his boss's actions, however difficult the personal consequences. It is a deeply indoctrinated ethic; very hard to dislodge.

Telling the truth in this situation would be to say, "We are changing our position because EPIC has instructed us to do so. We disagreed and tried to get it reversed, but were unsuccessful. Personally, we don't like this decision but we have no choice."

The debate shifted from who should make the statement, and what exactly should be said, to when the event should take place. Since tomorrow's all-day bargaining session is scheduled to start at 8:30 a.m. it was decided that the announcement should be inserted at some intermediate point. Furthermore, since Quinn is already on call to meet with the union, his presence is anticipated. This completed the logic for him to make the announcement.

The actual message would go as follows, "We are in trouble. We agreed on September 15 to a union-security clause. Now there are difficulties. For many years our company has supported the idea of free choice with respect to union membership, and has opposed its becoming a condition of employment. Most of our September 15 agreement violates that principle and this has created a strong negative reaction throughout the company. Part of this negative reaction is our fault. We did a poor job of preparing other people for accepting this break with tradition. Confronted with this negative reaction, we now have to withdraw our earlier agreement to a union-security clause." An additional optional paragraph is, "We still think the idea has merit. We will continue to encourage new employees to join the union. We will also take advantage of future opportunities to generate further discussion of this issue and to create better understanding around the company."

As evidenced by this quotation, the eventual decision was to make relatively vague references to external forces in the situation, without naming them man by man and without indicating whether they were in EPIC headquarters, in super-headquarters, or in other company production centers.

The interesting question here is how to predict the union reactions. Various members of the management group are making "educated guesses." Here are some of them.

Quinn feels that there will be no walk-out, and only a minimum of fuss. There will be a little emotional barking at the beginning, but he will be able to talk the union officials through to acceptance. Van, on the other hand, feels that the retraction will cause the situation to worsen drastically. Rather than blowing off steam, the boiler will blow up. The union very well may withdraw from bargaining, for some indeterminate period. Wes is of the same mind, though he is somewhat less worried than Van. He feels that the reaction will be more intense than Quinn anticipates, but not as militant as the one Van foresees. Hal feels that future negotiations are surely going to be affected but can't really anticipate the outcome.

And what do I predict? First, I think the union-security issue, as viewed from ERA and EPIC, has been blown out of proportion. It can be argued that the union is part of the legal apparatus through which decisions of plant-wide significance are made, and that each member of the work force has as much responsibility to take part in union affairs as he has for discharging other aspects of his work. Furthermore, as Van said, "The great majority of present-day contracts routinely carry this particular clause." I predict that the union will feel outraged when management reneges on the agreement. My second prediction is that, since the reason for retraction is vague rather than specific, the union will not swallow it. It will sense partial truth wrapped in a lot of fudging. Third, since this retraction, which kisses off one of the union's principal objectives, is to be made after weeks of heavy bargaining that have produced few other—and minor—agreements, it will only point out to the IEW its fundamental weakness, as an independent, in influencing management.

Based on these three considerations, my forecast is that immediately after the announcement is made and its implications discussed, the union will "take five" and go into caucus. During this caucus, the union officers will talk through the implications for future bargaining and will come back and break off negotiations. It is difficult for me to perceive how the union can do otherwise. To accept the retraction with a "more in sorrow than in anger" statement of regret would be like the union saying it is prepared to kowtow, to kneel, to stoop, to do whatever it can for the noble purpose of relieving Lakeside management from pressures coming from elsewhere in the organization. If my forecast is correct, union leaflets will be handed out on Friday morning, and this event will signal the beginning of open warfare between IEW and Lakeside management.

There is another reason for this prediction. The union came to this bargaining series with serious misgivings and deep distrust regarding management, a set of attitudes based on observation of management's activities during the fairly recent union elections. Management's hands were not clean in an industrial-relations sense. No legal violations were involved, but management was seen to have slipped into tricky, manipulative behavior. Since the initial period of distrust, and particularly during the past two months or so, there has been a dawn of feeling that perhaps this management has become reasonable and is genuinely committed to problem-solving relationships. The union has slowly and with difficulty reached this conclusion—or, at least, some of its members have. They want to believe it. They hope it is true. Now then, what will the retraction do? It will undermine whatever elements of trust and confidence in management's integrity the union has been able to generate up to now.

If the union does *not* break off negotiations, I, for one, will be surprised. Breaking off is the only way it can maintain its self-respect, mobilize and test its strength, and challenge management. Furthermore, the union will say that when management cancels out its retraction and is ready to act in accordance with previous commitments, the union will return to the bargaining table.

Even though I predict a walk-out, consider what might happen if negotiations continue. Now, with heightened distrust and a desire to punish management, the union will begin making many demands, several of which would seem inappropriate and unacceptable even under more impartial canons of judgment than management will apply. Negotiations will be formal, often on a brusque yes-no basis. On many issues, the union will try to force compliance. It will receive from management many more angry noes than submissive yeses.

What might be some of the implications for the union election next January? I predict the international ICEW will be able to point to the independent union's inability to deal with management. Whether the IEW walks out, or stays in negotiation, the new spirit of bitterness augurs great difficulty and probable failure in concluding any contract soon. Possibilities of concluding one which causes IEW members to marvel at their representatives' achievement are even more remote. The more that IEW, despite its militancy, shows evidence of weakness and failure, the stronger are ICEW's chances of persuading Lakeside's wage people that it, the huge international, can represent them better. I believe tomorrow's retraction will trigger a series of events resulting in the demise of IEW and its replacement by the brawny ICEW.

The problem is complicated in another way too, because many Lakeside managers, supervisors, and foremen will be pleased by the predicament in which the top executives now find themselves. These frustrated people, who would rather fight than solve problems, will use this occasion to embarrass management's bargaining committee and to ridicule its "silly" behavior of at first—as they see it—"giving in" to Dan and his cohorts as a weak gesture of goodwill, and then having to be shaped up by Headquarters. The outlook is bleak. A fluke of politics has let loose forces that no member of management has sufficient stature or statesmanship to deal with. The result of this sorry headquarters intervention, based as it is on an unthought-out mass of traditional premises and prejudices, will be internal strife and disorganization at Lakeside.

It is not only the wage union which will be affected by the retraction. Identically the same request for a union-security clause had been made by the salary union and agreed to by Lakeside management. Headquarters' countermand applies there too. The decision is to deliver the *coup de grâce* to the salary union at 1:00 p.m. tomorrow. My prediction here is not the same as for the wage group, though it takes essentially the same direction. Salary unionists too are likely either to start dragging their feet when negotiating and even, eventually, to resign; or they will, after the edict, communicate to their membership the impossibility of conducting problem solving with this management.

Factors in this particular issue point directly to the reason why men turn to international unions. The "independent" unions are relatively powerless to deal with so-called "decentralized" management whose members are prone to shift, hedge and fudge whenever headquarters' displeasure is felt, or when personal career considerations override a manager's interest in promoting good industrial relations. Workers notice this, and then take what, in these circumstances, is the most intelligent decision: namely, to *centralize* their own representative organization so that it will have the necessary clout to confront its real adversary—big-daddy headquarters.

"Don't Do Anything Till We've Thought Some More"

Retraction of the clause was to have been made this morning. Telephones jangled all night. The sun has risen, eight o'clock has come and gone, and the retraction has yet to be made. There is a stalemate between Lakeside and EPIC.

Yesterday, after Quinn and the others worked out how to phrase and explain the retraction, they decided to notify EPIC of the exact message which Quinn would deliver to the union. When this information reached EPIC headquarters, it stirred up strong feelings there. A local management was saying to its coordinative superior, "Look, you can direct us to reverse our position, but that doesn't mean that you can change our thinking. No evidence which you have brought to our attention shows any defect in our earlier decision to accept a union-security clause. We will shift our position according to your instruction, but we have not changed our thinking."

At this point, headquarters management is confronted with a dilemma. Should it, in the midst of contract negotiations, force local management's hand to bring about an action with which management disagrees? If so, can it then confront local management with the "thought enforcement" obligation to alter its attitudes? The headquarters point of view at this moment is quasi-democratic in its tone, and circular in its logic: "We will not require the retraction until you have changed your minds and come to think as we do."

Lakeside management has said, "We will execute the reversal according to instructions, but we remain unconvinced." Such a stand is indeed a precarious one for Quinn. For in effect, he is agreeing to acquiesce against his better judgment. It also puts headquarters in an awkward position by spotlighting its clumsy and ambivalently motivated coerciveness.

Now there's an interesting reaction. Headquarters management scratches its head and says, "This is not the way that Lakeside management usually behaves. There must be some alien influence causing them to have these heretical opinions. Who is the subversive satanist? Where is the fly in the ointment?" So headquarters management searches for someone to blame. Who does it find? It finds me. And so last night someone said to Quinn, "You must be spending too much time with Bob Blake; you're getting brainwashed. You'd better watch out." To which Quinn replied, "That's an unintelligent remark for an intelligent headquarters person to make." Whether such a retort is effective is rather doubtful, but at least it demonstrated Quinn's sense of intellectual autonomy.

The fact is, I never took a public position on the union-security issue. That issue was debated to consensus in the union-management bargaining committee more than two weeks ago. I was not even in the meetings, for indeed, I have to abstain from involvement in local *content* issues. My mission is to help improve problem-solving processes. Moreover, it was only yesterday that I worked through some ideas of my own regarding the relative desirability of union-security clauses.

I didn't react to the "brainwash" crack. The present excitement in EPIC will fade in due course, and Quinn's freedom from "under threat" feelings will increase my opportunity to intervene constructively in process problems[2] at Lakeside.

In addition, it will open wide the opportunity to work with the headquarters group. The way this will come about is twofold. After the retraction problem has been resolved, headquarters management will feel guilty regarding its momentary feelings about my allegedly brainwashing influence. Second, by then, they will see my Lakeside activities in a different light and, therefore, will undoubtedly want to get better acquainted with me. This provides an excellent opportunity for me to review with EPIC and ERA the bigger stakes that are involved in union-management relations.

What are the attitudes of the various management people toward the dilemma currently confronting the general manager? Quinn is frustrated. From his point of view, this issue is minor as compared to the win-lose power struggle it has created between himself and Irv Irwin, the headquarters coordinator to whom he reports. It is important, from his standpoint, to correctly decide whether or not he should capitulate. If he does change his mind, he thereby gives headquarters management the impression that its logic has caused him to change his attitudes. On the other hand, if he fights, he is putting his career on the line for an issue which seems minor.

Van Gray feels compassion toward Quinn, but is uneasy about the retraction explanation. He considers it a violation of loyalty and principle to "blow the whistle" on EPIC. According to his view, a good manager always protects his boss. To do otherwise is to pass the buck, and that is a crime of mammoth proportions according to his personal ethic.

Carl O'Brien feels that it is honest and right to identify the source of the retraction order. It is his conviction that this will clear the air and make it possible for people to continue working together in an honest and open manner. He feels that if management states its problem honestly, the bargaining people will soon close ranks and get on with the job.

Wes Stratton sympathizes with Quinn, but he also sees the dilemma at EPIC. If headquarters does extract a reversal on this union-security, it says, in effect, that local bargaining is an illusion; a theatrical "divide and rule" performance by which management bedazzles a number of independent unions at various plants and thereby keeps them from joining forces or going international. If EPIC fails to extract a reversal, then it gets in dutch with ERA super-headquarters.

I don't know Hal Harvey's attitude, but Calvert Carroll is convinced that both headquarters are acting foolishly. They should wake up to recognize that Samuel Gompers is no longer around, and that a new age of union-management relations came into being 20 years ago.

But a fascinating thing that has come into clear focus today is that Lakeside management may be strengthening its position with EPIC.

In response to Quinn's position—that he would *do* as headquarters desires, but is unconvinced of the validity of headquarters' position—EPIC management has given an appearance, be it ever so small, that its own convictions are weakening. Its confidence in its demand for retraction is not so strong today as yesterday. As the headquarters executives begin to question their own position, Lakeside's top management becomes more certain of its position. This seems vaguely analogous to the workings of a hydraulic pump. It would appear that—momentarily at least—the fortunes of Quinn and his associates are on the upturn.

In any event, headquarters' intervention has confronted Lakeside management with its own weakness. It has to bargain with the independent under such a tight rein that the area in which its bargaining group and IEW can genuinely resolve problems is quite narrow. In my view, the rude awakening as to its own weakness will stimulate Lakeside's management to try to influence headquarters; the aim being to gain the conditions of local autonomy which will permit it to act with greater strength and flexibility.

I think Lakeside probably will emerge from the "retraction crisis" stronger than at any time in the past. Quinn has become unwilling to take sole responsibility for breaking the agreement; instead, he wants at least part of the responsibility to be borne by the countermanders themselves. The point hopefully will be reached when Quinn will be able to tell the union that he was overruled, and that he is in no position to challenge the order. If he does this, indicating that his own approach has not changed, it is my view that he will receive cooperation from the union to help him to exert influence on headquarters in the future. He may be able to present the retraction without causing headquarters to become a common enemy. Rather, he might foster the perception that headquarters creates a common problem both for Lakeside's management and for its union. Such an outcome would be most heartening.

In this context, it will be recalled that six months ago, the Green Acres conferences took place. At this time, the top executive group felt it would be appropriate to assess the prospects of adopting the Scanlon Plan,[3] the Weirton approach,[4] and other ways of strengthening local unions to make them better problem-solving segments of the organization. From the second-level groups, a different mood prevailed. They said to upper management, "We have told you enough times what you should do. What we want is feedback concerning what you have done." Next week, on Wednesday and Thursday, the Lincoln Lodge meetings will begin. These have been designed as an "application laboratory" for measuring where the organization is now and to establish human relations goals for next year.

It is now apparent to Lakeside's top management that middle management's criticism was realistic. Upper management has not done its homework, either on the Scanlon Plan or the Weirton approach. It has not analyzed its own attitudes toward such innovations, nor has it worked toward creating appropriate attitudes on the part of headquarters management to enable these innovations to be tested and perhaps put into effect. In other words, the Green Acres conferences provided a clear demonstration to me—and, I hope, to the remainder of the organization—that upper management really ought to examine its own behavior. At Lincoln Lodge next week management will be encouraged to ask itself why it felt complacent and failed to do the homework assigned to it.

References

1. Factual backing for Van's viewpoint is contained in a U.S. Bureau of Labor Statistics bulletin issued in March, 1960. See: Beal, E.F. and Wickersham, E.D. *The Practice of Collective Bargaining* (3rd Ed.). Homewood, Ill.: Richard D. Irwin, Inc., 1967, p. 253. Nonetheless, it is noteworthy that while 74% of the surveyed workers were covered by union-shop clauses, a mere 7% were subject to "maintenance of membership" provisions. So Van might have been arguing at cross-purposes to Wes' position.

2. See Chapter 4, Reference 2.

3. For descriptions and evaluations of the Scanlon Plan, see: Shultz, G.P. "Worker Participation on Production Problems: A Discussion of Experience with the Scanlon

Plan." *Personnel, 28,* 3, November 1951, pp. 201-210; Lesieur, F.G. (ed.). *The Scanlon Plan: A Frontier in Labor-Management Cooperation.* New York: The Technology Press, 1958; Buffa, E.S. *Modern Production Management* (3rd Ed.). New York: John Wiley & Sons, Inc., 1969, pp. 431-432.

4. The "Weirton Plan" originated in the Weirton Steel Division of National Steel Corporation.

9

Bargaining and OD Under External Conditions

These are my notes of October 10. The enforced retraction of Lakeside management's contract-clause agreement is temporarily suspended. Tomorrow there is a meeting at EPIC between Quinn, Wes, and two headquarters executives, one of whom is John Edwards. It was his instruction to retract the union security clause that was relayed to Quinn a few days ago by Irv Irwin. Since then, the situation has gone into a fairly well defined boss-subordinate intergroup conflict.

My prediction is that the four who meet Friday will react to one another in personality terms, although the behavior of both twosomes is perhaps better explainable in "intergroup representative" terms. I predict that the headquarters people will move slowly but with the clear goal of getting Lakeside to retract. They will want the retraction made in such a way that Lakeside union people see it as being due to Quinn's changed concept of the problem. It could be that Quinn will *actually* have changed his mind by that time, and so will speak to the union with some degree of conviction. I have the uneasy feeling that he's now searching for a way to capitulate to headquarters' wishes, even though recognizing that to do so may end the collaborative efforts which have been underway since July. If he reverses field, headquarters will be able to perpetuate its policy traditions, rather than Lakeside exerting constructive upward influences with regard to the larger stakes involved. I remain convinced that capitulation to headquarters, at this point in time, could have most pernicious consequences.

Wes Stratton, the other Lakeside representative, may be a potent influence at the meeting. As a personnel specialist with basic behavioral science insights, who is usually effective in his interpersonal relations—even though he can be provoked into win-lose orientations, as we saw during the crane crisis—he is dedicated to seeking "everyone can win" modes of collaboration. Also, he is fearless and doesn't appear to respond to the narrow view of political wisdom by accommodating his behavior to the prejudices and pressures around him. Rather, he pushes for systematic understanding of problems, and seeks solutions via considerations of statesmanship and human values. Whenever he sees this kind of solution taking shape, he aims for that goal. My prediction, then, is that he may be harder to influence in the direction of retraction than Quinn.

Another aspect of the crisis relates to certain attitudes appearing among other members of Lakeside's management bargaining team. These attitudes seem closely associated with individual executive standpoints.

Basically, if the retraction request is perceived as a challenge to the wisdom and problem-solving skills of individual executives, some may try to salvage whatever they can by seeking favorable recognition. If this is the case, probably a number of internal reorganization factors will begin operating. I think these are already evident.

During the past few days the most conspicuous break in team continuity could be seen in Van Gray. His immediate reaction was, "Whatever the boss says goes." In this sense, the boss is EPIC. "Let's reverse field and take the brunt of the responsibility as loyal subordinates should." Why did he take this position? I personally think that his rationale was, "Working out our problems at Lakeside is unimportant in comparison with being well regarded by EPIC." He was ready, as I saw it, to capitulate, sacrificing opportunities for constructive resolution of the problem. This sacrifice would be made on the altar of a "higher" goal: to keep himself clean and acceptable. He'd do it in spite of the fact that he also knows that such a capitulation, while it might relieve a momentary tension point between plant and headquarters management, would produce widespread disruptive consequences within Lakeside in the future.

The dynamics of this way of adjusting derive from a military discipline concept that one never challenges a superior or goes in a direction contrary to what, you conjecture, are his wishes. In interpreting policy, and in the absence of specific instructions, the goal of the "good" Lakeside subordinate is to forecast what his superior wants and to give it to him. I'm convinced nothing could be farther from "the law of the situation."[1] The goal of a good subordinate should be much more comprehensive than that. It would be to do what needs to be done: to accept legitimate influence from those above—and below—and to attempt to modify the thinking and attitudes of one's boss when his perceptions appear narrow, inappropriate or otherwise unconstructive.

On Friday John Edwards will be spokesman for EPIC. I have met him only once. He stepped in unannounced and unexpectedly at a session when I was describing to a union and management committee some basic research on intergroup relations. He and I had brief background discussions when we accompanied the two groups to dinner.

Edwards is described by others as a brilliant engineer. He is about 40, which is young for his rank in the company. He is anything but a forceful individual when one first meets him. Indeed, he appears shy and withdrawn, but he is always watching events and, seemingly, thinking and analyzing. In addition to being brilliant, he is also described as a highly meticulous person who never makes a mistake and in whose presence it is unwise for others to make mistakes. Technical blunders are deemed inexcusable and their perpetrators are remembered. He is said to be a "hard driver" who keeps long work hours and is a dedicated company man. Finally, although he is seen as a man of strong convictions, when he is confronted with new and relevant facts, he will change his mind and shift to a new direction, pursue a fresh course of action with the same dedication, drive, and determination as before.

So Quinn's and Wes' mission target will be his lively, critical, yet not impenetrable mind.

But Quinn and Wes themselves are being subjected to diverse influences and points of view from fellow members of the Lakeside management bargaining committee. Hal Harvey's reaction to the headquarters edict was observably one of private pleasure beneath a publicly expressed attitude of consternation and disturbance. What does this mean? I see Hal as a mixed-up person who is ambivalent between love and hate, or between peace and war. Maybe he can't decide which to value more: those parts of his personality that enjoy fight, or those that seem to favor collaboration. When collaboration is being mooted, he seems attracted to it, but gets anxious. He seems to find potential conflict enjoyable too, but again he gets anxious. So, he swings back and forth. Currently, part of him is pleased by the pickle Lakeside finds itself in, and another part resists complying with EPIC's edict.

Carl O'Brien is reacting to the situation as a true practicing Christian whose ethics are functional rather than verbal. He is neither criticizing headquarters nor whipping the committee. Instead, he is formulating to others the way he sees the problem and what he thinks is appropriate, which is to be honest. He doesn't militantly force his opinions upon others, nor does he hide in the bushes so as to come out at the last moment and agree with the final position. Having viewed so many under-the-surface behaviors recently, my feeling is that an internalized Christian ethic, combined with seminar training, is likely to produce a statesmanlike individual. Carl, prior to seminar training, was anything but a statesman. He was way back in the Old Testament somewhere, and, as a department head, used to lower the boom in ways quite disturbing to the organization. He was described in a number of union handouts as one of the enemies of the people. Since his seminar experience, he has changed more profoundly than anyone else, and is now a stabilizing influence. Even if he and Wes don't click personally as a pair, they exert powerful positive influences on the management committee.

Mac Anthony is a relative newcomer to personnel work. In my view, he is head and shoulders above the rest of the management bargaining group, with the possible exception of Wes. His stature is more obvious to me now than at first. Early along the way, when I began consulting at Lakeside, I had only brief conversations with Mac. Then at the beginning of August when the union submitted its contract proposals, he threw up his hands and said, "Hopeless." We had a long discussion at that time, and I came to see him as a fact-oriented individual who reacts to situations without much sensitivity to the "transformation possibilities" that may be present even in an emotion-laden context. Nonetheless, I was impressed by his determination to be objective rather than an exponent of his own "psychological needs."[2] It was following our talk that Mac, along with Wes, began to work creatively on intergroup problem-solving designs.

Since Mac and I have become better acquainted, I have discovered that he is a brilliant student of history. Though perhaps no older than 35, he can provide an exciting verbal movie of critical events in the U.S. Civil War. He knows where all of the battles were fought, their chronology, who led the military forces on each side, each general's campaign plans, why particular strategies and tactics succeeded or failed, and for each side the consequences of each event. He also is an excellent student of current affairs and reads the *New York Times* as though it were a thorough but unsystematic formulation of personal, intra-group, intergroup, and organizational conflict situations. He reads in such a way as to listen for the melody and to interpret these ongoing events in terms of systematic consideration of the issues. Also of great interest from the standpoint of understanding Mac is that two or three times a week he comes in and says, "Did you see that TV show last night?" The TV shows he describes are always newsfilms, documentaries, interviews, panel discussions, or "specials." His way of viewing them is as systematic as his newspaper reading. He listens for what is *not* said, as well as what *is,* and interprets against the background of the speakers' political intentions as distinct from their expressions.

Six months ago, you might have described Mac's clothing as flamboyant. But now his apparel is tasteful and tailored; quite an impressive and dramatic shift.

Another interesting aspect is that Mac is a dedicated family man. He has mentioned on several occasions that seminar training caused him to rethink his concept of discipline and control at home. I later discovered he has six children. In our conversation he has never mentioned his wife or where he lives nor has he invited me to visit his home. I interpret this as indicating that with his mature adjustment, he doesn't feel the need to talk about home life, and with a family of such size he devotes time to them rather than to political gambits such as entertaining those who are not friends in the social sense.

In the Personnel Department and in the bargaining team, I see Mac continuously developing strength and influence among other management members. Save perhaps for Wes, he currently has the best perception of the consequences of emotional rather than reasonable behavior. He can face a problem and struggle through until it is resolved, rather than becoming frustrated and fatigued and looking for an easy way out.

The Meeting at Headquarters

Today, October 12, Quinn and Wes met with John Edwards and Neal Young of EPIC to review the present relationships between the IEW union and Lakeside management, and in particular, whether or not to retract agreement on the union-security clause.

The outcome of the meeting is that the Lakeside bargaining committee will execute the retraction as headquarters, since hearing of the agreement, has wanted it to. However, the committee will indicate that the reversal is not due to changes in its own thinking but is being made because of external pressure.

When this is said, I do not think the union will break off relationships and use this issue as a test of strength against management. However, the retraction will restimulate old doubts about management's trustworthiness. My prediction is that negotiation will continue, but on a less spontaneous basis and with more doubletake. This event will smolder in the background for a long time, and probably the union will use it to embarrass management whenever possible.

Something else occurred during the headquarters session. The origins of this are traceable to a discussion between Wes and myself a few days ago. Our concern had been with the relations between EPIC and its several decentralized plants, one of which is Lakeside. In my view, it is necessary for headquarters and the plants to develop a common understanding of "who should handle what" when union-management problems arise. Until there has been some fundamental rethinking in headquarters, there is little scope for meaningful bargaining or problem solving at the local level. For example, union-management relationships at Lakeside are likely soon to regress and deteriorate, not that anyone wants them to, but simply because they have to be carried on under external controls which are so rigid that even when "two try to tango," one of the partners seems forever to be dragging and stumbling.

As a forward step, Wes proposed that a committee be formed to examine union-management relationships throughout the ERA/EPIC-controlled organization. Apparently this proposal was well received. It may establish the mechanism for exerting upward influence to get a new framework of thinking and to arouse new creativity in personnel work and industrial relations.

The committee is to include one plant general manager, two personnel managers from different plants, and two invited outsiders, possibly Douglas McGregor and myself. Wes will probably be one of the personnel managers on the committee. It is not yet known which of the plant general managers would be asked to join this group.

For two main reasons, this is an opportune time to establish the committee and begin its study. In last week's "representation election"[3] at another EPIC plant, the independent union lost. This is significant because it was a runoff election. The other main reason is that a basic company reorganization, which is expected to involve John Edwards, is to be announced in a few days' time.

Lincoln Lodge Gets Snowed Under

As I have mentioned, Lakeside is supposed to operate under EPIC's broadly stated policy goal of "running a sound business consistent with good human relations." My observation is that the operational side of Lakeside business is being run in very sound fashion, although, at many points, in a manner inconsistent with good human relations. As a result of management's recognition of a need to improve these relations, the "Lincoln Lodge application series" was proposed and sessions were scheduled for October 14 and 15. The schedule was announced well in advance, and the whole effort was previewed with the 52 senior and middle managers assigned to participate.

During the last few days we have had an arctic storm, and this has provided a wonderful opportunity for me to evaluate these managers' depth of commitment to sound business as distinct from "good human relations." While Lakeside continues to operate at near optimal efficiency, the storm, nonetheless, has presented certain hazards, which more cold weather may accentuate. These hazards come from the fact that certain hot-liquid transmission pipelines are likely to freeze. Thus there could be operational emergencies tomorrow, October 14, which is the day scheduled for the first Lincoln Lodge conference. The question therefore becomes, "Should management reconsider its commitment to the application sessions and postpone them until a later time so that all 52 can be on hand at Lakeside to take care of any emergency, or should tomorrow's session go ahead as scheduled?"

Fail-safe maintenance of production represents sound business. Going ahead with the Lincoln Lodge series would demonstrate deep concern for improving human relations. To go ahead with Lincoln Lodge under the assumption that lower echelons of management, if well briefed, are fully competent to deal with whatever emergencies arise would be a blow for better human relations. To cancel so as to provide extra safeguards for effective production would be a decision more weighted at the "sound business" end of the policy plank.

When talking with Wes yesterday afternoon, I inquired, "Do you think the storm will have an effect on Lincoln Lodge?"

He said, "Oh, no. There's no reason why it should."

I said to myself, "I have my doubts." The doubts had prompted my question in the first place. Today I queried again, and discovered that postponement was being considered. The first test question that arose was, would it be possible for Lincoln Lodge to park the cars of the 26 people who would come? I think the question was predicated on a wistful hope that the Lodge's parking lot would be covered by several feet of snow and that because of this "act of God" the sessions could be postponed.

We phoned Lincoln Lodge. The person contacted said, "Let your minds rest easy: we have already cleared our parking area and there will be no difficulty." Then additional high-level private discussions took place at Lakeside, and I have not yet been informed of their outcome. Meanwhile I am going to make some predictions. The first is that Carl, Quinn and Wes will opt for Lincoln Lodge and Van and Hal will prefer staying at Lakeside. A further prediction is that Van, as operations superintendent, carries the most weight on the scales of decision. His voice, grave with concern for production, will arouse anxiety in others and finally a decision will be made to postpone the sessions.

Another factor that modifies my initial prediction is that Quinn has been invited to a plant managers' meeting at headquarters tomorrow. This is expected to involve some important announcements regarding company reorganization. At last Friday's interview with the EPIC executives, Edwards and Young, he indicated that he would be unable to attend, and this was taken by the headquarters men as an indication of the importance he attached to the Lincoln Lodge sessions. It is beginning to look as though Quinn has a secret desire to be in both places. Last Friday, Lincoln Lodge seemed more important than the managers' meeting. Since then, the more he speculates about reorganization, the more importance he attaches to tomorrow's headquarters meeting. So, if Van today tolls the "productivity in danger" bell—as I predict—it will strike a responsive chord in Quinn. Rescheduling Lincoln Lodge will not only seem a "sound" way of assuring continued production, but it will also provide a means for him to attend the headquarters meeting. If the sessions are postponed, the test of my prediction, therefore, will be whether Quinn stays in the plant actively masterminding solutions of any production dilemmas, or goes to the headquarters meeting.[4]

This morning, October 14, I am at Lakeside instead of Lincoln Lodge. After discussing matters with Van, Hal, Wes, and Carl, Quinn did indeed postpone the Lincoln Lodge application sessions. The weather forecast has proven accurate and today Lakeside is a snowbound, icy industrial tundra, with eskimo-garbed figures anxiously checking the pipelines. Quinn, rather than remaining on station as chief, has gone to headquarters to attend the managers' meeting.

After the Lincoln Lodge postponement decision late yesterday, all 52 participants were phoned. Betty Ross, Quinn's secretary, was assigned responsibility for doing so. The information she conveyed was, "Lincoln Lodge has been cancelled." She did not say it had only been postponed, nor did she give any information on the rescheduled dates, November 4 and 5. This represents either one of two things: poor communication between Quinn and Betty, or an interesting transformation of perception and understanding; the transference being from postponement and rescheduling, to nothing. It is a minor but interesting example of a motivation-communications problem.

Perspectives in Labor-Management Relations

In a recent discussion with Quinn, he made the following points concerning the current perspective in labor-management relations.

"Independent" unionism is a tradition which seems to have very little future. For example, the international ICEW already represents two of this company's eight plants. Independent unions in other large companies within the industry are presently on the brink of going international. Also, if the Democrats win next month's election with their strong labor backing, the next administration undoubtedly will interpret labor-management relations differently than the Republicans.

Within EPIC, the lack of creative efforts to find new patterns in labor-management relations is causing further erosion of the effort at Lakeside to develop and strengthen collaborative relations with independent unions. Headquarters pressures are premised upon traditional thinking rather than in positive and creative terms. The less that a labor contract changes from one period to the next, the better a plant manager looks from headquarters' standpoint.

These and other factors are leading toward a future in which decentralized negotiation and problem-solving with an independent union are no longer possible. The trend seems inevitable unless some truly dramatic actions challenge and transform headquarters' thinking.

References

1. See Chapter 4, Reference 5.
2. The contrast here is between Mac's attempt to act upon facts (even though, at that time, he was not considering feelings as facts), rather than permitting himself to "use" situations to satisfy his private needs—for example, in terms of the "hierarchy of needs" postulated by Maslow, A.H., *Motivation and Personality.* New York: Harper & Row, Inc., 1954.

3. Representation elections are conducted by the National Labor Relations Board for the purpose of determining which particular union the majority of a unit's employees wishes to appoint as a representative. Following such an election, the Board may certify the majority-selected union as the exclusive bargaining agent for all employees in that unit. See: Beal, E.F. and Wickersham, E.D. *The Practice of Collective Bargaining* (3rd Ed.). Homewood, Ill.: Richard D. Irwin, Inc., 1967, pp. 111-112; Linke, W.R. "The Complexities of Labor Relations Law." In Moore, R.F. (ed.). *Law for Executives.* New York: American Management Association, Inc., 1968. p. 150.

4. These predictions of Quinn's behavior are an example of Lewinian "force field analysis." For a description of the method, see: Fordyce, J.K. and Weil, R. *Managing WITH People.* Reading, Mass.: Addison-Wesley Publishing Company, 1971, pp. 106-108.

10

The Great Headquarters Reorganization

At headquarters yesterday, Quinn and other plant managers were given the outline of a significant reorganization. Today, October 15, he convened the department heads and assistant department heads, and announced that EPIC no longer existed. He went on to present a vast format of the new inter- and intra-company organization, one which involves a highly complicated regionalizing concept on the one hand, but a functional integration concept on the other. In addition, the designers and their legal advisers obviously have had to accommodate the myriad nuances of anti-trust regulation.[1] Nonetheless, an important impact of the reorganization is that it was presented as a *fait accompli* which people could do nothing but accept.

All of this produced an interesting atmosphere typified by surface jocularity. The jocularity was not fun based; it seemed more motivated by frustration and needs for tension reduction. Also, there was a considerable degree of disguised hostility in queries such as "Who is going to report to whom?" "What's *that* guy doing there?" "Have they got two people in the same slot?" "Why isn't *this* box filled—don't they know who they are going to put in it?"

This is an understandable reaction because neither Lakeside nor other plant managements had been asked to give their thoughts on what might constitute an appropriate organization. Instead, they were given a packaged prescription to be swallowed. There is no appeal machinery or recourse to higher authority to change any structural detail. So, since they had not worked through a rationale for the reorganization, the immediate reaction was to find fault with it. Maybe it had faults, and maybe it hadn't—but clearly the motivation was to find its weaknesses rather than identify strengths.

The meeting lasted about an hour and a half, and by the end, jocular hostility had turned into hopelessness. Depression was clearly evident in private reactions expressed to me. The reorganization will probably produce many problems for Lakeside, one being the increased centralization the plan implies. ERA, the new super-headquarters, is now for most practical purposes, the *only* headquarters. Lakeside is now a subcomponent of an ERA-controlled company to be known as EPOCH. So management's attitude at this time is, "We have to suffer more centralization—at least until we can find out how to protect ourselves."

I queried a number of people as to why the reorganization took the shape it did. According to them, the grand strategy and overall aim of this reorganization is to wipe out the old subsidiaries which have been either autonomous or quasi-independent. One theory is that the best way for a new headquarters group to integrate a number of formerly separate or quasi-independent companies is to eliminate the old corporate entities.[2] By the same token, managers from the old corporate identities, when displaced to other positions in the new structure, will no longer think in terms which characterized the now-defunct subsidiaries. The speculation is that ERA reorganizers had this theory in mind when they restructured along geographical rather than corporate lines and grouped functions into unified organizations directly responsible to Headquarters.

From here on, no manager can make a decision by saying, "In the EPIC company we handle this kind of problem in the following way." EPIC was one of the older quasi-independent companies and is now extinct. In Lewinian terms,[3] an "unfreezing" of a traditional organization culture and the associated individual attitudes is being accomplished by eliminating the old EPIC company as a source of authority. If widespread unfreezing of this kind actually occurs, then ERA's own criteria, whatever these may be, have a better chance of being applied in all areas and functions.

Executing the Retraction

Today was a big day indeed. Not only because of the massive reorganization plan but because October 15 was also "bite the bullet" day on the union-security clause. This obligation was imposed with EPIC's "last breath" before it expired. But as several former key EPIC executives are now ensconced in ERA headquarters—and, like many philosophers, are not personally influenced by theories they formulate for others—Quinn must have had a lively awareness of the supposedly defunct EPIC tradition as he set about his pious task. The results were fascinating to observe.

It had been decided to make the retraction on Monday, but the blizzard and other interruptions made it impossible to get the appropriate groups together until today, the 15th. Soon after the department heads' session ended, the wage bargaining committee met. Dan Ives was not present due to a serious family problem. From management's side, one item on the agenda was to announce the broad outlines of the reorganization. Another was the retraction, and the third was to discuss arrangements for paying people who had worked continuously during the blizzard for 16 to 24 hours.

The reorganization generated a good deal of interest on the union side. Then came the retraction. Quinn pointed out that the agreement had run into staff resistance. The union officials gave him a sympathetic hearing. They were concerned to test the implications of this retraction, but seemed surprisingly compassionate about the problem that headquarters had created for Lakeside management. But then a new issue was mentioned, one which had not previously been known to Quinn and his bargaining committee. It was that IEW had been running into some resistance from its own membership with respect to the "maintenance of membership" portion of the union-security clause. As soon as Quinn mentioned that management had run into difficulties, some of the union delegates responded that they, too, had been running into comparable problems with their membership. Reactions from the union side were very reasonable, and the situation tonight looks better than at any time since bargaining was initiated.

Quinn was extremely pleased and, after the meeting, began asking, "What were we worried about? Why have we wasted so much time and energy—not to mention almost putting our jobs on the line—agonizing about the union's possible reactions and then quarreling with Headquarters?" "Who said there would be static?" This line of questioning really misses the point. There is an age-old reaction I have seen so many times. When Quinn handled the problem truthfully, he got sympathetic results. Now he acts as though he hadn't been disposed toward deception that probably would have brought a far less positive outcome. Van, too, was quite pleased, and his attitude was implicit in his remark, "This is golden." Mac felt that it would go well, and was not surprised. Wes, maybe, best understood the factors in the situation that produced a constructive-looking outcome. Carl was happy and somewhat surprised. I don't know what Hal's reactions are.

The prevalent feeling is that there is now a better basis for bargaining than has ever existed. Today, in fact, management came under pressure from the union to speed up bargaining so the committee could pinpoint areas of agreement as well as where the negotiators will be unable to come to accord, given their respective positions at present.

This afternoon the salary union was invited in to go over the reorganization, and to hear the union security retraction. A third matter concerned a seniority ruling which had been distasteful to the union, and which Quinn wanted to reverse.

The salary union showed great interest in the reorganization. It had almost identically the same reactions to the retraction as the wage union. Members were pleased with Quinn's reconsideration of the seniority issue. Again, management was requested to step up the pace of bargaining. The salary union was particularly interested in making progress because it had scheduled a membership meeting for the evening of October 23.

So we've gotten through a big day. I attribute this outcome primarily to the fact that management measured itself against the urgency of the problem and decided to tell the truth. It is a sad commentary on American industrial management that it is *unusual* for managers to behave in a truly honest manner that can generate a context in which people listen with openness and understanding. A hopeful conclusion might be that the lost art of being honest is slowly and falteringly being rediscovered. Management people don't trust it. They feel more secure in being "cute" and in exerting influence by manipulation rather than through openness and respect. Nonetheless, on each of these occasions, when honesty pays out as the best policy, it seems to encourage management to be more honest on the next occasion.

A Double Take

Looking over those notes I finished yesterday, and with the knowledge I have since obtained, I realize that optimism led me to make an inaccurate prediction about a dawning era of honesty in Lakeside management.

Here is the way Quinn reported to ERA headquarters after he had completed his retraction meetings. He said, "John, I have just finished my two sessions with the unions and both of them were highly successful. The unions listened with commendable understanding and appreciation of the deep issues involved. They respect and accept our position. In fact, I now feel quite embarrassed about all the telephoning, arguing and special meetings with you. I was concerned at that time because everyone was telling me that the union would fight back. What *you* thought would happen really came true, John. The people around me misread the situation completely. So I'm delighted to report that I've successfully retracted that unfortunate agreement."

Now let's analyze this one. The reactions that the people around Quinn had forecasted were what they had estimated would happen under "Plan A"—his original one—when, covering up the real cause, Quinn was going to say he had evaluated his bargaining team's tentative agreement on union security, had judged it to be unsound, and was now, on his own authority, annulling it. But yesterday, during the actual retraction, he used "Plan B," which accurately identified EPIC/ERA as the source of the trouble. It is to this revelation that much of the mildness of the union's attitude must be attributed. In his discussion with John Edwards, Quinn generated false understandings on the part of headquarters management. At the same time he characterized his bargaining committee as a bunch of nervous Nellies.

Why would he do this? Maybe to make points with John and the rest of ERA, with a shrewd eye to his career. But what he has actually done is reinforce in the headquarters executives' minds that they had been right all along.

This makes them say, "See, we understand how to handle that union. We have superior perspective on these union-management problems, and we can't afford *not* to quarterback contract negotiations."

This represents one of those communication *faux pas* that create worse side effects than the immediate favorable reaction they provoke. Headquarters attitudes toward IEW officials are exactly the same as Lakeside management felt up to two months ago! Over many years, Lakeside management communicated to headquarters its own antagonism, frustration, and disrespect of the union. It is only natural that headquarters came to see IEW in the same light. Then, after having created these attitudes, Lakeside failed to take the next step and continue to communicate its new attitudes of collaboration and the favorable union response. Thus, when headquarters management decreed that the union-security clause must be retracted, it thought this decision would please Quinn and the rest who would see it as another way to hit at the union. When Lakeside management resisted, headquarters was shocked because it had been unaware of the shifts in local management attitudes. Now, John Edwards and the others are probably congratulating themselves on having cured the Lakeside "temporary aberration." As for Quinn's kind words about the union's "understanding and appreciation," John and the others may smile knowingly and say, "Those IEW characters knuckled under when they saw our strength."

Reverberations of the Retraction

Bargaining commenced again today, October 16. Dan returned and this gave me an opportunity to study the effects of his particular approach upon the union bargaining group, in contrast to the way things went yesterday when he was away.

On returning to the plant, Dan had discovered that not only had management retracted its union-security agreement, but more remarkably still, his colleagues in his absence had accepted with relatively good grace. He immediately proceeded to brace up the union committee. This morning, as the meeting opened, he stated, "We know you're under the gun and we don't want to cause you additional trouble, yet we do need some kind of an arrangement that will keep us going as this plant's officially recognized union. We won the NLRB election and kept the International out—which should have pleased headquarters—but currently we're strapped for finance, and there are a lot of non-member employees who would like to go on having a free ride as we represent their interests. And you'll realize, of course, that the terms of the contract—whenever we've agreed to it and signed it—will make *us*, the union, responsible for its observance by all wage employees. So we request that a service fee clause be put into the contract. This will mean that no one is compelled to join the union, but in all fairness, a non-member will pay the equivalent of our membership fee as a service charge for the work we do on his behalf. This matter is so important that we want to schedule a discussion of it with Quinn and yourselves."

Currently, as the request for a service fee[4] is being evaluated in the councils of management, two responses are being voiced. The "freedom lobby" feels that a service fee is in the same category as enforced union membership. It puts management in the position of obligating a man to take some action not directly associated with his work. Another belief that weighs heavily with Lakeside managers is that headquarters will take the same negative, adamant position toward the service fee that it did to the other variety of union security. So it would appear that while yesterday's retraction was effective in that there is no longer an acknowledged "maintenance of membership" agreement, the basic issue is by no means resolved. Indeed, the union might intend to pursue to the ultimate point what it regards as a legitimate request to become a more effective representative of the people, with the strength to fulfill the contract responsibilities it will incur—such as preventing wildcat strikes. Members of the "freedom lobby" at Lakeside and headquarters seem blind to this.

So, in effect, the retraction problem continues, but now in different terms. The union has formulated a new position, and unless Lakeside management becomes somewhat freer and more open, its answer still must be "No," which will have an undesirable consequence in terms of future collaboration. Another bargaining session is scheduled for Monday morning.

Brownie Points for Maintaining the Status Quo

One of the things I've learned from the retraction problem is that the less that Quinn, as Lakeside's general manager, permits changes from traditional practices, the greater the rewards bestowed on him by headquarters.

Ostensibly, in terms of its policy slogan, headquarters has a goal of good labor relations. But its actual concept is "good labor relations without change." At headquarters, where daily pressures of rules and regulations that don't fit the situation are unknown, the static assumption is easy to preserve. This assumption will be invalidated only if it becomes evident to headquarters that bad labor relations exist. Then, obviously, change—for the worse!—has occurred. Then headquarters might do some dynamic thinking regarding how to change relations for the better. But if it notices a subsidiary doing this in the here-and-now, its immediate inference is that "something must have gone gravely wrong down there."

An enlightened headquarters would stimulate plant managers to look beyond where they are today and toward gaining some new and improved basis of relationship with the work force. This pressure to stick with tradition, as pushed by headquarters, is a strong and determining constraint on local management.

But headquarters is not the only influence toward inertia. If Quinn is a representative example, plant managers aren't exactly straining at the leash to create new patterns. For example, this morning when Van "took five" from the bargaining session and communicated Dan Ives' request, Quinn replied that he didn't really want to thrash out the issue again. He felt since he had already accomplished the retraction in a way that was pleasing to headquarters, why should he go back?

In collective bargaining, from a legal point of view the union is exactly equal with management. Therefore, there was no particular reason why Quinn should not honor the request by the union president. However, Quinn hedged.

"Look," he said to Van, "I don't want to go back over there. We've retracted and they understand that the retraction is complete. See if you can't get me out of it."

Van went back to the meeting, and said nothing about the request in the hope that maybe it would die a natural death. Dan said nothing about it until after the coffee break. Then he repeated the request. Van said he'd phone to see if Quinn were available. Quinn heard the second request as a nagging repetition, and he responded, "Look, I still don't want to go. I'd hate to go. Why don't we leave it this way? Let sleeping dogs lie, unless they ask again." Van scrambled the message and fed it to Dan. "He's just too tied up today, I'm afraid."

It was left this way until today, Monday. Over the weekend, Quinn thought up a stratagem which, in his view, was rather clever. His idea was that since the groups are scheduled to bargain all day, if the union made its request for the third time this morning, then Van was to say, "Yes, I mentioned it to Quinn, and he plans to be over this afternoon," giving the appearance that a busy general manager had always had the intention of complying with their request. It might even look like a lack of faith by the union not to believe in his second coming.

However, if the "dog" didn't bark, obviously it would be sleeping, and they'd kindly let it lie. Quinn would not have to come to today's meeting or any future one. Discussion of the service fee issue, if it ever arose again, could be handled by the management bargaining committee; the general theme probably being, "No way."

Quinn was proud of his brainchild. After the meeting when I went in to see him, he described the plan again and pointed out what a clever strategy he had worked up.

At this point in the presentation, I said, "Look, Quinn, let's turn the tables a bit. What would happen if the union had reversed itself, and you wanted to get a straight version from Dan. Through a middle-man, you made an appointment for him to drop by and talk it through, and he didn't show up. And then, getting a little impatient, you made the request again through your middle-man, and again Dan failed to show. What would you do? Would you make a third polite request?"

"No sir, I would see to it that he got his tail up here, but fast," he replied.

"What does this imply with respect to the legal equality of two groups when one group thinks itself superior to the other?" I asked.

He said, "I get your point."

I didn't let it drop here. "What do you think you are *really* communicating to the union when it has to make one request then another request, and then another? They form their attitudes by evaluating your actions, not your words. If you demonstrate your lack of readiness to participate with them equally, particularly on an issue where your own action caused the problem, they surely don't fail to see the point. Is this one of the causes of an historic lack of trust and confidence? Could this kind of behavior be the source of some of the unhappy attitudes between these two groups?"

Quinn said, "Okay, I'm sold. I'll go this afternoon."

My prediction in that conversation with him turned out to be dead right. During the bargaining session today, Dan indicated that they hadn't heard when the meeting with Quinn would be, and he would like to request that it be on Thursday.

Van said, "Okay, I will ask the chief to see if he can do it." Now, as far as I can see, Quinn is concretely obligated to comply with the request.

References

1. See, for example: Malina, M. "Antitrust and Trade Regulations." In Moore, R.F. (ed.). *Law for Executives.* New York: American Management Association, Inc., 1968, pp. 27-48.

2. A concise delineation of post-merger organizational issues is given in Hennessy, J.H., Jr. *Acquiring and Merging Businesses.* Englewood Cliffs, N.J.: Prentice-Hall, Inc., 1966, pp. 228-229. Associated problems are described and discussed in Mace, M.L. and Montgomery, G.G., Jr. *Management Problem of Corporate Acquisition.* Boston: Division of Research, Graduate School of Business Administration, Harvard University, 1962, Chapter IX.

3. Lewin's concept is that, "A successful change includes . . . three aspects: unfreezing (if necessary) the present level L_1, moving to the new level L_2, and freezing group life on the new level. Since any level is determined by a force field, permanency implies that the new force field is made relatively secure against change." Lewin, K. (1947), "Quasi-Stationary Social Equilibria and the Problem of Permanent Change." In Margulies, N. and Raia, A.P. *Organization Development: Values, Process, and Technology.* New York: McGraw-Hill Book Company, 1972, p. 68.

4. Another term for this is "agency shop." See Chapter 4, Reference 1.

11

Contract Complications and Management Mentalities

Largely due to pressure which ICEW, the big and brawny international union, has exerted over the last several months, patterns of industry-wide general wage increases seem to be forming. ICEW has been plugging for 18 cents an hour across-the-board. In other ERA-group companies, as well as for non-ERA competitors, the patterns seem to be shaping up at around 14½ or 15 cents, which equals about a 5% general wage increase. A number of companies have already made an offer, and in many the proposed increase has been accepted.

In the EPOCH company, a different story is being written. Being one of the largest companies now, it seems to be reviving EPIC's tradition of being the last to make any offer. This creates problems for local plant managements, as well as the entire organization. Because EPOCH is currently on an economy drive a general wage increase is quite unpalatable. Nonetheless, EPOCH's president only yesterday announced that earnings for this year will be better than any since 1957. This situation points up a contradiction; at least in the minds of wage earners.

The Lakeside plant has an even more disturbing problem. It has just made the largest return on investment[1] in its history. Although publicly there has only been silence about a wage increase, a tremendous amount of whispering in headquarters and double checking on the part of Lakeside management has been going on.

Against this general company background, the following local problem arises. In Lakeside, the craft-consolidation program a few years ago began a tradition concerned with "red circle" pay, which is granted under the following circumstances. A man is earning, say, X an hour, but as production requirements change—for example, if his job is automated in a way that makes his craft skills inapplicable—the man is no longer able to perform the function for which he was paid X. He gets backed down to a lower skill classification which rates a lesser pay. Since the man was backed down through circumstances outside his control, the craft-consolidation agreement specifies that his name should have a red circle placed around it. The red circle indicates that even though he is presently performing a job that involves lower skill, he continues to receive the rate of the highest skilled job to which he had previously been assigned.[2] This "red circle" clause of the agreement was the basic condition under which the union received the craft consolidation program.

At Lakeside by now, red circle rates contribute significantly to the total cost of the wage contract. If manufacturing economics were the only consideration when a man is backed down, he would be paid at the rate of the job into which he is moved. From a human angle, though, he has become accustomed to living at a higher level. Whether or not managerial kindheartedness might have played some part in formulating the red circle agreement, a definite fact is that this agreement obviated the potentially powerful roadblocking tactics that the union could have employed against consolidation. Now Lakeside managers are taking a hardheaded economic point of view. The red circle rate is a thorn in their sides which they want removed. If the red circle payments were to be phased out, Lakeside wage rates would come more into line with those in the immediate area, with those in other EPOCH plants, and with those prevailing industry-wide. Presently, Lakeside rates are higher than any in the surrounding area. The prevailing area rates which other local plants pay are higher than rates elsewhere in the United States and throughout the world. Therefore, this Lakeside plant probably has the highest wage rates of any place in the world.

So it's also a big thorn in the side of headquarters executives. They would like to see the Lakeside rates brought into line with rates paid in other segments of EPOCH; consistent also with rates at other companies' plants in this industry located in the Lakeside area.

How does all of this relate to a general wage increase? Management is buzzing with the thought that, "Here is an excellent opportunity—if we *have* to grant a general wage increase—to do so for all job classifications for which *pro rata* increases are allowable in terms of the contract, but not to apply the general increase to red circle jobs." Indeed, this has been written into a previous contract, which contained a proviso that a general wage increase granted during the contract period would not automatically be applied to red circle rates. The idea was that "red circle people" would get half of the first general wage increase granted, and on the second increase they would get nothing. This procedure would have brought the red circle rates into line with general wage rates over the long term. By now, that contract period has elapsed; but from management's point of view, the *spirit* of the past agreement is what should be considered.

From the union's point of view, the time period of the contract has run out and, therefore, no one presently is bound by what was in it. But the earlier bargain, under which red circle rates were established, remains in force; for if they had not collaborated in the craft consolidation program, unionists say, Lakeside's efficiency and profits would not be looking so rosy.

Another consideration is, how many red circle people are there? Is it a minor source of economic irritation or is it a real major problem? By now, as a consequence of much automation since the agreement was signed, roughly 12% of the wage membership is red circle. Seen from this angle, red circle differentials contribute significantly to operations cost.

Quinn is eager to apply the previous contract's rule of granting the red circle people one-half of the general wage increase. From his standpoint, it is sound and just. He feels they are already overpaid, so he would like to take this opportunity "to correct a very bad situation." In this respect, his wishes parallel those of Headquarters.

He began talking to me about the problem this morning. As he did so, a new rationalization occurred to him. Here is how he spelled it out. The next general wage increase is intended to offset a rise in the cost of living. Since the last general wage increase, the cost of living has only moved up 2.6%. Therefore, why not give 2.6% as a cost of living adjustment to the red circle people, and 5%, which is the industry average, to those being paid at the going rates? "By doing this," he argues, "we are not penalizing anyone. An adjustment, consistent with the change in cost of living, would be made to everyone but, by this very method, the objective of getting our rates in line with the area average could also be accomplished."

One thing he'd glossed over is that people usually regard themselves as deserving a *pro rata* general wage increase that is based, percentage-wise, on their actual earnings. So I asked Quinn, "You've had this red circle thing for a long time; what have you done previously? I know that in the past you have wanted to use general wage increases as a means of phasing out these rates."

He replied, "Yes, on each occasion we have tried not to extend the general wage increase to those who are red circled. But each time, we have eventually given up and granted it to them."

I pressed the implications further. "What are likely to be the wage earners' attitudes if you start by withholding part of what you are offering others, and then, later, you yield to their demands? What have you gained? Nothing. You have lost, because first you acted like Scrooge, and then buckled under pressure. What about this time? If you withhold the full 5% increase from red circled people, will you stick with that policy or will you eventually yield?"

Quinn said, "I don't know. I have no idea what I would do if it came down to the wire. But I have to try to adjust these rates. Maybe this time the union will see that we can't go on paying premium rates indefinitely."

I said, "Don't bet on it. To me, resistance seems more likely than acceptance. If so, it looks as though you stand to lose less either by withholding and sticking with it, or by giving the full increase initially and not trying to correct your economic situation—both of which alternatives at least carry an aura of sincerity—than by being tentative about it. If at first you withhold, and then yield to union pressure, the public image of your own behavior, your understandings, your convictions, and so on, can only be that of a Scrooge who is forced by pressures to do what others think he should have done in the first place."

So Quinn is confronted by a predicament. All of the pressures from headquarters are directed at correcting rates of pay which are out of line. But the union will push for a general wage increase regardless of whether or not a man is working at the standard rate or the red circled rate.

Splintering in the Union Bargaining Group

The October 20 bargaining session produced a phenomenon whose earliest indications were noticed at the time of the crane crisis. What happened was that the union group began to splinter.

On the other side of the bargaining table there are three leading personalities. Dick Kelly, the chairman of the union bargaining group, is described by management committee members as a fellow who continuously talks off the top of his head, tells stories that are not relevant, and in general is unable to control his own need to talk, talk, talk. Dan Ives, the union president, sits as an ordinary member of the delegation. He is the disciplinarian who keeps the group in shape. The theoretician of the union is Max Daniels, a truly intellectual and competent individual.

Over the past month, Max has been feeling less and less satisfied about the meetings, not so much about management's actions, but more particularly the behavior of his own colleagues. While management has been seeking to engage in problem solving rather than win-lose bargaining, an interesting situation has emerged. The extent to which the union is incompetent to engage in problem-solving discussion is becoming visible. With the sole exception of Max, these union officers don't seem to have the discussion skills, the analytical powers, or the logical capabilities to follow a line of argument through to a sensible conclusion. The result is that management is becoming frustrated because it can't keep discussion moving in a straight line due to the many distractions introduced by individual union officials. The off-target remarks are not intentionally provocative, but occur simply because of lack of intellectual discipline.

In the past, Max has been a belligerent foe of management. But recently, irked both by Dick's waffling and Dan's obstinate stands on relatively minor points, Max seems to be viewing the union's problem-solving capacities in much the same light as members of management's bargaining committee. Even in some contract-bargaining issues, he sees management's point of view rather than his group's. The apparent result is a split within the union. Its members are not able to agree and to cohere.

In my judgment, two things are needed to produce anything approaching productive negotiation. One is that the management committee members, rather than being personally critical of the union representatives, must find how to help them with their present problem. Secondly, Max, rather than castigating his colleagues and separating himself from them, must learn to provide the aid they need to become effective.

Following this line of reasoning, I proposed to management's bargaining committee that it should have a process critique session tomorrow to investigate how it might become a more adequate collaborator with the union under present conditions. Whether the lack of problem-solving skills in the union can be remedied by Max, the one member who really does possess skills of collaboration and analysis, is questionable. Likewise, can management itself, by greater patience, succeed in helping resolve the union's problems?

A final point is that both groups, union and management, are under severe pressure to make better progress. The pressure comes not from outside the bargaining room, but from within. Management wants to step up the tempo; it can almost smell the possibility of agreement. The union is also frustrated by the lack of progress. Both groups are pointed in the same direction, but neither has the requisite skills to help the other unblock the situation to accomplish the desired end result.

Working with Headquarters

Because of the significance of "headquarters backing" from ERA and EPOCH, the proposal was made that I go to Atlanta to meet with responsible line officers and discuss the broad implications of what is being attempted at Lakeside.

Yesterday afternoon in Quinn's "manager's meeting," I opened the problem. I said I wanted to go, and hoped it would be possible for me to do so. Quinn said this would be very worthwhile. He contacted headquarters to see if it would be possible for me to fly down there in a day or two. Unfortunately, several significant honchos had just gone on vacation and would be unavailable for several weeks.

How Informal Managerial Norms are Established

Informal norms such as clothing, working beyond the formal quitting hour, carrying away homework, checking in on Saturday, and so on, get to become "established" in the following way.

Members of management, who usually dress in gray suits, black shoes, white shirts, and quiet neckties, stop by the plant awhile on Saturday or Sunday to check that things are OK. When they do so, they wear sport coats, pants of contrasting material, and tieless leisure shirts. What is the reason for this? The best answer that I know is that Quinn makes a practice of stopping in either on Saturday, Sunday, or both, to check operations. When he does, he wears a tweed sport coat and a plaid shirt. It is strictly a question of follow the leader.

Another informal norm governs the appropriate time to quit work. The standard quitting time for middle management is in the neighborhood of 4:45 to 5:15 p.m. Above a certain level of management, however, the time to end the day is 6:00 or 6:30 p.m. Why? Quinn rarely gets away before 6:00 or 6:30 p.m., and everyone knows that if you want to get a few minutes with him to talk over the neglected problems of the day, that is the time to do it. Also, everyone knows that in Quinn's eyes, to be on hand between 6:00 and 6:30 p.m. is an indication of an eager manager.

Another norm relates to doing homework and carrying a briefcase back and forth to the plant. The norm says, "Don't read reports at the plant during working hours. Do it at home. Carry a briefcase." Why? First of all, Quinn is a heavy reports reader. He likes the written word. He always packs a briefcase full so that he doesn't run out of things to do at home. He frequently remarks, "I got to your report last night and found it so and so." That tells people to read *their* reports at home, too. To say that you finished it between 10:00 a.m. and noon on Tuesday would indicate that you are using operations time for study. From 8:00 to 5:00 a manager is supposed to be an operator. When he gets home he can legitimately become a student of reports. It is my impression, therefore, that Quinn creates the expectations and model behaviors that underlie a number of prevalent norms. A summary of these norms would be, "Drop by to check your operations during the weekend, but be gentlemanly about it. Don't wear a business suit, wear a rough English wool coat and a plaid shirt. It is sporting. When you leave the plant, take a full briefcase with you. Reports should be examined at home. The hours from 8:00 a.m. to 5:00 p.m. are to operate the plant, not to sit and study. Between 5:00 and 6:30 on weekdays, be sure the general manager notices that you still have your nose to the grindstone. Furthermore, when you leave late, always drop a remark about it the next day if you have a chance. If you read any report at home, point out the horrible conditions under which you had to work; for example, the children were underfoot and the TV was on, so you went to your study to obtain quiet."

The rule is that if you stay late, be seen, and if you do work at home, let it be known. These are the properties that make a man into a promotion-worthy manager under local conditions.

Tool Time

When should a wage worker stop working? Is he through the moment the whistle blows, so that on hearing it he takes his equipment and tools to the storeroom, cleans up and exits? At the other extreme, when the whistle blows, should he be already at the gate, cleaned up and in his street clothes, regardless of where his work station happens to be? In other words, is a man paid from the time he enters through the plant gate until he leaves the gate, or is he paid from the time he gets on the job and starts doing work until, still engaged on his duties, he hears the whistle blow?

This is the age old issue of "portal-to-portal" versus "performance" pay.[3] It has been a source of perennial controversy at Lakeside, one that has had only incidental focus upon tools and returning them to storage. Rather, the controversy has centered upon "wash-up time." It concerns whether a man should be allowed to stop work soon enough to be able to go to the locker room and take a shower—or at least wash up—so as to be clean and presentable when the whistle blows. In previous contracts, wash-up time has been granted as a legitimate right of the worker. If a man got dirty while working the company was responsible for providing him the opportunity to clean up before leaving. Foremen have been administering wash-up time since in contract terms it can only be authorized if a man is grimy.

Numerous controversies have arisen over defining "How dirty must a man be to merit wash-up time?" Workers are irritated by a system which requires them to get authorization before they can leave the job and wash up. Even when a man has been given a wash-up slip by his foreman, he may be subjected to inspection by other company officials in the locker room occasionally to see whether he actually has been authorized to leave his job. To be asked to produce a wash-up slip when one is soaping up at the wash bowl or in the shower is inconvenient, if not humiliating.

This problem, and the bad feelings it generates, has been intensively studied by Lakeside management. As a result, and in contrast to what the union is seeking, they are planning to counter-propose that a 10-minute "tool time" be written into the next contract. This would mean that ten minutes before the end of the work day or shift when the whistle blows, every man would be authorized to stop work, gather up his tools and return them to storage. If time remained after a man's tools had been put away, he could use it for wash-up or for whatever else he felt like doing. The union's draft contract, however, proposes 20 minutes' "wash-up time."

In all innocence, one would think that a decentralized plant's management would be free to counterpropose and bargain with the independent union toward the kind of agreement which solves a local problem. The friction produced by the wash-up issue in past years is unique to Lakeside. Yet, against the background of the recent retraction that headquarters imposed, Quinn and the others are uncertain as to whether, if they put their proposal on the table and succeed in getting the union to accept 10 minutes' tool-cum-wash-up time, they might later face the possibility of another enforced reversal.

So Lakeside management has already contacted EPOCH, and has been referred to the appropriate decision maker there, Don Cooper. Thus, because of perceived implications for precedent-setting, what on the surface is a local problem must be resolved by the next-to-highest headquarters of the entire organization. The rationale is that if tool time were granted in Lakeside, unions in other plants would strive to achieve it on the next bargaining round. This would set in motion a cycle of change that ERA superheadquarters might not like.

All the more disturbing in this particular case is that many other things are interconnected in Lakeside's tool time and wash-up controversy. These are complex enough to bedevil the issue, perhaps beyond the scope for finding a good local solution. For example, at Lakeside there is no authorized coffee break for work people. In other ERA/EPOCH plants there is. Coffee breaks are not an issue locally, but a coffee break does constitute non-productive work time, as does the proposed 10-minute tool time. So an offer of tool time should be regarded as compensating for the coffee break allowed in other centers.

It seems, then, that one cannot look simply at the issue of ten minutes' tool time in an isolated way, nor can it be viewed from the standpoint of a general principle. Those modes of viewing the situation lead toward applying mechanical thinking to an organic problem. The "organismic" view[4] is that tool time is related to coffee break time, vacations, and many other things of a basically similar nature. In contrast, mechanical thinking uses concepts such as "precedents" and "the rule of consistency" across all production centers. I am beginning to see the quest for uniformity of policy and procedure as one of the blights of managerial thinking. What is needed is not uniformity, but thinking in terms of the situation so that procedures and policies that fit local circumstances in place X may differ from policies in Y for the simple reason that the problems of X are different than those of Y. To try to set a uniform policy that applies to X, Y, and Z when conditions in X, Y, and Z are different is the hallmark of narrow mechanical managerial thinking.

The tool time counterproposal has to reach the bargaining table tomorrow, or the union is likely to take for granted that its own 20-minute proposal has been accepted without demur. Both sides want to move into other segments of the contract and make progress. There has been so much previous stalling by management's bargainers that they see no way of stalling *beyond* tomorrow.

The phone jingled all day between Lakeside and EPOCH as there was an intensive examination of issues involved in agreeing to tool time in the Lakeside-IEW contract. The basic issue appears to be that even though tool time would entail only a standard ten minutes, which is presently granted on a widespread basis under the system of individual wash-up slips—each of which exacts "foreman time"—it would set a dangerous precedent. No one in headquarters wants to tell Lakeside that it can't have tool time, and yet everyone is doing just that. No one wants to take responsibility for, or feels comfortable with, the possibility that such a precedent-breaking agreement will be made, but everyone recognizes that the wash-up slip procedure is a mess and that tool time is an entirely appropriate solution.

This evening's result is a fascinating example of "Don't let your left hand know what your right hand is doing." The recommendation from EPOCH is, "Go ahead and grant tool time, but don't sign it into the contract. Just *do* it. Get an *informal* agreement that management and the union will honor but isn't written."

On the surface, this might appear reasonable. Grant the union what it requests, but in an informal manner. Give your word and live by it. But it's a subterfuge. The reason is that if Lakeside can avoid writing a tool time agreement into the contract, then there will be no opportunity for unions in other locations to scrutinize the Lakeside contract and demand tool time for themselves. If there's nothing in writing, every other management can stare at their respective union counterparts and say, "We don't know anything about tool time. What Lakeside is supposed to do is governed by their contract. If it is not in their contract, it doesn't legally exist—far less set a precedent."

Nobody is fooled for long by this kind of strategem, it's not even intelligent. Sooner or later the other side finds out what really is going on. In other words, here is just one more instance of managerial dishonesty, and, as an example, it shows why there are so many legitimate reasons for union officers to regard management as unworthy of their trust.

When the matter came up next morning at Quinn's meeting my position was that this was a dishonest approach which would produce many widespread difficulties in the future. This point of view was shared by Wes and Quinn, and the discussion was pursued by conference calls to headquarters. Finally, ERA acquiesced and sent word that it would be acceptable to grant ten minutes' tool time; they would raise no objections if local management were to sign this into the contract.

To some this may seem to have been an unimportant issue. Yet it has been a continuous source of conflict and controversy for 10 to 12 years. Only by a negotiated agreement will the problem be eliminated. It is only a minor irritation, but it tends to become mammoth simply because of its frequency of repetition. When wash-up time comes up at the next bargaining session, it should be a pleasant surprise for the union to find that finally management has seen a way to resolve this problem. Though just a little step of progress, it is likely to be very warmly received and appreciated.

I am appalled by the many examples of genuine management dishonesty that have come to my attention in the last few months. Were it possible for me also to have the inside view of union affairs, I might see comparable evidences of trickery. Even if a union were tricky, manipulative, and dishonest, this still would constitute no reason for management being the same way. Since management is the stronger member in the relationship, a casual guess would be that if a union is dishonest and deceitful, it has learned to be so from the very people who are skilled in the strategies of tricky politics. The union probably reflects in its behavior the kind of attitudes toward honest and straight dealing that it finds in its chief counterpart, namely the company.

If this is so, it means that management "trains" its union to be dishonest or honest, depending upon how it behaves itself. In any event, Lakeside has just missed getting into the throes of another battle over a picayune, unimportant, trivial issue. If this had happened as a result of buckling under to headquarters pressure, it would have been another defeat for local management's efforts to become not only honest with the union, but also to strengthen honesty within its own ranks.

The moral I am drawing from a great number of examples that I see is that basic early-American attitudes toward honesty as the basis for interpersonal and intergroup relationships have been almost lost. Nowadays the goal is not to be honest, but to gain your point. If this ideology has become widespread, it means that American industry is in a more serious basic difficulty than anyone has yet believed. Once conditions of openness have been discarded as bases of relationship, very little is left to replace them.

"Unfreezing" an Organization's Labor-Management Relations

One of the "invisible barriers" I sense at Lakeside is that labor-management relations have been a problem for so long that people have become accustomed to chronic conflict. After such a prolonged period of heavy emotionality with no positive outcome, it is difficult for people to invest more commitment toward bringing about a successful result. The labor-management situation here can be compared to the bad marriage about which one partner remarked, "Why speak of love? We were used to each other."[5]

The problem becomes, "How can the organization be unfrozen[6] so as to become more creative in resolving problems of labor-management relations?"

Here is a plan that I am mulling over. The first step would be to begin with Quinn and Dan Ives *together,* on a partnership basis, conducting a number of group interviews. Each of these sessions would be with fifteen or so wage people. The purpose would be to elicit frank statements as to the organization-related problems they find bothersome, as well as suggestions for improvements they feel would substantially contribute to improving working relationships between themselves and management.

If such a program were inaugurated, commitment would have to be present (1) to take action, wherever feasible, to bring about desirable results from recommendations made, and (2) to communicate clearly the reasons for not taking up any particular recommendation. If, as a partnership endeavor by Quinn and Dan, some 20 or 30 two-hour interviews of this sort could be conducted, at least three positive results can be expected. First, it would give Quinn an intimate view of the present quality of human relations around Lakeside, something which he simply doesn't have at this time. Second, it would identify many problems that people are not presently trying to solve. Third, it would begin to identify wage people who might be co-opted, as members of joint labor-management committees, to study these problems and come up with recommendations. In my view this partnership approach can immediately begin to unfreeze the organization. It can develop the kind of collaboration on the part of both management and the union which is essential for finding solutions to presently intractable problems.

Teaching Engineers to Manage

Lakeside employs many engineers. As a matter of fact, anyone here who wants to get somewhere in his career had better have an engineering degree or he'll be regarded as a flunky. The sustaining myth is that only engineers count in this world. Since Lakeside is part of a grand old blue chip company, it would hurt ERA's pride to employ an engineer who was not in the upper ten percent of his graduating class. This policy results in there being good engineers here. They are the cream of the crop. They are superb in engineering theory and application. They know how to formulate equations, how to automate processes, how to get results from a computer, and so on.

When it comes to supervising human effort, however, they are about as inadequate as any other technology-oriented professionals; perhaps more so because apparently they don't know what they don't know. When they first come to Lakeside, they are bright-eyed eager beavers. After two or three years, they notice that a few from their number are being groomed for manager positions. Up to this time, most of their work was technical and they were happy. Then this new anxiety-provoking ingredient is thrown in; that some become knighted and cast in a role of responsibility to supervise those who do the work. Hitherto the engineer has been paid a salary and told that he is a member of management, but in these first few years, he is more like a wage man.

Those who are promoted to supervisory positions are in trouble from the outset because without prior training they have to manage their former peers and the new engineers who come in. Those who don't go up must feel they're in trouble too, because they start looking for jobs elsewhere. It costs about $6,000 just to employ an engineer, if you count campus recruiting, visits to the plant, and all the numerous costs of this sort. Not only are continual financial losses caused by the outflow of disappointed engineers; the company also suffers a loss of pride when some of its finest engineering professionals leave because they have neither been groomed for nor given management responsibilities.

I was away at the time when they had a meeting to set up a management development program for engineers. The theme was, "We must train each junior engineer to be able to perform managerial tasks." When I came back, they had a perfect "circuit rider" project designed. This would put each new entrant under one division head for three months or so; then he'd be moved into another division for a period, and so on. Formal courses at business schools and lecture series at the plant would also be featured. Eventually, having made the grand tour of Lakeside and after imbibing from several different founts of managerial wisdom, any sound young fellow could expect to be fitted into some vacant supervisory niche.

Hal showed me the plan and asked what I thought of it. He was expecting a positive response. I told him I didn't even want to react. This perked his curiosity and he inquired further. I told him that I thought it was absurd, hopeless, useless; a program for rinsing money down the drain without any effective return. This caused considerable consternation throughout the top executive group. After some time, they decided to reevaluate the program in light of possible alternatives.

The meeting this afternoon is to redesign the program. I intend to draw a spectrum across the blackboard. At one end I am going to put the "Teacher tells, student listens" type of teaching psychology, and at the other end I am going to put "pure process—just mucking around in interpersonal behavior experiments with no definition of what aspect of human relations the training is designed to improve." From my standpoint, both of these are undesirable.

In the middle I am going to put a capsule summary of the following: a group of 12 or so junior engineer-supervisors assemble with a behavioral scientist, such as myself, as leader. On the job, from day to day, they would keep records of all "critical incidents" that occurred as consequences of their supervisory behavior. There would be incidents where they were successful and accomplished a good result, but also there would probably be a variety of other incidents where they had sought to succeed but had failed, perhaps dramatically. After a sufficient amount of material had been developed, this group would systematically analyze these real-life issues.

This would do two things. First, it would sensitize these engineers to what they are actually doing when they supervise people. During the weekly sessions, each person would get feedback from the others regarding how they saw his supervisory approach and how, in each specific incident, he might have gotten better results.

The initial period of the manager-development year might take about three or four months. The next period, of similar length, would be concerned with skill practice. Each person would design behavioral experiments in which he could, on a trial basis, change one or more aspects of his present supervisory approach and, afterwards, evaluate the results. By planning experimental on-the-job exercises of this sort, and by keeping a critical-incident record, it would be possible for each of the 12 to devise ways of testing and improving administrative skills, as well as getting feedback from others on how to improve his experiments. The third four-month period would include a heavier emphasis on theory regarding relationships and psychological phenomena in situations where one person has more power than another.

Ways of Reorganizing a Division

A division head recently put together some ideas about operational benefits that could be gained if the division were to be reorganized. Logically, these ideas make a good deal of sense. During the last two or three days, he has mentioned them to one unit supervisor and gotten his reactions, and then has run them by another unit supervisor to get further thoughts on the matter. The result has been that the rumors are beginning to fly. Anxiety undoubtedly builds under these conditions. People in the division have begun to take positions on what they think are the issues. Strangely enough, no one seems to suspect any intrigue, trickery, or politics involved in the division head's contacting people on a one-by-one basis. The best interpretation I could come up with was that this is the typical way of doing things and is accepted as such. People have come to expect that their bosses will be arbitrary and thoughtless. Perceived from this standpoint, they may appear so clumsy as to be incapable of guile.

The major thing that is wrong with this kind of approach to reorganization is that the "examining unit", the division head and one unit supervisor at a time, is inappropriate. The division head should get *all* of his unit supervisors together to discuss his ideas. At that time they could develop plans to involve other divisional people in studying the proposed reorganization. Under these circumstances each person has an opportunity to put his ideas into the pot as it is boiling. Every person knows what the score is; anxiety is not created.

There are two advantages of using group discussion. A better design is likely to emerge because many people will have bounced ideas off each other. In addition, as division people get involved, anxiety about reorganization disappears.

What is a Profit?

Around Lakeside, the profit statement generates considerable interest. Quite early each month, the operating performance report for the previous month is circulated to all department heads. In each department, figures for the various segments of the organization are put on the blackboard for examination. There is a broad spectrum of attitudes toward these profit and loss statements.

Nearly everyone at Lakeside agrees that, like motherhood, profit-making is intrinsically "good." Managers and union members would no more think of challenging profit as a fundamental motive than they would think about challenging godliness. I don't challenge the profit motive either. Receiving an appropriate return on investment is one of the strongest motives of management. It is the one motive that, if relied upon, will keep an operation muscular and lean and will provide a background for creative, innovative thinking. What is interesting at Lakeside, however, is a different aspect. Some managers, in comparison with others, experience much greater glee when a profit is shown. Some managers keep their eyes glued to the profit picture while others spend more time worrying about the human side of their operations and how to improve working relationships. I have noticed, too, that there appears to be relatively little correlation between the quality of a man's operation and the importance he places upon the profit statement. I am still searching for relevant comparative dimensions. At this point I will record some working hypotheses.

One such untested prediction is that the more devoted a manager is to scrutinizing solely his own monthly profit statement, the less is his skill in sensing and analyzing human relations problems; and the less is his skill, relatively speaking, in operating a sound organizational segment. This broad and sweeping generalization needs modification.

There are some managers at Lakeside who seem interested neither in profit nor operations nor human relations. They are men on the shelf, doing a repetitive job in a repetitive way from 8:00 a.m. to 5:00 p.m. Other managers are intensely interested in the profit statement as an indication of how the organization is doing and to use it as the basis for critiquing line segments of the organization which do not return a profit. For them, the profit and loss picture is a diagnostic indicator aimed at organizational improvement. In my view, these people have a meaningful perspective on the implications of profit.

My working hypothesis is directed toward the number of individuals I have come to know quite well who have an intense concern for profit but who do not use profit differences among the segments of the organization as a basis for diagnosing operating or human problems. They just like viewing the profit statement. A "good month" is an end in itself.

Also fascinating is the lack of any immediate connection between the operating profit and an individual's pay. A man's eyes are not drawn to the profit picture because it means more pay for him. It might eventually, but the connection is indirect, and, therefore, the motive to pay attention to the profit picture is not based on any selfish economic rationale.

From my point of view, profit-and-loss considerations are true motivators of efficiency, innovation, creativity, novelty and all the other ingredients that induce change, modernization and new thinking. It's hard to see how societies that don't work expressly on a profit-motive basis are able to keep themselves alive and press toward efficiency and improvement. I think I have noticed this lack of motivation in non-business institutions as well as in foreign countries where the profit motive doesn't operate freely. Instead, traditions tend to become encrusted. Old ways of doing things are perpetuated and prospects of efficiency are lost.

Is a Manager Penalized for Innovation and Creativity in Labor-Management Relations?

Sometime ago I suggested that a plant manager is regarded by headquarters in the following manner: the fewer the changes from one contract signing to the next, the higher the esteem in which he will be held by headquarters. Rewards come to those who maintain the status quo.

This prediction can be tested in two ways. The first is built into a proposal I have made: that a headquarters group be appointed to study a number of new and possibly relevant approaches to labor-management relations. My prediction is that Quinn would favor such an approach, but since it implies change, he would not want to be the source of the idea. So I suggested a number of concrete examples of innovative approaches to labor-management relations, and asked Quinn if it would be suitable for him to propose a high level committee of the company to study these and other possibilities.

He verified my prediction through the following remarks. "This sounds right. It is the way we must go, with the pressures that are building now, both locally and at the federal political level. There is no other good alternative. The point is, though, I would prefer the idea to come from headquarters rather than from me. If I present too many ideas, I am seen as someone who is out of step." This statement by Quinn I take as verification that the less change one is responsible for in the labor field, the greater is his acceptance.

The second test was by formulating the converse proposition: that the more change one is responsible for, the more disturbance is provoked in headquarters and, therefore, the greater the doubts on the part of headquarters regarding one's managerial skills. When I tested this proposition on Quinn, it received immediate endorsement. He immediately recognized that the silent motivation influencing his behavior is "to be responsible for as few disturbing changes as possible."

So, whereas present labor-management relations cry for creative, innovative thinking and for the search for new patterns, styles, arrangements or mechanisms which will *solve* problems, the reward system is constituted in the opposite direction. It very well could be that this explains the sad lack of creativity in the labor-management field at Lakeside.

References

1. The "rate of return on investment" concept and its technicalities are described in Horngren, C.T. *Accounting for Management Control* (2nd Ed.). Englewood Cliffs, N.J.: Prentice-Hall, Inc., 1970, pp. 364-372.

2. "Red Circle Rate" is defined, with source references, in Roberts, H.S. *Roberts' Dictionary of Industrial Relations.* Washington, D.C.: BNA Incorporated, 1966, pp. 360-361. The "red circle" demand by a union, and its relatedness to union perceptions of "rate of technological change" in industry, are discussed in Beal, E.F. and Wickersham, E.D. *The Practice of Collective Bargaining* (3rd Ed.). Homewood, Ill.: Richard D. Irwin, Inc., 1967, p. 289.

3. The problems associated with this issue center to a large extent around conflicting union/management interpretations of The Portal-to-Portal Act (1947) and its application to particular circumstances. See: Roberts, H.S. *Roberts' Dictionary of Industrial Relations,* Washington, D.C.: BNA Incorporated, 1966, pp. 328-329.

4. Organismic thinking takes as its reference point a conception of "the system as a whole." See: von Bertalanffy, L. *Problems of Life.* New York: John Wiley & Sons, Inc., 1952, pp. 9-22. Von Bertalanffy's pioneering work foreshadowed the approach now known as General Systems Theory.

5. Eliot, T.S. *The Cocktail Party.* New York: Harcourt, Brace, & World, Inc. (Harvest Books), 1950, p. 29.

6. "Unfrozen" in the Lewinian sense. See Chapter 10, Reference 3.

12

In and Around Both Camps

The biggest breakthrough in bargaining with the salaried employees' union came today, October 21. The initial feeling is that success for both parties has been achieved along with a solid foundation for long-term effective collaboration.

For a long time, the barrier to cooperation had been management's adamant refusal to accept a layoff clause which would invoke the seniority principle, one of the greatest treasures a union can have. But today, finally, the salary bargaining committee did agree to honor seniority in a layoff everywhere except in the medical department. This is a sharp break with management's tradition of using a recession imposed layoff to get rid of the least adequate personnel and keep the more competent. To the union this has always seemed manifestly unjust. They say to management, "You have your opportunities in prosperous times to tell a man to shape up or ship out. Then if you fire him, he at least has some chance of landing another job. But to wait until a recession—that's vindictive in the case of an incompetent man, and unfair to anyone who was performing satisfactorily even if he wasn't a shining star. Your sorting processes smack of a kangaroo court. People have been laid off, not because they were incompetent, but because of trivial incidents with supervisors in the past, or other irrelevant reasons. 'Due process' doesn't exist under those circumstances; it's more like the night of the long knives. We want justice under the simple and easily administered rule of seniority."

The salary union has a new lease on life. A general meeting has been scheduled tomorrow night, and it has only this point of major accomplishment to report, but several others as well; not of the same magnitude, but all in the same direction. It would appear that management has genuinely learned to listen with respect; to adjust its insatiable desires for efficiency to the reasonable demands of salaried personnel for security.

Evidently management's position has changed much more than the union's. However, management had much more need to change because of its heavy-handed and ill-timed emphases on efficiency while disregarding people's legitimate needs for security and dignity. Now that it has broken from its traditional approach, a number of new developments become possible. There are many areas in which the Lakeside unions and management may tangle in the future, but at least, the critical barrier to agreement has been broken.

A Visit with the Wage Union

I had arranged a meeting for 7:45 a.m. today, October 22, with Dan Ives, the union president, and Dick Kelly, the union secretary who also acts as chairman of IEW's bargaining delegation. Dan and Dick had said they'd stop by the Personnel Department and talk with me there. My aim was simply to see how the union is thinking and feeling.

I arrived at 7:30 in the bitter cold. The doors in the administration building were locked. I don't know when they ordinarily open, but I didn't want to miss this meeting just because the premises were locked. So I went to Dan's office. He wasn't there, but the coffee was on. A small man was sitting near the heater, but I didn't get his name. We chatted for a few minutes, and then another man came in. In his heavy coat and hat, I mistook him for Dan. We shook hands. Then another came in with a grocery sack. Before I had a chance to open my mouth, out came the rolls. Each roll had a slice of ham and a piece of onion. He called them "Dago buns."

Dan came in and was surprised to find me there. He immediately started joshing with the others. It was apparent that this group has a rich joking system built up over the years. He asked if I would like a cup of coffee, and poured one for me.

Another man, who is on the IEW executive committee, came in. I hadn't met him before, but he said that 35 years ago he had held some office in the labor federation. He was the most talkative of all. They all got rolls, and started eating. Several offered me one, but I figured that they had just enough to go around, and so I had better not accept.

The committee man turned to me and said, pointing to Dan, "You know this guy?"

I said, "Yes, a little bit."

Then he said, "You know what a Wop is? You know what a Dago is?"
I said, "Yes."

"You know what a slave is? You know what an Untouchable is?"
I said, "No."

He pointed to Dan again and said, "He's an Untouchable. That's what an Untouchable looks like."

They joked back and forth over their cups of coffee. Much of the conversation was cryptic, and I missed many of the subtleties that meant much more to the people who had the background than they did to me. Mostly I could pick up only the good old Saxon words they used for emphasis.

Then another man came in. I got up again to introduce myself, but before I had the chance, someone else introduced me. This time, the gray-headed committee man got my name.

He said, "Oh, Blake from BTS."

"Yes."

"I've heard a lot about you."

"That's too bad," I said.

"I have never heard one negative thing about you. You must be OK, but there's another one I knew at BTS who wasn't so good."

"Who was that?"

"Nutsy Glass. Everyone called him Nutsy Glass."

"Why?"

"Oh, I used to know a son of Israel from Detroit whose name was Glass, and everyone called him Nutsy Glass, and so we called this Glass, Nutsy Glass, too."

He turned to Dan and said, "Treat this guy OK. He's all right." I appreciated this.

Finally, everyone left to get to work except Dan and Dick. I said. "I'm leaving on a trip, but before taking off I'd like to get the picture from you as to how things are going. Do you feel there's any progress, or is it the same old thing? What do you look forward to? Is there a basis for cooperation yet?"

Dick spoke up. I could tell he wasn't reacting antagonistically toward me. He said, "Well, things are better, but only in a small way."

"What do you mean?"

"Oh, we're talking better. They get our point of view, but the big impasse comes whenever the dollar sign arises. Management simply can't conceive we're making progress when laboring people get a more secure position with a better financial stake." He made this point in various ways, but always came back to the general theme that management can't see very well because of the dollar signs always in its eyeballs.

Dick went on to say, "You know, back in the old days the Personnel Department was concerned with human relations. Nowadays, it's just legal stuff. Personnel is always telling us things that can't be done due to legal requirements, even though human considerations may be thrown away in the process. They're not concerned with human relations anymore. All they ask themselves is, "What can we get by with under the narrowest and most one-sided interpretation of the contract and labor law generally?"

Dan remarked that his general feeling was in the same direction. "Management isn't like it used to be in the old days. It's lost its personal touch. It's lost its feel for people. Quinn seems to avoid coming where the work gets done. Those sidekicks of his don't have the touch either. They're just engineers. Sure, they're smart. They know machinery. They know how to make a dollar, but they don't know how to treat people. They have no heart; they're engineers."

"This latest move of theirs, to deny the general wage increase to our red circle people, is par for the course. They're relying on an unfair clause in the last contract, one they forced us to accept when we were much weaker than we are now. They say the old contract is still in effect. We *know* it's expired and we're going to prove it.

"We can't continue bargaining this way, because management is not under pressure to produce a contract. It feels it has all the time in the world because, as they say, 'We still have the old contract.' We'll take them to court and test this one. If it turns out that no contract is in effect, those managers are going to be sorry they tried to pull a fast one on us, for two reasons. First, the court decision will open the way for another representation election between ourselves and the international. The issue there simply will be, "Which union is better equipped to wring a fair contract out of this heartless management?" After hearing about the runaround we've been given, the workers will want to draft Attila the Hun! Second, management won't be able to lean on the old contract. There will be *no* contract, and we or our successors will start from fresh.

"Furthermore, let me tell you, if management continues to come on like Scrooge, we'll do another thing. We hate the ICEW group, but don't think we wouldn't throw our support to them if we saw that it was in the best interests of our people. Maybe it is, after all. We've tried being reasonable and cooperative, and where's it getting us? Maybe force will get them off dead center."

At this moment, one of the persons who had been around earlier came back in just long enough to say to me, "Watch out for ICEW," and to Dick, "There's a tape recorder on the other side of the wall." He was joking, but for a moment I thought Dick and Dan were about to go outside and check.

Later, another indication of suspiciousness came in Dan's questioning of me. "Did Quinn send you?" he asked. "Are you going to report what's been said to you here?"

I reacted in two ways. One was, "You've said nothing to me here that I haven't heard a hundred times. I don't recall anything you've told me that I could report as news, even if I'd been asked to, which I haven't."

Dan replied, "Yes, you're right. Everything I said here, I say to the management. The only difference is, I say it to you with less emotion. When I say it to them, I really bang my fists on the table."

Then I got to my main point. "If there's been anything in the conversation you don't want me to mention, I certainly won't. You'll have to test me on that, whenever you want, simply by putting me under a condition of trust. As you've said, nothing's come up so far that you would want me to keep private. This could mean that we really haven't gotten down to brass tacks. I'm at Lakeside to help improve problem solving. The things I really want to know about are the things you wouldn't want communicated. The more I'm able to understand the more I'll be able to help the problem-solving process pick up strength. Perhaps another time we could get together and move toward a closer working basis, so that I could have some real insights into particular union problems."

Overall, I thought it was a good conversation. I wish I had been able to continue. However, a bargaining session was scheduled for 8:45 a.m., and they were already five minutes late.

I would like to make a few more observations about this meeting. The first concerns the general suspiciousness that seemed to be present. I have been impressed, here and elsewhere, with the amount of suspiciousness and double-reading that occurs across intergroup lines when a background of conflict prevails. Individuals with personalities of distrust are far more likely to emerge as leaders, under these conditions, than are men who feel unthreatened by conflict and who, therefore, are not so prone to look under the chip.

This is not to say that union officials may not have good cause to be suspicious of some managers' motives. This is evidenced by Dan's remark that the focal point of much conflict and difficulties is the behavior of Earl Higgins, an assistant department head in Engineering. We didn't pursue this particular issue, but I take it that Dan has substantive grounds for worrying about the antihuman relations forces which Earl is mustering.

Another thing quite apparent is the cohesion among the people who frequent the union president's office. The coffee, the rolls, the joking, the playful hurling of "Dago," "Wop," and other epithets which less intimate colleagues would hear as insults, indicate the level of emotional ties between these people. It may well be that IEW officials are not the only or even the foremost leaders of Lakeside's workers, but as a group of people they are fairly close knit.

For example, while Dan and I were having a chat, another man walked in. He said, "Did you hear that Joe had a heart attack and died?"

Dan responded with surprise and genuine grief. "No, you don't say! When?" The other man gave details.

"How old was he?" Dan queried.

"Oh, about forty-five." The other man began to muse, "Boy, I am sure looking forward to becoming fifty years old. That period between forty and fifty is a killer, heart attacks all over the place. I want to get to be fifty. I only have two more years to go and then I will be safe.

Dan griped back, "Friend, you're safe now. You have to have a heart to have a heart attack."

Time and Motion Engineering

The union officers today told me a delightful version of how they see industrial engineering. They said, "Time and motion study is pretty scientific.

It's a good way to analyze a job to find its components and how much time it should take for a man to repair a pump or any other kind of job. The boss can then evaluate whether or not he is getting a fair day's work for a fair day's pay. We subscribe to this in principle. And it's true that some of the new engineers really know how to do time and motion study. They're pretty sharp cookies and conscientious about doing things by the book."

The union officers went on to say, "Our problem is that we don't know how to read those books the engineers learn from. We have to assume they understand what's in them. For our part, we rely on common sense, and so *we* don't understand why, when it's ten degrees above zero outside and the ordinary rules don't apply, the engineers don't know it. A fellow just can't produce in subfreezing temperatures according to the same formula that applies to work in an air-conditioned garage at 70 degrees. Furthermore, those formulas don't apply when the temperature is 99 degrees, and the humidity is 100%. Now, either the textbook fails to say that these formulas should not apply under abnormal conditions, or it says something that engineers never learn, because they seem to think these formulas apply under all conditions. It annoys us to have educated clowns giving us stories like that. Even Taft-Hartley didn't try to repeal the laws of nature. But you can't teach an engineer that his formulas need a human element in addition to whatever scientific component they may embrace."

So then it occurred to me to interview one or two of these smart engineers. I questioned a couple of them on using formulas in a mechanical manner. They said, "We know better than that. We know that a man working in grilling heat or near-zero temperature has to adjust his pace. The trouble is that our *bosses* don't seem to know that. They expect the same efficiency in the heat or cold and in rain, snow, or dry weather. Our bosses want production according to the formula. They read the data we submit. They see that we operate at 40% rather than at 70% efficiency. They say the trouble is due to poor supervision. The standard report sheet doesn't mention whether it was hot, cold, wet, or dry when the work was done.

"Another aspect is that there are some guys who really try to do you in for every iota they can get. Those jerks are just trying to get out of work, and we are man enough to see to it that they don't. So occasionally we put the heat on in a way that might be a little inappropriate."

I went back to the union and said, "Just for the heck of it, I decided to double check what you told me about time and motion study. A couple of engineers explained it this way." I gave them the two explanations.

The union man said, "Oh, yeah? We'll give you examples." They came up with about a half dozen examples, extending over a four year period. I asked whether there were more, but these six were the only ones they could recall.

A wage man's mind is not something that comes with an eraser. An event of the distant past remains just as poignant and meaningful and threatening as though it had happened yesterday. The memory of a person who has been treated unfairly continues to rankle. Stories told to others about the man who was treated unfairly can't be blotted out. The mind is not that kind of device. It remembers. Management has failed to realize the extent to which a single impulsive decision may become a classic which is never forgotten. In many situations, the union never forgets the mistreatment, or what it perceives to be mistreatment.

Is "The End" Ever Reached?

A fascinating phenomenon can be seen operating among Lakeside managers with respect to the future of contract bargaining. The argument goes this way.

"Our industry isn't in as good a shape as it used to be five or ten years ago." (A day or so ago, EPOCH indicated that it was in the best shape it had been in the past several years.) "We cannot afford to give any more. It's impossible. The union has to learn that this must stop. We just can't continue in this way forever and stay competitive."

Management is saying that the industry has come to the end of the road; that there is little room for improving the economic lot of workers. Interestingly, this point of view is a repetition of the views of a different plant management group in the same industry I listened to five years ago. At that time, management also proclaimed that the end had come; that there was no possibility of continuing a policy of give, give, give. The union's real options were said to be limited to getting better working conditions, not more pay or vacation.

Management frequently talks itself into the position that it has reached the end and there is no room for further give. Over the years, there has been a continuous loosening and upgrading in rates, improved safety conditions, and so on. All of these have cost. As long as industry goes on there will be improvement. There can be no other way. As long as the mind works, it is striving for a better life, and pressuring those who control the resources to share them in a more equalitarian manner. Union power is such that it can exert bargaining pressure, and the whole key to the human success of American industry is in this feature.

Unions exert pressure to improve their members' situation. This creates a wide area of conflict. However, management is not *only* production oriented, nor is the union *only* human improvement oriented. There are many examples of unions persuading their members to take pay cuts to have continuity in work and to gain other benefits as well. Many managements have modified their formerly single-minded production orientations in recognition of values that exist in human interaction, of which profit is only one very important aspect.

Politics, Production and People

If I were to sum up my first year at Lakeside, I would conclude that there are three major forces that interact to dictate the outcomes of many basic decisions. These three forces are politics, production, and people—like the corners of a triangle. The way a decision is made and implemented is a function of how much weight is placed on each of them relative to the other two.

Politics has reference to prestige, status, power, privilege, prerogatives and a host of other factors relevant to an individual who seeks either to gain something for himself or avoid losing. In organizations, political awareness identifies a perennial win-lose situation for the individual player. Many of the political considerations that bear on a decision are stimulated by headquarters if a plant manager is involved. For example, Quinn is continuously thinking how he will look in the eyes of headquarters if he takes some action. Will it increase his prestige and further his career? Similar issues are involved down the line in operational and staff departments. Each person is looking out for himself and examining the political impact of his next decision, and how it will influence his future.

Production forces, in comparison, are concerned with efficiency, profit and performance. The question becomes, "How can we increase our overall effectiveness?" Effectiveness is almost always a critical consideration in a manager's mind as he goes about making a decision. He may emphasize production without concerning himself with political repercussions, or he may emphasize production because demonstrated effectiveness may have a particularly strong political outcome for him. It can't be anticipated which way the two forces will combine or be exerted separately.

People forces come from the third corner of the conceptual triangle. The question here is, "What will be the impact of the decision upon people?" "People" in this sense may be subordinate managers, members of the work force, or union representatives.

For example, in last month's crane crisis, the major influences operating within the engineering department at the managerial level were a positive force toward production, and I believe, an antagonistic force toward union and wage people. Bringing in the crane would contribute to production, but would also frustrate people. Only as others observed the wider dimensions of the problem did it take on company-political overtones. Nonetheless, it is possible for the likely "people impact" on different individuals or groups to be assessed before taking a decision which will affect them all.

The red circle issue can be stated as, "How do you implement a general wage increase for people who are already making more than the rate that would be paid had they not at some previous time held higher-classified jobs?" This one is surely a dilemma produced by a clashing of political and people forces. From a political angle, the plant manager can gain by bringing his rates into line. From a people standpoint, he may lose over the longer term by alienating the work force. From the production point of view, he is attracted because by not adding the full 14 cents to red circle pay, he hopes to moderate the added production costs.

So Quinn is still confronted with the dilemma of whether or not to grant a 14-cent increase to red circles. If he withholds, he gets plusses from headquarters, but criticism from local wage people. If he capitulates, he will be seen as a "regular guy" by local wage people, but viewed as weak by headquarters. If he first withholds, and then yields, he is seen as a Scrooge who, when you put the screws on him, finally comes to his senses, and does what people ask. Scrooge is not reasonable, but he can be forced into taking stock of the problem he is creating and then, if you push him hard enough, he will shift. That kind of plant manager hardly fits EPOCH's preferred image of "sound business consistent with good human relations."

What will Quinn do when the chips are down? Will he yield, will he withhold, or will he first withhold and then yield? These, it seems to me, are his only possibilities. There is a remote possibility that he might go for a smaller trimming of the red circle rates this time, with another little bite next time, and so on. He could get his rates back into line that way, but headquarters would undoubtedly interpret this course of action as weak.

13

Give and Take

Today, October 27, EPOCH published its decision to grant a general wage increase of 5% for salaried personnel, and 14 cents an hour for wage people, which is about 4.2% of the average worker's pay. Thus a first provocation is that wage earners are being treated less favorably than salaried people.

After receiving the message from EPOCH headquarters, management requested meetings with the two unions. The salary union meeting took place this morning; the one with IEW in the afternoon. For the salaried group, the offer was in line with what people had more or less expected, except for one proviso which is said to have astounded and irritated the union. This was that anyone hired in the future would not have the 5% added to his entering salary.

Quinn came to the wage union meeting and announced that a 14-cent general wage increase was being offered by headquarters. Next, he gave reasons for his own decision to offer only 7 cents of this to red circle personnel. In response to a question, he mentioned that Lakeside's salaried personnel were getting 5%.

The union caucused and quickly recognized that a 14-cent increase was inferior to 5%. It indicated that it didn't like this discrepancy, but more than that, it was gravely concerned with the plight of red circle personnel. A meeting was requested for tomorrow. Overall, today's proceedings were relatively quiet.

The Union Attempts to Shift Management's Position

The bargaining committee met again today, October 28. The atmosphere was more heated than yesterday and the results were different. After discussing the difference between 5% and 14 cents, the union came to its major point of contention: Quinn's withholding of one-half of the general wage increase from the red circle personnel. Most members of the union delegation are on red circle rates.

The discussion became intense as the union tried to dislodge management from its apparently fixed position. The argument went, "After all, you promised us that you would do nothing to hurt us if we accepted consolidation. Look at what you are doing now. You are penalizing the very people who helped you out."

Management continued to resist, pointing out that the present contract's terms provided for this first step in phasing out the red circle rates.

Then Dan said, "This brings up the issue as to whether or not a contract is in effect. You have been saying that the old contract continues because we never gave notification that we wanted it cancelled. We maintain that the old contract is *not* in effect because its specified time period has long since lapsed. So, we're going to take the matter to court to determine whether or not a contract exists."

A third point the union made was that Quinn's action in withholding the 7 cents would encourage the international union which wants to move in at Lakeside. The independent unionists' view is that management's niggardly behavior can only substantiate ICEW's allegation that the independent is unable to protect its people. Incidentally, the ICEW presently has no contract in any plant where red circle rates exist.

Dan made his concluding points. "Since we are in an impasse, I am not going to put this particular issue before the workers for a vote. You management people could probably whiplash a majority of employees to vote for acceptance. But I, as union president, have the prerogative of *not* calling a meeting. So not only do I refuse to accept the general increase offer, I won't call a membership meeting either.

"The final thing I want to say is this. Since we are deadlocked on this matter, with your side still arguing in terms of a dead contract, and with no evidence that you are ready to bargain in good faith for a new one, I see no reason for continuing these sessions. Therefore, unless you change your minds and let the full wage increase apply across-the-board to everyone, there will be no more bargaining."

The meeting broke up. The situation is so delicate that it is difficult to predict which way things will go. Quinn has scheduled a meeting for tomorrow when department and assistant department heads and other top ranking people will discuss the crisis.

Firming Up Management's Attitudes

Management met this morning, October 29, to discuss whether or not to grant the entire 14 cents to the red circle people. After much debate, a vote was taken. It was close to a tie, but the majority voted not to restore the withheld 7 cents, whatever the consequences.

All of management's bargaining committee, except Wes and Mac, feel that today's position is right: that management must hold firm. At the meeting

Wes and Mac had argued for either a compromise offer or granting the full increase. After a "one more look" discussion on November 3, management will give the union its final position.

Quinn told me today that withholding the 7 cents from the red circle rate is an application of the principle of "running a sound business consistent with good human relations." He said that in the past he has had to make many firm decisions that were not well received at first; in each case, years later, the union has indicated that he was right. Of course, what he fails to report is that employee disillusionment with the IEW union which permitted these things to happen has been steadily on the increase. This red circle issue may be the one that takes it over the top. Even Quinn is uneasy about the eventual outcome. It could mean the end of collaborative efforts and the reopening of warfare, with the possibility that ICEW will replace IEW at Lakeside. He remarked that maybe, regardless of his red circle decision, internationalization is an inevitability which will come to pass in the next few months anyway. He sees this particular issue as symptomatic of a more basic economic illness that calls for a firm treatment regime. He wants to be seen as a man who, once having made up his mind, is resolute in holding to his position. Yet at the same time he is worried, realizing that this particular event could precipitate the end of some promising steps toward cooperation.

Another point is that this blossoming red circle controversy constitutes another external pressure that disturbs bargaining. It is not directly associated with difficulties of cooperation between the two groups. It is on a par with the crane crisis, the membership-maintenance retraction, and similar events outside of the bargaining situation which have had negative impacts. I'm beginning to see that many of the difficulties in bargaining are not due to interaction nearly as much as by harmful external forces.

One final point: although everyone's take-home pay is to be increased, no one feels the increase is associated with his individual work contribution. An industry-wide general wage increase, made in response to an international union's pressure, is producing local unrest and causing animosities which might not have developed had there been no wage increase.

Despite Dan's outburst, the IEW union still has not formally rejected last week's offer, but instead has asked management to reconsider the red circle decision and the fact that salary personnel were offered 5% while wage personnel were offered the equivalent of 4.2%. Management's answer was to be given this morning, November 3.

Meeting early, Lakeside's top management and the bargaining committee had a "feedback session." This was management's way of finding out how the wage people were feeling and it showed what flimsy evidence management has to work on.

Hal Harvey said he had only been able to get dribs and drabs of information. One of his sources was a foreman who car-pools to and from work with three pipefitters. They felt Quinn's treatment of red circle people was right—it was about time they were taken off the gravy train. Hal had heard very little from the boilermakers. The instrument people, who were offered 10 cents, "seem happy since they said it was better than nothing." Someone in the Process Division who wears a 30-year button had said that as far as he could see, process people were happy and complacent. Only five process people are on red circle rates. But a general reaction from the Engineering Department people, according to Hal's informants, was that the 14 cents in comparison with the salaried employees' 5% was another example of wage men getting something of a "hosing." The general mood seemed to be, "Grab what you can and fight for more."

Hal mentioned also that Engineering Department managers were arguing against giving the full wage increase to red circle people. There seems to be a unanimity among Engineering's division heads on this point. The reasons are twofold. One is that the provision that red circles would not receive the full general wage increase was written into the contract three years ago. So there have been three years of conditioning on this point. To shift now would be to respond to local political pressures created by Dan Ives. The engineers see Dan falling apart quite soon, rather than being able to maintain a strong position on this one.

Now here is my prediction. The general result, influenced by one invidious difference created between the wage and salary unions—making the wage earners look like second class citizens—and another invidious difference between the treatment of red circle people and people receiving standard pay, will be to bring the issue of *whether a contract exists* to a legal test. If the court finds that no contract currently exists, there will be a new NLRB election, in which case the international union will win. If the contract is found still in force, there will be no further contract negotiations. It will take quite a while to evaluate whether these predictions are valid. Many other things are in the fire that can influence the final outcome.

My rationale for this prediction is founded on observations that there is somewhat of a general industrial-relations erosion going on. The first indication came with the benefit plan mentioned sometime ago. Here, IEW was confronted with a *fait accompli* so that there was no alternative other than accepting it. Now a general wage increase has been offered on condition that it must be accepted by November 16 to be paid retroactive to October 27th. Both of these management actions erode the strength of the union. Management gives the union no basis for bargaining in terms of local requirements, only something to take or leave. Of course, the union can't reject the general wage increase, because it would alienate the people. On the other hand, the offer gives the union no basis for searching for a more optimal adjustment. My impression is that EPOCH management is moving in the direction of a design where management decides what it can and will do and makes an offer. If the offer is accepted, well and good. If it isn't, the offer is retracted, with no discussion as to other patterns that might be better or more acceptable.

At the end of this management feedback session, there was an extensive discussion concerning which management member should announce the final position to the union. As usual the choice was between Quinn, Van, and Wes. In this case, Van had been on vacation during the last week and was not familiar with the continuity of the discussion. Wes seemed like a logical choice, but he was passed over in favor of Quinn. The union frequently asks for answers from the "Old Man" anyway, and it might as well get this decision from him firsthand. Quinn was reluctant to be spokesman because he felt it weakened the bargaining committee which should be working continuously with its union counterparts rather than calling on him to deal with "important matters." Cal's private opinion was that Quinn was reluctant because he finds it extremely unpleasant to do anything that is negative or that brings on an unpleasant reaction.

In any event, in an impulsive moment, just at 10:15 when the issue was in deadlock, Quinn rose and said, "OK, let's go. I'll do it."

The session started with trivia regarding the last football game. Van pulled the discussion around to the point where Quinn could present management's point of view, which was not to modify the previous offer. He presented it briefly, requiring perhaps seven or eight minutes. Dick Kelly, the union secretary, said that he was sorry that management had taken this position because in the new draft contract there was a proposal for a 10% raise, and had management been able to come through on the red circle, the union might have settled for a little less than it had requested. But as of now, the full 10% remained on the table.

Several management members quickly noted that the union neither accepted nor rejected Quinn's offer. Dan Ives said nothing. Thus, an interesting situation is created. A few days ago Dan declared he would not even take this offer to the membership, and threatened to test by legal action whether or not the old contract is in effect. At present, management is unable to interpret his silence. However, he did not call off the bargaining as he had threatened last week. Negotiations continued through the morning and terminated at the regular time.

Last Friday, Dan told Mac that the governing committee of the union was behind him all the way, and he would fight this one through to the finish. The present situation constitutes an interesting dilemma for management. A number of them think that Dan's bluff has been called, and he had been found to be as thin as a piece of papier-mâché. They say that when he is told where the line is, he is not ready to stick by his guns and fight. Other managers see him as playing a clever game. They believe he is counting up the negatives and eventually will point out to the wage membership all the items on which he has been unfairly treated by management. The wage issue then is simply another notch in his belt to be placed beside the other grievances he's lined up.

Mac's own theory is that Dan may be engaged in a "scorched earth" program. The analogy is to the Russians who, during World War II when forced to retreat, destroyed everything in sight, not to help themselves, but to hurt the enemy. If Dan is planning a "scorched earth" policy, then he can make management look unattractive and recommend to the wage membership that they throw in with ICEW. This could very well be the outcome.

It seems certain that Dan is still trying to use power strategy to achieve his ends. It doesn't appear that he has really accepted or comprehended the possibilities released by applying a problem-solving orientation. Yet one of the important reasons for his adopting a win-lose power orientation is that he has been well and truly provoked by the thrift plan and the general wage increase, where management has delivered a power package.

Area Patterns of Wage Increases

The pot is boiling on the general wage increase problem, and up to now, November 5, results are quite consistent with my predictions. However, I have a new item of information. This concerns two patterns of wage increases which have developed over the United States during October. One can be called the West Coast pattern, and the other, the Midwest pattern. The West Coast pattern is 5% for the salary union and 14 cents to the wage union. The Midwest pattern offers 5% increases to salary and wage people.

The EPOCH Company production centers were the only units in the Midwest to follow the West Coast pattern. This means that EPOCH is locally out of line with all other companies.[1] The important thing here is that for years Lakeside management has been trying to pound into the heads of the union the importance of making "relevant area comparisons." Now EPOCH offers a general wage increase which disregards area comparisons. This further antagonizes the union for what appears to be management's inconsistent behavior.

The aftermath of the general wage offer is beginning to emerge. Whereas the union's initial reaction was one of disdain, now it has shifted its attention to having been treated with less consideration than similar plants in the area. In addition, within Lakeside the wage personnel have been treated with less consideration than the salary people.

In Dan's mind, the situation is bordering on hopelessness. He feels that it is silly to play the game of local bargaining since Lakeside management is controlled by its headquarters to the point where plant-level bargaining is like tussling with puppets.

Among Lakeside managers, though, the general impression is that Dan's actions will alienate him from the union's membership. This obviously disturbs management. The fear is that Dan will refuse to have a membership meeting in which the offer can be accepted in time to qualify for retroactivity to October 27. This would mean that while contract bargaining over the union's 10% increase demand could continue, the retroactive pay available under the Quinn-modified EPOCH offer would be lost.

This morning, November 6, Mac Anthony of the Personnel Department met with Dan and Max over a technical matter in the benefits program that has been a source of friction between the company and the union.

During the meeting, Max went to the bathroom. While he was gone, Dan expressed disgust at the way the benefits program and the general wage increase and the year-end contribution had been handled. Then he casually mentioned that he was going "OUB" (outside on union business) to Washington tomorrow for a conference with Wilson, head of the international.

As he was doing so, Max returned. He picked up Dan's remark about going to Washington to see the ICEW president. They pursued it casually for a short while before getting back to discussing the benefits program with Mac Anthony. He and the two union officials eventually came to agreement on the disputed topic.

So evidently Max had not known, up to this morning, that Dan had decided to go to Washington. This probably means that Dan was acting on his own initiative rather than under a mandate from IEW's executive committee. Of course, it could be that Max was not in the meeting when Dan was told to confer with Wilson. Further details may emerge during tomorrow's bargaining session. The most credible indication at present, though, is that Dan is flying solo. Even more mystifying is what Dan might be trying to accomplish.

Mac duly reported to Wes that Dan was seeing Wilson tomorrow. Wes passed this data on to Quinn.

Two further points need to be made with respect to the general wage increase. An important reaction among Lakeside salary and wage workers is, "Why did they give us an increase at this time? Everyone knows that before the ink is dry the cost of consumer goods in the local area will jump to cancel our increased buying power. Therefore, all we do is to pay more taxes; we don't really gain more purchasing power from this offer." This may not be a widespread reaction, but it is sufficiently frequent to be worthy of note.

Another reaction, one which came from Max today and which Wes and Mac particularly want to pursue, is that real creative thinking applied to the problem of wage and salary administration probably could result in an entirely different way of increasing remuneration. It is not necessary simply to put it on top of a regular check. For example, the same amount of money made available through union collaboration for increased health insurance, retirement benefits, or for a number of other purposes might represent, in the wage man's eyes, a much more equitable and useful contribution to each man's security and welfare.

A meeting is scheduled tomorrow for Van, Quinn, Cal, Wes, Mac, Hal and me to go over the union's reaction to the general wage increase offer. For perhaps the first time, managers are wondering what they could do to help Dan think through what he might be doing to himself and to Lakeside's wage earners if he takes one course instead of another. Management quite clearly feels that Dan could make a fool of himself and themselves as well.

References

1. Beal, E.F. and Wickersham, E.D. *The Practice of Collective Bargaining* (3rd Ed.). Homewood, Ill.: Richard D. Irwin, Inc., 1967, pp. 347-357.

14

Win-Lose Relationships Within Top Teams

A few people at the vice president and general manager levels, who have been with a company for an extended period of time, presently are near the top of its pyramid. Each has thought of the possibility that he someday may take the final upward step to the pinnacle position in the organization. Since there may be several peers competing for the throne, and since there can be only one king at a time, the situation is ripe for interpersonal competition, conflict, and win-lose strife. So a unique human relations environment is found at the top of an organization.

Top-team strife can take a number of forms, depending upon how the chief relates with his senior deputies. If his relationship is on a one-to-one basis rather than as a group, he may incite intense interpersonal competition. This is particularly true when he shows, or appears to show, favoritism to one member. Then all the cut-throat strategies imaginable can appear. Top team members have already achieved their high positions because of their long discipline and skill in winning battles under conditions of competition to move "up." The final step to the very top is the hardest and yet the most coveted. The most classic indication of win-lose competition for succession to the throne is found in intense distrust of one another. Each candidate looks at the other and speculates about his motives.

Another symptom is when all or some challenge the adequacy of others. Remarks, insinuations, or overt actions have the effect of demonstrating the inadequacy of someone else's operations. Difficulties of cooperation and collaboration are pointed out, and it is suggested that one's peer and rival has become unable to perform effectively. These insinuations can have a penetrating effect. A frequently heard remark is that the situation would be hopeless were a certain peer to be anointed as the top man.

For example, in the Frontier Company, which makes a technical product, the Director of Operations, who ranks as a vice president, is technically qualified. The other vice president is highly competent as head of Sales, but has little background in the technical operations. Both are well qualified for their present jobs. Each is broad-gauged enough to mastermind the entire company as its president.

Competition between these two men is intense and destructive. Each can and does point to numerous instances of the inadequacy of his counterpart. Both recount examples of sheer stupidity on the part of the other. Each professes to be at a loss to understand how the other operates his "show."

Why do these individuals see only the "negatives" in each other? Neutral observers inside and outside the company can describe strong features in the performances of both men.

In another setting, Atlantic Associates, the vice president of operations finds nothing good in the performance or personality of another vice president who is financial controller. The controller, not to be outdone, points to numerous incidents in which operations management has goofed.

An interesting sidelight is that both of these men have been with the company for 25 years. They grew up together with it and during the first 15 years, were the staunchest of friends. After 15 years of happy and warm relations, however, they became aware that they were the ultimate competitors for the top position.

At Lakeside there is a comparable situation. Calvert Carroll, Quinn's second-in-command, is a highly energetic, aggressive, and self-oriented man who has worked tremendously hard during the 11 years he has been here. He gets into the plant at 7:00 a.m. and leaves between 8:00 and 10:00 p.m. seven days a week. He has climbed to within one step from the top by sheer effort. He is not happy-go-lucky, nor is he easy to know. Six months ago, Cal was struck by a heart attack and was out of commission for so long that it appeared he might never be able to return to Lakeside.

With Cal in the hospital, it was necessary for him to be replaced on a temporary basis. The result was that Van Gray, then acting head of maintenance division in the Engineering department, was elevated to be acting operations superintendent. Van took hold and plowed. He did so with personal modesty and interpersonal skill. He caused no conflicts but, rather, made considerable contributions to resolving conflicts left in the wake of others. He has the broad picture, and is oriented to constructive ends. He has tackled many problems that formerly constituted plant-wide issues, and has resolved them with the people who were actually involved rather than allowing them to continue reverberating.

Six months ago Cal and Van were close and warm work partners. Then Cal had his heart attack. Now Cal's state of health permits him to return, at least on a part-time basis, to resume some of his previous responsibilities. Van still is in overall charge of managing operations. Nonetheless, Cal is back on the job.

If logical factors were dominant, one would predict that Cal would have reason to feel considerable appreciation and gratitude for the excellent job done by Van during his absence. Also, it might be predicted that with the assurance of Van's capabilities, Cal would be content to move slowly back into the job and so avoid placing a heavy burden on himself, which he is as yet unable to bear. At the same time, a gradual piece-by-piece resumption would help avoid duplications of effort between Cal and Van.

Against the background of what might be expected, what has happened? Cal can find nothing for which Van should be congratulated. Cal has reviewed, one by one, Van's decisions during the period when he was entirely responsible. In doing so, Cal has not found one action by Van which was as well done as he, Cal, would have handled it. This situation is so ludicrous that people in lower echelons joke about it. The only person blind to what is going on is Quinn. Cal's behavior with Quinn is different from his behavior with Van. While Cal routinely criticizes most of Van's decisions to his face, he is much more selective in pinpointing items of administrative imperfection when he talks with Quinn. He is highly accurate in only bringing to Quinn's attention those features in Van's decisions which could more objectively be regarded as less than adequate. During the period of six months Van made literally hundreds of decisions and, therefore, by screening each one it became possible for Cal to find some that were clearly imperfect. By only bringing these to Quinn's attention, it becomes possible for Cal to cast an air of suspicion over Van's general administrative competence.

Why is Cal so anxious to accent in Quinn's mind Van's administrative bloopers? In terms of what has just been described the answer is obvious. Cal is insecure. He feels threatened. If Van looks adequate to Quinn, then Cal may be shelved, or given assignments appropriate only to his limited physical stamina. From Cal's point of view, this would represent failure in the supreme battle of career competition.

Lincoln Lodge

Rescheduled Lincoln Lodge sessions for the top 60 members of the Lakeside organization begin tomorrow. Quinn and his five principal managers will attend sessions on both days.

The program has been designed so that participants, particularly Quinn, will take responsibility for defining the content issues. My responsibility will be restricted to procedural contributions. This arrangement differs from the Green Acres series. There, I did quite an extensive job of helping diagnose what appeared to be the problems of the organization. Apparently this was quite helpful. However, according to the theory of consultation being applied here, there is a distinct advantage in the line organization's taking greater and greater responsibility for doing its own diagnosis and problem definition.

Therefore, as we formulated the program, I strongly recommended that management define the issues while I help with the mechanics.

Quinn will define the broad issue as one of extending the progress made since Green Acres. He will not attempt to diagnose Lakeside's current problems and opportunities. Rather, the point of emphasis is for management to plan for the next year. Quinn insists that the entire organization go through similar sessions this time, not only the top 120 as was the case on the last go-around. He hopes that the union will participate during the coming year.

I suggested that one person from each session be named programming representative of that group to insure that various members are made accountable for executing the plans that evolve. I think it was accepted, but the onus will probably be upon me to demonstrate how such arrangements can be set up.

Each session begins at 8:30 a.m. Quinn will kick off the proceedings by speaking for 10-15 minutes and will then ask other members of the top five to make some remarks. Groups will then work in separate rooms until 11:00 when they will reconvene in a general session to compare progress and findings. After lunch, participants will again work in groups until 4:00 when they will meet in general session for a summary, comparison, and review of positions and recommendations. The next day, Quinn's opening statement should summarize in broad outline what was accomplished the day before. This program seems sound and could set the direction for next year.

In certain quarters, particularly in Engineering, there is some resistance to what is called "going off in the woods to discuss human relations." The organization is accustomed to spending one day every six months talking about human relations and all of the remaining work days dealing with matters of operation. To some, a single day devoted to human relations is excessive, but from my standpoint the real issue is that human relations are by no means to be regarded as separate from everyday work.

Ripples of Negativism

The problem of administration created by the general wage increase offer becomes greater and more widespread hour by hour. Because of recent developments, it was decided that management should meet this morning, November 7, to discuss the general wage increase situation. The issues are the invidious comparison between the wage people's 14 cents an hour and the salary people's 5%; and, the 7 cents Quinn has withheld from red circle people.

As we mentioned yesterday, Dan, the union president, reacted to Quinn's offer with a disgust that is reflected in his decision to visit Wilson in Washington.

At another EPOCH plant, Hilltop, the union president, Chuck Hendricks, has also decried the offer and is stirring up trouble. There is a ruckus at Mountainview where, besides the invidious comparison feature, no general wage increase whatever is being offered to red circle personnel. The problem is also coming to a head at Seashore, where a special meeting is scheduled today between the union governing board and Will Grigg, Seashore's general manager. The wage union at Coastline, which is affiliated with Wilson's international, has accepted the offer. But Coastline's *independent* salary union is against acceptance. At Plainfield there are only a few red circle people and local management did not withhold part of the general wage increase from them. The union accepted.

In addition, the union officers from EPOCH's raw materials division are "marching on Atlanta" today to demand a 5% across-the-board increase with a floor minimum of 14 cents. If the demand is met, it will mean that wage people will receive something above 5%.

Under the terms of EPOCH's offer, all units are required to accept by November 16, or the offer will not be retroactive to October 27. In Lakeside, however, the contract (whose present existence is in dispute) states that the union has one month in which to decide whether or not to accept any general wage increase. Since (a) the offer was not made until October 27, (b) management has argued that the old contract is still in effect, and (c) no court has yet determined that the contract in question has expired, IEW has until November 27 to answer. Thus, Dan and his colleagues cannot be held to the coals on this one. They can hold out for 10 days past the deadline, and still be within their contractual rights.

At this morning's meeting, Quinn predicted that before this complex, poorly handled matter is satisfactorily resolved, EPOCH's board will yield on the 14 cents, and come to a standard 5% across the board. It will be two or three weeks before this prediction is fully tested. Quinn also said that the situation is in such a confused state now, that Lakeside's management bargaining committee should take no action to influence it one way or another. Therefore, this morning's meeting was more of an information conference than a planning session.

On October 27 the salary union was offered 5% with the reservation that this increase would not be included in the salaries offered people recruited in the future. Management's reason is that starting salaries are already more than competitive, so why add to them? The salary union is having a membership meeting on the 10th to decide whether or not to accept the offer. In the interim, salary union officials are bitterly protesting Quinn's withholding the 5% from starting rates.

I anticipate that management will yield on this one, at least to some extent. Quinn asked Wes this morning if he thought yielding on this would have an unsettling effect on the wage union. Wes said he would like to take time to think about the question. The mere fact that Quinn considered this possibility indicates a weakening of formerly resolute convictions.

Plenty of rumors are floating around Lakeside. Some have it that IEW is planning a membership meeting for the 12th. No one is sure if this is true. The other day, Dan vowed not to call such a meeting.

At Seashore the union president indicated he would recommend that the membership reject the offer. It will indeed be an interesting situation if Seashore, the largest EPOCH plant and with the best wage union relations at the present time, repudiates the offer. If it does, then what will EPOCH do? Can it retract the offer and not reissue it? This seems unlikely. So it is highly probable that headquarters and some plant managers will be forced to their knees before all this is over.

Although there is no federation of independent unions within EPOCH, most of them are taking a remarkably similar approach. In effect, they are doing company-wide bargaining even though they have not gotten together formally to develop a party line. I wish I knew how much they are chatting with one another long distance regarding the position they should take on this matter.

As of today, my predictions regarding the final terms of the general wage increase are:

1. The final basis of agreement will be 5% across the board.
2. Red circle wage personnel will be given the full increase.
3. The provision for withholding the 5% from the entering grade of salary personnel will be withdrawn.
4. The basis for both salary and wage personnel will be 5% with a 14 cent per hour minimum.
5. Even if a final agreement between management and the unions is not completed by November 16, October 27 will remain the effective retroactive date.

There are two shortcomings to making a restrictive offer and then yielding when resistance arises. The first of these is management's inability to diagnose potential points of resistance which will generate opposition strong enough to cause management to modify its behavior. The second is that management looks at the initial problem almost exclusively from its own point of view. For example, when Quinn and his executives formulated their position on the red circle matter, the primary consideration was that they would be able to bring their rates into line. Due to pressure from headquarters to get rates into a competitive relationship with other units in the area, this was a compelling consideration. The possibility that various plant unions might get together to force management to modify its position was given only minor attention. In making its predictions as to what would be acceptable, management overweighted its own interests and failed to give sufficient weight to the opinions and attitudes of the recipients. It is this general failure to make an accurate assessment that has produced so much conflict in past and present situations. The syndrome is that management puts together an unsalable proposition and simultaneously deludes itself that others will gratefully accept it.

15

Plans and Predictions Which Shape Outcomes

The latter part of this morning, November 7, was devoted to a management meeting to review the Scanlon Plan.[1] Last summer George Shultz and Bob McKersie of the University of Chicago made a feasibility study as to whether or not the Scanlon approach could be applied to a plant such as Lakeside. This afternoon a general review by Shultz and McKersie will be given at EPOCH headquarters. Quinn and others scheduled to attend the afternoon meeting used this morning's session for briefing.

Predictions are spread throughout the Scanlon literature. One of them is that any management, in its initial review of the Scanlon plan, will find many reasons why the program seems unfeasible. Managers usually argue that "While it may work in a small plant, it won't work in a large one"; or "It may be optimal for certain kinds of production, but not for 'our' kind." The person who might feel most threatened by the Scanlon approach is the first-level "bull of the woods" supervisor. Once he begins to glimpse the implications for openness to wage people's suggestions, and for a corresponding reduction in dogmatic foremanship, this kind of supervisor tends to feel that ruinous revolution is being preached.

In the review this morning, all of these and other unfavorable reactions occurred. It was argued that the program was an "unrealistic" one for Lakeside. It was reported that supervisory personnel in particular thought the program would do more harm than good. Furthermore, since so many operations cost reduction plans were already underway, adapting to the Scanlon plan would impose additional costs—more than would be saved by implementing established plans. Many other arguments were given, none of which said "Generally it looks feasible; let's explore it in detail." Rather, the prevailing theme was, "Let's come back again a year from now and review it, and continue to do so annually until we make up our minds."

Dan's Mystery Trip, and his Personal Situation

Something quite interesting occurred during the bargaining session today. Soon after it began, Dick Kelly, chairman of the union delegation, asked for Dan's whereabouts. Max, apparently realizing that Mac Anthony, on management's side of the table, already knew where Dan was, kept an awkward silence. Mac also said nothing. When a phone call for Max came in later, Dick said, "That's probably Dan telling us why he hasn't been able to come today."

These two points clearly confirm a previous speculation that Max was surprised when he overheard Dan telling Mac Anthony that he was going to visit Wilson in Washington. This definite indication that Dick knows nothing of the president's trip is further evidence that Dan is acting without mandate. So if Dan is disgusted and disturbed enough to take solo action, this is a bad omen for the future of bargaining.

There are two other significant points concerning Dan. During the week between October 25 and November 1, Dan came to the bargaining sessions unshaven. The reason for this was that he had some kind of rash on his face which made it painful to shave. Management people regard Dan's rash as indicative of a nervous condition.

Dan is a large man. He is of Italian descent and is "warm" in both appearance and manner. The reaction that I have to him is that you can't help like him the moment you see him. For others, though, it seems to have been a case of hate at first sight.

In late September Dan's wife bore his fifth child. The baby arrived without incident, and Dan was at the bargaining table that day and also the next. Negotiations were going well at that particular point. About two weeks after the birth, however, there were indications that something might be wrong, and specialists were brought in. Dan's reactions were very mature, I thought. As he put it, "There is nothing *we* can do. The specialists have the problem in their hands and even though there may be nothing *they* can do, they are trying." Now all indications point toward the baby's being afflicted with a serious bone disease. Consequently, Dan is searching for a hospital whose expenses he can afford and where the baby can be given the kind of attention it requires. He thinks it best for the baby to be separated from the other children because the situation can only be unfortunate and traumatic for them as well as the parents.

I do not want to draw unwarranted conclusions at the psychodynamic level. I do, however, think it worthwhile to assume that there may be some internal connection between the unfortunate birth experience, the rash on the face, the feelings of weakness and hopelessness, and Dan's turning outside the organization to a strong man to find the help which no one else seems able to supply.

Hal Bows Out

At the end of bargaining today, Hal Harvey made an announcement. He is the head of the Engineering Department and historically has been known as a tough operator. An Annapolis graduate who likes to run a taut ship, he demands and achieves high loyalty from his immediate subordinates. As I have mentioned previously, he has always been intensely responsive to intergroup conflict, yet can almost simultaneously be swayed by peacemaking sentiments.

Over the last several months, Hal has undergone quite a transformation of his onetime approach. He is treating people today much more according to their perceptions of what is fair than by his old quarterdeck notions of what is shipshape.

As the meeting came to an end. He quietly announced that this was his last day of participation as a member of the management side of the committee. Everyone knew there were medical reasons for his decision.

This disclosure came as a tremendous shock to the union. As a then-and-now contrast, it was fascinating to see the deep warmth for Hal that was shown by the IEW men. Six months ago, they hated him bitterly. More recently, they have come to see him in a different way. Dick and the others expressed great concern, deep compassion and sympathy, and hoped that he would return soon.

I think Hal will be missed even more by the union than by management. This is one of those pathetic situations where in quick succession, one member on the union side, Dan, has had a traumatic experience in terms of his child, and now someone on the management side has his life hanging in the balance. These unpredictable happenings undoubtedly will have impacts on the progress and effectiveness of bargaining.

Programming after Lincoln Lodge

Toward the end of work today, Wes, Mac and I spent a few minutes pondering some critical problems. Lincoln Lodge sessions for the top 60 or so people at Lakeside have now been completed. In my judgment these were good training experiences, highly valuable in bringing key organizational issues into focus. They also disproved others' predictions that the one-day design would fail. Each of the two days went off smoothly. Work ended about 5:45 p.m., and then cocktails were followed by dinner. People left between eight and ten in the evening, having put in a full day's work and then enjoying fellowship.

The main problem that we are confronted with is, Should the rest of Lakeside's membership be provided the same design? After the Green Acres programs there were reservations about having such sessions at lower levels.

Certain line persons felt that this type of format would weaken their control over subordinates, whether singly or in general.

Before the Lincoln Lodge series, Quinn insisted that we should not repeat the mistake of only going halfway through the organization. The question now in my mind is whether or not Lakeside is ready to make the necessary effort to schedule numerous people for one-day off-the-job sessions. Wes believes that the whole organization has to learn to think together in order to gain the maximum effort in the human relations field. Mac agrees. The difficulty, though, is that these two are "staff" persons. Neither has any substantial responsibility for production or problems of operations. Quinn, who does, is in favor of the program. But he is uninvolved with its "nuts and bolts." If others see me pushing it, then it becomes "my" program in which they might participate, but without a sense of ownership.

In the end, my proposal was that it should be discussed in Quinn's managers' meeting Monday afternoon. If the "downward programming" of further Lincoln Lodge sessions is favored there, then it can be thoroughly debated with all of the department heads. Then if the plan is implemented, it will have full and favorable support from the top of the organization. Anything less is too risky to portend success.

Surveying the Climate of Lakeside

The climate in Lakeside at the end of work today, November 7, was as different from the climate some weeks ago as any two could be. If anything, I think we see today the lowest morale and the highest discouragement at the top of the organization that I have observed during my year here.

Let us briefly explore a few of the factors that are responsible for it. One is the matter of the general wage increase. This situation is in a state of flux. All of the EPOCH plant unions are resisting the 5% for salary bargainable people and 14 cents for the wage union. One group from another production center is resisting so strongly that the phrase coined this morning was "they are marching on headquarters." That phrase captures the spirit of the reaction, and incidentally it is interesting to note that during the Lakeside management meeting, some members applauded and whooped it up at the announcement that the other plant's union officers were confronting headquarters. In retrospect, this very group may realize that if the march is successful, it will create all kinds of embarrassing circumstances for Lakeside management.

Another source of concern to top management is that Dan Ives is in Washington today, closeted with the redoubtable and notorious boss of the international union that "wants in" at Lakeside. What does this mean? The answer is that nobody knows, but no one seems to feel that it means good.

Another thing that I think is demoralizing is that so many things came up at Lincoln Lodge which seem difficult to accomplish. This contributes to a sense of powerlessness to control one's own fate. Probably it is this very phenomenon that accounts for much of the prevalent demoralization, disgust and disappointment. Surely this hypothesis is sustainable: such a sense of weakness does not promote an interpersonal climate of conviviality and esprit de corps. When people are unable to see the conditions under which they can pull together successfully, they lose any contemporary spirit of cohesion.

A further element which helped to generate the present sense of weakness stems from what occurred during bargaining today. Management took the position that it wanted to be precise and restrictive in defining matters subject to arbitration. The wage union approached the problem from an entirely opposite direction, saying that it wanted to be loose and wide open in defining what is arbitrable. Why management wants a narrow and tight definition is obvious. It would then have a broad perogative to manage, retaining the right, in most cases, of making the final decision in a grievance rather than transferring the power of judgment to a so-called neutral person.

The union doesn't want management to combine the role of defendant or prosecutor with that of judge. In a sense, there is no more justice in management's being the final arbiter than there would be if the union were granted this right. In my view, the logic here is indisputably against management's position. No agreement has yet been reached, even though bargaining on this issue lasted all day.

Management committee members feel that the union was deaf to what they were trying to say. The union apparently feels that management was dictatorial in its demands. Failure to make any progress on this point—which is a most important one to management—is a further jab at morale.

Bargaining is scheduled for four days next week. Dan will be back in harness and Max also will be back from the OUB he has requested on Monday, so that bargaining probably can resume with the entire committee present.

I predict further clarification of the general wage increase issue next Tuesday. Although the scheduled topic is to be the issue of arbitration, the general wage increase will be given priority. The developing frustrations of union and management will produce aggression and antagonism during the meeting. There has to be some movement, either on the general wage increase or on arbitration, before real constructive steps become possible.

My general prediction is that management will gain no benefits whatsoever from this general wage increase. As I understand it, the Lakeside wage increase will cost about $1.5 million a year. It was offered in response to the international's demands, and to compensate for recent rises in the cost of living; it is not something that employees could truly feel they had "earned" by dint of hard work and personal accomplishment. Instead, issues of "unfair treatment" have come to the forefront of a deepening dispute. If the wage union loses, in that IEW officers are unable to correct what they consider to be injustices in the "salary/wage distinction" and "red circle" areas, they will see management as rigid and arbitrary as ever. If they win, they will see themselves as strong, and view management as having reluctantly yielded under pressure.

Either way, Lakeside management will be worse off than it would have been had there been no general wage increase at all. It is incredible that management could make an offer worth $1.5 million and receive nothing in return. The Lakeside bookkeeper ought to open an account headed "Clumsy behavior and lack of foresight," and charge it with this annual sum.

The Role of Prediction in Management

I am ever more impressed with how extremely important it is for the individual manager to be able to predict the consequences of his own and others' actions. Without predictive skill, a manager is lost. Even if possessing it, he is not automatically "made"; predictive skill must be integrated with the other managerial skills. A person with a lot of initiative together with inaccurate prediction skills is horrible to watch. He is always stubbing his toes because he takes inappropriate actions which he has to follow through with or back off from, and neither course is good.

There are several areas of prediction skill that are separable. One of these relates to technological considerations, such as long-term planning. This is one prediction area which can be supported by technical studies, so that forecasts are rational extrapolations from known conditions. Something more than an intuitive personal theory of operations is needed if one man is to make predictions of this character. It does take a great deal of technological information and disciplined intellectual accomplishment. Long-term planning for plant operations which offer a number of alternatives for materials conversion and by-product utilization—and where the market is growing and changing—represents one of the greatest challenges to the policy levels of management.

It is fascinating to study the manner in which long-range technological planning discussions are conducted. One of the standard features, for example, is the concept of the "case." This means defining a possible situation as a case and then looking at what kinds of plant, personnel, procedure and policy changes would be necessary to meet that case if it appeared to be a sound one from a market point of view. By exploring whole ranges of cases, or by projecting many alternative possibilities and intensively examining each one, certain cases can be identified as more desirable or likely to occur than others. Then the case is examined from a long-term point of view and evaluated in terms of short-term effects. The latter can also be analyzed as sub-case situations. In general, then, the job of technological planning is one projecting a future situation and then testing near-term possibilities for their immediate impact on profitability; but equally, or more importantly, evaluating what the near-term change would contribute or take away from the long-term case.

It is thought-provoking, also, to notice the number of assumptions that have to be made to build up a case. Assumptions made in connection with the case sometimes resemble the facts as they later develop and sometimes do not. It is a matter, however, of taking what appears to be the most valid present assumption as to conditions that will exist in the future and building cases premised upon them.

This procedure many times tends to resemble the "blind leading the blind," because the deeper question is, From where do these assumptions come? Some assumptions appear to come from predictions by experts. Others are made on the basis of information about competitive plants in Lakeside's marketing area. The third source comes from projecting linear trends from the past and present. Examples include population growth, the trend of market penetration corrected for population growth, and so on. Extrapolations of this sort constitute assumptions rather than predictions because they are incapable of forecasting, to any great degree of accuracy, upturns and downswings in economic activity.[2]

Lakeside's long-term planners are said to be among the best in the business. For comparative purposes, they try to get access to planning studies from competitive organizations or other EPOCH plants. Then they analyze them down to their projective bases. Many times, through an exercise of this nature, it becomes possible for the long-term planners to recognize that their current assumptions are different from those being made by other professionals. When these assumptions differ radically with respect to the same basic problems, it always constitutes a challenge to reinvestigate.

Another aspect of long-term planning also merits consideration. It is the use of computers for programming a set of hypothetical conditions and coming to quantitative projections for periods of five, ten, fifteen years, and even longer. Computer technology in this setting sometimes gives an unjustified appearance of validity to long-term planning studies because of its quantitative nature. Of course, before computerizing a long-term planning study one must have quantitative values. The same kind of assumptions have to be built into the computer as are built into logical analysis. The search for numbers to express concepts and trends forces even more rigorous analyses. Nonetheless, the computer technique is still subject to whatever weaknesses the assumptions contain.

People who have gravitated into long-term planning slots tend to be highly verbal, coldly analytical people who can bind tensions.[3] They consider an endless range of hypothetical possibilities, most of which will never come into existence. For them it is a career without action. Other engineers who like the hot experience of production and operation give the impression of being more impulsive.

Another significant area of prediction skill emerges from analyzing the existing and potential environments in which the company can operate. Market research is the discipline which is basically concerned with analyzing the sales environment, the likelihood that a product will be able to penetrate it, the depth of penetration, and other factors. Predicting future sales is even more complex than technological prediction. Sales environments expand and contract, and have their multi-causal peaks and valleys, booms and disasters.

Technological and marketing prediction areas are connected, but the "interprofessional" connection for the most is mechanical. Market researchers' estimates of the probable sales environment two, three or five years hence, are received and assumed as "givens" by technical product planners. Not being investigators of the sales environment, their job is to take those estimates, treat them as though they were real, and do the technological product investigation, predicting the kinds of changes in products, equipment, processes, procedures and so on, required to satisfy the demands predicted in the sales environment. Both technological and sales forecasting are essentially cognitive and logic-oriented areas of prediction skill.

The third area of prediction skill is far different because it involves the direct prediction of human reactions to others' decisions and plans. In this area, it is necessary for the persons making the predictions to comprehend individual personality dynamics, the phenomena within groups, and intergroup relations. Only then will he be able to assess, with some accuracy, consequences of an intended action.

Almost all problems of *inaccurate* prediction at Lakeside are in this human area. The analyses of technology and sales environment seem excellent; in fact, there have been no great difficulties up to now in these areas. The people who operate Lakeside, for the most part, are engineers highly competent in technological forecasting. The analysis of the sales environment is done mostly by EPOCH specialists. Lakeside, however, is studded with examples of human prediction errors. It is amazing how many times top management has had to shift its position when the actual reaction differed from the one anticipated.

One of the most significant problems of our times is, How can conditions be generated under which a person can increase his prediction skills in the human area? Yet the formula for doing so is relatively simple. It involves two program functions. One of these calls for a vast increase in basic behavioral science research to make available a more relevant and better validated set of theories. With these, more effective predictions will come from applying the theories to data. The other program function requires greatly improved training media for communicating knowledge to operational specialists. In a way,

I feel that far more behavioral theory exists than is being used in managerial predictions. From another standpoint, however, I have the feeling that the theory available is too impoverished to provide a sound basis for systematic generalization in terms of making concrete predictions. In the next decade, a great deal of work is needed to upgrade the skill of managers in predicting reactions of individuals and groups to alternative decisions and actions.

Again with respect to prediction in the human area, it appears to me that there is a fundamental background consideration related to predictive accuracy which has to do with fairness and the violations of expectations. If an action is taken which is not perceived as *fair* by those upon whom it has an impact, then it produces a negative reaction. This appears almost too simple to dignify as a theoretical concept. Yet it is fundamental, if only because of the frequency with which it is overlooked. From the union point of view, fairness is another way of saying "our dignity and security." Fairness underlies the pressure for seniority. In addition, respect accrues to anyone who is seen as fair and square.

Operational decisions at Lakeside are very frequently resisted because those involved feel the actions are not fair. Management emphasizes efficiency. The wage man places fairness first and efficiency second. From management's point of view, if efficiency had to be sacrificed for fairness, that would be wrong. From the wage man's point of view, if fairness had to be sacrificed for efficiency, that, too, would be wrong. Managerial inability to predict which of its actions will be regarded as fair and which ones will not is the septic source of many decisions and actions that generate undesirable side effects.

Where does this supreme attachment to fairness come from? How is it that people are so sensitive regarding what is fair, and what is not fair? Freud's book, *Group Psychology and the Analysis of the Ego*[4] provides the key. His thesis is that, in the family, the children watch the actions taken by the parents—but mostly the father's—toward each of them. If any differential treatment is experienced, it is immediately regarded as unfair by the disadvantaged sibling(s), and serves as the whole background against which one or more of them take counteractive measures in the interest of achieving fairer treatment. In other words, the criterion of fairness arises from early childhood experience within the family. It is related to actions taken by the parents toward the children. Obviously the fairness criterion is elaborated in many other situations. But children use direct intra-family comparison as the first basis for judging fairness. Later, they use observations of how other parents treat their children.

In our local bargaining situation, a major element which concerns fairness is that the management team doesn't see the union delegation as an equal partner, even though labor law tends to support the equalitarian idea. Instead, management takes the posture of superiority. This is not good because immediately the union people feel that they are being unfairly patronized and treated like children. And from deep down, the child's resentment resurfaces, even though some very sophisticated adult thinking may be conjoined in the emotionally charged quest for ways of getting back at Big Daddy.[5]

Lincoln Lodge: A Basic Cleavage Opens

For some time, as I observed it, bargaining was going quite well. Just prior to the wage increase hassle, real problem-solving orientations were observable on both sides of the table. But in management's background, and in the lower reaches of supervision, to collaborate successfully with the union is a sign of weakness. It is also taken as a sign of a person's being on a drunken giveaway binge.

Months ago I noticed that this attitude runs deep in the blood of many managers and foremen. Their point of view can be characterized as, "If you want to run a sound business consistent with good human relations, there is one way to do it: Keep the hired hands so hard at it every minute of every hour of every day that they don't have any time to complain or to get together and gripe. When people are that busy you don't have human relations problems, and you certainly are running a sound business."

The next great debate in the management ranks will center around plans for additional Lincoln Lodge conferences for people lower in the organizational structure. The Engineering Department, which has a "party line," is quite likely to feel that additional Lincoln Lodge conferences would not be worthwhile. Other members of management are likely to take the opposite point of view. The stage is set for another great debate next Monday afternoon at Quinn's managers' meeting.

References

1. See Chapter 8, Reference 3.
2. See: Samuelson, P.A. *Economics* (8th Ed.). New York: McGraw-Hill Book Company, 1970, pp. 247-249.
3. "The ability to bind tension makes it possible for a person to inhibit inappropriate role behaviors." Sarbin, T.R. "Role theory." In Lindzey, G. (ed.). *Handbook of Social Psychology*. Cambridge, Mass.: Addison-Wesley, 1954, p. 245.
4. Freud, S. *Group Psychology and the Analysis of the Ego*. (trans. by J. Strachey). New York: Bantam Books, 1965.
5. Typical reactions to "paternalism" are described in Blake, R.R. & Mouton, J.S. *The Managerial Grid*. Houston: Gulf Publishing Company, 1964, pp. 214-216. See also: Eric Berne's depictions of the Parental, Adult, and Child ego states in *Games People Play*. New York: Grove Press, Inc., 1964.

16

Decentralization: Myth or Reality?

Decentralization, one of the sacred cows in modern management's theoretical menagerie, has prompted the popular idea, "To have a sound organization, profit centers should be located near raw material sources and the market. Men can run these profit centers autonomously, requiring only the basic external controls of personal responsibility and accountability." The argument further proclaims that a manager be given relatively free rein by chartering broad responsibilities which outline his job. By doing this and freeing him to employ his talents, energy, and judgment, it becomes possible to develop the breadth, depth, perspective, and sense of personal responsibility which make great managers.

In contrast, the more a headquarters supervises its subsidiary production facilities, the greater the centralization. Since centralization, according to the argument I have cited, seems relatively undesirable, it becomes even more important to devise ways and means which free local plant managers to operate in a manner consistent with their own convictions about efficient performance. Yet they also need to develop, both for themselves and for their subordinates, a degree of morale based on personal security and the worthwhile nature of one's work. This in turn promotes dignified treatment of individuals which is much desired in a society where profit is mandatory yet where labor peace is also prized.

It takes a deep and analytical penetration of an organization to discover the *true* extent of decentralization. In fact, headquarters' pronouncements—regarding a plant manager's freedom to operate consistent with sound business logic, human relations concepts, and his knowledge of the local situation—might not correspond to actual circumstances and practices.

There are several ways to examine the extent to which decentralization does in truth exist. Four might be called critical. One asks, "Where are decisions made regarding plant modifications or expansion?" Another is,

"To what extent are local plant managers free to commit corporate funds for new equipment?" A third is, "To what extent does a local plant manager have to submit his decisions to headquarters' review prior to announcing them?" A fourth is, "Besides—or in the absence of—formal review, how much informal clearing goes on between a local plant and its headquarters management; and also, how much clearing occurs between a local plant and one or more company plants some distance away?"

Decisions on Plant Modification and Expansion

In EPOCH plants rarely can a local manager commit corporate funds to a major plant modification or expansion without approval from headquarters. The reason for this is that only headquarters has an overall point of view. One headquarters procedure is to initiate and work up a new-product proposal—or, sometimes, to adopt a proposal suggested by one of its plants—and then request bids for the project from its various subsidiary plants. The new-product proposal usually entails modifying or expanding existing production facilities. Under these circumstances, each plant bids against the rest. The decision as to which one gets the "plum" depends on a host of social and economic factors. Social factors include local tax rates, labor availability, and projections of population increases and of expanded local markets for products. Economic factors involve the proximity of raw materials and supplies, the distances involved in moving finished products to the market, and the cost of land if an expansion requires a new site or more space adjoining the present site.

This way of proceeding is routine among companies that have headquarters coordinating subsidiary plants[1] and although there may be variations from company to company, the similarities far outweigh the differences. The point is that a local manager can rarely, if ever, launch any plant modifications or expansion under his own initiative. Therefore, evidences of decentralization must be sought elsewhere.

Plant Manager Autonomy in Purchasing New Equipment

In many items of operation a plant manager is given budgeted limits for his equipment-purchasing and maintenance. The amount varies with a number of factors, but the range is probably between annual totals of $25,000 and $250,000, according to the plant size. Before authorizing expenditures beyond such limits, a plant manager must get headquarters' approval, even if the expenditure represents neither modification nor expansion, but simply replacement of an expensive piece of equipment.

Therefore the question to verify or disprove the existence of decentralization is, "To what extent is the plant manager free to commit funds for new equipment without headquarters' approval?"

Headquarters' Review of Local Decisions

The third test for decentralization is whether or not local managerial decisions need official approval from headquarters before they can be announced and implemented. It is the trickiest of all to apply.

EPOCH's organization operates according to policies and procedures specified, in broad terms, by headquarters. Since no policy statement can cover all contingencies, managers must, of necessity, interpret them in the light of specific situations. But if several plant managers interpret differently, particularly with regard to union contracts, then cross pressures are created between the plants and undesirable consequences can occur. The same is true for salary and wage administration, and benefits programs. Generally, these are not within local plant managers' spheres of independent decision making. Administration of these programs is regulated by detailed rules and procedures which are uniform throughout the company. Decentralization doesn't apply here—any hazy points of interpretation must be referred for headquarters to clarify.

Contract policies involving the union are spelled out in broader outlines that allow the plant managers more personal discretion. But here the real trick appears. You might think that if there is only the most general supervision of the major decisions made by plant managers, and that reviews by headquarters are rare, such circumstances would indicate that decentralization exists. However, the sneaker in this situation is that people don't become plant managers unless they have deeply internalized, and habitually express, headquarters' point of view spanning the widest possible range of factors. They are qualified to inject headquarters' points of view into local decisions; thus, no need for close supervision exists. Often the local plant manager can anticipate the headquarters attitude toward some particular issue. The easiest way to avoid appearing deviant is simply to avoid making decisions which would be contested by headquarters.

Thus the apparent conditions within which local decision making seems to be quite autonomous—since Quinn makes and implements most of his decisions without having them reviewed at Atlanta beforehand—mask the real conditions of dependency. There is no reason for Quinn and other plant managers to get their decisions okayed in advance because they have already spent a lifetime studying the kinds of reactions that can be anticipated from headquarters. By making decisions consistent with these attitudes and unstated policies, there is rarely any happening at the local level which causes headquarters eyebrows to be raised.

Informal Checking with Headquarters

The fourth point concerns the degree to which plant managers and other local executives have confidants in headquarters whom they can contact to get advice on problems. Generally, lower echelons in production centers that operate under a headquarters organization routinely set up their own private channels for finding out what is going on in headquarters and what the reactions to various proposals will be. Informal friendship communication lines sometimes border the official channels. Thus the Lakeside plant lawyer is in fairly routine contact with the legal department of headquarters. The head of business services double checks with his counterpart in headquarters any anticipated revisions of procedure. Personnel executives commune with their respective guardian angels at headquarters. And so it goes. In addition, there seems to be a well-developed lateral communication network through which people in different plants informally keep in touch.

How Quinn Views His Position

Quinn seems to feel that he has a high degree of autonomy. He has told me that headquarters is committed to the idea of decentralized operations, and, indeed, EPOCH frequently stresses the importance of decentralization and its contributions to effective operations. In my observation, however, decentralization is a cherished myth rather than a reality. Let's summarize the evidence. There is continuous checking, double checking, and cross checking between headquarters and plant, or vice versa. Few significant actions are taken without asking, "How would headquarters react to this?" or without previously being worked through with appropriate headquarters personnel. This goes on even though many EPOCH and Lakeside people would stoutly maintain that "autonomous local decision making under conditions of decentralization" accurately describes the present situation.

In this connection, I am reminded of a Caribbean freighter trip I once took. In my naive way, I had presumed that the captain of a freighter would be about as free as any man could possibly be. On the surface he appears to make numerous significant and critical decisions. As I became acquainted with the captain a variety of external controls that I had not anticipated became evident. For example, the rules regarding working hours, rest periods, conditions of employment, and living quarters for the crew are for the most part rigidly determined by contract arrangements which the captain can only disregard in serious emergencies. The internal operation of the ship is largely out of his control except for seeing to it that the rules, already agreed to by others in other places, are obeyed.

Then there is the matter of movement from one port to another. Does the captain decide for what port he will depart? The presumption is that he does but the facts are otherwise. On a Caribbean trip, for example, he may have any one of a dozen ports of call. They may or may not be dictated in advance. If they are dictated in advance, he is already restricted to the sequence as well as arrival and departure times. If they are only roughly outlined in advance, it would appear that the captain has a free choice. This is not so either, for the radio operator is continuously receiving messages on available dock space in the proposed ports of call. Where the captain goes is determined by the available dock space for unloading. Therefore, external instructions, and not the captain's choice, determine where he goes. Beyond these matters, you might say that the captain remains free to determine his speed, but this is not so either. Speed is conditioned by the ship's capacity.

Traditionally a ship captain was thought to be the master of his own fate, the fate of his ship, and the fate of his crew. Twentieth-century facts, however, are quite different. The ship captain is a person whose personal authority is much less than his responsibility, except when serious emergencies arise. Only emergencies can produce local circumstances so complicated that headquarters offices are unable to do the planning for the captain.

The same is true, too, in a local EPOCH plant. It may be that the only time when true decentralization exists is when an emergency, such as a hurricane or a flood or a blizzard strikes. Then decisions can only be made by people whose eyes and ears are actually in the situation. Then, and only then, does headquarters acknowledge that they have whatever it takes to know what to do. Genuine decentralization, then, whether at Lakeside or at sea, seems to be a relatively short-term phenomenon.

References

1. See: Buffa, E.S. *Modern Production Management* (3rd Ed.). New York: John Wiley & Sons, Inc., 1969, Chapter 10.

17

The Prospects Worsen

Two weeks ago an important meeting was held in headquarters regarding the next steps in corporate reorganization. It was decided that all of the "light production" plants would be grouped into a single functional organization to be headed by Neal Young, who has been the head of a sub-group of EPOCH plants with John Edwards as his immediate colleague. Both Neal and John are being made corporate vice presidents, and will soon move from Atlanta to Chicago. It was also announced that a committee was being set up to plan the integration of the various plants into a functional organization. Quinn is to be on this committee, whose work is likely to be very arduous and time-consuming. This may mean that Quinn will be unavailable to deal on a continuous basis with Lakeside problems.

Quinn, who is about fifty-five, has been in his present position for at least five years. He has brought the plant to a level of effective operation in terms of running a sound business. This calendar year, Lakeside will make a larger profit than at any time during the past thirty years, even though much of the U.S. economy is in a slump. There are some indications that Quinn is not in the best of health; he has been working himself to a point of near exhaustion recently. I often get the feeling, too, that the seemingly endless union-management hassling at Lakeside has him fed up to the craw. Now that Quinn is on the committee which will design the new light production coordinating structure, this total combination of circumstances provides him an excellent opportunity to move upward. He seems to have high motivation, a solid reputation, and means of access. It very well could be that within six months he will be appointed to some position in the Chicago headquarters.

From the standpoint of the organization's being able to take a fresh look, there is much to recommend in this. When industrial relations have been on a continuing conflict level, as with Lakeside, it's reasonable that the general manager would eventually want to escape from them if he could not improve them. Another possibility is that headquarters might expect a new manager to bring an altered approach to the situation. In EPOCH, it is unusual for a person to be promoted to general manager from within the same plant. This indicates that headquarters' theory requires the top man to be a person who enters his post as a relative stranger. The reason for this, probably, is that the new general manager is in no way committed to the policies, practices, and procedures established by his predecessor. With regard to EPOCH-specified policies, he may bring in different emphases and interpretations. He has few, if any, personal commitments based on friendship or a sense of obligation to repay past favors. As a result, he is more free than the previous manager to take a fresh approach to solving the plant's contemporary problems. Yet, the probability is that, after a period of time, he too will have settled into an interlocking system of personal relations and commitments, with his effectiveness being correspondingly diminished. It is easy for a manager to gradually become less productive of organizational improvement the longer he stays in a position, because he becomes more and more committed to the conditions that were present when he arrived and thereafter he has helped to create.

Combining all of these considerations, I would predict that Lakeside might have a new general manager within six months. I make this prediction quite tentatively, because I have no conclusive evidence that Quinn feels the time has come for him to move onward and upward; nor am I sure that a new higher-level post may be available. Thirdly, I have no actual grounds for assuming that headquarters thinks it desirable to replace Quinn with someone who could take a fresh approach. Indeed, there are many indications that the opposite could be true, because of Quinn's demonstrated success in moving this plant from being a deficit operation to becoming an efficient and profitable one.

Wage Increase Woes

The Mountainview plant's management has promised that by Friday, it would give the union its final answer on the "5%—14 cents" problem. The Mountainview union wanted a straight 5% across-the-board general wage increase. On Friday, just before the meeting was due to be held, Neal Young, EPOCH's production coordinator, called Mountainview's general manager, Allen Eastman, and said, "Allen, go ahead and have your meeting if you want to, but don't give a final answer. We are running into static on this problem at Lakeside, Seashore and Hilltop, and I want to explore it further before we make a final position known." The Mountainview meeting was held, but Allen gave no answer on the across-the-board increase request. Instead, he announced a fundamental change in position on the red circle issue. In the initial Mountainview management communiqué, red circle people were told they would receive no general wage increase at all. Now they were reinstated to the extent of being offered a 7-cents-per-hour "cost of living contribution." Allen bargained hard with the union, emphasizing that he was making a significant concession on the red circle issue, and implying that he would hold the line everywhere else.

At Seashore, EPOCH's largest plant, a meeting with its union had also been scheduled for last Friday afternoon, but Neal Young gave Will Grigg the same instructions as Allen, and the meeting was cancelled. A unique circumstance exists at Seashore. This is that one union represents both the salary and the wage personnel, and negotiates their respective contracts with management. The postponed meeting was held this morning, November 9. Will Grigg, following precepts that have been employed by all plant general managers, indicated to the union that he had closely studied their request, but in fact was unable to change his offer from the 5%—14 cent pattern. At this point, Abe Baker, the head of the Seashore union, said, "I'm mighty sorry, Mr. Grigg, that you can't see it our way. Now let me tell *you* something. You can take your little wage offer and shove it. If you ever come around to seeing things sensibly and wishing to treat people fairly and equitably, let us know, but as of now, we want nothing to do with your picayune little wage offer." Thereupon, Abe and the other union officials got up and walked out.

It should be noted that Will at Seashore, Allen at Mountainview, and Quinn at Lakeside, are quite unable to act autonomously. Yet each of them is talking to the union in me-and-you terms as if to imply that he is capable of setting local rates on his own initiative. This is a sham and a farce and everybody recognizes it.

Dan stopped by this morning and talked to some people in the Personnel Department about another matter. During this discussion he said, "I have nothing more to say about that lousy offer. My people told me a long time ago to push for a 10% raise, and this isn't even 5%; and then there's your miserable cutback on the red circle rates. The bargaining positions are so far apart that I don't have the slightest reason to call a membership meeting."

So Dan is playing a sharp game. EPOCH is adamant in a different way, saying that if the offer is not accepted by November 16, it will not be retroactive. Abe Baker at Seashore isn't worried by this, and Dan isn't fretting either.

When another union "marched on Atlanta" recently, its officials got to see EPOCH's board of directors. The president, Elliott Long, said, "Our first and final offer was 5% for salaried personnel and 14 cents per hour for wage earners. Your counter demands won't be considered. Whether you take the increase or leave it is up to you." Then, with the ritualistic emphasis which is becoming a standard feature of labor-management relations throughout EPOCH and its plants, Long and his executive group got up and walked out.

Gary Cooper, the general manager at Hilltop, is having union troubles, but his position is not clearly understood at the present time. At Plainfield, whose employees are mostly blacks, the 14 cents offer is equivalent to something in the neighborhood of a 6 to 8% raise. Presumably this is why they have already accepted it.

In the past, when faced with a union that has stubbornly taken a stand on an issue, management has turned away to "bargain directly with the people." The strategy is one of persuading employees that their union is pigheadedly obstructing management's genuine efforts to benefit them. Then the people will pressure union officers to do what management wants them to do. Currently at Lakeside, some engineer-managers, who see negotiating and problem solving with the union as equivalent to mollycoddling it, consider that now is the time to build "heat" under the union officers and force them to accept the wage increase offer and the red circle decision. This is a power strategy pure and simple.

Among Lakeside's communications media there are two publications: *Newsletter to Management* and *Lakeside Today*. Both, in the past, have been used as anti-union propaganda carriers. Those managers who want to incite the union are pressing to have both publications used for this purpose again. Wes, the personnel chief, whose department is responsible for publications, is placing a notice in tomorrow's issue of *Lakeside Today* to inform wage people that the offer needs to be accepted by the 16th if the wage increase is to be retroactive to October 27. Wes' aim is to make the announcement in as factual a way as possible, thus undermining future criticism that wage people were not informed. Uninfluenced, as yet, by the "inciters," he is trying to make the facts known without u sing *Lakeside Today* as a pressure device. The developing situation illustrates the extent to which jockeying occurs in an organization whic h presently is half committed to power strategies and half to problem-solving strategies.

Today is the 9th of November. My feeling is that people are doing a kind of stationary shuffle. Nobody is running, but no one is standing still. It is a recess period while people wait for the November 16 deadline. It is a vacant and uneasy time. People need closure, and here the situation is open ended and will be for another week. It is easy for the union to take a standoffish attitude when it still has eight days available.

EPOCH wants to keep bargaining on a local plant basis so that each management takes responsibility for dealing with its union, and there is no centralized bargaining. Some years ago, various plant union officials tried to form a bargaining coalition group which could deal more firmly with headquarters. This play was effectively blocked by management, and bargaining continues to be a local activity. The situation seems unfair, because management is an integrated coalition group. It gets its final orders from one office and then everyone falls in line and marches in unison. On the union side, however, there is substantial evidence that an undercover coalition exists and is active. Chuck Hendricks, the union head at Hilltop, keeps in touch with Johnny Johnson of Mountainview, with Dan Ives, and with Abe Baker at Seashore. They are apparently in daily telephone contact. While they may be unable to develop a concerted public strategy for dealing with management on the wage increase issue, it is my impression that their efforts are coordinated. For example, in his contacts with John and Abe in particular, Dan has discovered that different red circle withholding patterns are being applied.

Earl Higgins

Two or three weeks ago, Dan told me that Earl Higgins was the storm center of Lakeside. To the union, Earl is seen as a real sour apple, a trouble maker, a dishonest, deceitful, manipulative member of management. Earl is assistant department head under Hal Harvey.

Last Friday, when Hal Harvey resigned from the bargaining committee, management indicated that Earl would be moved up to become department head; that Jack Smith, who unionists see as a "hard nosed work pusher," would be made assistant department head, and that another of the most hated members of management would become division head in place of Jack Smith. Of course, Van and Hal commented on each of them with pride and enthusiasm, but the unionists winced as each name was mentioned.

Dan, back from Washington, appeared bright and early this morning and asked for a meeting with Van and Mac.

When they met, Dan said, "I want to tell you fellows what I am going to do. I don't know how your people will react, but I will go along with what my people have decided. Some time ago, we had a suspicion that you would put Earl Higgins on the bargaining committee. We voted to a man that if you ever did that bargaining would end then and there.

"I hear you're going to make the announcement tomorrow morning, when bargaining starts. If and when you do, we will caucus, and I will ask my people, 'Do you or do you not want to continue bargaining with Earl as one of the members of the committee?' If the officers vote that they want to, we will continue. If they vote that they don't want to, we will engage in no further bargaining until Earl Higgins is removed from the management bargaining team. But if you're wise, Van, you won't have Earl on the team in the first place." Van, a friend of Earl's, argued bitterly with Dan, challenging him to justify the major positions of his attack on Earl.

Dan's ultimatum uses power for trying to guard against what, to the union, appears to be an intolerable situation. Earl Higgins, indeed, has taken many actions which are not okay from a wage earner's standpoint.

However, according to labor law, management has an absolute right to place on its bargaining team anyone it chooses; and the union has a similar right. In principle, the union has no more right to dictate membership of the management team than management has to dictate the membership of the union delegation.

The union officers were OUB this afternoon. They left the plant with Fred Henry, the union's legal counsel. Management thinks that if the Earl Higgins problem is mentioned to Fred Henry, he will advise the union to avoid this precipitate action, because there are no legal grounds for it. Also, the hard nosed members of management are skeptical, saying that if the union officials were to break off negotiations, they would have to "go back to work." According to these managers, bargaining is a kind of vacation away from the work station, which no union official wants to bring to an end.

There are two main reasons why Quinn and his executives want Earl to join the bargaining committee. One is that Earl is the member of the Engineering Department who knows the most about labor contracts and therefore makes it possible for him to bargain effectively from an engineering point of view. The other reason is more important. Earl is at a significant turning point in his career. It is known that he has developed a very hostile attitude toward union and wage people alike. He has a single master-servant philosophy of supervision, and reacts with shock and anger if his decrees are questioned. Although unsophisticated at this level, he can be very ingenious in devising provocations and springing traps against those who have annoyed him. The wage people, of course, have a more detailed acquaintance with these talents of his than Quinn, Van, and Hal have.

Quinn and the others see him as a bright engineer-manager who, to qualify for bigger posts in the future, needs to improve his human relations capabilities. If he can't become more acceptable to wage personnel, his career might be stunted. If he can, then he will probably be able to move up further, and because of his drive and intellectual brilliance, he could go very far. The decision to place him on the committee is a test case for his own career as to whether or not he will be able to make the required adjustment.

When Dan's ultimatum was reported to Quinn, he gave it little thought. He merely remarked that Dan's tirade was par for the course and not worth worrying about.

Maybe it isn't, but if the union does take a vote to terminate bargaining, the breakdown of negotiations could be interpreted at headquarters either as proving that it is hopeless to try to deal with IEW, or that Quinn doesn't know his people well enough to avoid placing on the bargaining committee somebody who is personally objectionable to the union. It doesn't matter too much which interpretation is adopted or whether it is right or wrong. What does matter is Quinn will be viewed as having failed.

So although legality is clearly on the side of management in this issue, labor and functional relations, and a person's career, hang in the balance. It is a very complicated situation.

What Has Gone Wrong with Union-Management Bargaining?

Two months ago, a hopeful atmosphere permeated the plant. Everyone who had the relevant facts at their disposal saw the union-management bargaining proceeding at a good pace, with sound solutions being achieved on several basic issues that had been sources of conflict for many years. At that stage in bargaining, one would have predicted that further success was inevitable. Today, the situation is vastly different. On two occasions the union has threatened to terminate bargaining. The hurling of threats is symptomatic that things are unexpectedly going wrong; and I want to figure out *why*.

The earliest disturbing issue was the crane crisis. The union considered it a violation of trust and past practice for management to replace an IEW member with an international union member as crane operator. Management at first stuck to its guns, then decided to shift its position, then was unable to find someone qualified to do the work. In the end, the international crane operator sat in the crane cab. Management had failed, and the union had gained no satisfaction.

The next thing that came along was the benefits program. This should have been a bargainable item, but because EPOCH has one of the world's finest benefits programs, headquarters attitudes always have been, "We will work out the details, and they'll be so good that you should accept them wholeheartedly. We would prefer not to bargain, because a comprehensively designed and company-wide benefits package is much superior to what would be possible if each separate plant or other entity were to bargain and set up its own benefits program." The union protested and fought management to get details. Management itself was very vague about what the new benefits program would be. Nonetheless, it practically forced the union to agree on accepting a virtually unknown program.

As of today, certain features of the new benefits program are becoming evident, and they are much less beneficial than the terms of the previous program. This is exactly what the union had feared and tried to find out about before it was pressured into on-faith acceptance of the new program. Word came through today that there has been a retroactive increase (to November 1) in the interest rate on any loans that a member of the organization takes out under the benefits program. The loan rate is now at a higher level than it has ever been before. Another hidden feature which is now coming out is concerned with the conditions for receiving an uninsured loan, and the interest rate that will apply. Both of these items lessen the value of the new benefits package, but neither of them was disclosed when the union was confronted with a deadline for accepting the new program. The union is not only bitterly resentful of headquarters' trickiness; it is furious with Lakeside management for giving what have turned out to be false assurances. The Personnel Department is accused of having been too timid, or lazy, to have run a check with headquarters before propositioning the union to "Trust us, for all will be well." So the fury at being tricked by EPOCH headquarters is supercharged by rage with local personnel managers such as Wes and Mac who, it seems, just wouldn't take the trouble to check things out on behalf of the wage man. "You see what happens when we trust those clowns to go to bat for us?" Dan and others are saying.

A third item which has caused trouble is the maintenance of membership issue. At first, management agreed to a clause in the contract. Then, due to headquarters pressure, it reversed its position.

A fourth item has to do with the "year end contribution" that the company customarily grants to each employee. EPOCH has announced a record-breaking profit. Lakeside's efficiency and productivity is better this year than ever before. Yet the year end contribution has been reduced, relative to previous years. Again, the wage people, through their union, have been given no information as to why the reduction has been made. But Dan and his colleagues can see Simon Legree Quinn and the engineering cohorts basking in the warmth of headquarters' approval and piling up career brownie points while, down on the plantation, the wage slaves get a kick in the teeth as their Christmas bonus.

A fifth matter concerns EPOCH's announcement of a 5% increase for salaried personnel and a 14 cents per hour (equivalent to 4.2%) increase for wage people. This is viewed by the union as being very unfair. The union argues that if this is a general cost-of-living increase, the prices of bread, milk, and so on, have gone up the same amount for everyone, so it should not matter whether a person's collar is white or blue; everyone needs to get the same proportionate raise. Thus far, Lakeside's and other plants' unions have been unable to shift EPOCH's position on this one. They have to contend, too, with the specious counter-arguments of local managers who, under the decentralization myth, claim that they are key decision makers in wage and salary matters.

But in a way that further confuses and enrages the unions, local management does seem to have some discretionary powers, under the general principle that what's bad for the wage earner is "good" in the eyes of headquarters. The prime example at Lakeside is Quinn's decision to withhold 7 cents of the wage increase from red circle people. At Mountainview, Allen Eastman initially withheld the entire 14 cents, though he has recently come around to offering back 7; which puts his position in line with Quinn's. The earlier discrepancy indicated that individual general managers were acting autonomously, but the subsequent shuffle raises the question of whether some EPOCH coordinator is calling the shots. If so, the further question for any union is, "Who *do* we bargain with?"

At Lakeside it is clear that, although union and management are far from being a Romeo and Juliet duo, they have an intimate relationship going, and are indispensable to each other. Through bargaining negotiations, in theory, they are trying to coexist more satisfactorily than in the past. Now the stage directions say, "Enter Earl Higgins." From IEW's point of view and in

Shakespearian analogy, this is like qualifying Tybalt as a marriage counselor and bringing him in to shape the future action of the drama.

All of these issues have emerged during the last few weeks. Every one of them represents a management action which was experienced as being characterized by arbitrariness, rigidity, ambiguity, and a general lack of compassion. On every one of them, the union has protested. On none of them has the union been successful in moving management toward its point of view.

If the union examines headquarters' actions, and compares them with Lakeside management's actions, a common theme emerges. This is that the actions are all negative and seemingly unfair. Management has blundered on through, taking haphazard or opportunistic positions one by one, often standing firm on them, but in some instances backing off or side-stepping. The problem is that the union feels confused and weak. I believe that the sum total of Lakeside and EPOCH managerial actions—which really are so eclectic and ill-coordinated as to approach randomness—is viewed from the union side as a huge and supersubtle strategy being masterminded by some Machiavellian genius in headquarters. IEW officials are very uneasy because they have no way of predicting what's likely to happen to them next, except that more shocks can be anticipated. Union officials feel that although they have "people power" to throw around, doing so brings no effective result. Power is measured by its effects. When an organization begins to throw power around, but no one pays any attention, it doesn't take that organization long to realize that it doesn't have any influence, and has been squandering its energies.

The union has made some gains through bargaining, but all of these are relatively minor and do not affect the pocketbook. Nor indeed are they items that really improve one's sense of security or dignity. They are mostly ones on which management is correcting its own past lapses rather than solving contemporary problems in ways that are helpful to the union.

As of tonight, bargaining relations are shaky. The union is hurling empty threats and weak challenges. Intensive bargaining is scheduled for the next four days. There is a sense of demoralization in management and in the union. Headquarters has forced Lakeside management to take positions that neither it nor the union agrees with. When bargaining begins, and for a period of time things go well, and then a number of negative actions occur that make you feel weak and ineffectual, what is the next step?

I predict the union will act tougher to test whether it can budge management in any way. This is not a union that would accept being a rubber stamp to endorse headquarters' or Lakeside management's decrees. It will fight for what it feels is right. If it becomes gravely frustrated by not receiving what it considers equitable, it may take much more extreme actions.

One dramatic action would be for the IEW officials to resign en masse. Another option would be for IEW to affiliate with one of the international unions.

Another factor, one which looms in the background, is the possibility of prosecution of the union for an alleged violation of the Title IV election provisions of the Landrum-Griffin Act. This issue is filled with hazards, too. If the union is brought to trial and found guilty, the faction in management which has avoided bargaining with this group will think they were right, and that the other managers, who were trying to create a mature and aboveboard relationship, were wrong and soft. If the union is found not guilty, it is not really in a stronger position or better able to deal in a problem-solving way with management, for Quinn and his men are weakened by external pressures upon them. Certainly this situation is more difficult than I imagined a year ago. My greatest surprise this past year has been to see the pitifully implemented reality of the EPIC group's most cherished and publicized principle: decentralization.

Earl Higgins Awaits Admission

The big procedural issue before the bargaining committee this morning, November 10, was whether or not the union delegation would agree to continue bargaining if Earl Higgins joined the management team. Earl was supposed to have joined the bargaining session this morning, but he didn't show up; the reason being that Earl did not want to join the meeting and suffer the possible embarrassment of the union's getting up and walking out. Instead, he stayed in his office, awaiting their decision. This uncharacteristic tact indicated that Earl recognizes he is on probation.

The morning proceedings began typically, with a quick summary of outstanding problems. The issue of arbitration was worked on without any real consensus emerging on what might become final grounds for agreement. Nothing was said by the union regarding Earl Higgins, though they had started the day with a caucus for the purpose of discussing their position on this matter.

At the coffee break, around 10:00 a.m., Van and Dan got together. Van said, "Do you have anything to tell me regarding Earl's coming in?"

"Oh yes," Dan replied. "We talked about it in our caucus, and the fellows were most unhappy at the prospect of seeing Earl on the other side of the table. Anyhow, eventually we felt we should continue in spite of him. So let's go on, and hope for the best." Then Dan went on to make a remark which could have substantial implications. "It does appear that we are making some progress. At least, we are finding our areas of disagreement and occasionally we find something on which we can agree, and it seems worthwhile to keep plugging away even though the pace is slow and tiring."

Apparently, through the union's need to discuss Earl and what his presence might portend, they had effectively pressured themselves into examining the present position—whether or not progress was being made. When it appeared they wanted to continue and did feel they were making some progress, their spirits were lifted. The morning discussion was a useful one. There already seems to be enough flexibility, in the union's understanding of the arbitration problem, to presage some eventual agreement.

Earl will be joining the meeting this afternoon. I asked Van if Earl had been told of the union's misgivings about him. Van said that he had. I don't know the substance of their conversation, but Van has made it clear that he fully intends to censure Earl if his actions change the present atmosphere of gentlemanly disagreement back into a hell's kitchen of conflict.

Since Earl has already been shaken by recent events, such as being carpeted for his part in the crane crisis, he may be searching for ways to become more acceptable to the union and to his colleagues and superiors in management. He knows that future career prospects hinge on his developing the skills and tact that will induce wage people and their union to cooperate with him, rather than dreading and shunning him as they have done for over three years. It is a difficult situation, when not only does the union rate you as objectionable, but also your colleagues and higher-ups are identifying you as hampering their efforts to achieve the objectives to which they are committed. Among his fellow engineers, Earl is seen as a reasonable and collaborative person even though, to me, it appears that he has great difficulties in accepting a wage earner as a fellow human.

It will be interesting this afternoon to learn how Earl made his debut as a bargaining team member. One way he might behave is to be relatively silent and unparticipative, which would be quite uncharacteristic of him. If he remains his usual self, he will play his favorite game of one-upmanship, telling the union why they are wrong and why he is right. I am not sure that Earl can enter a potentially competitive situation without polarizing it and fighting to win. My guess, though, is that only by finding a constructive orientation will it be possible for him to consolidate his new position and establish himself as a credible candidate for higher executive posts.

Where Are Problem-Solving Methods Best Attempted?

The question has frequently been asked, Where in a large industrial plant can behavioral science methods of problem solving best be attempted with a view to expanded use? Many different answers can be given, such as working directly with the president or general manager, or with some functional segment of the organization such as a department; but from my standpoint, none of these are as satisfactory as starting with the union-management bargaining committee as a problem-solving facilitator. If it is impossible to work with both parties, to work with either one of them would be worthwhile. If a choice is possible, it is preferable to begin with the management bargaining team, because usually these people consider themselves to be socially and intellectually superior to the union officials. Therefore, management has great difficulty in seeing the problems it is creating for itself through arrogance and ineptitude vis-á-vis the union.

It is a favorable situation if the management bargaining team is composed of line executives as well as staff people such as personnel specialists, and better still if the team members are of high rank.

There are two main reasons for this. First, if the managers learn to see and utilize the advantages of collaborative problem solving with the union—in contrast to engaging in battle with it—and if they gain some skill in initiating this with the union, they are the very people who, by virtue of their formal positions and authority, can institute a similar change of approach in resolving disagreements and improving relationships within their own departments or other areas of responsibility.

The second and allied reason for the management bargaining team being a good point for applying behavioral science concepts and methods is that the union is the only major group connected with an organization over which the management does not have direct control. Even though the union is seldom treated by management as an equal group, in a legal sense it *is*. And being autonomous, it is, in the final analysis, uncontrollable from the outside even though attempts may be made to coerce it. Obedience by the union cannot easily be extracted by the threat or exercise of power. Theoretical and experimental work in the intergroup field suggests that the most successful way for autonomous groups—between whom there is an area of mutual interest as well as potential friction—to collaborate is for them to solve the problems that keep them separated.

It can be predicted that since neither group can control the other and since the strategies of win-lose and "give a little, get a lot" haven't worked well for either side, management will eventually notice and take the option of relating with the union in such a manner as to solve problems. It appears, then, that the most effective point of application for bringing behavioral science concepts and insights into an organization involves the management members of the bargaining committee.

18

Grappling With Internal and External Problems

This afternoon, Earl Higgins joined the bargaining session and it became evident that he was on his best behavior. In fact, as someone remarked afterward, he had no more than ten words to say all afternoon.

I attended the management team's post-bargaining session, which turned out to be one of the longest postmortems ever held. Here Earl was quite active. In a series of masterful maneuvers, he practically became the leader of the group. One of his tactics was to complicate issues that had already been discussed with the union to the point where further questions were needed for clarification. Then, having the floor, Earl would inject new ideas and expand on them very persuasively.

He also exerted leadership by confidently telling Van and the others what hidden motives the union members had for asking certain things. His interpretations of the IEW officials' ideas were clearly predicated on his own distrust and suspicion. He gave no indication that honorable intentions might be present. Rather, he focused his remarks on what he alleged were manipulative intentions of the union. This was disturbing to the other members of the bargaining team, for he implied that if management were to accept the union's proposals, it would be "sucked in."

A third feature of Earl's approach was that he frequently used the words *win* or *lose* as he discussed the negotiating issues. Other members of the team, who are oriented in a problem-solving way toward negotiations, never use these terms. Earl was saying things like, "If you agree to that, you will lose your shirt," or, "If we can get them to buy this, we will really win." His mind is heavily anchored in a win-lose orientation, and he seems unaware of its effect upon his thinking.

I can't speak for the other members, but as I sat in at this session, I found my stomach tightening up. His distorted statements and the suspicion with which he analyzed and criticized the union quickly put me in a tense mood. I could readily feel that a union official, hearing Earl's tirade, would immediately regress into a fight orientation, no matter how dedicated he might be to problem solving.

Van, the chairman of the team, evidently leans on Earl for moral and intellectual support. It seems unlikely, then, that he will prevent Earl from polarizing the bargaining teams. After the meeting, Wes remarked to me that Van doesn't realize the extent to which Earl can manipulate him (Van). Mac said it is very likely that Carl, who has been a constructive influence in bargaining, may find that Van will not be as receptive to Carl's thinking as before.

Possibly a rivalry relationship will arise between Carl and Earl, since both are competing for attention and credibility with Van. This is the kind of win-lose situation in which Earl can be very clever. He is helpful to the man in charge and operates in such a way as to make himself indispensable to him.

Another matter was that last night the salary union had a meeting during which two important events occurred. One is that the salary union voted to accept the 5% increase. The second thing is that the present slate of independent officers in the salary union has decided to run again in a December election against a slate of ICEW candidates.

Long's Opportunity to be a Man of Character

It is now evident that the 5%-14 cent pattern of general wage increase has been offered in almost all cases where the ICEW is the recognized bargaining agent. The 5% across-the-board has been offered in all situations where independent unions represent the wage personnel. The one significant exception is in the EPOCH company. In EPOCH, the ICEW pattern characterizes offers to independent unions. Furthermore, in EPOCH, the 5%-14 cent pattern has already been accepted by the largest ICEW unit, the one at Coastline. No explanation for the reversal of patterns has been given, but it may mean that Elliott Long, the president of EPOCH, is determined to demonstrate that no outside influences can dictate the situation within his company. This, in turn, would indicate that EPOCH leadership has become heavily oriented toward economic and efficiency aspects of problems as contrasted with personal welfare, security, and dignity considerations.

Long recently met with the union officers who had "marched on Atlanta," and rebuffed them, saying that the "5% and 14 cents" offer was the final one. No one at Lakeside knows Long, but because he has put his foot down firmly, the presumption is that he is a man of strong character, ready to live with the consequences of imposing tough terms upon others.

November 16 is the deadline for accepting the general wage increase with retroactivity to October 27. The 5%-14 cent pattern has already been accepted at Plateau, a plant which is under survival pressures; and at Plainfield, where, since the rates are lower, the 14 cents works out to around an 8% increase.

Four other plants' independent unions—those of Seashore, Lakeside, Mountainview and Hilltop—are holding out for 5% across the board. Mountainview and Lakeside have red circle problems as well. In all four plants, exactly the same procedure is being applied by the union presidents. Seashore's Abe Baker told Will Grigg to "go shove that miserable offer." Yesterday, the Seashore union had a handout which was described as being very nasty in its tone. Today Dan is having a handout printed for distribution tomorrow. The IEW caucused for about an hour this morning to check out the draft.

The Mountainview independent union has not called a meeting of its membership to ratify the offer, and neither has Hilltop. It is known locally that Dan is intimately acquainted with the actions of the three other plants. All of this suggests that deadline day, the 16th, will arrive with none of these four having accepted the 5%-14 cent offer. Then what will be the reaction in EPOCH company headquarters? At this point in the game, the initiative returns to Elliott Long. If he authorizes a 5% increase, he exposes himself to future upward influence because he will be known as a man who responds to pressures from below. If he doesn't authorize it, and the unions back down, he will thereby establish himself as a strong minded man; people will conclude that when he says something, that's how things are going to be.

Lakeside's wage and salary administrator predicts that if the four plant unions give up and accept Long's offer, the order of acceptance will be Mountainview, Hilltop, Seashore, and Lakeside. He gives several reasons for this prediction. On some previous occasion Mountainview has held out beyond a retroactivity feature. The wage and salary administrator believes that the Mountainview plant union will remember its loss under these conditions, and so it will be the most likely to break ranks and give in. The reason for predicting Hilltop to be the second one to go is that with Mountainview gone, Hilltop is in a less favorable position to go on resisting than is either Lakeside or Seashore. It is a smaller plant where management can bring pressures to bear on wage personnel more directly and thereby arouse employees' anxieties regarding what they stand to lose.

The prediction then is that Seashore will be the third to go, but this is simply an intuitive forecast. Seashore is placed in third position only because the attitudes of Dan Ives at Lakeside are known to be highly antagonistic toward accepting this particular offer. It is thought that, out of the four union presidents, Dan will be the last to buckle under.

The agenda item for bargaining this morning, November 11, regarding whether all agreements made by union and management representatives should be written, was debated through to some degree of reconciliation. Much further work is needed on this particular issue; as well as on the next, which is concerned with disciplinary action.

There are two indications of Earl's effectiveness in terms of the union's present preception of him. Max Daniels is a union official who has great intellectual competence and comprehension of the issues. As far back as two months ago, he recognized that management was beginning to behave differently. Since then, he has formed a good deal of respect and trust for management and believes that its bargaining team members are making a constructive effort toward resolving problems that have been sources of friction for too long.

Today, however, he said to Frances Dunn of the Personnel Department, "Earl Higgins is going to bust up this bargaining real fast."

Another reaction came from Dick Kelly, the union team's chairman. He got with Wes at the end of the morning to discuss an incident that occurred during bargaining.

Recently, not wanting to miss any of the bargaining, Dick arranged to postpone his vacation—which was to have been taken before the end of the year—to sometime in the next year. To make the arrangements, Dick and Dan met with Hal Harvey and Earl Higgins, who were Engineering's department and assistant department heads at the time. The four of them came to a private agreement that under the circumstances Dick's vacation would be carried into the next year. Since this was such an unusual procedure, which technically breached an existing agreement that annual vacation should be scheduled within the respective calendar year and not carried over, both the union and the management members agreed to keep the arrangement private. A few other members of management such as Wes and Mac from Personnel were apprised of the action, and all agreed that it was an appropriate and proper thing to do.

This morning one topic was whether or not all contract agreements should be in writing. The union wished to reduce the number of oral agreements or, hopefully, to eliminate them completely. As long as they are oral agreements, management can put pressure on weak union representatives to make exceptions to the contract, or even violate its provisions repeatedly. The union doesn't know what is going on unless it gets a record of whatever transactions constitute side agreements to the contract proper. In debating the issue, Earl used the example of Dick's postponed vacation to test with the union group whether this is the kind of thing they would like in written terms, or whether they would prefer to keep it as a gentleman's agreement in verbal terms outside of written contract language. Dick immediately felt that there had been a violation of trust, but was at a loss to know how to react when Earl made the announcement. Dick finally rose to his feet and said, "Look, you fellows can't understand what Earl is saying. Let me tell you what the story is . . ." They tested it and determined that this was the kind of thing they would like to maintain as a verbal agreement rather than putting it in writing.

At the end of the morning, Dick came to Wes and said, "We just can't put up with this kind of behavior by Earl. You know that it was a gentleman's agreement. He violated confidentiality in the presence of all the members."

Wes said, "I agree it was an inappropriate thing for Earl to do. Would you like for me to talk to him about it?"

Dick said, "I certainly would." So Dick is burned up after only two bargaining sessions with Earl.

What was Wes to do under these circumstances? If he went to Earl directly, who is an agressive fighter, Wes would be backed into a corner. Rather than doing so and having his actions misinterpreted by others in the bargaining team, Wes correctly went to Van, repeated the story and requested Van's reactions as to whether he, Wes, should go back to Earl and give him some feedback on Dick's grievance.

Van said that if Wes wouldn't mind, he would prefer to do it himself. Van has committed himself to managing Earl, and he insists that he can easily keep Earl under control. But Earl never takes a reprimand on the chin. He always ducks and comes back fighting in one way or another, twisting to his own purposes what others see as truth.

Demoralization in the "Backup Committee"

At the end of the morning period, the management bargaining team got together for a brief postmortem to look at issues connected with upcoming topics. It found itself in considerable disagreement regarding the determination of job content, including definition of qualification and the use of progression programs to evaluate the competencies of individuals. Obviously, the management committee was not unified in its consideration of what constituted an effective negotiating position in its impending discussions with the union. The meeting concluded with managers saying to one another, "We need to get together and thrash these matters through." As of now, they have been tabled, or what the unions calls "MacArthured," meaning matters to which "we shall return."

The bargaining team members left and the backup committee remained to discuss further a technical problem on which it was advising management. It was very noticeable that these specialists and junior executives were demoralized. The flavor of their feelings was evident from the way people were slouched in their chairs and the floating nature of the conversation. Rather than debating the technical issue that confronted them, I suggested that they discuss their own feelings and attitudes.

Their reactions were of the following character. "We've spent endless hours debating the issues, developing suggestions and recommendations, and providing the bargaining team with alternatives to consider. These materials are dittoed and made available for discussion and further clarification, but they get neglected. The bargaining team gives itself insufficient time to use the materials we provide. One reason is that bargaining is so open-ended that the team simply does not do its homework. They won't sit down long enough to take an analytical orientation to these materials and debate the issues among themselves and with us. A result is that we find ourselves working with the bargaining team for only the last hour of the day. They're full of what's just happened, and haven't studied tomorrow's topic at all. Instead, they expect us to give them a lightning-fast appreciation of the material and then offer suggestions of positions they can take in tomorrow's session. Consequently, the management bargainers are inadequately prepared to debate with the union the issues that confront it on any day, be it problems of today, tomorrow, or next week. Presently the team appears 'punch drunk.' It has been hit so often that at bargaining sessions it grasps for straws rather than having a clear goal and methods to achieve it."

The overall impact on bargaining is that problem solving is impaired and critical issues are being tabled and postponed. This MacArthurism problem of "we shall return" appears again and again. Since problems are not being resolved, the bargainers must return to them on a second or third go-around; and we are getting a "Panmunjom effect." It is becoming somewhat like Colonel Joy returning to the truce discussion table and talking through the same old problems with the opposition for nineteen months, but never coming to an effective result. Some members of the backup committee said they can see the same kind of punch-drunk fatigue hitting the union, but were unable to supply concrete examples of this. Nonetheless, the feeling that the union is getting tired is the important thing to be considered at this point.

In one respect, there could be an advantage from this fatigue. People can get so tired that they no longer have intense emotions about any of the issues that are involved, and can discuss them more objectively and analytically. But it is more likely that the two sides would crawl wearily to the first convenient mutual solution that presented itself.

As a result of having examined their own attitudes, the backup committee members' tensions appeared to be somewhat relieved.

At this point the discussion took a different and interesting turn. I asked the question, "What is the responsibility of the backup committee in terms of what it does and the difficulties that it faces?" We explored the responsibility of the backup committee to be a "mirror," reflecting back to the bargaining team the image it is creating in the backup committee's eyes. If the backup committee could get with the bargaining team on a process level, then it might be able to confront these issues squarely and to produce a constructive result.

Backup committee members agreed that they should help the bargaining team to see its own dilemma. Although the backup committee recognizes that its perception of the bargaining team may not be accurate, its outline perception is realistic. A full day's bargaining is scheduled for tomorrow, and little time is available to accomplish results. Several members of the bargaining team are in a meeting from two to four and then the bargaining team is committed to a session with the backup committee.

Apparently, time is so limited there is little opportunity to help the bargaining team prepare itself for an adequate job of problem solving; nor is there enough time, if an effort is made in the process direction, for the backup committee to deal with background matters that would help the bargaining committee in the long haul. The following plan was developed. Rather than dealing with this matter between the two groups, it might be best for Mac Anthony to help Van after lunch and before the 2:00 p.m. meeting which Van must attend.

Mac and I went to lunch and talked about how, in his discussion with Van, he might orient the backup committee's problem. Our talk put things in an adequate perspective for getting a realistic examination of the core problem. The plan broke down at this point because Van was so tied up with bargaining, it was impossible for Mac to get with him during or after lunch. Several others needed to see him regarding operations and other problems, and so Van spent lunch dealing with a number of administrative issues with different people rather than being available for Mac.

While Mac was trying to get a word or two with Van, I went to finish off my lunch with Earl Higgins. I asked him how things were going.

He replied, "Reasonably OK."

I asked him about the atmosphere of bargaining.

He said, "The union isn't getting to the point. They know that as long as they keep talking, they're not working." His whole mental attitude towards the bargaining was on the negative side. He had nothing to mention in a positive vein.

We discussed a manager's predictions, because a manager frequently has to make predictions which become actions. He evaluates the accuracy of the predictions through the consequences and reactions that his actions generate. To modify or shift his initial action to some new position means that the prediction was only moderately accurate; a subsequent one has suggested otherwise. If he makes a decision which subsequently does not need to be changed because of the positive results and reactions it produces, then his initial prediction must have been essentially accurate.

I then asked Earl how he personally felt in the bargaining sessions. This did not produce much reaction. I went on to query point-blank how he felt coming into the bargaining sessions when the union had protested his participation.

This still did not bring the response I was after, because he said, "Well, apparently they had agreed to give me the cold shoulder."

I asked, "Do you have concrete evidence that this was an agreement that they made?"

He said, "No, it was just indicated in their behavior."

I shifted the topic again and said, "Well, I really am not asking about their behavior toward you once you got in; rather, I am asking about their threat to quit bargaining if you came in." This was getting down closer to home, and I could tell that Earl was shaken by this question.

He replied, "I don't much care one way or the other. Some people like you and some people don't."

I began digging in fast and deep. I said, "Earl, you aren't squaring with me on this one. You know you cared. It was a matter of serious concern to you."

He said, "To tell the truth, what did concern me was how Quinn, Van, and the other people on our team were going to react to the union's behavior. After all, the union should not have any effect on a man's career, yet this kind of behavior could have a lot of effect on mine."

I said, "Let's not try to paint the picture of an ideal world. If the union, by its reactions to a manager, influences the kind of progress he makes in his career, obviously they do have power. You can't erase this power simply by saying that it is wrong for them to have it. Anyway, I am not too sure that it is wrong for them to have it."

He became more tense as I talked. One thing led to another, and then I said, "Earl, I want to put it on the line. The next three months will make or break your career."

He began to qualify. "It can't make my career, but it sure can break it."

I went through the self-fulfilling prophecy concept. Every time he told me that it is only possible to get agreement from this union group if you give, give, give, I pointed out that he'd made a self-fulfilling prophecy. I tried to shift his mind in the positive direction: toward realizing what would follow if he led the union and management groups back into a fight orientation, as contrasted with the impact on his career were he able to generate the conditions of true statesmanship, and thereby offer leadership to the management and union teams alike in collaborative problem solving. This was really getting to his core. All of the smart staff and phony politics began to look less like the fuel of career progress and more like a lot of baloney.

He finally acknowledged that he had a tremendous job to do and a terrific opportunity, but that he felt woefully inadequate regarding some areas of the opportunity. Nonetheless, he kept arguing that he had had a lot of experience in bargaining and knew the way to go.

I kept telling him that sure, he had a lot of experience in win-lose bargaining, but did not yet know the way to go. My suggestion was for him to keep his eyes open and his mouth shut until he knew the rules of the game and how to react in a collaborative manner under the conditions of relationship now existing.

As we left, I also told him that if I saw him confusing the situation, he could anticipate immediate feedback. He said he would be genuinely appreciative.

My project for the next few days was to create conditions under which Earl could become an effective contributor in labor-management problem solving.

Earl has had nine years of intensive bargaining experience predicated on win-lose theory. From his remarks to me regarding the present bargaining, I don't think he can tell the difference between win-lose bargaining and intergroup problem solving. This is amazing, because Earl has been present at all the bargaining sessions, and knows about the attitudes and unstable circumstances.

This situation is one where Earl can make or break himself. There is little doubt as to which direction he will go: Earl will make himself. Eventually he will become one of the most trusted and respected members of the management side. I have this feeling of confidence because the management team is very committed to constructive collaboration instead of fighting. When it sees one of its members leading it in a fight direction, the team will not accept a disruption of its efforts because of someone who doesn't comprehend or appreciate what it is trying to do. My central hypothesis is that the goal of collaboration, once people form it and start moving toward it wholeheartedly, becomes irreversible. The management bargaining team has already adopted that goal.

Another prediction is that the union will not tolerate being manhandled by Earl. If the other members of management don't get him to shape up, the union delegates will.

Lincoln Lodge Continuation

This afternoon, Quinn's management meeting debated the recommendations that came out of Lincoln Lodge. One suggestion was that there should be additional training, throughout Lakeside, to improve human relations during the coming year. However, a string was attached. It was that the training should be "under local autonomy"; that is, supervised by the respective department, so that the design would meet the peculiar needs confronting each one.

These kinds of conditional statements are always difficult for planners and policy makers. If the general proposition is accepted, there seems to be an accompanying obligation to accept the conditional premise associated with it. But the "strings" often connect to strategy levers that are at cross-purposes to the general intent of the broader proposition. For example, I believe that Engineering Department sees this as an opportunity to spend more time on worker technical skill training. Even though such training may have human relations overtones, it will really be undertaken to increase productivity. This was not the intention of the initial proposal. Increments in productivity are certainly desirable, but the human relations situation at Lakeside could worsen if the Engineering Department re-aligns the training program to give it a crude productivity emphasis.

This situation also illustrates the conflict that can arise when bargaining-type proposals are made. The Engineering Department is manned by several people who have had extensive win-lose and give-a-little/get-a-lot bargaining experience. They are now using these tactics on managerial issues rather than trying to solve problems on an organization-wide basis. They are jockeying. Rather than saying outright that human relations training is not worthwhile, they are saying, "Training is good, but we want it only under conditions that we can prescribe to our liking."

The discussion today in the managers staff group questioned the future of Lincoln Lodge type programs for people lower in the organization. The feedback on the recent Lincoln Lodge sessions ranged from the extremes of "waste of a day" to "the best learning day that I have had in the company." This spectrum of reactions generally indicates how much responsibility an individual feels for organization-sponsored human relations activities, or his comprehension of how attitudes are formed.

It was decided that the top 13 people of the organization should go to Lincoln Lodge for a one-day "leveling" conference. However, this has been scheduled for January 10, nearly two months away, because of various conflicting commitments. I anticipate its success, and I intend to push hard for a real examination at the relationship level. This would not be an examination of "what our operational problems are," but a discussion of "what our relationship problems are," and "Why is it difficult to work effectively with one another, and give one another enough mutual support for programs to have full organizational impact?" Though there were no precedents for how to do it, this was the beginning of team building as a systematic applied behavioral science idea.

We have heard the last of Lincoln Lodge until January 10, and then we shall hear a great deal more about it.

At four o'clock, the meeting of the backup committee with the bargaining committee began. Materials needed by the bargaining team for next morning's meeting with the union were reviewed, but the digestion was not very smooth or effective.

The issue, which the backup committeee had identified earlier, then popped into the open, because Carl O'Brien felt uneasy about the bargaining committee's nonchalance in preparing itself. This resulted in more general discussion and recognition that the bargaining team now needs to step back from its intensive interactions with the union and discuss its own ways of operating.

More attention should be given to long-term goals and to a schedule for mastering the problems of effecting a new contract. My suggestion was for the bargaining committee to leave the negotiating table and spend a full day discussing its own internal situation; problems of team cohesiveness and joint action, its relations with the backup committee, and members' problems of being, simultaneously, both bargaining representatives and line or staff managers with ongoing responsibilities.

Mountainview Union Strategy

Word has reached Lakeside that Allen Eastman, general manager at Mountainview, and Johnny Johnson, the union president, met today, but failed to agree on acceptance of the general wage increase offer. Johnny's attitude was interpreted as being that the union would accept EPOCH's offer—rather than going for 5%—if management would grant the full 14 cents to red circle employees. It will be recalled that at Mountainview, management began by withholding the entire general wage increase from the red circle people, and then it restored half of the increase to them. The union is hinting that if management would restore the 14 cents to the red circle people, it probably would swallow the discrepancy between salary and wage personnel that is represented by the 5%: 14 cents differential.

George Jackson, the head of the personnel department at Mountainview, feels that the union would accept the EPOCH-dictated pattern even if management did not fully restore 14 cents to the red circle personnel. But as there are not many red circle people at Mountainview, it is conceivable that Allen Eastman may agree to restoration so that he can be assured that the union will accept the GWI offer by next Monday, EPOCH's deadline date. The interesting question then is, What will be the impact on Lakeside? Will Lakeside hold firm on its 7 cents withholding from red circle people when its sister plant has granted the full increase?

Possibly, Johnson is bargaining for full restoration of the 14 cents on the assumption that if Lakeside, Seashore, and Hilltop successfully hold out for a 5% across-the-board general wage increase, then Mountainview will also get the 5% when that is granted to all EPOCH plants. If this is the Mountainview union's strategy, Johnson is playing a very clever game. Not only might he be able to change Mountainview management from giving red circle people nothing to giving them all—thus setting a precedent which other unions will exploit—Mountainview wage people will also reap the benefits of a future 5% across-the-board adjustment which other unions, using greater numerical strength, might force EPOCH into granting. This is power operation at its best, and it shows the great strategic and tactical skills Johnson possesses. It is one indication why, in a recent election, he won 80% of the votes.

19

The Union Comes On Strong

In the last Lakeside union election, there were two groups of candidates. The incumbent group, headed by Dan Ives, was known as the "international independents." They pledged that if reelected, they would affiliate with the big ICEW international. The opposition, known as the "independent independents," was headed by Ted Rogers. Though not a forceful chap, he was widely respected as a loyal independent unionist.

The election, held at the beginning of this year, was a bloody affair. It involved intrigue, double-dealing, trickery, and alleged monstrous misdealings. Ted Rogers received management endorsement prior to the election. Taking the broadest possible interpretation of the labor laws that regulate management's involvement in union elections,[1] Quinn went on TV with a pitch for Ted. The international independents barely won the election.

Before the election, Dan and Ted had agreed that they or their representatives would meet at a given place and time on election day and count the ballots. On the actual day, however, when Rogers and his men arrived, they found that the ballots had already been taken from the polling booths, and that the count was underway, with Dan presiding. He claimed that Ted was an hour late and that everyone had gotten tired of waiting; but it appeared to Ted and his supporters that "dirty work" had been perpetrated. The only evidence available, which could not be immediately contested, showed Dan and his candidates received the majority of votes.

There was speculation about ballot box gymnastics, and some affidavits were sworn by people who declared that they had voted for Rogers. In one area there were so many that had each of them voted as his affidavit indicated, Rogers would have easily won in that precinct. Meanwhile, NLRB recertified IEW as Lakeside wage employee's exclusive representative.

Rogers eventually filed an official complaint. He charged that he had been defeated unfairly and asked for an investigation. There was a momentary stir, but the discussion of ballot box trickery eventually simmered down.

Then, in June or July, there were reports that several wage personnel were being interviewed outside the plant, by "government men" who were investigating the allegedly fraudulent election. Rumors circulated for about ten days before dying down.

The wheels of justice turn slowly. Today, November 11, Lakeside scuttlebutt says that Ted Rogers' accusation has top priority in a government regulatory agency. If true, this would indicate legal fireworks in the near future. If Dan and his allies are found guilty, the election will be declared null and void. Then, when a new NLRB-supervised election is held, the "independent independents" may again run for office. Facing them would be either the IEW as presently constituted, or—if Dan's recent visit with Wilson is any indication—even an ICEW affiliate.

All these developments, of course, are conjectural at present. But there is a possibility that six months of intensive bargaining might go down the drain. That is not a pleasant thing to look forward to.

Lakeside management was well aware of the accusations of ballot box trickery that were being bandied about. From the Engineering Department in particular, there came strong pressures to "avoid doing business" with Dan and his associates. I felt that management in general took a posture of statesmanship. It said, "We should prejudge no one. A man is innocent until proved guilty. Dan and the other officers are certified representatives of the people in good standing until some regulatory body decides otherwise. It is our responsibility to act maturely by proceeding to bargain." However, if the election results are nullified, the price of management's naiveté will be six months of wasted effort.

The situation is very uncertain, because consequences are extremely difficult to predict. Academically, it is a fascinating situation. There is so little definition that no one can plan a course of action. Under these circumstances, the management bargaining team can only continue, reluctantly and dejectedly, to do what was appropriate from yesterday's standpoint.

Reactions to the Union Handout

As I predicted yesterday, the union was handing out pamphlets at the gate early this morning, November 12. The handout expressed IEW's position regarding the general wage increase offer, and it also took potshots at Basic Training Services and the TV program that management presented before the last union election.

Early in the day, Dan showed up in the Personnel Department. Wes, Mac and others, in a sportsmanlike way, complimented him on a good handout. Indeed, in terms of hitting power, it does surpass previous ones he has published.

Dan was extremely pleased, and said happily, "We treated you pretty easy in this one. The ones you'll see from here on out are going to be a lot tougher."

In some ways, Dan is like a mischievous and pampered child. He loves to be cuddled and accepted for puckish exploits such as pricking management. His aim is not so much to make management mad, but to make management say, "Well, Dan, you are really quite a clever fellow."

I met him in the hallway this morning and said, "Look, Dan, I am proud to take responsibility for Basic Training Seminars, but I had nothing to do with the TV show." This caused him and some others to snicker. Later on, I ran across Dick and said the same thing to him. He chuckled a bit. Pete Collins of the union bargaining team, who was accompanying Dick when I said this, also got the point—whatever it was, for I couldn't fathom it.

The handout is having quite an effect. Management sees it as a very well written piece, perhaps Dan's best. It is hard-hitting because it emphasizes unattractive features of EPOCH's proposals, such as the discrepancy between salary people's 5% and wage people's 14 cents; and also Quinn's chopping the red circle increase to 7 cents instead of coming through with the full 14 cents. Another reason for its effectiveness is that it doesn't say, "*We* accept . . ." or "*We* reject," but says instead, "To reject it would not be a sensible solution, but on the other hand, to accept it would be to break the backbone of the union and everything that unionism stands for." The implication, then, is that the next step is for management to take, and that to make a sensible and acceptable proposal, management should eliminate the discrepancy between wage and salary treatment and grant the full increase to red circle people.

In the first paragraph of the handout it says, "Time and time again, Quinn has told us there are no problems that cannot be worked out. He is right, providing that you work them out *his* way." When Wes gave him a copy to read, Quinn reacted angrily. "This is a low blow. It is unfair. It questions my integrity." He was very disturbed and hostile.

Wes suggested to Quinn that he shouldn't take that comment as a personal slur. "It's for rhetorical convenience, and because they don't know what really goes on among us, they're blaming you for everything. They're reacting to several setbacks they've experienced lately. Some came from EPOCH, and in each case either you've had to be the hatchet man, or we've had to announce the decision as yours, or we've had to seal our lips to keep EPOCH's role a secret.

"Look at the benefits program, for example. Someone in headquarters set a deadline for signing; someone else, without telling us, was revamping the loan interest rates. So here we were, persuading the union to sign on faith. Now that the interest rates have been hiked, we've been made to look like a bunch of tricksters. We're taking a lot of flak, but we can't tell Dan to aim his fire at headquarters, nor would it be any use blazing back at him. Until EPOCH rectifies that interest thing, our credibility isn't likely to improve. The union sees the general wage increase, the salary/wage anomaly, and the red circle cutback as your arbitrary decisions."

"Look Wes," replied Quinn, "Aren't you willing to support me? Those rates are way out of line."

"The union's tagging *you* for imposing your own solutions. Now, for better or for worse, you *did* come into the bargaining room and announce the 7-cent reduction as your own decision."

"Okay then, I did. It was an important point, and I've intervened only in one instance. Is that enough to portray me as Machiavelli?"

"They can't separate your actions from EPOCH's, so naturally most things are attributed to you. But in some instances you *are* confirming their impressions. For example, it's several weeks since they asked your reactions to the service fee proposals. They've received no answer, and to them it appears you're saying, "Forget it!""

"Hmm. I guess we'd better touch base with Neal on that one."

A Change in Earl

Earl Higgins exhibited a radical shift of orientation in the bargaining session today, November 12. He is being unbelievably quiet and really trying to listen to every word. Earl had a slight misunderstanding with Dick Kelly, but he seems to be getting along relatively well otherwise. Thomas, the black member of the union delegation, understands Earl, and is trying to help him be a more effective discussant.

During lunch with Carl and Van, Earl remarked, "There is a tremendous difference between this bargaining and the bargaining that we did last time."

Carl asked, "What do you see different?"

"It's much less emotional, and there is better listening. People make better sense as they exchange views. It's not vicious and destructive like the old kind of hassling. It is a real effort to look for new and better perspectives, which enable swift agreement when possible and provide an opportunity for negotiation when circumstances warrant it."

Previously, Earl's experience with the bargaining had been vicarious, but since he has become personally involved in the negotiating, he is more able to understand what is going on. When he came in, he had no perception of the management bargaining team's shift from a win-lose to a problem-solving orientation. His initial effort was to add his weight to the fight, intending, after demonstrating his leadership and combat skills, to take credit for the victory once it was achieved. But now, he realizes that victory might not be as rewarding as problem solving; and that the union is not a despicable band of rebellious serfs, but an equal, negotiating partner. He may even realize that rewards of problem solving result from collaborating for mutual benefits, not from closing ranks and going to war.

More Reactions and a Surprise

During the morning a couple of wage people phoned the legal department and indicated their desire to resign from the union. They did not give details, but apparently something in the handout had provoked them into thinking of getting out of IEW. They sought legal advice for disclaiming membership.

About 3:30 this afternoon, I visited with the three Personnel Department people who are responsible for keeping a finger, morale-wise, on the pulse of wage earners. Although busy preparing material for the next round of contract negotiations, they did not know how workers were reacting to this morning's handout. I asked them to tap their sources and discern the general reaction toward the handout. Evidently, they obtain information by questioning supervisors, sometimes high-level ones. The findings indicated little reaction one way or another. Indeed, at two or three places, some individuals had no knowledge that such a handout even existed. The contrast between certain union members' sharp disapproval of IEW policies and actions—as evidenced by the "want out" inquiries—and the general lack of interest by supervisors is one that invites further investigation.

It seems that the handout is only one of several new initiatives that the union is taking. Quinn received a letter in legal language from Dan, which detailed an official complaint that the benefits package had not been offered in good faith. It stated that despite Dan's efforts to procure precise information about the content of the offer, such data had not been made available. Instead, a deadline—with its implications of duress—was set, and the union was given unsubstantiated assurances that the new benefits package would be no less favorable than the present one. It was upon this basis that Dan and Dick signed the agreement a week ago. Now that tightening of loan conditions and hiking of interest rates have undermined the agreement, the union intends to file an "unfair labor practice" complaint with the regional NLRB director, citing the company's pre- and post-agreement actions as instances of failure to bargain in good faith.

Douglas Fowler, Lakeside's legal advisor, who has been studying the letter, says that he has found a technical defect in the union's case which could get the charge ruled out of order. Wes, unimpressed by the legal research, doubts whether the technicality would be much of an impediment, and he foresees an NLRB hearing at which some damning points of evidence will clinch the union's case. One of them is that he, Wes, was unable to answer Dan's specific inquiries, prior to signing, about what the new benefits package would contain. Wes was given very few details by the EPOCH executives who were urging him to get the IEW signed up before the deadline. Yet, well before the signing, as he has since found out, a pamphlet describing in layman's language the ingredients of the package was already being printed!

Obviously this means that EPOCH has prescribed, without prior consultation or negotiation with Lakeside's and other plants' wage unions, exactly what the package was to contain. EPOCH had taken its customary position, "This company knows what is best for you. So we aren't *offering* a benefits program to you, we are announcing it to you."

The Independent Unions Confer

Early this morning, Dan flew to Atlanta, where he met with three other union presidents: Chuck Hendricks of Hilltop, Johnny Johnson of Mountainview, and Ned Lee of Plainfield. In two of the plants, Hilltop and Plainfield, new early-retirement programs, which are less generous than the programs they replace, have been announced. At Mountainview and at Lakeside there is strong resentment toward the 5%-14-cent offer. Since all of these union officers have common areas of concern, it seems to me that EPOCH's behavior is pushing them in the direction of a coalition.

At Lakeside this afternoon, the personnel men are predicting that the wage earners' expectations that "management will do the right thing" will be seriously transgressed if, because of non-acceptance of the general wage increase offer by the deadline date, they lose the retroactive provision that would have given them back pay to October 27. According to this analysis, then, Dan stands to lose very little support if he doesn't meet EPOCH's deadline; instead, management will get the blame. In these circumstances, the personnel men feel that management should get into an active compaign aimed at persuading the wage earners to pressure the union into obtaining retroactivity.

Earl Is Put to the Test

Wage bargaining continued on throughout the afternoon. It is interesting to see the union's new approach to Earl, whose attitudes have become more and more constructive. His relationships with the IEW delegates are rapidly building up.

Frank Graves, a big, hulking, but reserved man, is one of the union delegates. One of his favorite tricks is to take the cap of a soft drink bottle and bend it between his fingers. As the bargaining went on today, he took a bottle cap, and put it between his thumb and forefinger, and crushed it. Then Frank gave Earl a bottle cap and whispered to him, "Let's see you do it."

Earl is not one ever to refuse a challenge. He put the cap between his thumb and forefinger in the same way that Frank had done, and squeezed. He squeezed and continued to squeeze until he seemed close to breaking his fingers. He was defeated and he knew it.

He handed the cap back to Frank, as other members of the union watched. Then, Frank took the cork insert out of the cap's inner side, and turned the cap around so that Earl could see a penny inside.

All Frank said was, "See!" Maybe this was something of an initiation ceremony, with its own subtle message. I don't think they would have pulled this kind of trick on any other member of the management team, and I doubt whether they intend to haze Earl in the future. Today's incident seems to indicate their readiness to enter into relationship with him, even though the relationship is not all on the up and up.

Earl took the revelation of the penny under the cork in good stride. He laughed about it in his warm way, as if to say, "Okay fellows, you win this time, but there will be another round later." I wouldn't be surprised if Earl doesn't come back with another test of physical strength with the same kind of cleverness about it.

The afternoon negotiations were quite constructive. Earl said that in his ten years of bargaining he had never seen anything like it. It was more fun than work. Indeed, this is one of the indices concerning what actually is happening. To the best of my knowledge, no member of management has missed a bargaining session for anything except an out-of-town assignment. They have missed all other kinds of meetings and had many different kinds of excuses, but everyone turns up for bargaining.

The Human Relations Measurement Project

At Green Acres, some time ago, we found that one of the difficulties in getting improved human relations was that there was no system of measuring the status of human relations. It was recommended that an adequate human relations measurement index be devised.

A committee was composed for this purpose with Calvert Carroll as the senior managerial person responsible for servicing the project. Tom Archer was retained as the professional consultant to this project. The committee members agreed that they needed to identify the critical variables involved in human relations. Wally Franklin, one of the line members of the committee, suggested keeping diaries. The assumption was that committee members' own human relations problems would be fairly representative of the problems confronting others. By keeping diaries, and logging the frequency of various problems, an index of critical variables could be constructed.

The project was initiated about six weeks ago, and proved to be a laborious one. The diary was written at night and on weekends. Each Friday, the members exchanged diaries and categorized incidents. At first, it was difficult to expose their diaries to one another, because each diary usually indicated failures in dealing with complex human problems.

As they proceeded, a side effect occurred, one that had considerable significance for each of them. They discovered that after they had broken the intimacy barrier, they began to get useful insights into their own everyday difficulties and relationships. These insights into their own interpersonal and intergroup problems fascinated the members, and revealed to them the importance of an index.

Last Friday, they summarized the group's present position and discussed future action. they concluded that the process of teaching one another, with each learning how to be more effective in his own behavior, was the most important aspect. They decided that this process is so fundamental to improving managerial skills that instead of developing a human relations index, they should design conditions which disseminate these learning routes. Their point, I think, is that if human relations are effective, there is no need to measure them.

One important recommendation was that the best way to create a human relations program for Lakeside would be for the top management group to take the initial action and thereby set the model for the rest of Lakeside. If the top management group realizes its own human relations problem, a critical step will have been made. In a conversation with Cal, I learned that Quinn intends to study the committee's findings at a meeting scheduled for Wednesday morning.

Today, November 13, completes Earl's first week of bargaining. Already I can see a considerable change in him. Earl now seems fully aware that wage earners can think, feel and respond as maturely as do engineers and other human beings. At post mortem sessions he has been booted around by the management team for his tactless blunders, and has been punishing himself quite a bit for his errors. Earl is also trying to understand the basis of conflicting opinions, and I think he is realizing that there are dimensions of relating to wage people and to the union which he has been missing. Soon he should direct his creativity to constructive human relations.

At Lincoln Lodge the proposal was made that the various departments should reinstate the regular meetings with the union for the purpose of surveying department operations, problems, and opportunities for better collaboration. Earl has already restarted these meetings in the Engineering Department. This is a very good step.

I had the opportunity to counsel Earl this morning after one of his combative backslidings. I said, "Earl, here's a proposition for you to think about. You have no equal among your teammates in figuring the union officers' strategies and what their bargaining positions mean to production. But also, I know of no team member who understands the union's attitudes less than you. No doubt about it, the union's positions continually involve win-lose solutions. That doesn't mean that they don't want help in resolving their problems. But first they must know that you're not trying to beat them out of something. It's your periodic hostility, Earl, which puts them on the defensive and stiffens their opposition to reasonable solutions. You're laying a self-fulfilling prophecy on them. Actually, though, they are as subject to change as you are or anyone else is."

Earl said, "I know, I know, I know."

This again tells me that he is troubled and is presently undergoing an "unfreezing" process of reshaping his values. I think Earl's human relations problems might be nearing resolution. In spite of some lapses, he is rapidly establishing membership for himself. He is seeing alternative ways of working. As soon as I have the opportunity, I want to discuss with him the implications of a collaborative approach to operating his department. If we can get the Engineering Department moving, tremendous progress is possible for the coming year.

Before driving to the plant this morning, I went to the hotel to pick up Tom Archer, the Measurement Project consultant. I was sitting in the coffee shop with Tom when I saw someone, whom I seemed to recognize, come in. More as a bold guess than with certainty, I said, "By golly, it's good to see you, Ned," and sure enough it turned out to be Ned Lee, the union president from Plainfield whom I had met on a previous trip there. We chatted a bit, and he said he was coming to Lakeside to see the new computer. I said, "Fine, maybe I will see you around." Tom and I finished up and went out to the plant.

Later in the day, Ned, escorted by Dan, met with Van and Wes to talk about plant problems in general. Ned soon began probing into the current EPOCH-wide industrial relations issues, asking how things were working out at Lakeside.

Wes gave him a rundown on the situation. He had hardly finished his opening remarks when Dan, smiling proudly, chimed with, "Y'see, fella, any time you and Apley can't get your troubles squared away, come down to where we have a good relationship between the union and management. If you really want to find out how to hack it, you have to come to where people know things and are on their toes."

Yesterday, Ned, Dan and other union presidents were conferring in Atlanta, presumably about their common and unresolved disputes with the company. Now, Dan was closing ranks with Wes, Lakeside's personnel manager, as though they were on the same team.

Ned did a double take and said, "Look, I thought you fellows were at one another's throats."

Dan replied, "Oh, we have little family problems. We fight among ourselves, but as far as visitors are concerned, we want you to know that we have the best union and the best management that you can find anywhere."

Wage Increase and Benefits Program Issues

Last night at EPOCH's biggest plant, Seashore, there was a meeting of the union council at which delegates voted 49 to 9 to approve the union president's rebuff to the general manager. Abe Baker had told Will Grigg, "This is a ridiculous offer; it is beneath our dignity to react to it, and we await management's return to its senses." The union council also authorized Abe to call a plenary meeting of the union membership.

So Abe now has great freedom of action. He can ignore the deadline of Monday, the 16th, and if management does not improve its offer, he can call a membership meeting to test reactions. If the assembled members reject the offer, then he can confront management again; but if they vote in favor of it, he can then simply accept the offer.

At Lakeside, Dan can rely on a provision in the contract: that in respect to any general wage increase offer, the union can take up to one month to deliberate before signifying acceptance or rejection. Under these arrangements, Dan is not bound to answer until November 27, so he can wait to see the outcome at Seashore before holding his membership meeting.

In a handout today at Seashore, Abe Baker described the benefits program and the present situation of the general wage increase. He interpreted it as meaning that the local plants have lost their former semi-independence. Atlanta is now exerting centralized control, and so it seems necessary for the union officers to bargain directly with EPOCH headquarters. This implies that a coalition of independent unions may be forming. EPOCH executives would probably view that as a very undesirable development.

One of the fascinating things I've noticed is that people have no clear perception of the thinking and attitudes that are present in EPOCH headquarters, and therefore they cannot anticipate how their own actions will be interpreted. This is "decentralization by policy vacuum." You don't know how to act in the way that the centralized power wants you to, so you must act in terms of your own convictions about the situation.

This morning Dan and Wes discussed the unfair labor practice charge. Wes said to Dan, "I want to make it clear to you that if you take this accusation to NLRB and it comes to a hearing, we will do our level best to lick you."

The unfortunate thing is that if the union loses, this would indicate that the management *did* bargain in good faith when, according to my best information, it didn't. If the union wins, it will have to start bargaining for a better benefits program than Lakeside employees had before the recent cutbacks—which seems almost impossible.

Dan knows that he got taken, though he doesn't know why. He is sore about it and wants justice. Emotionally he is right, yet if he is victorious, he really gains nothing except the moral victory.

It would be unfortunate in a way were the union to win, but it would also be unfortunate were it to lose.

The "Exceptional Actions" Issue

One of the knotty problems on the contract bargaining agenda concerns management's scope for taking exceptional actions, like transferring people temporarily to do work which is not in accordance with the contract's seniority provisions; having foremen do work wage people normally do, and so on. Everyone acknowledges that management should not be bound by protocol in emergency circumstances. In the past, union officers granted management a "free pass." Over the year, however, management has become careless and callous and now typically acts in the following manner. Whenever it has a problem that needs solving—and perhaps the "problem" is only due to poor planning—it immediately hollers "Emergency!" and then takes whatever action seems suitable for solving it.

The union has been saying, "We just don't want to buy your loose misuse of the word *emergency*. If you can give us a definition of what the word means, in terms of which we can test whether or not an exceptional action is permissible, grievable or arbitrable, then we will be ready to settle these matters. But until you tell us what you mean by 'emergency,' there will be no agreements on this point."

Earlier, the union had been genuinely helpful in creating conditions of flexibility under which management had every opportunity to solve genuine emergency problems. In a hurricane or a blizzard, for example, such flexibility of action is indispensable if the plant's functioning is to be maintained.

But management has misused the privilege. So the union reaction is, "We are sick of your taking advantage of us, and now we are going to force you to define 'emergency' and abide by it as a regulatory reference. Then, whenever you propose or take an exceptional action, we will be ready to evaluate whether it is appropriate or inappropriate; and if we find it inappropriate, we will call you down. We will charge you money for it, and do whatever we can to force you back in line. This is the only way that we can ensure we won't be mistreated."

Management's bargainers did not say so in public, but they did indicate among themselves in private that the union is dead right on this one and that they have to tighten up and stop this loose behavior on emergency.

Earl, in one of his efforts toward constructive relations with the union, said that he, too, agreed that the union had a big point on this matter. He suggested management send the problem of defining "emergency" back to the operating units, such as the Engineering, Process, and Chemical departments.

My reaction to this—one of my few interventions—was, "If you ask the operating departments to define 'emergency,' without stating the ethical ground rules that govern your interpretations of the term, you will be dead. Several of your managers who have not been exposed to bargaining still operate on the principle, 'Give as little and get as much as possible.' Their definition of emergency, in accordance with this principle, would allow them to call a flat tire or a rain shower an emergency if they so desire. If you ask the operating departments to do this job, you must also explain your intentions with respect to union-management relations."

I think the point was well understood by the bargaining team. The union wants a definition which is tighter than the bare generality, *operating emergency*. Managers want something which is more restricting on their bull-of-the-woods colleagues than a loose definition which allows lack of foresight to be declared an act of God. It is not a particularly difficult problem but it is a situation to watch.

References

1. These are the Wagner Act (1935), as amended by the Taft-Hartley Act (1947) and the Landrum-Griffin Act (1959). In particular, under Wagner, it is deemed an unfair labor practice for an employer "to interfere with, restrain, or coerce employees in the exercise of their rights under law," or "to dominate or interfere with the . . . administration of any labor organization or to contribute financial or other support to it." Issues of "free speech" versus "unfair labor practice," in terms of Taft-Hartley, are depicted in Chamberlain, N.W. *Sourcebook on Labor.* New York: McGraw-Hill Book Company, 1958, pp. 494-501. See also: Linke, W.R. "The Complexities of Labor Relations Law." In Moore, R.F. (ed.). *Law for Executives.* New York: American Management Association, Inc., 1968, p. 142.

20

Promoting Progress Amid Storm Warnings

Last Wednesday, at Quinn's administrative meeting, it was decided that the top group should go to Lincoln Lodge on December 8 for a one-day leveling session.

Already, Lakeside managers are calling it the "Summit Conference." The Human Relations Measurement Project group, whose recommendation sparked the decision, is most enthusiastic for top management to seriously introspect. The members of the Measurement Project feel that it will create a model for others to do the same. I, too, think it is a very important step, and to explain why, I must examine the impact of my efforts on the organization to help the top group study and improve its teamwork. First, who are the senior executives who have been influenced up to the present time?

Quinn attended a Basic Training Seminar conducted at another place. He understands leveling[1] and the human relations approach because it fits his way of life, but occasionally he bobbles a problem by either talking too much or in non-managerial ways. Nonetheless, he tightly controls his subordinates and keeps close surveillance of minor details. In December, I plan to compare the same months of several different years and study the number of meetings, appointments, and control sessions that Quinn has had. I project he has held far fewer daily meetings than in past years.

Van Gray, chairman of the management team, probably has been as deeply influenced by problem-solving methods as any person at Lakeside. As an indication of my esteem for Van, let it suffice to say that I would select him to head any crucial production operation which might arise.

Although some of Van's personal strengths might constitute limitations in a higher job slot, these strengths find full scope and make valuable contributions within Lakeside. He is a good team member, and never challenges Quinn's thinking. Van is the one person who, on the "locus of causation" issue involving management's retraction of the membership-maintenance agreement, felt that it would be inappropriate for the Lakeside team to reveal that it was acting on headquarters' orders and against its own best judgment. His idea of correct procedure is to accept the conditions of your operation, find the limits of your freedom, and then buckle down to implementation. Once a decision has been made, he does his best to make it work, stimulating team action all the way. He is respected by the younger men, and is frequently imitated.

Calvert Carroll has been criticizing Van's performance. As was mentioned earlier, Cal, Van's former boss, had a heart attack which has limited his activities. He sees Van's success as a threat to his becoming heir apparent to Quinn. Yet, Cal does realize the need for more openness, more commitment, and less complacency among the top group. He has been affected by his BTS experiences, by the Lincoln Lodge programs, and most recently by the measurements program.

Fred Jackson, the administrative superintendent, is quieter and plays it cozy. He is the kind of warrior who never gets involved in the fight, but is always there to divide the spoils. He is never defeated, because he never charges into the jousts. He went through a BTS program sometime ago, but I did not know him then.

Earl Higgins, who is getting a trial by fire as head of the Engineering Department and bargaining-team member, is rapidly acquiring a constructive attitude. He will be a prime target for a lot of leveling criticism at the summit conference, and this will be very helpful to him. In contrast, Carl O'Brien, the head of Chemical Products, has already adopted a progressive attitude by making constructiveness the keynote of his managerial behavior.

Sam Allen is the head of Staple Products. His department's "development group" convened last night and he came under strong pressure from Wally Franklin, his assistant department head, to improve the department's human relations. Wally is a member of the measurements committee.

Bill Jones, head of business service, will also be in the leveling session. He has participated continuously in the salary bargaining and has learned a lot.

The department heads who lack exposure to my personal influence are Wilson Jennings, head of the technical department; Burt Porter, head of services and warehouses; and Paul Simpson, head of the medical department. Paul, although not directly involved in operational decision making, was very much influenced by the development of the Green Acres program. Lastly, there is Randall Cox, who heads the distribution activities and who has a broad knowldge of the total EPOCH organization. He has been mentioned so little previously because he has very few *people* relations within Lakeside. Most of his work is done through direct over-the-phone contact with headquarters and with operating centers of various sorts. Randy Cox has great intellectual depth, and he is one with whom I prefer, almost more than anyone else at Lakeside, to debate. These debates are not controversial, but are of the problem-solving, give-and-take sort.

These are the principal management personalities with whom I have been in contact and have influenced in varying degrees. Looking ahead to the

December 8 leveling session at Lakeside's top management, what would characterize it as an important next step? First, there is the opportunity for each participant to examine and describe to his colleagues his basic assumptions, attitudes, and approaches to problem solving. They, in turn, will feed back to him examples of his behavior. Discrepancies between "self" reports and "others" reports can then be examined to clarify misunderstandings on the part of the individual himself or between him and his colleagues. When this is done, the emphasis will shift to consideration of how *all* team members can interact more productively. Harmonious interaction will result from deeper individual self-knowledge and the positive utilization of such insights; but beyond that, team members—hopefully by now "unfrozen" from their habitual routines—will develop a collaborative culture conducive to creative initiatives. Progress now deemed impossible may be made in Lakeside's problem-solving relationships with EPOCH and IEW. Then perhaps headquarters or the union, or both, noting the new cohesiveness and zest of Lakeside management, will themselves get into the leveling and team-building processes that in turn may lead to further breaks from contemporary organizational and labor-management stalemates.

Bluff or Warfare?

Last Friday afternoon, Dan and Wes discussed the "unfair labor practices" charge in regard to the non-bargained benefits package. Wes asked Dan about the extent to which IEW officers had considered the implications of an NLRB hearing; and what it was that Dan believed he could gain by challenging the company in this manner. Wes put on a convincing "more in sorrow than in anger" act.

But by now Dan was in a confiding mood. He said that Fred Henry, the union lawyer, had told him, "It's unwise to pursue this charge even if you have a fair chance of getting the board to order bargaining, because it would only be a hollow victory. It would not directly improve the security, dignity, or personal welfare of the people. The present benefits program is as sound as anything you could get. All you could do by negotiating on a local basis is end up with a package which might be of poorer quality."

Dan said he had raised the benefits issue on his own initiative, because of Quinn's crackdown on the red circle rates. He then said, "I sent a nasty letter to Quinn but I have not filed a formal charge with NLRB. I am planning to wait awhile. If you fellows restore the 7 cents per hour that you've withheld from the red circle people, then I will overlook the benefits issue. But if you stand frozen like snowmen and don't restore the red circle rates, then I'll go to NLRB and make every effort to get you crucified for your failure to bargain in good faith. So think things over and make your choice.

"I don't want to be unreasonable, but *we've* been treated unreasonably on two counts. One, you did not bargain the benefits package in good faith; and two, you trimmed the general wage increase to correct what *you* consider an improper wage structure. The general wage increase is supposed to compensate for cost-of-living increases and not to be tampered with like Quinn has done. If you are agreeable on the red circle rates, I will be reasonable and tear up the unfair labor practice charge." Later on Dan said, "I am about ready to accept the 5%-14 cents differential between salary and wage increases as inevitable. I think it's an unfair and stupid distinction, but I'm ready to go along with it if the company will restore the 7 cents per hour to our red circle people."

There's a weak point in all this, which Dan did not touch upon: apparently, the 7 cents withholding, which involves some 200 people, is popular among the *non* red-circled. They agree with Quinn that red circle rates are out of line and constitute an injustice to them. In other words, up to 1500 of the regular wage employees think that Quinn's action is appropriate, while only 200 think it is not. But most of the union officers are red-circled. So here is the dilemma: Management stands to lose many employees' respect if it accommodates to the pressure and grants the 7 cents, but it stands to gain collaboration from the union officers if it does so.

Wes discussed this matter with Quinn. Quinn said, "We have got to be men of our word. We said that we would handle this inequitable rate structure by withholding half of the 14-cent general wage increase from those who are already ahead of the others. Do we stand by our policy, or do we act in a soft, spongy fashion, responding to every pressure that comes our way and yielding? I want us to be men."

His attitude is interesting in two ways. One is that it does represent a position of conviction and so merits respect from that standpoint. The other is the belief that to take a firm position and stick to it steadfastly is the sign of a *man*. This personal psychological need of men in a controlling position to give full evidence of their strength is a very interesting phenomenon in itself.

So it looks as though management is bracing itself to hold to its general wage increase fiats, while letting the chips of the benefits-package issue fall where they may.

Early this morning, November 16, I had a chat with Quinn regarding team development of the top management group and the critical importance that I attach to the December 8 summit conference. On my way out of his office, I bumped into Dan Ives, who had a real head of steam on.

He said, "Hello Doc. Now they're going to get it!"

"What do you mean? They're going to get *what*?"

"We're going to file that unfair labor practices charge and we're going to rub their noses in what they've been giving us!"

I said, "Dan, what's up? What's wrong?"

He raged on, "They're rotten from top to bottom. They're a bunch of dishonest, deceitful, scheming mavericks. You can't trust them as long as my finger," and he stuck his finger up in the air.

I winced and shook my head and said, "I'm sorry you're feeling this way."

He stared me in the eye, did a retake, and replied, "I'm not blaming you, Bob; in fact, I'm sorry for you in that hopeless job of yours, trying to shape up such a rat pack. You can't help them; no one can help them. They're a bunch of thugs. We're going to take this one to a hearing and we're going to win, because this time we have government men on our side."

I have no clear idea what the issue was that caused Dan to be so stirred up at nine o'clock this morning, but he surely was. My guess is that he'd gotten word, through Wes, of Quinn's refusal to make a deal. I may hear more about it later on today.

A sidelight here is that there are signs of serious tensions—if not outright conflict—within the union. Last Friday, Sol Sommers, one of the union bargaining members, phoned Wes' secretary, who is responsible for scheduling the bargaining sessions, and said, "May I ask you a secret and confidential question?"

Pausing only to review her private life, Mollie replied, "Sure, what is it?"

"Was Dan up in your building yesterday for a conference with someone?"

"Yes, he was."

"Was he alone?"

"No, he was with Max."

Sol asked, "Who did they go to see?"

"Mac Anthony."

"Oh, okay. Thank you," said Sol, and he hung up.

The interesting question here is, Why was one union officer checking on what other union officers had been doing the previous day? This is symptomatic of something going on, but it is very difficult to know what the clue implies.

Today is the deadline date set by EPOCH. This means that if the unions have not accepted the general wage increase offer by now, the retroactive feature expires. Various unions in EPOCH stand in different positions regarding acceptance.

Lakeside's IEW has, under the terms of its present contract, until November 27 to accept or reject the offer. Mountainview's union is having a meeting tonight. Allen Eastman, the plant manager there, believes he has persuaded the union executives to recommend acceptance of the 14 cents per hour offer—together with a 7-cent downward adjustment of red circle rates—for the sake of gaining retroactivity. The wage unions at four other EPOCH plants have already ratified acceptance of the offer.

At Seashore, union officers met this morning with EPOCH's chief personnel coordinator. He has gone there in response to the union's complaint that it finds local management powerless to bargain, and therefore needs to confront the source of its frustration: namely, headquarters. No word has come through yet on what happened at this meeting, but Abe Baker does have a strong mandate from his union's executive council to persist until it gets a 5% across-the-board increase. At Seashore, the same union represents both salary and wage personnel, and Abe's argument is that it is morally inappropriate for the plant manager, Will Grigg, to treat one part of its membership one way and another part another way. The same argument has been used, but apparently with less success, at Mountainview.

At Coastline, where the ICEW international represents the wage personnel and where bargaining is currently underway on a new contract, the general wage increase offer provoked serious difficulties to the point where last Friday the union gave management notice of a strike to take effect this morning, the 16th. There must have been some progress during the weekend, however, as the notice has been withdrawn and union and management bargaining groups are back at work trying to resolve their difficulties.

At present, it looks as though the 5%-14-cent pattern will stick, except at Seashore and Lakeside. It is less certain that the 7-cent reduction in offer for the red circle people will remain, but with resistance to it collapsing around the entire EPOCH circuit, it appears that Seashore's position will be substantially weakened. Lakeside's union is, maybe, in the strongest position of all. It has an authorized extension of time for consideration, during which it can see what happens to Seashore during the week. Then it can make pertinent recommendations to its own membership meeting.

The Unaccountable Consultant

At two o'clock this afternoon, Quinn's administrative meeting began with Van, Cal, Wes, and myself in attendance. A few matters of minor consequence were being debated, and little in the way of constructive results had been achieved when about 2:30 I received a phone message. Quinn's secretary, Betty Ross, came in and passed me the note. It said, "Earl Higgins is having a meeting and would like to know if you could break away from this one and come to his. Phone him back immediately." I got up, went to Betty's outer office, and phoned him from there. I asked what was on his mind. He said, "We are talking about one of the recommendations from the last Lincoln Lodge conference, and we don't want to bobble this one. It might be useful if you could drop over. Can you get out of the meeting?"

I said, "Sure. I'll leave now." The administrative meeting was scheduled to end at 4:00.

I returned to Quinn's office, and said, "They are having a meeting over yonder, and I think I had better go." They broke up in laughter, and I had no idea what the jocularity was all about.

As soon as Quinn recovered, he turned to me and said, "Now, that is a concrete, descriptive remark. They called, over there, yonder, and you think it might be worthwhile for you to join them!"

I said, "Yes, I think it would."

"Who called, over where, and about what?"

I replied, "The organization isn't exactly open, and the social contract under which I am operating says I do what I can, where I can, when I can, and I don't tell anybody, including you, where I am, at what time, or what I am doing." I said these things in a humorous way, and again guffaws arose from everyone present. I left. Later in the day, I happened to run into Betty.

She said, "You sure have the people confused."

"Why?"

"They don't have the slightest idea of what you are doing, with whom, or why."

"So what?"

She said, "I mean, they don't understand this kind of behavior. After you left, the meeting never got back to its topic. They just swapped jokes."

I asked, "Why?"

She answered, "They see you as totally unaccountable. Whatever you do; they don't know. It keeps them in suspense. They don't know if what you are doing is good, bad, or indifferent. They think it is helpful, but they're not certain. They're not too worried, but curiously enough, they've gotten from your behavior a clearer indication of what is meant by accountability."

"How?" I queried.

"To anyone else, they ask, 'What are you doing?' If they ask you, all they get is, 'I am going over yonder.' They don't know where *yonder* is. They're frustrated, but fascinated."

I said, "We discussed this when my contract was drawn up. Lakeside is riddled with suspicion. An organization ought not be suspicious. I told them then that I wanted the opportunity to free wheel. I am wheeling freely."

She said, "They know it, and they are charmed by testing their own tolerance to allow an individual the freedom to be unaccountable."

I cherish this particular experience as a relevant one, for it defines one of the fundamental problems of organization. Perhaps no one, save for the Lakeside medical director and myself, is free to act in accord with professional criteria. The medical person, because he can read x-rays that the line person is unable to comprehend, feels free to show the x-rays and to tell the organization what they mean. I have no x-ray negatives; all I can do is say, "The situation is this way. I think I want to go and to participate in what is occurring."

Definitions of Respect in Union-Management Relations

At the last Lincoln Lodge conference, Randy Cox, the department head for supply and distribution, made the following point. "We say that we want to treat the union with dignity and respect; but to be more analytical about it we ought to look at the dimensions in terms of which respect can be expressed. There are at least three kinds of respect. One is *social* respect, another is *procedural* respect, and a third is what I would characterize as *true* respect.

"Let me define what I mean by each of these. Social respect is easily exercised in a mechanical way. All you have to do is perform everyday courtesies. You create conditions under which the union can have a decent office at the plant. You say, 'Good morning.' You do several routine things that express your respect for their social situation. Furthermore, you introduce visitors to the union officers, and one indication of how well you have established social respect is the extent to which the union reciprocates. So there are various ways in which social respect can be expressed and understood by everyone. everyone.

"A second kind of respect is *procedural*. Here you avoid tricks, like setting up situations which bamboozle the other side and produce the result you want. For example, it seems unfair to use superior procedural skills of Robert's Rules of Order to corner your adversary. Under procedural respect, you avoid that kind of approach. Instead, you begin negotiations by discussing with your counterparts the rules of the game by which you will establish a problem-solving relationship. Doing this will at least fulfill the legal requirement to bargain in good faith.

"But then to underpin social and procedural respect there is what I describe as *true* respect. Instead of thinking along traditional master-and-servant lines, you acknowledge that duly elected union officers have co-equal status with management in negotiations. With true respect, there is no need to consider the pros and cons of juggling the situation. Rather, you are open, manifesting an integrity which is essential for stimulating others to respond in like terms. Also, you need not remind yourself that 'we have some visitors today, so we'd better phone the union and make an arrangement for them to meet'—but, rather, it comes naturally. You react spontaneously toward your union counterparts as peers, and therefore you're not forced to continually guard against discourtesy. Openness becomes natural and replaces trickery. Similarly, so does respect. For us, at present, social respect is perhaps easiest to exhibit because one can be most deceptive with it. Moving toward procedural respect will be more difficult, and internalizing true respect will require fundamental shifts of attitude for most of us."

A rare opportunity to shift an attitude presented itself a few minutes ago when I bumped into Max Daniels, the "intellectual" of the wage union. Up to now, I haven't gotten to know Max particularly well. I referred to the recent handout which suggested that the money expended on Basic Training Seminars and the pre-election television program might have been used to make the general wage increase more equitable than the 5%-14 cents salary to wage differential that was actually offered.

I said, "Max, do you think I had anything to do with the TV show?"

He winced and replied, "No, and if you look at the handout closely you'll see that it doesn't say that."

"Not outright, certainly. But it *can* be interpreted either that the controlling hand behind BTS was the same one behind the television show, or that two different hands were working separately."

Then I asked, "Max, what are your impressions of what I am doing here at Lakeside?"

He said, "I really don't know."

"I can tell you clearly what my purpose is. The issue basically is whether or not it is possible to enter an intergroup warfare situation and help the people on both sides to convert it into constructive and mutually beneficial intergroup collaboration. In the last few months there *has* been an improvement of relationship between union and management, and I doubt whether this could have happened without the BTS program and my work with management and its bargaining team in the interim."

He said, "Yes, I agree, they're listening better, and both sides have begun to see many areas where we can improve the contract itself and the way it should operate. In fact, I'm personally more interested in administrative procedure changes than in the economic items." He grinned, and added, "Of course, some of my brother delegates aren't this way at all."

I said, "I don't know the details of what you're debating at the bargaining table, but I'm glad, because that's not my concern. Rather, in the issues under discussion, I'm focusing on the question, 'Is management listening as well as it might?'"

"Oh yes, not only are they listening better than ever before, but I think they're really trying to understand what we regard as some basic issues."

I remarked, "I'm only sorry that, as yet, I haven't had the chance to work with the union. Maybe it didn't seem advantageous to do so before, but I hope an opportunity might be provided sometime."

"It'd be fun to try, that's for sure," he responded cryptically. "But look, Bob, we've had a real bad setback with our bargaining relationships in the last weeks."

"What was that?"

"Oh, the subbing in of Earl Higgins for Hal Harvey. That was real bad news for us."

"Let's talk about that some more."

"There's nothing to talk about. It's obvious that he's a slippery, slimy character. And he's too smart for me even to try to contest with him."

"Let me give you another way to look at the problem of Earl."

"OK. What?"

"How can he be helped? How can the union help Earl become a more effective member of management? This is the chance of a lifetime. You see Earl almost every day that you bargain, and each time provides you the opportunity to exert influence on him and help him see the bigger issues of management. Imagine the results of bringing him to a more collaborative point of view. He's an important man in the line organization, and if you could help him examine some of his underlying attitudes—which he currently accepts without question—and to see alternative ways to think about problems, your efforts might pay off in a more reasonable and humane interpretation of the contract."

I am reasonably sure that the thought of helping Earl had never passed through his mind. It was so novel that he did not react to the proposition at all, and so I repeated it using several different points of view to maximize its impact. I think that Max will now look at Earl in a very different way whenever they meet across the bargaining table. Sparked by Max, their interaction may then improve greatly.

Ideally, my suggestion will illustrate to Dan and the union my statesmanlike attitude in asking them to provide the kind of educational contribution to Earl Higgins' career, which only the union can supply. I hope this will have systematic impact on the union by pointing out to it the opportunity to become more influential. Perhaps these suggestions will show the union that I might be able to offer it newly constructive ways of defining its situation and opportunities.

Now we move on a few days. A meeting of the union executive board took place last night, November 18. No clear report has emerged regarding the points of issues that were debated. Wes indicated this morning that apparently the union has no intention of calling a general membership meeting to ratify acceptance of the 14 cents aspect of the general wage increase offer.

The bargaining item this morning concerned the problem of "qualification." The union wants to be able to exert some influence on correcting injustices that may be created by management's decisions regarding which wage earners are qualified for particular jobs and which are not.

Before the bargaining began, however, Dan stated that he wanted to spend the entire day dealing with the general wage increase problems. Immediately, Dick said, "Dan, you got your answer the other day from Quinn. Why do we want to spend another day dealing with this thing?" At this point, the union took five.

When the groups got together again after IEW's caucus, nothing more was said about the general wage increase. A few points regarding layoffs and so on were discussed. Then, the conversation became essentially an interlude of free association on issues irrelevant to the contract proposal. Why this happened, I don't yet understand. It would appear to be a "flight" reaction.[2] In terms of Bion's theory, motivated groups tackle the basic issues that separated them, but frustrated groups talk about irrelevancies. In recent months, successive issues such as the crane, work sampling, the general wage increase, and the benefits program have all mounted up, each adding more frustration to the last one, to the point where a sense of hopelessness is shared by both groups. Even so, there is sufficient communication and understanding to prevent frustration by one another, but not frustration of their impotence to remedy the situation.

It seems that the two groups are collaborating for the purpose of wasting time. They can't go forward, and intuitively they recognize that they have a common enemy—namely, EPOCH headquarters. Whether this is a true explanation of their behavior will have to be determined by more detailed inquiry.

The bargaining this afternoon returned to relevant issues again. In the management team's post-bargaining session I checked out the hypothesis that both groups had been intuitively seeking comfort in one another because of a disproportionately powerful common enemy. The team members did not think this interpretation was correct. Glossing over the morning's resultless interlude, they emphasized that the session this afternoon was productive and useful.

By five o'clock today, I was able to establish what happened last night in Dan's meeting with his governing board. Dan recommended that the union should not call a membership meeting to ratify the 14-cent offer, rather, they ought to let the November 27 deadline pass—and accept the risk of losing retroactivity—in order to concentrate on forcing management to erase the 14-cent offer and replace it with a 5% already offered to the salary union. From what I have heard, the governing board endorsed Dan's proposal, and so there will be no plenary meeting of the membership.

Yesterday afternoon, Earl firmly predicted that there would be a membership meeting. Van predicted just as confidently that there would be no such meeting. One more week is left to determine which of the two is right. As of tonight, it appears that Van was on the track, and that Earl, the authority on wage-earner mentality, was completely off in his forecast.

References

1. "Leveling" is "giving accurate *feedback* to a person concerning his impact on others." Blake, R.R. & Mouton, J.S. *Group Dynamics—Key to Decision Making.* Houston: Gulf Publishing Company, 1961, p. 115. This meaning, of course, is entirely different from either the industrial-engineering or historical and political connotations of "leveling."

2. Bion, W.R. *Experiences in Groups.* London: Travistock Publications, 1961.

21
Onward to the Summit

When unexpected events affect an organization's entire membership and when management decides that intervention is needed to facilitate the actions of individuals and groups, there are two contrasting orientations that can occur: one is "paternal" and the other "fraternal."

Paternalism operates under the premise that "daddy knows best." It implies that one should take father's advice, for he has the best perspective of things. Fraternalism, on the other hand, claims that if you give people relevant information, they can usually combine it with their own problem-solving logic and take appropriate action. Fraternalism operates under assumptions of mutual respect and de-emphasizes status differences.

Although a blizzard has left up to eighteen inches of snow in parts of the Midwest, the Lakeside plant has been operating close to normal production levels. This is an amazing performance because the personnel available is vastly reduced from normal operating conditions. Today only about 65% of the work force has been able to get to the plant. In the last few days, some people have been working sixteen-hour shifts, and management has arranged for them to sleep in nearby hotels because they were unable to get home. A more skeptical explanation I have heard is that by doing this, management keeps them immediately available for work.

In any event, the paternal-fraternal issue is more clearly illustrated by the communication of a special bulletin of weather conditions. How should a special bulletin be written?

A paternalistic management bulletin, in these circumstances, would begin as follows. "All employees are advised of the extremely hazardous weather conditions prevailing. It is strongly suggested that people who must travel do so with extreme care as the danger of accidents is great." Beyond these remarks, additional suggestions would be made to impress on people the arctic terrors confronting them. Then, almost as an afterthought, the management bulletin would list which roads were clear of snowdrifts and those that were impassable.

A special bulletin written under the fraternal assumption of respect and assistance would contain no opening paragraph of advice to employees to be cautious—the kind of advice that an anxious father might give an immature child. Instead, it would assume that licensed adult drivers are fully aware of the hazards involved in blizzard conditions, and give them relevant information that they otherwise might be unable to obtain. So it would start, for example, "The noontime report from the police department indicates that the following road conditions prevail in this area." The bulletin would then report which roads did or did not provide access between the plant and people's homes. Thus, advice would be eliminated. In its place would be factual information that people could use to plan their activities. Under the fraternal orientation, the justification for a bulletin is that people exchange relevant information because of mutual respect and concern for each other's welfare, and do it without patronizing.

I stopped by the office of a communication expert on Wes' staff who had written a beautifully composed paternalistic bulletin. We sat down and discussed what it meant. The communication expert said, "Rather than attributing these attitudes of caution to management, why don't I say the police advise that highway conditions are extremely hazardous, and that *they* urge individuals to be ultracautious during this critical period?"

My reaction was that it merely ascribes a paternalistic attitude to the police force, still implying that people are not capable of protecting their own interests. Responding to this critique, he then put together a special bulletin of the factual type, giving concrete relevant information to help people who needed it.

Deadline Deadlock and Benefits-Program Backfire

Dan Ives met with the governing council of his union last night. Today, November 20, reports are that the 14-cent increase was seen as an unfair offer in comparison with the 5% given to the salary group. The council gave Dan unanimous endorsement for his position.

At this point, there are two interconnnected deadlocks. One of them relates to the invidious distinction between the wage and salary offers. Another is between the Lakeside and EPOCH managements. Quinn and his executives were not in favor of the salary-wage differential decided upon by the EPOCH headquarters group.

But Lakeside management is to EPOCH management as a nail is to a hammer; the nail may not go into the board on the first swipe, but it can't pound back on the hammer. With enough blows, the nail goes in and stays there. Lakeside management knows it can only offer token resistance, even though it feels that the treatment given the wage union is unfair. And with regard to its own situation, management is sensitive to and resentful of its weak authority under so-called "decentralization." EPIC's official and oft-proclaimed doctrine seems to have only superficial influence on operating realities within EPOCH and its far-flung plants.

I am noticing how hopelessly complicated the social-psychological phenomena are that a managerial decision-making group must consider if it wants to maintain credibility among its employees. The context in which Lakeside management must work obliges it to juggle unanticipated, critical situations, thus making the course of events unpredictable even to the people who are most directly involved. Rather than constructively implementing clear-cut policy goals, they are usually groping in the misty swamps of expediency and opportunism.

Quinn has gone to EPOCH today, probably to discuss the wage situation. Wes intended to contact Quinn at EPOCH earlier today to point out to him that the major issue here is not the 7-cent withholding from the red circle people but, rather, the distinction between the salary and wage offers. It is possible that some upward influence might be exerted on EPOCH management to shift its stance, but it is not likely because many other plant unions have yielded and accepted the 14-cent situation. Wes predicts that Quinn, with EPOCH's backing, will succeed in withholding the 7 cents per hour from red circle people. For IEW members, it will be a "siege until starvation." Eventually, when they can't get more, they will accept what has been offered. I predict EPOCH's invidious wage/salary differential and Quinn's red circle cut will remain unamended, but that even if the acceptance deadline for achieving retroactivity is passed, retroactivity will be granted whenever the agreement is made.

A necessary condition for an individual to act responsibly is that he feels he has sufficient authority to implement his responsibilities. People who possess authority but no responsibility are likely to feel weak and ineffective in exerting influence. Irresponsible actions need not be the result of a person's personality problems, but instead may be caused by an individual's inability to exercise the kind of authority necessary for certain areas of responsibility. The benefits program needs to be examined from this point of view.

The benefits program was designed and packaged in EPOCH headquarters with the motive being that if they had a program that covered the entire company, they could thereby take advantage of more favorable rates and other considerations that would apply for fifty thousand people. Details regarding its specific provisions were not released, but a brief outline indicated its superiority over the existing program, which was in effect up to November 1, last year. It was presented to each of the plant unions, via local management, on a "Please accept this" basis.

What the EPOCH designers did *not* consider, until a very late stage in the process, was that benefits packages, insofar as they affect the terms and conditions of labor contracts, are bargainable items. If EPOCH had a single multi-plant union—such as an international union or a confederation of independent plant unions—the overall package could have been bargained and confirmed at the headquarters-union level. However, EPOCH and its predecessor, EPIC, have for many years discouraged internationalization and have actively prevented coalitions of independent unions. Therefore, under the venerated doctrine of "independent unions collaborating with decentralized managements," (cf. Chapter 1, The Shadow of Headquarters), the obligatory next step was for each local management to go through the motions of bargaining in good faith with its respective wage and salary unions and somehow come up with *identical* ratified agreements which, *in toto*, would legitimize the prefabricated EPOCH-wide benefits program.

At Lakeside, Wes sat down with Dan and Dick to get the IEW union's consent. When Dan requested detailed information regarding the package's provisions, Wes was unable to provide it; but on the strength of his assurance that "This package is going to be better than the last one," and his entreaties about meeting the deadline, Dan and Dick accepted it. A few days later EPOCH announced loan interest rates had been raised. Other emerging details tend to confirm the union's belief that it has been sold a bill of goods.

When the union has been completely frustrated in trying to fulfill its responsibility as the bargaining agent of Lakeside's wage earners, the issue is, Do these conditions facilitate industrial statesmanship or do they cause an individual to react in an irresponsible manner? I think the latter is true. Suitable conditions for collaboration were not provided and frustration resulted. If frustration cannot be discharged by direct confrontation, then it seeks discharge in other ways, such as indirect blocking tactics, criticizing, undermining, and any number of things which give the appearance of irresponsibility.

In general, when union officers act with apparent irresponsibility, two explanations can be offered. One is that union officers *themselves* are irresponsible in a personality sense and therefore they are "no good" and impossible to work with. The other explanation, the more valid one in my view, is that so-called irresponsibility represents symptoms of interpersonal or intergroup malaise rather than ingrained individual propensities. When viewed as symptoms, the question becomes, "What are the causes promoting these symptoms?" If such causes can be identified and corrected, then the symptoms should disappear.

Happenings During My Absence

Today, December 7, I came back to Lakeside after a two-week absence. While I was away, routine bargaining took place during the first week and many MacArthur items surfaced momentarily. On Monday of the second week, Van Gray visited the Seashore plant. I do not know the purpose of his visit.

On Tuesday the bargaining exploded into an emotional confrontation. The union men said they'd had enough of haggling with third-class flunkies who were masterminded from Atlanta. Dick charged that EPOCH was using bullfight tactics—sending in its picadors first to harass and weaken the union until some headquarters matador saw his opportunity to step in and deliver the final thrust. Other delegates, referring to Lakeside's industrial-relations history, cited what they saw as instances of management's perennial hatred and active subversion of the union. Management's alleged manipulations during the last union election were described in detail. Dan claimed that he had receipts from the Michigan Restaurant where Earl Higgins had entertained Ted Rogers and other members of the anti-incumbent slate of candidates. This revelation apparently was very disturbing to Thomas, the union official who has been most sympathetic to Earl. Indeed, Thomas, in a brotherly way, has been helping Earl to build better human relationships at the bargaining table. So Dan's disclosure might have caused him suddenly to wonder whether he hasn't, in fact, innocently been playing Uncle Tom to an anti-union serpent.

In turn, the management team exposed many of its background attitudes. They told the union that they'd distrusted its motives in preparing the contract proposal, because management felt many of the demands were so extreme that the union was not trying to bargain, but rather to block any possibilities of agreement. "We're still not sure what you're up to," Cal continued. "Do you *really* want to be a sound independent union, or are you using these negotiations merely as a device for getting your members so frustrated that they'll go international? Who's masterminding *you* fellows—Wilson, up there in Washington?"

This angered the union and they fought back strongly, emphasizing that they had put in a tremendous number of hours, from January through July, preparing the contract proposal. They intended to use it as a constructive basis for bargaining, and were dedicated to independent unionism.

Dan and Dick led the union in a bitter personal attack on Earl Higgins, accusing him as the problem confronting management. Earl remained silent throughout these diatribes, but Van finally cut off Dick in mid-sentence with a curt "Now, hold on!" He said that personal abuse had never accomplished anything and that he, Van, like everyone else, would like to forget certain incidents and try to find an alternative to warfare. The union men, all of whom have high respect for Van, did a retake, and moved to a new topic.

The union officials feel that plant supervisors and foremen disrespect them and unnecessarily complicate their responsibilities. It was charged that, once again, supervisors were making the "springing" procedure unworkable.

Any Lakeside wage man who must be away from his work station for several minutes has to get authorization from some member of management. When the absence is of several hours, such as for bargaining sessions, the man is supposed to put in a written request a day or so in advance. Then the manager contacts the man's supervisor and tells him to release the man for the specified time. When the specified absence is ended, another member of management has to sign a slip of paper, indicating the time at which the contact was terminated. This is called the springing procedure. The technical justification for it is that supervisors must ensure that all key work stations are continuously manned. Yet there are unfortunate overtones of penal control in this system, and for union officials who often must attend meetings elsewhere, it is very onerous.

Six months ago, there were considerable difficulties in "springing" members of the union bargaining delegation from their work stations. The union complained bitterly, and Van indicated that he would investigate. For a short while there were fewer difficulties, but now there are again as many if not more. Dan and the others indicted some of their supervisors in a very personal and vitriolic manner.

The final topic of discussion Tuesday concerned the conditions of history which had served to generate ill feelings. On Wednesday morning, Mac Anthony reviewed the entire course of union-management relations over the last ten years. He and other members of management now feel that painting this broad historic perspective did more to put issues into correct perspective than anything that has been done in the past six months.

When union and management got back to bargaining, around Wednesday noon, relationships seemed somewhat relieved. However, Thomas became more dissident, probably because he had been shocked at the misbehavior of management which was revealed to him during the Tuesday confrontation. Being a person of simple mind and earnest dedication he was horrified by these revelations. Consequently he has been acting in a very maverick fashion and is at odds with his own colleagues.

Part of the problem arises from the following circumstances. The union delegation often schedules a skull session in a local beer hall and tells Thomas where the meeting will be. He says that he will come but then doesn't. His reason for not coming is that being black, he doesn't want the embarrassment of either being refused admittance or sitting in a white-clientele beer hall and being exposed to snide remarks by the more prejudiced patrons. Therefore he has little opportunity to engage in the development of union positions. In the past he sometimes felt that the union was taking an unfair attitude toward management. At present, however, his mood seems to be, "A plague on both your houses."

In any event, during the bargaining last Wednesday he continued to make disruptive remarks, and Dick called for a five-minute caucus. When the bargaining session reconvened, the atmosphere did not improve. The bargaining broke off at 3:30, presumably so that the union could talk further with Thomas about the difficulties he is creating for them. There is a strong feeling in management that the union is trying to dump him. According to management, this is because he won't be a party to union manipulatory tactics. Another reason is that the other union members have found him to be stupid. A deeper reason, in my view, is that he has a pro-management orientation, or at least did have until he heard about the bad things that management had done in the election-warfare period.

Harking back to Tuesday's confrontation, it is interesting to note that when management was harangued about its inability to bargain due to pressures from Atlanta, no member of the team felt free enough to be honest and to level. This occurred in spite of the fact that the secretary had already been instructed not to take notes. Nonetheless, it seems that management is keener than ever to get out to Lincoln Lodge for its own leveling session tomorrow.

Generally it seems to me that the management team has lost its sense of security. This may be because it has been subjected to a heated reflection of its own behavior. Another thing that greatly disturbed management was the union's exposé on supervisors and foremen who treat union officials and other wage men with disrespect. Team members seem to be thinking, "If we are unable to create conditions under which supervisors accord union officials and other wage people dignity and respect, there is little hope of relief from chronic strife." In any event, I get the impression from what has transpired that significant steps were taken during the period of my absence.

Sometime ago I told the management team that before effective work could be done, it would be necessary to come to terms with the union at an emotional level. In turn, they had suggested to the union that a leveling session would be mutually useful. The union rejected the offer, but the management members seem to have kept the leveling possibility in the backs of their minds. When the opportunity presented itself, management did attempt some interpersonal leveling rather than ignoring the union officers' emotional attacks. Of course, management did not acknowledge that it was as hog-tied by EPOCH as it actually is. Nonetheless, this mutual leveling on the emotional plane represents an essential step toward improving the relationship. I am hopeful that more factual frankness will begin emerging now that pent-up feelings have been discharged.

Today's Problem Mix

Being away for two weeks and then returning to the situation and listening to what people tell me provides me with an opportunity to evaluate my role at Lakeside. First, there is no doubt that my point of view has found acceptance there. It is now widely recognized that honesty through leveling is the only way in which effective problem solving can be achieved.

Another example of feedback I have received involves two aspects. One is how much confidence the entire plant management, as well as some union people, derive from my presence. My being here somehow gives everyone the courage to continue the policy I had prescribed. This is not dependency; rather it denotes readiness to experiment with new ideas and to consolidate positive results.

The second aspect presents me with a dilemma. I review what I am doing and planning to do with Jane on a weekly basis, and as a result she is as much of an OD pioneer as I am. This is a critical contribution because she is in a position to see trends, themes, and the "big picture." But there is no one to answer my questions and double-check my actions on a day-by-day basis. If I blunder, the consequences may be extremely widespread. Not only are there numerous problems between these 2500 people and the various groups in which they have membership, but each diagnostic intervention and each development strategy has to take into account the help or harm it may contribute to other local issues. The entire network of personal, interpersonal, and intergroup problems is sensitive and volatile so that correct selection and timing of interventions is crucial.

A third impression I get concerns the primitive nature of the theories available to me for structuring my present activities. Usually, I am working beyond the present-day frontiers of behavioral science, formulating and testing and refining applied theories as I progress. It is necessary to go step-by-step, never letting my uncertainties disturb anxious Lakesiders. Because of the importance of my actions and the difficulty of being confident with my decisions, the Lakeside assignment is both challenging and threatening.

Today Mac Anthony and I discussed the springing problem. I said it was reprehensible for Lakeside management to know about this situation for six months, to be aware of its antagonizing effect on the unions, and yet being unable to solve it. I was convinced that something should be done about it, but not necessarily in an autocratic or dictatorial manner. The problem is that plant supervisors are harassing union officers by failing to pass on work-release messages to them. Making supervisors answerable for such conduct is a matter of simple decency.

I suggested that Mac discuss this matter with Van. Supervisors or foremen who fail to execute their responsibilities in this area should be invited to Quinn's office to explain why the failure occurred.

Mac took my comments seriously. He saw Van and made the point, as Van listened, stone-faced and silent. When Mac began to reiterate, Van said, "You don't have to repeat it, Mac; I understand what you're saying and you've sold me. But I have one suggestion. There is only one difference between what you propose and what I would like to do. I don't want those supervisors to be called on Quinn's carpet; I want those supervisors to come to *my* office, not Quinn's, and explain their behavior to *me*." It remains to be seen whether Van will take the needed actions to set up this taut-ship procedure, but I predict he will.

Leaving work today, I ran into Mac again. He said that Anderson, the secretary of the management bargaining team, is convinced that there has been a general stiffening of management's position since Earl Higgins replaced Hal Harvey. Anderson feels, and Mac agrees, that this is because of the "chemistry" between Earl and Van. Earl Higgins began with the company many years ago as a carpenter's helper, and only after some years did he go on to complete an academic education. Out of this background, two conflicting themes have emerged to typify his behavior. One is that he conceives himself as the expert on how the average wage man thinks. The other is that he tends to reject the wage man. In a way, I think he is repudiating his own origins. The odd contrast between his apparently genuine feelings of friendship for Thomas on the one hand, and his edgy relations with the white officers of the union on the other hand, might support the rejection-of-origins theory. Thomas is not visibly what Earl might have become but the others are. In any event, Earl seems to have no awareness of these mechanisms.

Being a magnetic person, vocal and aggressive, he is able to exert a stiffening effect on Van, who—though not having risen from the ranks himself—is similar to Earl. Van was a famous baseball player in college. Thereafter he joined one of the toughest construction outfits in this country; a company where you produce or perish. It specialized in building immense and complicated industrial plants under tremendous efficiency pressures and deadlines. There is a deep rapport between Earl and Van which, from Van's side, seems to flourish undisturbed by Earl's frequent departures from constructiveness during and after the bargaining session.

As the bargaining has gone on, a most interesting series of events have happened. During the first part of October, Max Daniels, the theoretician on the union staff, began showing signs of demoralization. He told Mac that he was dissatisfied with the bargaining, because he felt that although management was honestly trying to take a new and better approach, the union was not responding constructively. He hinted to Mac that he was thinking about resigning. After his holidays, though, he decided to return and has since been an outstanding member of the committee.

Then Dick Kelly, chairman of the union delegation, became highly frustrated and aggressive and spoke of resigning. I don't know how the union dealt with this internal problem, but Dick is still chairman. Whereas previously he was criticized by management as being a person who couldn't use common sense, he is now seen as something of an elder statesman; a person who has his eye on the big picture and is making a constructive effort toward cooperation.

In the past few days, it has been Thomas who, due to the Tuesday and Wednesday confrontations, became alienated from both groups and wanted to withdraw. Yesterday afternoon, he planned to write a letter to Quinn expressing his feelings, and also to send another version of the letter to Dan tendering his resignation.

Last night, Thomas phoned Earl, and after a long talk Earl persuaded him to overlook Earl's and other managers' tactics during the union election several months back. This morning, Tuesday, at the beginning of bargaining, the union took another caucus and spent an hour and a half discussing its problems with Thomas. When they returned, Thomas seemed considerably relieved. We have since heard that he wants to remain as a member of the delegation, having been assured that his contribution is substantial.

In the same period as these problems have developed, Dan has become more vocal and in some respects more abusive. I discussed this with the management team, and we concluded that Dan is still oriented to win-lose terms. He feels threatened because members of his group, who previously were under his discipline, have now gained a certain freedom and perspective under which they act differently. Dan is the last important union official to change. He is still acting as all of the others used to, but even more intensely. He battles at the bargaining table, and elsewhere, with more fervor and animosity than before.

I think he is doing this because he no longer feels the security of colleague support. If so, he is undergoing an unfreezing process too. Presently he doesn't know which way or how to shift his behavior, and perhaps is threatened by the thought of doing so. Like the others, he might soon exhibit a dramatic demoralization. Then, if there is a pattern to these phenomena, he should reorient himself to the idea that management intends to work earnestly with the union to produce an excellent contract. Then he too will shift to adopting a problem-solving approach.

Pre-Summit Considerations

The management leveling session, originally scheduled for December 8, is to be held the day after tomorrow. For several weeks it has been referred to throughout Lakeside as the Summit Conference. An interesting aspect of individual preparations for it is that tomorrow I have been asked to hold separate interviews with Quinn, Wes, Carl, Fred, and a couple of others. Apparently, they want to have a pre-think of the issues at hand, because there is a general feeling that great chips are involved.

Tonight I am thinking seriously about the kind of kick-off statement I should make on Wednesday morning. It seems to me that Lakeside management has gotten almost to a point of no return and is circling undecidedly. It has gone some way toward humanizing its behavior and developing a constructive relationship with the union, but at present it lacks the vigor and determination necessary for completing the journey. The territory over which it is now hovering is too marshy to settle upon; management must either regenerate enough impetus to continue forward or else turn around and go back.

From this halfway hovering point, the past state of affairs may seem more attractive than the future. Notwithstanding all its defects, the past is at least familiar. The future hides the unknown; and the longer management circles around at this halfway point, the more uninviting such a future might seem.

Yet if management could gain a clearer idea of its purposive destination, such doubts would vanish. Minds presently immobilized by anxiety would grasp the positive necessities involved in achieving progress. After all, these are mostly line managers; they are committed to and thrive on "doing things." As engineers they are highly competent in "going to" machinery and materials. As managers and by natural analogy in a production sense, they have tended to "do to" people as well, with unfortunate consequences. Their present uncertainties center in the novel domain of "doing with" people. I will use these points in my opening on Wednesday morning.

Even Mac Anthony was apprehensive about the prospects. He insists that the situation will not open up, and even though it is a "summit conference," there will be no leveling. It will resemble the 1955 Geneva fiasco[1] with participants playing their cards close to the chest and retaining a deceptive covering. Why? According to Mac, "Nobody could criticize a man in a year for having said an honest thing, if he didn't say it. But everyone a year from now could criticize a man for saying an honest thing if what he proclaimed did not develop. If you do a force-field analysis, I think you stand to gain everything by being closed; and all you stand to gain by being open is that you might improve the present situation, and even then you may not receive credit." Beyond these considerations, according to Mac, it is expected that Quinn will start the conference with a speech that will do little to ease the task confronting Lakeside management.

As of tonight, December 8, there is a good deal of hesitation, concern, threat, anxiety and uncertainty with respect to tomorrow's meeting. During the day I conferred with eight of the thirteen participants, each trying to discover what he would be risking if he opened himself up. Tomorrow will decide whether Lakeside management is ready to abort its "hovering circle" and move toward an enlightened new era of labor relations.

References

1. The course of events leading up to the 1955 Geneva conference of heads of state is described in Rostow, W.W. *The United States in the World Arena.* New York: Simon and Schuster (Clarion Books), 1969 (originally published, 1960), pp. 346-347. Contrasting accounts of the conference and of one another's approaches, by leading participants, are available in Eisenhower, D.D. *Mandate for Change.* New York: Doubleday, 1963, pp. 511-527; Khrushchev, N.S. (translated and edited by Strobe Talbott), *Khrushchev Remembers.* Boston: Little, Brown and Company, 1970, Chapter 13; Macmillan, H. *Tides of Fortune 1945-1955.* New York: Harper & Row, 1969, pp. 616-623.

22

The Summit Needn't be the Ceiling

I had proposed a simple procedure for use in the initial "summit" leveling conference. Each individual would provide a thumbnail sketch of his methods and problems of operations. He would also be required to describe how he feels he is seen by those present at the session. This would allow the other members to give him constructive feedback on how *they* see his performance and problems.

The rationale for this procedure is that from the standpoint of interpersonal and team collaboration, every man needs to understand others and needs others to understand him. Of course, this merely perpetuates the *status quo;* the bonus benefits of individual and team development begin to emerge as colleagues suggest and discuss improvements.

The "leveling" concept inherent in this procedure helps to unfreeze a problem-ridden group. The informal social structure, the web of interrelationships, and the self-perceptions of individuals need to be evaluated in a plenary meeting to provide the opportunity for constructive action. When a group has explored its own interpersonal perceptions and attitudes and has reached some level of openness, people become more direct in expressing themselves. There is less motivation for covert manipulation. Anyone who has reservations about suggested actions is more likely to speak his piece rather than shrug his shoulders and fall in step with the rest. Moreover, he and the others will address the issues and not get sidetracked into endless bickering. Openness in debate means that personality traits no longer block group members from resolving objective problems. A situation of "everyone can win" replaces one that was formerly characterized by win-lose.

The first one to level and be leveled with on Wednesday morning was Wes Stratton. He said that he had joined Lakeside to help improve its personnel work and industrial relations, but ran into a wall of resistance. He remarked that if he can't accomplish his objective through collaboration he generally uses power. No one disagreed with this self-analysis. All did agree that he had given an accurate portrayal of what he had done and that this pressuring and power pushing had produced considerable trouble.

The other people added several more things that they felt had caused trouble. "What you do in a decision-making session is to push hard for your point of view. If the final agreement doesn't go your way, you refuse to do what has to be done. For an organization to be effective you have to close ranks with the others and make things work. Rather than following through, Wes, you sit around and hope it will fail. Maybe you even give it a little help in that direction. Then you say, 'See, you didn't listen to me. If you had done it my way, you would have gotten the desired result. You didn't. Now you're in a mess and have to bail yourselves out.' "

Other members went on to say, "This behavior makes it very hard for us to work together. We always feel that we are under your microscope of judgment. You put your magnifying glass on every decision we make. You are always criticizing and looking for failures and bad side effects from decisions which you participated in but didn't commit yourself to. This lopsided viewpoint makes for tough relationships."

Wes agreed.

Someone else added, "One of the difficulties of working with you, Wes, stems from your 'know-it-all expert' type of attitude. You don't confer with us when your personnel expertise is overridden because of more salient operational necessities; you instead have a tendency to appeal to higher authorities, even if this means going out of channels."

In accordance with the ground rules of the leveling session and my non-membership role as its facilitator, I abstained from commenting. However, my own diagnosis is that Wes represents a different thematic orientation than those around him. He is a personnel specialist, a staff man; whereas they are engineers and line managers. His main focus is on human relations, yet he is working with people for whom efficient production is the means and ends, and to whom human relations aspects often appear irrelevant or even counterproductive. Furthermore, as engineers, they belong to this great corporation's "chosen race." So basically there is an *intergroup* staff/line problem affecting Wes' integration into Lakeside's top team. His own inability to deal with the intergroup problem causes it to get worse. When this intergroup conflict appears—particularly when efficiency/human relations cleavages appear—he withdraws from team membership and has heightened feelings of being a member of a rejected outgroup. He then aligns himself to the *power* rather than being a good *peer,* and tries to manipulate authority. In these ways, he continues to keep himself separated from the team, and sits in judgment on its performance.

The next leveling candidate was Cal Carroll, the former operations superintendent and currently part-time. As I've already related, Cal is a very intense, driving person. Before his recent heart attack, he was a fourteen-hour-a-day man.

Cal began his self-characterization by saying he was the group's oldest member. He has been at Lakeside for about 16 years. Confidently, yet without bragging about it, he depicted himself as a very competent and knowledgeable person from the standpoint of plant operations. From that point onward, though, he had difficulty in portraying himself to the others.

The picture that he got back carried one significant theme. "Cal," Carl O'Brien said, "once you adopt a position, you become rigid and opinionated. Then it's impossible to get through to you or get you to look at new facts and circumstances. You end with the same answer you started with."

Generally though, according to the other members, Cal has good peer relations. His only other problem area is his impatient exercise over subordinates. They suggested that possibly this constitutes a problem in his confidence in them. "However," they added, "apart from that, Cal, we've seen your working relationships steadily getting better."

"Every day, in every way . . .," I felt like interjecting at that moment, but consistent with the game plan, I stayed silent. Neither Van, nor any of the others who knew of Cal's months-long jealousy-inspired harassment of the operations superintendent, mentioned the problem. Maybe their delicate hints regarding Cal's impatience with subordinates were intended to open up the subject, but if so, the diplomacy failed completely.

Maybe Van and the others were reluctant to risk stirring up Cal, fearing another coronary. At all events, Cal's session concluded in a warm, fraternal way.

It appears to me that Wes and Cal have a problem in common. They both affiliate with authority in that while being highly respectful of it, they respond to authority figures more readily than to the other people. Both are rather opinionated. The difference is that Wes sits around and double judges. When people won't play the game according to his rules, he takes his marbles and goes home. Cal, on the other hand, never quits. He fights back. He retains his opinion under extreme pressure to change. Because of this, he has angered other members of the organization.

Van Gray was next and he indicated that he tried to give leadership to the organization and at the same time consider the thinking of those beneath him. The major feedback that Van got was that he is, in the most literal kind of way, a true leader. When he wears his aluminum safety helmet into a meeting and leaves it on, five younger men do the same thing. He is open. He puts it on the line. He withholds nothing. He really makes an effort to be a constructive and sound force.

The other side of the coin, though, is that while Van has a manly willingness to "take it on the chin" during the rough-and-tumble of operational problem solving, he will also take a stab in the back with equal fortitude and without complaint. Again, as during Cal's session, there was no mention of what Van has been undergoing for several months. So there may still be several layers that need peeling off before genuine all-round frankness becomes characteristic of Lakeside's top team.

The next member discussed was Carl O'Brien, head of Chemical Products. Carl described himself as a person who liked to move along and get accomplishments as fast as he could. He felt that his major weakness in managing operations was that when he encountered heavy opposition he would throw in the sponge and say to himself, "Oh, what's the use? If that's the way they want to go, let's go that way." He felt that this was a weakness; that he should be more firm and stand by his guns when controversy arose.

Others did not agree. They said, "Carl, that is the way you may have been in the past, but it's not the way you operate now. We see you as the most open member of our group, a person who can communicate emotions as well as thinking. You contribute to group effort by becoming a part of it. Your performance makes for minimum difficulty and maximum contribution." They closed out with a mention of some inter-department lower-level conflicts between Chemical Products and Randy Cox's area, Supply and Distribution. Carl and Randy get along well together, but they both need to inspect what's going on down below.

Sam Allen, head of Staple Products, was the next to speak up. He found it very difficult to say anything about himself, critically or constructively. Yet, he appeared to be well acquainted with himself. I was fascinated that others could contribute very little to a picture of him—this in spite of the fact that he has been at Lakeside for many years.

In fact, Sam didn't get the full treatment at all. Unfortunately for most of the day the labor situation had lurked in the background and there had been a lot of pulls in this direction. At 4:00, Mac suggested that since time was running short, they should move on to the next step for improving labor relations. It was unfortunate, because the eight members who have not yet been dealt with, want to be dealt with. Consequently, another leveling session must occur in the near future. As today's summit conference broke up, a number of members spontaneously indicated that this had been the best session of the management committee they had ever attended; albeit that some of them had been at Lakeside from ten to fifteen years.

Today, December 10, there are already indications that the summit leveling session has had positive impacts on several members of Lakeside's top management. The first person I ran into this morning was Sam Allen. Though Sam got some feedback, he was not satisfied and would like to return for more. Nonetheless, this morning he conducted a long human relations session with his division heads in Staple Products. Sam described the leveling concept and the flavor of yesterday's conference, and then suggested that they launch similar efforts to improve mutual understandings and collaboration in their area. Bill Jones, head of business services, also wants some feedback about himself. Like Sam, he got together with his key supervisors for a review of leveling and team development possibilities.

I also saw Wilson Jennings, head of the technical department. He is in a similar situation to Bill's, in that the group did not get around to him at all yesterday and he wants another leveling session so he can share the feedback time. Likewise, Randy Cox insists on having another session to complete the summit conference. Randy remarked to me that he had never dreamed this management committee could get down to brass tacks the way it did yesterday.

Earl Higgins, another of the non-leveled members, also had a meeting with his Engineering Department division heads this morning, and presented them some specific issues for consideration. One was, "How well do our foremen personally know the people they supervise?", and "How can we accelerate the flow of information from ourselves to the foremen and workers, and vice versa?"

Earl told me later in the day that he was also considering the feasibility of having a leveling conference between himself and his division heads. He also mentioned to me confidentially an aspect of interpersonal relations which is well-known throughout Lakeside, but never openly discussed. For the past seven years he and Calvert Carroll have had a feud. Earl told me that during Cal's leveling session, he'd been mulling over this problem but failed to reveal it. By evening, though, he'd decided to bite the bullet and as the conference broke up, he surprised Cal by offering him a lift home. In the spirit of leveling, they arranged a series of private conferences to correct their bad mutual history so that they could thereafter work together on a better basis.

When I saw Cal this morning I noticed that he seemed very chipper, and now I realize why. Hopefully he will also consider closing out his other and more one-sided vendetta against Van. Anyway, his comments this morning were very positive. He felt it had been a fine session and that we should return to those relationship problems we did not examine yesterday. Cal also said that he was seriously considering taking his subordinates from Lakeside for a day to really explore their relationship and operational problems.

Fred Jackson—who true to form had contributed no more to yesterday's leveling than a bronze Buddha, apart from nods and "Yes indeed"—type bromides—said, "Good conference, Bob!" as he encountered me in a corridor today. Apparently Quinn is the only person who is noticeably dragging his feet at the prospect of further leveling sessions. Perhaps he anticipates some undesirable feedback.

My general conclusion is that we have begun to move on a broad front toward tackling deep-lying problems which historically have hampered the effectiveness of the entire Lakeside organization. The leveling concept is fundamental to resolving these issues. Leveling appears to be the panacea for individual management development, team development, intergroup development, and in an overall sense, *organization* development.

While the summit conference will help Lakeside in many positive ways, I don't think I can continue along present lines of conducting a large-scale organization development project that would constitute, to fellow professionals, an uninterrupted "metered" experiment. My main reason for this is that members of Lakeside's senior-management group may go to Atlanta headquarters in the near future. The great reorganization will result in an outflow of some of Lakeside's best qualified men. I would not be at all surprised if by next April 1 Quinn went to EPOCH as Neal Young's number two man. Cal, if his heart problem continues to clear up, might also go, understudying John Edwards. Wes might also be transferred on promotion, to fill an industrial-relations vacancy in Atlanta. Even Fred Jackson, whose supreme achievement has been to keep his nose clean, may soon be gone. Any of these changes would entail a major reshuffling of other Lakeside managers; while if all occurred simultaneously, an across-the-board reorganization of Lakeside would be required. During yesterday's summit conference these uncertainties permeated the background, but they could not be dealt with in any constructive sense.

Another session of the summit conference has been scheduled two weeks from now. I predict that the leveling concept will act as the key that unlocks organizational change at Lakeside. Already all kinds of interpersonal and subgroup conflicts have been exposed and currently are being corrected. I expect that the next big step forward will be to have leveling conferences within departments. Then, similar conferences can be held *between* departments. After a number of these, the organization should be fully unlocked so that the major step of progress, to bring about improved management of operations, can be taken.

I believe that what I am now formulating has essential validity as a basis for bringing about real organization development. The sequence of steps is as follows. First comes laboratory training for the entire organization, which places emphasis upon and gives deeper definition to the concept of leveling. The next step is a series of leveling conferences involving the chief executives, and all of those managers immediately subordinate to him. The third step is departmental leveling sessions, several in number; between department division heads, between division heads and region and unit supervisors, and, finally between unit supervisors and foremen. These would be designed to improve relationships in the operating structures that are charted on the table of organization.

The next stage would involve a series of intergroup sessions, where each department—first, at the policy level—formulates its own values explicitly and its own attitudes towards, say, another department with which it has a conflict. It does this to clarify among its own members where it stands. The contending department does exactly the same thing from its own particular standpoint. As a second step, the two contending departments get together and begin to share intergroup perceptions. As these emotionally saturated stereotypes and norms are examined, it becomes possible to plan changes which will resolve problems in working relations among the departments.

23

More Bargaining

Bargaining was relatively conflict free for the last several days, but today, December 15, it moved into that part of the union's contract proposal which demands a 10% wage increase. Attention then focused upon EPOCH's still unaccepted general wage increase offer of 14 cents per hour (less than 5%), from which Quinn has lopped 7 cents in the case of red circle personnel.

This morning, issues quickly became heated. At 9:30, the union took a caucus to discuss what its next move should be. The management team invited me to join them as they talked things over. Most of them were predicting that the union was about to "take a walk," ceasing negotiations because it saw no possibility of honest bargaining with a local management group that doesn't have delegated authority from headquarters. Dan took these parting shots: "Look, why, in the hell should we go on like this? It's as plain as the scowls on your miserable faces that as a so-called bargaining team you're nothing but a bunch of puppets masterminded from Atlanta. It's sad because on the job most of you are upright and honest men. But you come into this room and start playing games, trying to con us into believing you've got scope to bargain. Well, boys, we've checked around and we know damn well you haven't got *any*!

"Any one of us blue-collar stiffs has more dignity in this room than the entire bunch of you. Y'know why? We *believe* in what we've come here to do. But *you,* Van, I *respect* you everywhere else, but in here you've got *me* feeling ashamed on *your* behalf! Why have you let Long and Quinn turn you into a bargaining phony, a spouting puppet? We know full well that EPOCH's told Quinn not to give one inch or one cent and that he figures to make some more brownie points by robbing the red circle people. If only you'd come in here and said so, we'd still *respect* you. But oh, no, they've given you extra instructions to come to us and make with the froth and bubble, pretending you're bargaining in good faith!

"How does it feel to be a phony and a flunkey in here, Van? Are you having a nice break from running the plant? And the rest of you, how would you like to be brought before NLRB on a *second* unfair labor practice charge?"

There's no doubt that Dan can lower the boom. The impact is augmented by the amount of truth in his remarks. During the coffee break, Van's face was a mask of silent suffering.

The management members asked me how they might keep discussions continuing. I said that there were several approaches which may prevent a union walk-out. They could level and say that they were unable to raise the general wage increase offer above the present 14-cent level because of headquarters. They could also point out that on many matters local management does have complete autonomy and anything gained from bargaining in areas other than the general wage increase will be lost if the union breaks off negotiations.

Management can improve the red circle situation. It could reverse field and offer these people the full 14 cents. This is completely within Quinn's authority. The question is, why is management so firm about the 7 cents per hour withholding from red circle personnel? There are two answers. One is because the wage structure of this plant is out of line with those of comparable plants in the geographical area; the red circle reduction is one means of bringing rates back into line. A related and even more important reason for management's position is that Atlanta headquarters has been critical of the fact that Lakeside's wage structure is out of line. If Quinn achieved a red circle reduction, he would be a hero at headquarters. It would show his responsibility and effectiveness. Headquarters would say, "Here is a general manager who can take firm and definitive action to correct a negative situation." Quinn's desire to please headquarters may explain his obdurate stand on the red circle issue.

The union knows that Quinn could, if he wished, come to terms on this issue. Earlier Thomas had remarked that the union should bargain with Quinn on this point. They feel that the management bargaining team is only echoing Quinn. The union's complaint is that it has no access to Quinn, the person whom they must influence if the mandatory "bargaining in good faith" is to be a reality. The interesting question here is, if the union files another unfair-labor-practice charge, *which* particular breach of good faith will they emphasize? At present they have two options. One is that the 14-cent general wage offer, which represents less than the 5% increase simultaneously offered to salary personnel, has been dictated by headquarters and is not presently being "bargained" against the union's 10% increase proposal which preceded it. The other matter they can bring up is Quinn's arbitrary 7-cent slash in the red circle area, which, according to headquarters, was intended to compensate for cost-of-living increases. He slashed it for reasons unrelated to the union's contract proposal, and the union can claim he is hiding behind his subordinates, refusing to discuss the problem he has created.

Quinn told me earlier he would try to get the rates down, but if he lost the contest he'd take it philosophically as one of life's little setbacks. The second time we talked, he was much firmer, proclaiming that his red circle decision would be implemented.

The morning bargaining session ended at 10:45 because Quinn was to hear employee grievances. However, the management team returned to the bargaining room after the caucus to hear Dick express the union's position, "First of all, we can't MacArthur this general wage increase issue. It has to be dealt with now. Secondly, we feel that over the past few months this bargaining committee has corrected the conditions that used to produce distrust and suspicion. However, on this general wage increase, we know the problem is not between ourselves and you, but between ourselves and Quinn. We want Quinn to face the issue. We know that you are not able to bargain on it, and that's why we want to discuss it directly with Quinn."

The management bargaining team then met briefly with Quinn. They told him that the union wanted some straight talk out of him. He said that he did not want to deal with the matter right now, but would mull it over in his mind. It is this inaccessibility and his lack of spontaneity, clarity, and directness that disturbs the union men. They are insistent on getting Quinn out of his god-king remoteness and into the bargaining arena for a showdown.

This morning, Dan tried to move the bargaining session into a win-lose showdown but was unable, either in open meeting or in caucus, to get the rest of the union members to follow his lead. Odd as it may seem, Dan and Quinn are in similar positions. Dan hasn't worked through his win-lose orientation, nor has Quinn. Both believe they have much to lose if they change from a win-lose orientation. If Dan moves to collaboration, it tells his people that he has gone soft. If Quinn moves to collaboration, it tells people in the higher echelons of the organization that he has gone weak. The bargaining committee members of both sides have found it much easier to collaborate, because it is the leader who takes the rap for failure. They can afford to be more open and collaborative because they have nothing to lose.

At 2:00 p.m., the general manager's meeting convened. In attendance were Quinn, Van, Wes, Cal and myself. Van again described this morning's bargaining impasse. He speculated about IEW's line of thrust tomorrow regarding the general wage increase. "The union says it won't accept a MacArthur type solution to this one. We can't table it for later discussion, saying, 'We shall return.' Tomorrow, they want to know clearly and definitely what your final decision is. And they want to hear it from Quinn himself.

"The union fellows said how pleased they have been with the negotiations, not that a whole lot of agreements have been reached, but rather that a spirit of openness, leveling and hardworking collaboration has been produced. But they see you standing aloof from all this. They want you to come in and come to terms with them."

I suggested to Quinn that he level with the union about his and their emotional attitudes prior to discussing details of the general wage increase. I said that what he communicates to them is the general superior attitude of paternalism based on the plantation-master concept that he brings from Virginia. I told him he ought not to present himself as the Dalai Lama of Lakeside, but as a man dealing every day with other men, frustrated by them and frustrating to them. He should explore with them the reasons why they do not trust him as they do most members of the management bargaining team. Quinn then agreed to attend tomorrow's bargaining session.

There were three issues of the day. One is concerned with the invidious salary-wage distinction in the general wage increase offer. Local management has no leeway on this point, and it seems improbable that exerting upward influence can obtain for the Lakeside wage people the 5% across-the-board increase.

Red circle rates posed the second issue to be discussed. Quinn gave another reason for withholding half the general wage increase from the red circle personnel. This was that the same position was taken by the general manager of Mountainview, Allen Eastman, and was eventually accepted by the union. Were Quinn to capitulate now and restore the 7 cents per hour to the red circle people at Lakeside, he would be traitorous in the eyes of Mountainview. Moreover, it seems that the lower echelons of Lakeside management firmly believe that the red circle differential should be reduced. While citing these reasons for sticking with the 7-cent reduction, Quinn hinted that he would sell out on this one if he could buy a contract with it. It is this slippery aspect of Quinn's behavior that disturbs the union. You can't tell for sure on what grounds he stands at any particular point in time.

The third issue was retroactivity. The original offer to all wage personnel was made by EPOCH on October 27 stating that if the general wage increase had been accepted by November 16, the offer would be retroactive to the October 27 date. However, IEW at Lakeside already had a clause in its contract which stipulated a consideration period of one month. Just before November 27, the union held a meeting of its executive committee, which approved Dan's strategy of pressing for meaningful negotiations on the two outstanding issues—discriminatory wage-salary treatment, and the red circle reduction—that the offer and Quinn's interpretation of it raised. Accordingly, they did not call a plenary membership meeting to decide on ratification or rejection. The matter has stood at that point until the present time. Currently Dan is receiving a great deal of pressure from wage earners who are impatiently awaiting their additional pay. These people are also well aware that EPOCH's retroactivity deadline has come and gone.

Today some Lakeside employees who are members of the international union have been circulating petitions which request an NLRB election, which would empower ICEW to resolve the general wage increase issue.

Management Reworks its Position

At the general manager's meeting, when the issue of retroactivity arose, Quinn took the firm position that there could now be no back-dating of the general wage increase. He said he had been told by Neal Young that the union had lost its chance for retroactivity when it let the November 27 deadline date go by without having accepted EPOCH's general wage increase offer. Wes then mentioned that Atlanta had granted Seashore, the other "hold-out," the privilege of eventual retroactivity to October 27. Quinn was now confronted with a considerable amount of pressure to contact Neal and to find out actually how matters stood. He placed a call and switched on his desk speaker so that we could hear both parties to the conversation.

Neal thought that no retroactivity would be provided either to Seashore or to Lakeside, but added that he wanted to get an official answer from Atlanta. Quinn got annoyed and said that he wanted to take authority himself and grant retroactivity without Atlanta's say-so. Neal indicated that this would be a quick way for Quinn to get himself fired, and advised against it. He told Quinn to hold until he, Neal, got an answer. While Quinn fumed on "hold" and the rest of us sat silent, Neal contacted George Ingle, an EPOCH vice president, whose immediate reaction was, "no retroactivity." After telling Quinn, Neal said, "That's it, then!" and hung up.

Quinn called Will Grigg, general manager of Seashore. I still couldn't understand why Quinn had suddenly reversed field and was now, apparently at some risk to his career, campaigning so vigorously to get the workers' back pay reinstated.

"Sorry, no way," was Will's initial response. Undeterred, Quinn went on pressing him to change his mind and tell EPOCH that he was now in favor of granting retroactivity.

"The important thing from Allen's and my point of view, Will, is to get our red circle rates back in line. The Mountainview union's already seen reason, taken the 7-cent cut, and has accepted EPOCH's general wage increase offer in time to get retroactivity. Dan Ives has held out past the deadline, but he'll yield on the red circle too, if he can get retroactivity. I want to get this nailed down just like Mountainview's deal, and then your troubles should be over too, Will. But headquarters is being shortsighted as usual...."

Will grumbled that he was facing a different set of wage increase problems with the Seashore union, and that giving in on retroactivity wouldn't help him with Abe Baker. "But it *could* turn him around, if you've cleared with Atlanta beforehand and have it ready to offer at the right moment," counseled Quinn. Within minutes, Will was sold on the proposition, and decided to call Atlanta. At Lakeside, we sat around for a while until a call came from Atlanta headquarters saying that they needed to have a three-way conference with Seashore and Lakeside concerning the retroactivity issue.

Quinn and Will began successfully working on George Ingle and Neal Young. From the opening refusal, they shifted to something between full retroactivity to October 27, and no retroactivity. So the four conferees eventually settled on retroactivity to a date halfway between October 27 and whichever date the general wage increase offer eventually would be accepted at Lakeside and Seashore respectively. Quinn put down the phone and turned to us, smiling happily over his figurative half loaf.

Van, Wes, and Cal didn't seem to share his pleasure. What is the situation now confronting the union? First, it has been unable to budge EPOCH from its 14-cent wage-increase offer which is inferior to the simultaneous 5% salary offer. Secondly, it has been unable to prevent Quinn from chopping the red circle rates by 7 cents. Thirdly, because of the time it has spent trying to get into direct negotiations with those in headquarters who made the initial offer, and with Quinn who made that offer even less satisfactory, it now stands to lose at least four weeks' retroactivity, which is a large financial loss to wage earners. These people are likely to get the impression union officers are not effectively representing their interest, which would suggest that they need a stronger union than IEW. And at this very moment, Wilson's muscular international is collecting signatures for an NLRB representation petition!

The situation seems to be moving toward a climax in which the independent union will suffer those three relatively severe defeats in quick succession.

The next topic at the meeting related to how Quinn should deal with the union in the morning. Quinn's initial attitude again reflected his unique interpretation of "bargaining in good faith." The penny-in-the-pocket approach was that if the union didn't bring up the retroactivity issue, he wouldn't either. If it were brought up, he would say that there could be no retroactivity, and then, if they pushed hard enough, he would gradually move to the position now authorized by headquarters management; namely, one-half of the time between October 27 and the date of IEW's acceptance of the offer. He implied that by putting up a good sham fight before granting them half of what they wanted, he could get them to feel that they'd made a significant gain. "In fact, he quipped, "they'll be so busy congratulating one another at having faced me down, they'll hardly notice that 7 cents of their red circle rate rolled away the moment they accepted."

My comment was that these histrionic tactics represented the very kind of bargaining of which Lakeside had been trying to rid itself. I predicted, too, that an opening "No retroactivity" announcement would produce consternation and a raging reaction that may *really* end the bargaining, at least for some time.

But Quinn didn't seem to hear me. Instead, he wanted to add another hooker. This one was that the one-half retroactivity would only be valid if the union were to accept it within one week. In effect, he is offering a condition defined by himself that others must either accept or suffer the consequences for rejecting. We explored this with Quinn and made him realize that it would be more appropriate for him to explain the new retroactivity conditions, and then to explore with the union what would be a reasonable time limit to place on the situation. He saw, eventually, the technical importance of this.

I get the feeling, as do others, that Quinn has an intellectual comprehension of collaboration, but still fails to have emotional commitment to the openness, mutual acceptance, common trust and joint confidence necessary for making it work. This morning and early this afternoon, he was reluctant to meet with the union. Then his mind began to change, and with growing excitement acting as its own fuel, he became combative.

Tomorrow should be a crucial day. It may be the day when local management's weakness and lack of autonomy will emerge. The union will notice more evidence of Atlanta's minute control over significant matters as well as headquarters' sharp win-lose, take-it-or-leave-it attitude. I am getting the feeling that Atlanta's attitudes toward unions is of the nature, "This is our position and you accept it; or, if you reject it, suffer the consequences."

A second thing likely to appear is whether or not the mutual trust between Lakeside's union and management bargaining representatives will furnish enough emotional support for getting the two groups through this difficult period without fundamental loss of constructiveness in their relationship.

One of the most frequent complaints of managers, regarding an international union as distinct from an independent union, is that an ICEW local cannot get into local problem-solving type bargaining because it answers to a headquarters that is far removed from the in-plant scene. This complaint can justly be lodged against large international unions that are structured along fixed organizational lines.

It should be recognized that this is the same complaint that independent unions can legitimately make against a local management, which answers to a distant headquarters where people have little comprehension of the local situation. For example, the telephone conversation between Quinn and Ingle took no more than perhaps 20 minutes. George Ingle cannot be cognizant of the delicate balance between Lakeside or Seashore managements and their respective unions, nor could his position be based on a thorough assessment of the situation. Thus management is guilty of the same "long distance dealing" for which they criticize the union.

Quinn Participates in Bargaining

Bargaining resumes at 8:30 this morning, December 16, and there is anxiety among the management group. My initial impression this morning is that the retroactivity modification will blow the joint sky-high. Noontime will tell, maybe. . . .

It's now 11:20. The union and management are still deliberating. Their agenda includes the general wage increase, union-management relations, a discussion of Lakeside management's autonomy as a company-authorized "bargainer in good faith," and pre-set guidelines imposed by Atlanta. This undoubtedly will be one of the most critical conferences of the entire year.

Now it's evening, and I can review what happened earlier today. When Quinn and the management bargaining team met with the wage union this morning, the issue of the general wage increase came to a head. The union delegates did not want to discuss 14 cents per hour, much less 7, but wanted to talk about the 10% across-the-board increase demand in the contract proposal. Their chairman and official spokesman, Dick Kelly, said that the union would conform strictly to the advice of its legal counsel, Fred Henry. This was to firmly reject the 14-cent offer, and to discuss any misunderstandings management might have about the present impasse. While the union did not want to terminate the negotiations, it wanted to make some points perfectly clear to Quinn and the others. "First of all, the general wage increase in the contract proposal is not a MacArthur item. It needs to be cleared up now before we can go forward. Secondly, we are prepared to meet as often and as extensively as your management bargainers desire, but we have nothing more to say. We have made our position as clear as we know how. Having done so, and until there's movement, we see no need to talk with you further until you modify the present rigid Atlanta-dictated position. We will remain available and indeed eager to bargain, if necessary, directly with your kingpin at headquarters. This is not a walkout. It's not even a recess. It certainly isn't a power or pressure tactic of the sort that unions are frequently criticized for using."

Having given this official bulletin to the other side, Dick settled back in his chair and reminded Quinn that this was the first time they'd seen him since October 27 and that, since then, the union and management bargainers had spent many long hours getting nowhere on the general wage increase. According to Dick, though, some of this time expenditure had been productive.

"We think we've removed some of the old crusts of distrust. We've also made substantial progress in discussing some very complicated matters. If this present issue hadn't been injected into the contract talks, we'd be close to a wrap-up agreement. However, there *is* this issue, and the people whom we represent want it resolved. They're fed up with waiting, and they can't accept the position you've taken. It contains the 5%-14 cents salary/wage differential. We're being discriminated against. You'll never convince us that the cost of living has increased 5% for white-collar and two-and-a-smidgen for red circle people. It's absurd! We've invited you to try to prove to us that there is no injustice in this invidious distinction, and you can't. So it's up to you to rethink your position and to contact us when you are ready to continue."

The management team sat quietly awaiting a tactical signal from its chief. Members were wondering which of the available options he'd adopt. Yesterday, he'd *said* he'd hold firm on the red circle, even though he'd hinted that if it came down to the wire, contract-wise, he'd be flexible. Or would he broach the retroactivity question and bargain toward the halfway compromise that yesterday's Lakeside-Seashore-Atlanta telephone conference had recommended? Above all, was he going to be frank about his bargaining options?

Quinn began to talk, and it was soon apparent that he was giving the same kind of speech he'd made on October 27 when announcing and explaining the general wage increase offer and his red circle pruning. As they listened, his team members dutifully looked attentive and serious, while the union men manifested boredom and frustration. At one point, when Quinn was repeating the EPOCH point of view, Dan turned to him and said, "I don't want to understand you." When Quinn finished, the other delegates packed their papers and put on their coats. Van glanced uneasily at Quinn, then, with sincerity addressed them. "I want to compliment the union representatives. I want to take my hat off to you fellows. In the last few months we have made a lot of progress; we have understood one another's problems and attitudes which is superior to anything achieved previously." There was no response, except from Dan, who said, "Fifty-one sessions for nothing!" in reference to the fact that today's meeting was the fifty-first in this round of contract bargaining.

The character of the present negotiations is unlike that of any previous negotiations. The battle has been to achieve collaboration which would allow both groups to win. Collaboration efforts have now been broken off. The question is, who is the victorious and who is the defeated? As of now, the union is clearly in the position of the victorious group. Its behavior has been superior, its position more flexible, its attitudes more understandable.

Management realizes it is a defeated group. It has only been able to communicate fixed positions handed to it by EPOCH. It has had little freedom to use problem solving in meeting local requirements. This is obvious in the cases of the benefits program, maintenance of membership, and on the 5%-14 cents wage offer. Thus management is the defeated group in the sense of having failed to win constructive collaboration by bargaining in good faith.

It would be expected, then, in management's postmortem sessions, to observe aberrations in a defeated group. First of all, team members turned their hostilities on EPOCH, but soon after, the guilt-seeking discussion began focusing within the team. Members started bickering over the 7 cents vs. 14 cents issue, and it was argued that the red circle issue was central to the present impasse. Some members of management were saying, "This is the only area in which we have flexibility, let's reconsider it."

Others were saying, "No, we are ideologically on solid grounds on this one and to yield on this point would knock wage rates out of line with local area levels forever." The bickering went back and forth on this point for awhile.

Then Earl Higgins opened up on Dan Ives, whom he called "the bully." Immediately, Earl was attacked by Mac who said, "The issue is not that Dan is acting like a bully. We have put him in a position where bully tactics seem to pay off better than reasoned negotiation."

Then Earl opened up a new line in this discussion which was his old line until a month ago. "We might as well meet the issue head on. We can't give and give and give. If relationships have to be broken off, this is as good an issue as any."

Others reacted negatively to Earl's lack of faith. It seemed that Earl doubted the possibility of long-term success. Cal spoke up and said, "It comes right to the question, do we want to develop a strong independent? If we do, are we willing to pay the price of having an independent?" This idea stuck a chord with everyone, but was palatable to none. The *we* implied by this hypothetical statement involves the management of EPOCH, not merely that of Lakeside.

Seashore, the only other plant where an independent union hasn't accepted the EPOCH offer, is in somewhat similar position with its union on the 5%-14 cents issue. There seems to be no more basis for resolution there than here. A difference between the two situations is that, at Seashore, the independent union represents salary as well as wage employees.

As a contrast, it should be noted that a most interesting situation is developing at another EPOCH plant, Coastline. Two years ago, in an NLRB runoff election, the independent was beaten by the ICEW international. In a new election six months ago, there was a tie and again it was necessary to have a runoff. ICEW rounded up 200 more votes, and won for the second time. Management was not happy with this situation. During ICEW's first year, there had been a sweetheart situation with very few points of difference between ICEW and management.

But when bargaining began just after the election six months ago, ICEW got tough. Presently, there are three major points of controversy separating ICEW from Coastline management. One concerns "work flexibility" (otherwise known as "craft consolidation"). The union is holding out for no crossing of specialized lines. Management is saying there will be contract without flexibility. A second issue concerns contracting of work. The union said, "No contracting of work"; management wants complete freedom to take whatever necessary economical steps work-contracting will facilitate. A third issue relates to matters of seniority.

Recently a mediator was brought in and recommended the number of people involved in the bargaining be reduced to three on each side. It looks as though some progress has been made in the past few days. However, last week the union had a membership meeting where they concluded that it would be premature to take a strike vote. However, a strike is definitely threatened.

On the management side there are different complications. EPOCH's board of directors have told the local management at Coastline, "Bargain in good faith, but don't yield on these three points. If it comes to a strike showdown, take a strike rather than capitulate."

Don King, Seashore's personnel chief, predicts that there will be no strike at Coastline. He said, "The international will back down. In the final analysis, it doesn't want to strike. ICEW represents only 60% of the people, and if the other 40% were to break the picket line, the strike could go on indefinitely, but plant operations would proceed without interruption."

Of course, management usually thinks that a union is bluffing. Its threat is not intended to be an eventual action. It's only a scary preview of what they might do, not what they *will* do. I am reminded of the present situation at Lakeside, because Don King also indicated that he saw no other solution except for the union to say, "Okay, we will take whatever you offer," and then go to its membership and say, "We fought a good fight, we got as much as we could; it's not as much as we wanted, but it's the best we can do under the circumstances. The problem is not in the local plant management, our real enemies are in Atlanta."

The three production centers can be thought of as different points on a curve. Coastline is in a win-lose, warfare, slugfest with its ICEW local. Anyone who yields, loses, whichever side it may be. At Seashore, the situation is better, though not much. The salary-wage independent union is telling management, "You are treating us like scum. You have created an unfair condition which splits our membership ranks. We find ourselves in an intolerable situation which is unjust and unfair. We will not abide by your pronouncements."

At Lakeside, the union is saying, "We recognize that with the exception of the general manager, local management is doing as much as it can do in bargaining a sound contract. We, too, are searching for conditions that can promote long-term collaboration, but the offer that EPOCH and Quinn have given us is so objectionable to our people that it wouldn't be ratified even if we recommended acceptance, which we can't do. Try to understand our position and create conditions of basic justice under which we can work together constructively."

Coastline, Seashore, and Lakeside are three of the largest production centers in America. All are coordinated by EPOCH, and all are in union-management trouble. It would appear that a great amount of the trouble stems from inflexible positions taken at the highest level in EPOCH's board of directors.

What we are seeing, therefore, is a very rapid decay of union-management relations generated against the background of uneasiness that has existed for decades. All of the in-plant relationships are deteriorating, and there is little opportunity for the exertion of upward influence from plants to headquarters. Instead, plant general managers have learned that they are representatives of headquarters who carry messages downward, rather than representing their plants and providing information for headquarters to evaluate regarding what its policy positions should be. In other words, the direction of influence exertion is from the top to the bottom. Once EPOCH officers have stated a position, no further debate is tolerated. The only information communicated upward is the "good news" that Atlanta likes to hear. This means that headquarters' policies become less connected with problem-solving requirements existing in local situations. It looks to me as though EPOCH is headed for serious trouble, perhaps proving that a large integrated company with power concentrated at the top earns itself a large integrated union where power is likewise concentrated at the top.

24

Let's Impress Headquarters

About six weeks ago, Quinn conceived the following idea: "Because of reorganization, some key people at headquarters won't know much about Lakeside and the efficiency of our operations. We need to have them learn about us as quickly as possible; otherwise, there is a danger that we will lose new production facilities to Seashore, Coastline or Mountainview. So let's put on a show. We'll have our department heads report on their operations and really impress these EPOCH people."

Quinn announced this to the management committee, which reacted to its quarterback as any good football team should do. "Okay, boss, if that's the signal, that's what we'll do." As the preparation and practice sessions continued, a few team members became discontented with the game plan, and they told the quarterback about their concern. Actually several department heads were trying to outdo one another by developing charts, graphs and specialized texts. Each person was out to prove how wonderful his own department was, with no attention being given to problem areas.

At the summit conference, the department heads decided to informally discuss the matter with Quinn. They told him, "We agree with explaining our situation to the EPOCH executives, but we are uncomfortable with your format of a formalized speech, graphs, figures, and charts. We would prefer to sit down with six or eight people from EPOCH and answer any questions they might have. After all, giving unrehearsed answers should indicate our capabilities to them."

Quinn is of the old school, and wants to put on a performance. You don't trust to luck or to mutual candor an effective discussion on pertinent topics. Rather, you define topics and structure conditions so that the right questions are asked. This ensures successful, impressive results.

Yet, nearly every member of Lakeside's management committee believes that the group from EPOCH will quickly diagnose what is going on: that a show is being staged, exhibits are being unveiled, and that all failures and unresolved problems have been covered up.

With their insights from BTS and later developments, the other managers look askance at Quinn's showmanship. They dislike the constrained atmosphere and the ceremonial routines of putting on a show. They would be glad to help the headquarters group become acquainted with them, but they resent being forced to be dishonest by this format.

When Quinn discovered their feelings, he remained adamant. There is a "sound" way to do it, and as general manager, he wanted it done that way. He wasn't nasty, but he was firm.

The date for the presentation is December 28, a Monday. So far, we have had two dry runs, which have been extremely interesting to me for what they reveal about engineers. Every department head has numerous graphs and diagrams on flip charts with hundreds of bits of numerical information. Everything has to be numerical. The department heads read from their text folders as would a graduate student presenting a term paper—maybe not quite so well; they're stiff, formal, and artificial. The department heads refer to the charts with a pointer, which creates an uncomfortable atmosphere because of its rigid, mechanical nature. To watch these presentations is to sit through an unintended farce.

My first conclusion is that these department heads, each a middle-aged, highly educated engineer, are ill-equipped to sensibly interpret their respective areas of responsibility. The use of prepared texts indicates that the operational details are not sufficiently well fixed in their minds. If they truly grasped these details, they could throw their texts away and just talk. Again, their model of reporting is not give-and-take, show-and-ask, or ask-and-tell, but simply tell-and-show or tell-and-sell. It is a primitive nineteenth-century concept of how you communicate knowledge. Everyone is uncomfortable with it, and yet it is part of the tradition.

Even more indicative of an engineer's mental attitude are the contents of his charts. First of all, there's the question of their honesty. Although they might present some major points of operations performance in a valid way, they cannot be relied upon. For example, no two department heads use the same financial or calendar year in their presentation. Each department head uses the worst year for his area over the past decade to show dramatic improvement. Everyone recognizes that each department head is choosing his worst year, and they laugh about it, but each is acutely aware that his responsibility is to tell a *good* story, not necessarily a true one. It is the opposite of leveling.

Also, charts with any year-by-year irregularity have been rejected. If there was a bad year, followed by a good year, followed by another bad year, and followed by three good years, this chart would be rejected because it has an irregularity. It does not show a steady progressive trend of improvement, and therefore is subject to criticism. Several of the charts do not meet the minimum of a first year graduate student in psychology. Many of the charts are based on highly unreliable indices and the managers know it. The *trend* is the important thing, not the actual points on the curve. Points on the curve are taken to one or two decimal places, even for trend data that are of known low reliability. Everyone recognizes intuitively that it is inappropriate to carry the trend statistic out one decimal point. But since it is customary, everyone does it without exception.

Another criticism of the charts relates to the style of their composition. Raw data are presented except when the information can be "adjusted" to produce a more favorable picture. Many of the adjustments are legitimate, since they reflect cost increases produced by inflation. For example, in order to compare expenditures made on tools from year to year, adjustments are needed to remove the tool price-inflation effects which are not being compared. Nonetheless, the decision to use an adjusted chart, or to have a raw-data chart, is based on which of the two versions has the most steady line of improvement progression. The decision is not in terms of which one makes more sense.

A further criticism is that the charts *are* either raw data, or data as adjusted by a constant factor or annual price index. Consequently, some of them look like forests of spines and prickles, and one can only guess what the ongoing trend line is. Headquarters management, in reviewing one of its plant's performance, would need trend lines calculated and displayed as smooth curves that would not show every minor monthly fluctuation, but show the representative trend over a series of years. This would permit an approximate extrapolation of what might be expected five years hence. When I asked the question why smoothed data were not presented, I was told that headquarters people are very suspicious of smooth lines. They want to see raw data points. I asked why. "Because headquarters people have been tricked too many times by 'treated' statistics," was the answer.

Other evidence of naiveté of mathematical treatment by engineers is in the following consideration. Several graphs were presented in which there were year-by-year fluctuations. The engineer presenting the data had the chart drawn so that the hypothetical line showing the the trend connected the topmost pinnacle of year "A" with the highest point of year "B," and so on. A least-squares computation, of course, would produce a trend line that ran *beneath* the "peaks" as well as above the "valleys."[1] No single engineer in this situation presented a single least-squares trend line to compare with the jagged raw data profile.

I attach considerable significance to what I have seen. These engineers, it seems, are naive about the valid interpretation of statistical material. Up to now, my stereotype of engineers has been that whatever they may lack in human skills they certainly substitute for by specialized competencies in math, chemistry and physics but now this stereotype has been shattered. The general conclusion that I draw, therefore, is that as plant department heads, they are not only relatively incompetent and unskilled in dealing with human affairs, but also their competencies in dealing with engineering and quantitative matters are far below tolerable levels. Although this plant uses complex chemical processes to manufacture its range of products, I know from other situations that there are few people here who have a basic comprehension of chemistry and physics. Once production facilities have been installed by contractors on a turn-key basis, many engineers have merely to function as meter readers, button pushers, production and supply clerks, and maintenance patrolmen. "What happens" within the stills, vats, and pipes is preprogrammed, and so does not evoke either intellectual interest or ongoing concern.

Additionally, to the best of my knowledge, there are only a few in this group who have anything approaching an adequate comprehension of mathematics. Yet many make selective use of data to prove a point that they want communicated, instead of communicating a point of view which jibes with a valid portrayal of the facts.

A remark I heard today typifies management at Lakeside. Cal Carroll said, "We have an Alcoholics Anonymous type of management. We try to get through to the end of each day, and if we can just do that without encountering disaster, we are happy." Another quote comes from Van Gray. "EPOCH headquarters surely is pushing the stick in the spokes of bargaining." It is an effective image which illustrates the present status of bargaining, going neither forward nor backward.

References

1. The "least-squares" technique is described in Ekeblad, F.A. *The Statistical Method in Business*. New York: John Wiley & Sons, Inc., 1962, pp. 534-538.

25

Limbo and Ferment

I am trying to imagine what the EPOCH board considers an appropriate posture for a large integrated company with respect to its labor-management relations. When the raw materials division people marched on EPOCH last month, they were given a resounding "No!" by Elliott Long, EPOCH's president. The board would not change its offer from 5% for salaried personnel and 14 cents for wage people to 5% across-the-board for everyone. The board felt that the offer was suitable and was not open to further negotiation.

In the Coastline situation, EPOCH has told local management, "The three issues on which you're to stand firm—work flexibility, outside contracting, and our refusal to be bound by seniority—represent the conditions under which we intend to manage business. If the union doesn't like these conditions, that's too bad; we won't budge an inch. If they feel they want to strike let them try."

Seashore and Lakeside, the two independent-union plants, where the 5%-14-cent offer has been refused, are presently under the gun. EPOCH is saying, in effect, "You two plants have been giving your unions more than they deserve for years. The general wage increase offer is final; we won't consider changing it. It is your responsibility to convince the union to accept."

These examples of EPOCH headquarters' labor-management mentality are referred to locally as "Boulwarism."[1] This is a concept of collective bargaining under which management carefully studies the problem, comes to a conclusion, and then makes a proposal which represents not only its initial position but its final one.

This is called fair-but-firm bargaining. The message it conveys to the union is that "We have studied the problems thoroughly and our position is strong and unshakeable. In principle, you have the option of proving to us that our position is wrong, but with the data at hand, we see no possibility that you could do so. Yet we're open minded. If you can find pertinent new facts that we misinterpreted, we will reconsider our position; otherwise, it's final."

When the general wage increase decision was made, there were no conceivable circumstances under which the EPOCH board of directors would change its offer, nor has any group brought a new point of view to the EPOCH board that would shift its position.

I now see the conditions under which a large integrated company, centralized at the top, frustrates local problem-solving arrangements. The wage-earners are forced to seek comparable strength through a large and well integrated union group which has the power to strike all of the great company's plants simultaneously. It is obvious that this is the long-term consequence of what is currently going on.

Cal Carroll told me today, December 16, that Fred Jackson will soon be leaving Lakeside to join John Edwards' staff at headquarters. I learned yesterday that a personnel chief in EPOCH has discussed with Wes Stratton the possibility of Wes' transfer to headquarters. It is known that a personnel relations specialist is needed by one of the EPOCH vice-presidents.

Cal and I attended a meeting of the human relations measurements group, and, as an invitee, I formulated what I saw to be key steps that the Lakeside organization might take during the next phase of management development. Many group relationships can be examined and understood in terms of the medical analogy of a boil. The boil produces a tension, but the cause of that tension may not dissipate spontaneously for quite awhile; intervention is needed. It is necessary to lance the boil and remove the pus from the system. Only then is it possible for the organizational relationships, which were disturbed by this localized infection, to be healthy again.

The analogy isn't attractive, but I think it is quite apt, because a personal system under the tension of a boil is one in which vivacity and enthusiasm are reduced, where lethargy takes over. Full vigor will not return until the painful tension has been released.

Since Lakeside's human relations problem existed in various spots, rather than in a single large carbuncle, many separate beginnings could be made locally before each "treatment" affected the others. I cited the Engineering Department as a case example of solving certain problems of intergroup relations between two departments. Engineering's head man and his key members would first have a leveling conference, during which they'd confront and relieve any interpersonal tensions. Then they would identify what they considered to be the other department's perceptions of them. They would also explore the stereotype of the other department that they themselves shared. While these two action steps were being taken in the Engineering Department, similar steps are underway in the other department.

The third step is for an intergroup leveling conference to take place. Here, Engineering explores with the other department how each of them sees itself—its values, goals, efforts, and so on—and how it is seen by the other; as well as identifying each department's barriers to working effectively with the other department. This third step would also include exploring how to relieve certain tensions, and how to extinguish whatever informal and incompatible norms, peculiar to either department, that are hindering mutual collaboration.

The fourth step would be for pairs, trios, and quartets of people, who operate daily across departmental lines, to get together and plan how they can collaborate more effectively in practical implementation of the better understandings that have emerged.

What are the advantages of this complicated procedure in comparison with directly confronting problems of intergroup operational relationships? The rationale of the leveling approach is that until group members can candidly talk with one another, it is unlikely that they can candidly talk with members of another group. A corollary point is that until the two departments have talked informally and at an emotional level between themselves, identifying and eliminating negative emotional stereotypes and normative criteria, their cultures will remain mutually exclusive and self-sealing. If two individuals from different departments collaborate, they do so under the threat of being branded traitors, because each risks censure for violating the invisible, informal and yet highly valued norms that have formed within his own group.

I checked this with members of two reputedly discordant departments, Engineering and Staple Products, who were serving on the human relations measurements committee, and while we didn't go into detail, the intergroup leveling concept made sense to them. Up to now, they have felt blocked, in spite of the fact that they have been searching for the conditions of interdepartmental collaboration. They find themselves prevented from establishing collaboration because of certain differences in norms, attitudes, and stereotypes—differences that individuals can feel but cannot verbalize or objectify and take constructive actions to dispose of them.

On Friday I have a meeting with Earl Higgins, who recently polled his Engineering Department managers about their willingness to hold a leveling session with the Personnel Department. His group refused. I think they refused because they have never talked openly with one another. Probably neither they nor Earl know their real reasons for rejection.

Who's to Blame?

Later this afternoon, the management bargaining team will evaluate constructive next steps to end the logjam. However, this morning, Mac Anthony told Dan that management would place in its next supervisors' newsletter a factual statement saying that contract bargaining talks were in recess. The union immediately responded that it wanted to have a session with Van and Mac to discuss the matter.

Just as I was leaving at the end of the day, the meeting was getting under way. Dan, Max and Dick were there on behalf of the union; and Van, Carl, Earl and Mac represented management. I left before I could get any reading on how things were going, but Mac's secretary said it wasn't going too well. Nonetheless, I believe this could be a very productive conference, because it shows the union management's desire to avoid negative situations caused by inflammatory bulletins.

As of tonight, the Lakeside top team is highly demoralized. It has been defeated in what, since last August, had been a dedicated effort toward constructive collaboration with the union. It has been defeated not by the union, but by EPOCH headquarters, which, by coming in with its controversial general wage increase offer on October 27, threw the contract negotiations into aimless confusion. The Lakeside executives are receiving pressure from the wage union, which EPOCH provoked, and also from EPOCH for not having resolved the situation.

Management sees itself as the scapegoat. By itself, it cannot break the deadlock with the union, and it hasn't been able to exert influence on headquarters for help. It is a frustrated and distraught group, showing numerous evidences of defeat. The basic attitude is that "*We* haven't caused the trouble; *they* have," referring to headquarter's management. This may be a valid appraisal of the situation, but Lakeside management could have done some things which would have lessened the guilt for the present impasse. Had it attempted figuring the union's reaction to EPOCH's discriminatory general wage increase offer, it might have decided against trimming the red circle rates at this time. Also, it might have done a better job in researching the benefits program before asking the union to "trust us and sign up."

However, there are larger and more shadowy issues involved. Lakeside may be in the early stages of a transition period during which a large integrated company shifts from local problem solving to a Boulwarism concept of labor and management relationships. If so, it is a factor which I had not anticipated. Could it be that the massive reorganization is bringing into the company an entirely new set of values alien to local managements as well as the independent unions?

The IEW union at Lakeside feels weak, because it cannot influence Quinn and his managers, and because it knows that Quinn himself is weak relative to his EPOCH masterminders. Since it cannot exert direct influence on EPOCH headquarters, it must rely on alliances with the Seashore and other plant unions. There is relatively good communication between the managements at Seashore and at Lakeside, as well as between the presidents of the independent unions. In effect these two plants are closing ranks because under present circumstances both the management and the union see that they have a common enemy: headquarters.

Seashore management is as frustrated as Lakeside management. Neither it nor the union have had exposure to behavioral science concepts. The Seashore union is making accusations which provoke management counteraccusations, and so on. Recently the union, in desperation, contacted the

Federal Mediation Service. An arrangement has been made, though not yet agreed to by management because of Will Grigg's absence, by which a mediator will be available, from December 28, to relieve the impasse between management and the union.

The rationale of involving a mediator is unclear to me, because the power to unlock this particular impasse is at EPOCH headquarters, where the invidious distinction between salary and wage personnel was created. I don't see how a federal mediator can be of much help in this situation.

EPOCH could give in at this point, raising its 14-cent offer to 5% across-the-board. This would relieve what the unions consider to be unfair treatment of wage employees relative to salaried personnel.

Will headquarters management do this? Probably not. There are some 24,000 bargainable people in the EPOCH company and so far the offer has been accepted by 21,000. It is only deadlocked in three plants: Coastline, Lakeside, and Seashore. EPOCH can say to the three respective plant managers, "It's your bungling that has prevented us from making a clean sweep. We're not going to revise a proposal, already accepted by 21,000 people, to meet the childish desires of those who represent the 3,000. It's your duty to bring your 3,000 into line with the other 21,000."

Of course, the other side of this coin is that the 3,000 at Coastline, Lakeside, and Seashore are members of the company's largest metropolitan plants. The other units are either in the boondocks or so small and widely dispersed that they can't build bargaining strength either through ingroup cohesion or intergroup collaboration.

At Lakeside, in contrast to the other "holdout" plants, and from the union standpoint, management can't duck its responsibility to seek an equitable settlement, because it has spent six months improving its communication with the union. If management is not convinced that its package is a fair one, then management has the moral obligation to turn its influence in a different direction entirely, toward getting headquarters to amend an unjust and unreasonable offer.

Headquarters Report

The "upward influence," officially termed "headquarters report," conference is scheduled for December 26. There will be five people from headquarters: Jim Hall, EPOCH's highest-ranked vice president (manufacturing); Allen O'Dell, vice president in charge of operations; Don Cooper, a vice president, and EPOCH's chief production coordinator; George Ingle, a director and vice president who works closely with Don to supervise planning; and Larry Jones, formerly of EPIC, who is also a vice president. Lakeside will be represented by the general manager's staff group, which consists of Quinn, Fred, Van, Cal, Wes, and myself. Additionally, all department heads will be in attendance.

This conference was first envisaged by Quinn as a situation in which Lakeside management would demonstrate to headquarters how well they were discharging Lakeside's responsibilities as the "swing" plant of EPOCH: one which takes up the slack from various production centers and builds up reserves, which are available when needed by other plants that carry out specialized finishing processes. Notwithstanding these complex conditions of operation, Lakeside has managed to become a basically sound business entity, with good profitability.

The initial idea of trying to impress headquarters has been converted into an entirely different approach. The new theme will be that Lakeside is tackling many difficult problems, about which headquarters personnel need to know if they are to contribute to Lakeside's development toward greater effectiveness. Many changes in the design and format of the conference have been made. The morning was to have been spent on an operations analysis and the description of profit improvement. Lunch was to have been followed by a tour of the plant, with the last hour or so of the day devoted to human problems of operation. Instead, the whole morning will be spent on the human side of the enterprise. It will begin with a two-hour meeting on union-management relations, followed by a private conference of a half-hour or more between the headquarters people and the executive committee of the wage union, after which a similar period of time will be spent with the salary union. A "refocusing session," in which management will aid the headquarters corporate officers to diagnose the implications of what they have learned, will then be convened. The plan of having a tour of the plant has been totally eliminated. The last couple of hours will be devoted to operations problems, as Quinn says, "if we get around to them."

The Human Relations Measurement Project group met this morning, December 18, with Quinn to report progress. As has been mentioned previously, this group has essentially abandoned the measurements aspect of the project, but has become very enthusiastic about the process through which it passed as it sought to identify critical variables that might be amenable to measurement.

The "critical incident diary" method taught them a lot about the sensitivity-creativity area. They believe that if other members of the organization would experience this process, Lakeside's health would be improved. Quinn was impressed with their enthusiasm and permitted them to do whatever planning they think is appropriate for the next step.

Friday morning this group will reconvene to study problems of distribution and implementation of their proposal throughout the organization. This could be a very important session. Already one of the members, Andy Stewart of Chemical Products, is having intergroup conferences with the maintenance chief in Engineering, Jack Smith. These "organizational health conferences" are used to discuss certain problems of relationship which cause problems of operation. These meetings are not for problem solving entirely;

they are intended to create conditions of mutual understanding that could solve the operations problems. This appears to be a very significant step forward.

Dan and Max were away on union business and the implication is that they went to the NLRB regarding the unfair labor practice charge surrounding the benefits program. The union is having an executive board meeting tonight. No member of management to my knowledge knows what the main topic of discussion will be. Possibly a strategy similar to that employed at Seashore will be the outcome. If the governing board says, "Neither accept nor reject, but go on plugging for meaningful negotiations," then Dan Ives will let management stew in its juice. Alternatively, if the executive board recommends that a membership meeting be called, whether for ratification purposes or merely for evaluation of EPOCH's offer, Dan may welcome the opportunity to make a major "call to arms" policy speech to the IEW's increasingly impatient membership. EPOCH may look impregnable—but so, at one time, did the Bastille.

Sometime ago, Dan was asked by the Coastline ICEW president if Coastline were on strike and posted pickets at Lakeside, would the Lakeside workers respect the picket line? He asked the same question of the union president at Seashore. Dan mentioned this to Wes and added that no self-respecting human being would ever cross a picket line, and that he and his union colleagues would see to it that all Lakeside wage earners maintained their self-respect. Indeed, Dan went on to say, a Coastline strike and widespread picketing might solve the general wage increase problem and force management to be fair and honorable.

Today, December 21, Wallace Graham of EPOCH's personnel department informed Wes that the Coastline situation was looking better. As a result, it might be possible to get a contract before the retroactivity deadline, now extended to the 24th, has expired. If this happens, then the Lakeside and Seashore wage unions will be even more isolated as last-ditch holdouts. Indeed, their chances of getting the salary-wage differential settled are dim, and if they hold out past the Christmas Eve deadline, they also lose retroactivity.

Scanlon Approach

Recently, the ERA board of directors took an action which created a climate, and this is my record of it.

Last summer, George Shultz and Bob McKersie made a study of Lakeside and other EPOCH plants. The study was to determine how applicable the Scanlon Plan[2] might be to particular manufacturing operations. Shultz and McKersie got a twenty-minute hearing from Quinn when they had finished their study. Quinn has long been interested in the Scanlon plan, but could not experiment with it unless authorized to do so by headquarters.

When Shultz reported on the Scanlon plan to the employee relations group in ERA, he received much advice but only luke-warm endorsement of the basic idea. Yet Schultz is not a man easily discouraged. He eventually presented his report to the ERA board, the top level decision-making body of the entire system. He indicated that the Scanlon plan, with appropriate adaptation to this industry's production settings, would be very suitable for implementation in the company's plants.

Shultz is an unemotional, analytical kind of person who, although encourages, seldom arouses people. However, on completion of his report, the ERA board enthusiastically endorsed the Scanlon plan presentation. Their attitude was, "Here is something new, something different, and something that could be vital." They requested that the Scanlon plan presentation be made to the EPOCH board, and one of the ERA board members was asked to create arrangements under which Shultz would have the opportunity to do so.

These events are important for several reasons. One is that they indicate a considerable degree of openness on the part of the ERA board itself. Such openness and concern for innovation is of particular importance during a period such as this.

Also, what might happen in the present wage-increase deadlock if the EPOCH board, upon hearing Shultz's presentation, allowed the plants to implement the Scanlon plan? The next step could be for Lakeside to break the hopeless deadlock by some such strategy as the following. Lakeside management could say to the union, "Let's scrap the wage offer that's been made. In its place let's put in escrow the amount of money which employees would have received had the wage increase been granted with retroactivity to October 27. With this backlog of funds, let us consider the feasiblity of a Scanlon-type approach.

The union already has indicated willingness to look at other than general wage increase type approaches as the basis for enlivening interest among the wage earners. So the union is ready to move in this direction, management is just about ready, and super-headquarters has already indicated its readiness. Thus the top and the bottom are in agreement, and only the middle section is dragging its feet. EPOCH headquarters stands in the way of what could be a dramatic breakthrough.

I have received all of this information in a conversation with Fred Jackson. The members of management realize the situation which I am presenting, but they probably feel it too rapid a step to take. Nonetheless, Lakeside needs a dramatic reformulation of the kind that the Scanlon plan could provide in order to get off dead center and move into a new experimental era.

The Concept of Irreversibility

I have seen the following phenomenon repeated often at Lakeside. A person gains some understanding of the human relations field, but then he loses it and resumes doing business in the same old way. A new training venture enlightens him and changes his behavior for awhile, but eventually he slips back into his old ways. Then, perhaps, a crisis event, with training intervention, occurs and he gets new insights; only this time he does not relapse. He can no longer revert to the old way of doing business. He is irreversible. He can only go forward according to a new style and a new set of insights. However, the implication is that such a training approach, which intends to enlighten an individual, might last a year without any constructive input into the organization itself.

Not all human relations eventually convert themselves to a new, more understanding and increasingly creative style. The point is that in those areas where he has deeper insights, a person's behavior is "irreversible." The reason is that many human relationships are based on different assumptions, different information, and different feedbacks from others. Many such relationships produce no difficulty of operation. Under these circumstances, there is neither opportunity nor need to examine its "health." Therefore, the patterns of yesterday are perpetuated, sometimes to become problems of tomorrow.

I have seen numerous examples of behavioral scientists who were so impressed by "learning from feedback" ideas that they applied it to all dealings with colleagues. However, with regard to teaching and family relations they continued to use the same style as in years past, and ignored the feedback approach.

In other words, there are many functional sub-systems within a person's total realm of experience. A training insight may be incorporated to the point of irreversibility in any one sub-system, but not necessarily be extended to another sub-system, even though the other sub-system may be functionally interconnected with the transformed sub-system. This is an interesting human phenomenon and conforms in major aspects with the Lewinian concepts of a "differentiated inner-personal region."[3]

Quinn's behavior is a classic example of psychodynamic fallacy. The most pressing problem confronting him is the situation existing between management and the wage union. Management-union relationships have become a preoccupation with him. The *manner* in which this issue preoccupies his thinking is the most remarkable aspect of the situation. One moment he's saying, "We need to have a showdown with those union characters once and for all. They're insolent, negative, irresponsible, unreasonable, and they're trying to destroy us." On the next occasion he is saying, "There is no hope in warfare. Our only possibility for genuine progress is to collaborate and create conditions under which a working relationship with the union is possible."

Two things stand out as I see Quinn. One is his preoccupation. The other is his indecision as he shifts momentarily and unpredictably from the assumptions of warfare to the assumptions of cooperation. In psychodynamic terms there is only one diagnosis and treatment possible. The diagnosis is that this man is overly preoccupied and feels an acute, even painful self-responsibility for his actions. In the effort to exercise this personal responsibility and to shoulder the associated burdens of choice, he becomes indecisive, contradictory, and confused. As for treatment, an expert would have to investigate with Quinn the historical antecedents of his conditions and thus help him understand why he has these self-defeating swings in direction and motivation.

According to the psychodynamic position, given adequate intellectual comprehension and an emotional awareness of the antecedent conditions which produced this disturbing situation, Quinn would then be able to put relations between the union and management in perspective. He would be able to take a decision accepting whatever consequences came from its application.

But there is another way to diagnose these actions of Quinn, and also to treat them. It would give a very different explanation for his behavior and would also show that the psychodynamic explanation is fatally wrong. Let us remember that Quinn is the pinnacle of power at Lakeside. One of his great responsibilities is that of establishing the conditions of effective union-management relations. Because of the high premium placed on sound industrial relations by those above him, he is under continuous prodding pressure to bring resolution to the situation. This is one source of his preoccupation, and perhaps the primary explanation of it. His preoccupation is not due to psychodynamic factors, because the force to feel self-responsibility does not arise wholly from within. Although reinforced, to some extent, from within, the primary dimensions of influence are from without and above.

The next question is, why is he so indecisive and vacillating? Does Quinn fluctuate between the extremes of combativeness and conciliation due to psychodynamic reasons? Superficially, one would think so. A closer examination makes it clear that, in the effort to "do something" somehow, Quinn is imbedded with a system of interpersonal influences which are acting on him from *below*.

Two sub-systems within the Lakeside organization are clearly evidenced in the contrasting attitudes between two major departments, Engineering and Personnel. Engineering's attitude is, "If, by questioning our authority, people get in the way of production, force provides the means to straighten them out." Until Cal and Hal were medically sidelined and Earl was converted, the engineers had effective spokesmen who continuously pressed this point of view on Quinn. In fact, some of them may be still doing so, and there are authoritarian movers and shakers just one level down from Earl in Engineering's hierarchy.

In the Personnel Department, though, people say the opposite, "Collaborate, learn how to solve problems together, accept the present union and its officers for what they legally are: equal-status bargainers. There can be no denial of that. If you'll only accept them as equals, they'll respond as equals. The problem is in generating common respect and mutual trust." Wes, the spokesman for this point of view, also is a very effective person. Thus, within any two-hour period, Quinn may receive vivid formulations of opposite and contradictory positions as to how he should exercise his responsibility.

According to this second diagnosis, then, Quinn is not confused or vacillating because of internal factors. He is in a central position, with several people trying to influence him in setting the course, each in a different direction.[4]

If the second diagnosis is right and the first one is wrong, then the psychodynamic method of dealing with Quinn as a personality would produce a much worse situation, because it would lead him astray by placing emphasis on irrelevant sources of influence. What is the correct treatment according to the second diagnosis? Here the answer is simple to formulate. The production-valuing norms anchored in the Engineering Department and the people-valuing norms anchored in the Personnel Department need to be made congruent. Then Quinn can manage the affairs of Lakeside according to a creative and integrated production-people ethic that is acceptable to all. Under these circumstances, he would not be subject to contradictory influences, but rather would have a single reference point.

How might this be done? Well, at the Green Acres application sessions (cf. Chapter 1, "Management Efforts: Laying the Groundwork for Diplomacy"), we saw an experimental result which indicates the larger possibilities. By ferreting out the norms which were contradictory and conflicting and then by creating a single normative system shared by all, which formulated a new approach to union matters, a dramatic result occurred.

The week before the Green Acres conferences, Quinn was in trouble. He was saturated with neuroticism, indecisiveness and vacillating points of view. Yet his problem was not within himself; it was a function of the system of relations and influences within which he operated.

The outcome of Green Acres was a general statement which said, "We must treat the union and its officers with dignity and respect and create conditions under which collaboration in finding and implementing solutions of common problems is possible."

The following week, Quinn no longer showed signs of neuroticism. Now he had a single reference point. He had the support of the top hundred managers at Lakeside, and he had a plan which headquarters regarded as being potentially effective. The plan certainly was one that they could not improve upon.

Had Quinn gone for personal consultation instead of to Green Acres there would probably have been a gross psychodynamic fallacy in that consultant's diagnosis. The real problem was one of intergroup conflict among warring factions beneath Quinn in the organizational system. At Green Acres, the warfare between the contending factions was replaced by collaboration and understanding. With a single point of view, which was acceptable to the managers beneath him, acceptable to the organization above him, and acceptable to himself, constructive forces could be released.

Admittedly, "the spirit of Green Acres" has a long way to go yet before it permeates Lakeside. Over the past few months, various untoward events and influences have buffetted it like a beacon in a storm, but it still gives the light of insight as people see its resolving possibilities for their problems. I should not delude myself, however, with hopes that "when things get better," the Green Acres spirit will propagate itself more widely. Rather, it must be capable of applying itself to, and *changing* for the better, hard times such as we are currently passing through. The methodological problem facing me is ensuring the *irreversibility* of positive change. If I fail, the people may regress to their old self-defeating behavior, especially when they have struggled with difficulties which began to look insuperable.

For example, several months after Green Acres and his beginning an auspicious singleminded approach. Quinn shows signs of reverting to the "weather vane" way of responding to pressures. Setting aside important career development considerations, Earl once again wants to wreak havoc on Dan Ives; and so it goes. A psychodynamicist would say that each, in his particular fashion, was manifesting symptoms of interior disturbance—thus far, I would not disagree. But he would be interested in examining their emotional histories to find the underlying malady; whereas I am not, because I recognize the organization-engendered conflicts that are pressuring them from the outside. Perhaps the day will never come when EPOCH or any other organization is tension-free—how boring that would be! But it is surely advisable for policies and expectations to be internally consistent enough to avoid the irreconcilabilities which tear apart managers of the corporate mechanism. Obviously, EPOCH's double-binding is the cause of Quinn's present mental stress and ambivalent behavior; while at the same time, through reverberatory effects, it is influencing Earl and others for the worse.

It seems a tenable hypothesis that if executives at headquarters sought to fully integrate production and people considerations, they would obviate the divergent policy interpretations and tactical initiatives which for years have poisoned their labor-management relations. Or, if "decentralization of plant management under headquarters coordination" were a fully operative concept Quinn and his team could work toward implementing improvements, along both the "production" and "people" dimensions in relative freedom from unconstructive outside interventions.

Nonetheless, organization development presupposes an imperfect state of affairs; so we'll have to continue from where we are now. The Headquarters Report or "upward influence" conference on the 26th provides opportunities for acquainting Atlanta with how the problem-solving approach to labor-management relations formulated at Green Acres, has been faring both before and after the head office interventions. A few days later, there will be a second session of the summit leveling conference. These two neighboring events illustrate two "campaign fronts" of OD: attention to and critique of unhelpful aspects of the encompassing organization *culture,* with a view to improving it; and a companion emphasis on *individual development* in the realm of values, attitudes, and consequent behavior when working with others.

Independent Unionism

Max Daniels, the union theoretician, has explained to me some of the problems that confront an independent. He said, "Management always says that production has to be efficient to be competitive, and that Lakeside has to do better than the next EPOCH plant, not to mention those of rival companies, if it's to be respected by headquarters and given more capital in the form of new production facilities that, hopefully, provide more employment opportunities."

"What about an independent union?" Max continued. "It also must be competitive, because it has to compete with the internationals. If the independent is unable to demonstrate efficiency in its bargaining—efficiency, in this sense, meaning the production of human dignity and security, as well as improvement in wages, benefits programs, conditions of work and so on—then a competitor like Wilson's international tells the workers, 'We can do a better job for you than your incumbents. Look at what we got for the employees at Plant Center X! Your independent was unable to get it here, but we could get it because of our greater strength.'

"You might agree, Bob, that our union and Lakeside's management need each other. They need us to solve many existing problems and, I suppose, to make a good impression on headquarters. We obviously need them for much the same reasons, in the interests of the people we represent. On the other hand, we and the international are in truth antagonistic groups. If one wins, the other automatically loses. In a way, our situation with them is like the Lakeside plant's situation with Seashore and other EPOCH plants when new capital investment allocations are up for grabs. It's the win-lose competition that in the end shows which is the most efficient and effective unit.

"We know we have to achieve gains for the people we represent in order to win against the international. On the other hand, management knows that, to remain competitive with other plants, it must avoid making nonproductive concessions which would lower profitability. Since our union is in a win-lose struggle with the international, and management is in a win-lose situation with other EPOCH plants, the very means by which we could gain victory over the other union could possibly create conditions of defeat for Lakeside in its competition with other plants. The question is, under these conditions, how does it become possible to collaborate?"

"Well, Max," I said, "I guess it all comes down to what is 'productive' for both your union and Lakeside management. In principle, a general wage increase to compensate for cost-of-living increases may be justifiable; but it's not *productive,* either to your people or to the company, in the sense of generating anything that represents an improvement or an achievement from both your and management's angles. It's just a matter of the company paying out some extra money, and people feeling, maybe, that they're about even with the rate of inflation. There's no way that I can see it either as improving Lakeside's profitability or as giving your people a sense of greater dignity, security, or of being rewarded for accomplishment; far less, as satisfying both labor and management."

Max nodded agreement. "So we need to look," I went on, "for other areas where *both* Lakeside's union and its management can win. In your terms, Max, that's when the union wins against the international by demonstrating convincingly to the people that it's bringing home the bacon of greater human dignity and security, and better wages; and when, at the same time, Quinn and the rest are showing headquarters that Lakeside is such an effective operation as to be worthy of further investment. There are many details involved, but it looks as though the pathway toward such a situation involves everyone working together better to do better together. And for a starting point on the technical possibilities, I'll drop a name on you. Have you heard of Joe Scanlon?"

A word to the wise is sufficient. Max's broody face took on a grin, and he replied, "Yes, and I've heard of George Shultz too! I don't know too much about George, but Joe passes muster with me; and indeed you do, Bob. Okay, I'll do what I can, and I'm sure you'll keep on with the good work."

I asked Max, "If there were to be an election today between the international and your independent, who would win?"

Without hesitation, he replied, "*They* would, definitely. We haven't achieved any improvements for our people. Starting with the craft consolidation hassle, we lost. We also lost with area supervision. The contract talks started but got bogged down. Now, we seem to be losing on the benefits program and the general wage increase.

"Eight to ten years ago, we were able to gain. Now all we can do is lose. People don't remember or vote on past performance. Attitudes toward the present are shaped by what is going on *now,* and by what, in the immediate past, forms a background for interpreting the present. Our immediate past and present do not indicate that we, as a union, have been able to do anything which makes us a more effective bargaining agent than the international."

He went on to say, "It's discouraging when you're confronted with a situation like this. We get stepped on by management, which says that 'If we agree to this proposal, we lose our competitive position.' Then we get stepped on by the people we represent. If we can't produce, we aren't worthy of representing them . . . oh well, Merry Christmas, Bob!"

References

1. The "GE method" or "boulwarism" is described in Walton, R.E. and McKersie, R.B. *A Behavioral Theory of Labor Negotiations.* New York: McGraw-Hill Book Company, 1965, pp. 360-365; and in Herman, S.M. *The People Specialists.* New York: Alfred A. Knopf, 1968, pp. 184-190. In April 1963 an NLRB trial examiner found that GE, in using the Boulwarist approach, had not thereby bargained in good faith. See also: Northrup, H.R. *Boulwarism.* Ann Arbor, Mich.: Bureau of Industrial Relations, Graduate School of Business Administration, The University of Michigan, 1964; Boulware, L.R. *The Truth About Boulwarism.* Washington, D.C.: Bureau of National Affairs, 1969.

2. See Chapter 8, Reference 3.

3. Lewin, K. *Principles of Topological Psychology.* New York: McGraw-Hill Book Company, Inc., 1936, p. 181.

4. For a discussion of role "senders" and "receivers," and of associated problems of role conflict and ambiguity, see: Katz, D. and Kahn, R.L. *The Social Psychology of Organizations.* New York: John Wiley & Sons, Inc., 1966, Chapter 7.

26
Smoke

A few days before Christmas, Van, Carl, Earl and Mac met with Dan, Max and Dick to discuss a letter that management wanted to send to supervisors about the present suspension of negotiations. It was agreed that no letter would be sent to supervisors until after the contract bargaining had recommenced. After the meeting, the four management members reviewed the draft of the speech Van intended to give at the upward influence conference on December 26.

The opening paragraph of Van's draft conceded management's chicanery and hostility before the present round of contract bargaining began. Earl, who had been personally involved in the bargaining tactics, took violent exception to this. Apparently, Earl was still unaware of the assumptions which are presently under intensive examination by the wage and salary bargaining teams. His reaction provided an excellent opportunity for the others to explore his attitudes and his role in the history of union-management relations at Lakeside.

The next day they met again, and reviewed Van's revision of the draft. The parts that Earl found objectionable had not been eliminated, but in many ways had been extended, enriched, and clarified with more concrete examples, thus giving Earl a very different picture of himself than he had before. This will be helpful if he genuinely is seeking to be more flexible by examining his own historically rigid attitudes in the labor-management area.

Later, as the four discussed the red circle questions, a dramatic instance of how vested interests mar the objective evaluation came to light. When Mac suggested a re-examination of management's position of withholding half of the general wage increase offer from the red circle people, it immediately polarized with Mac and Carl arguing for a re-examination, and Van and Earl arguing against that proposition.

Earl and Van represent the Engineering Department. Earl is its acting head and Van, before becoming operations superintendent, had worked within the Engineering Department. The heart of the red circle question is located in the Engineering Department. Earl and Van have strongly vested interests in eliminating the red circle wage differentials. To these two managers, the 7-

cent reduction of the wage increase offer, as it applies to the red circle people, would correct half the problem of employees being paid at higher rates than are appropriate for the jobs. Mac and Carl argued that because of Van's and Earl's vested interests, their attitudes prevent them from asking the real question of, "How can a long-lasting acceptable solution be found?" But as the discussion wore on, it was apparent that Earl and Van, because of their strong emotional commitments to correcting the red circle anomalies—and particularly under the spur of Van, who was advising Quinn daily—had taken a fixed position and had gotten Quinn to present it to the union. Or, rather, their spontaneous recommendations may have so closely accorded with Quinn's own thinking and EPOCH's policy as to have been crucial in his resolve to make the 7-cent cut. Now, however, it is obvious to these two members of the bargaining team that they should have told the union, "The red circle rates have been in force since consolidating, and there comes a time when, in relation to the red circle people's production (which, in many cases, is identical to what other employees are being compensated for at standard rates), their existence is no longer justified. To us, the red circle rates represent a problem, and we would like to search for a proper solution. Rather than saying how we would like to do it, we want to point out the problem as we see it, and ask you to review it with us. Will you listen to our suggestions? Let's find out if we can come to an equitable settlement."

Mac said that instead of doing this, a prescription had been prepared and offered to the union in the spirit of, "Take it or leave it." The union rejected it, and left management in a quandary as to how to resume negotiations.

Into the evening over drinks and dinner, the discussion continued. Mac and Carl had a very open leveling session with Earl and Van, telling them that unless they could open their minds and disregard their vested interests, it was hopeless to continue talking about it either with the union or within management. By the end of the evening, Van and Earl had indicated their readiness to discuss the matter in a bargaining committee session before Christmas, to say, "Let's reconsider the red circle problem. We have used only our point of view in trying to solve it. Obviously it's not acceptable from your viewpoint. So let's explore the problem in its entirety to see if we can find some effective basis of collaboration without taking such final positions."

Van cleared this proposal with Quinn the next morning, and then got in touch with George Ingle in headquarters who contacted his close colleague, Don Cooper.

Interestingly, George now has a leery attitude toward Lakeside management's altering its position on the red circle question. He is anxious because what was done by Lakeside is intimately connected with what was done at Mountainview, the only other production center with a red circle rates problem. Allen Eastman, Mountainview's general manager, originally had trimmed the general wage offer to eliminate red circle rates entirely, but later took Quinn's position of offering half of the general wage increase to the red circle people. The Mountainview union, which represents salary as well as wage employees, accepted that offer.

If the 7 cents were ceded at Lakeside, Mountainview's independent union would immediately demand a similar concession from Allen Eastman. In a conversation with Don Cooper, Quinn learned that headquarters also feels that Lakeside management has lost the freedom to alter the red circle clause which is attached to the general wage increase offer. What started out as a local proposition has now become a headquarters-backed proposition. Don and George argued that if Quinn changed his position, he would restore to full intensity the old problems of Lakeside wage rates being out of line with other plants. George also felt that for Quinn to "give in" would violate a moral obligation to the Mountainview general manager. Thus another aspect of the "decentralization myth" has been clarified. A subsidiary plant, by taking an autonomous position, loses its option subsequently to alter that position.

The agenda of the December 26 Headquarters Report Conference has undergone the following revision. Quinn will begin by highlighting a graph, which shows that in a period of five years this plant has shifted from operating at a deficit of $11 million to operating in the black at around $12 million. A $17 million profit margin is predicted for next year. After presenting these bold figures, he then intends to say that Lakeside's management would like to explore the difficulties encountered while achieving this dramatic efficiency, and to discuss what they are presently doing to resolve the conflict and alienation produced by the layoffs and craft consolidation of the past few years.

Wes will then give a historical synopsis of the problems that have cropped up in the human field. He also will describe in broad outline the corrective problems that have been undertaken, and their relative degrees of success.

The Green Acres seminars, despite the union's refusal to participate, were a major step in eradicating these negatives, and he intends to point to my behavorial science consultant participation as another important contribution. His aim will be to cite changes in management thinking, strategy and tactics brought about by Green Acres and my continuing consultation on chronic conflict conditions.

Next, George Hall, chairman of management's salary bargaining team, will portray a shift in attitude, ideology, techniques and accomplishment in bargaining from the old days of warfare to the new days of collaboration. His presentation should be a dramatic reformulation of the differences in two types of relationships with the salary union representatives.

After a discussion of George's topic, Van Gray will present his picture of changes since Green Acres insofar as the climate of bargaining with the wage union.

The responsibility will then come to me to make whatever points seem necessary and relevant from my point of view. I intend to tell the EPOCH quintet that Lakeside is launched on a great experiment which can have far-reaching implications for the company as a whole.

The problem is this. Like many other managements, Lakeside has been trapped in the "pendulum theory" which swings from the extremes of "pushing hard for efficiency and then getting negative human results" to "being human, but generating conditions of low productivity." The real issue is, "How can an organization be both efficient and human simultaneously?" This is the solution-seeking experiment which the Lakeside plant has begun to conduct on itself.

Last week, Quinn, Van, and Wes had a meeting with Dan, Max, and Dick about union participation in the Headquarters Report Conference. In making the invitation, Quinn spoke of the big stakes involved in Lakeside's management and union working together to communicate to the group their achievements, concerns, and problems. The union officers immediately agreed to participate, and said they were enthusiastic about doing so. The union did not desire to use December 26 as a gripe session against either Lakeside's or headquarters' management. Rather, it wanted to take the same posture as Lakeside management intends to take; one of helping headquarters people get a better appreciation of relevant issues in the local situation.

All of this is good. Here are two contending groups, who are deadlocked over the general wage increase controversy, putting this temporarily aside and collaborating to achieve a goal which is common to both; that of enlightening the controllers who, through an apparent lack of understanding, have had a part in creating the situation besetting Lakeside's management and union.

After discussing the purpose and program of the upward influence conference, they turned to the inevitable issue of the general wage increase. The problem was explored in a very frank and open leveling session. The union officials said, "This is a double-boiler problem, and we can't do a MacArthur on it. Either we solve it now, or we can't go forward. One bubbling pot of poison is the offer to us of a 4.2% wage increase compared to the 5% given to the salary people. The other one is your red circle chop." Dick said that the only acceptable resolution would be complete restoration of the general wage increase to the red circle people. If this were done, then there might be grounds for coming to terms on the general wage increase even if the invidious salary/wage distinction was not completely erased. Dan mentioned that he and Abe Baker at Seashore have an agreement that neither of them will resolve the general wage increase issue in his plant without first informing the other of the situation. Dan and Abe, then, are swapping notes and helping each other to obtain the best deal that each can make with his respective management.

But as Dan concludes alliances and battles onward, his own organization may be unraveling behind him. One way in which management can deliberately or unthinkingly destroy a union's integrity and cohesion is to release selected information to friendly members of the union, so that they can use it to overpower their adversaries. There has been some such dirty work at Lakeside, as I now realize.

Quinn confided to Thomas that he would be willing to consider some kind of deal whereby the masons (whose rates, Quinn believes, are grossly out of line) would receive no wage increases, while the other red circle personnel would receive 10 cents rather than 7. Quinn wanted Thomas to pass the information to "the right people," and, with their help, prepare the union to make the deal without bargaining it. Quinn reported this to management's bargaining team the other day, and no one except myself raised an eyebrow.

I drew attention to what, at Green Acres, had been identified as the basis for creating constructive relations with the union (c.f. Chapter 1, "Management Efforts: Laying the Groundwork for Diplomacy"). I said that this involved a certain ethic of communication with the union, and that, accordingly, management should recognize that it must work through the IEW's committee chairman, its president, or its secretary, in the periods between plenary bargaining sessions. It surely should not use non-office-holding members of the delegation as a means of applying manipulative pressure.

We are now beginning to see the devastating impact of the general wage increase issue on the independent union. Since Dan has refused to call a membership meeting to hear his constituent's reaction to EPOCH's offer and Quinn's red circle pruning, he is left with one flank severely exposed. He is subject to criticism by union members and other employees who, if retroactivity to October 27 is lost, will later claim that they never had an opportunity to express their attitudes toward the offer.

Because of this, the union delegation is split. Dan Ives, Dick Kelly, and Max Daniels want to resist the offer and bargain for better terms. Another group wishes to accept the offer quickly, so that contract bargaining on the union's 10% increase proposal can continue. Sol Sommers, who seems to have taken over Ted Rogers' anti-Dan constituency, leads this faction, whose other members are Thomas, Maurey Link, a member from the process area, and Neal Downs, a delegate who has been relatively neutral. The presence of splintering, warring factions is a typical syndrome of a defeated group. The dominant atmosphere within the union is that it can't win, that it can't get EPOCH to grant more than 14 cents, and that it probably can't win on the red circle question either.

This internal union conflict became known to management when last Monday, Quinn, Van, and Wes met with Dan, Max, and Dick to preview their participation in the December 26 upward influence conference. During the meeting, the union talked about the present bargaining impasse, and said that the problem was not only the distinction between the salary people's 5% and their own 14-cent offer, but it also included the red circle rates issues. As the union put it, it is a double boiler. Management acknowledged the dual nature of the issue and understood that this information had been communicated to them in confidence.

The next day, Earl Higgins mentioned to Thomas that Quinn and the others had had a good meeting with the union threesome and that the matter of the general wage increase had been brought up. This made Thomas furious. Apparently, there had been some kind of gentlemen's agreement within the union delegation that their internal split would not be revealed to management. Thomas apparently got the impression that the differences in opinion about the general wage increase within the union had been recounted to Quinn; whereas, in fact, they had not. Feeling betrayed, he then spilled his guts to Earl, saying that half of the delegation wanted to quit and take what they could get, while the other half wanted to stick it out and take the consequences. Thomas then asked Max directly, "Max, did you mention any of our private business to Quinn, Wes, or Van?" According to Thomas, "Max said, 'no.' He out-and-out lied." On Tuesday night, Max saw Carl at a company dance in Chicago, and said he was disgusted by the snide behavior of management in violating the confidentiality of yesterday's conversation.

The friction between the two warring factions has been tremendously magnified by this incident. Sol has contacted a lawyer, who thinks that they have an excellent case to bring to NLRB against Dan, Max and Dick in order to have them disqualified. He thinks that their valid arguments are that there have been no union meetings for some time; that a scheduled election of stewards and representatives was cancelled; and that, against the union constitution, the membership has had no opportunity to express itself about the general wage increase offer. Thus, the lawyer feels that Sol, the political heir of Ted Rogers, together with Thomas and others, may now be in a position to unseat the IEW's head honchos, who have been in power for several years and who were re-elected less than a year ago.

In addition, the ever-hungry international union is presently conducting a very legal representation-petition campaign; only soliciting during free periods such as before work or during the lunch hour. At the moment, the IEW independent union's membership is a little more than 70% of Lakeside's wage earners. Out of the rest a very substantial proportion have already joined the international.

27

My Mini-Lecture to Headquarters

The upward influence conference took place yesterday, December 26, and it closely followed the revised agenda. Each Lakeside representative who spoke emphasized the accomplishments in his respective area and the obstacles which were surmounted to achieve these accomplishments. They poured it on heavily, trying simultaneously to illustrate the problems still facing them and to demonstrate their efficiency. They all knew that if headquarters were favorably impressed, Lakeside would be in a better position to receive contracts for capital expansion in the future.

But the visitors sat like "bumps on a log," not even batting an eyelid. There were no direct comments except for information. On the other hand, the EPOCH quintet made numerous remarks of a win-lose character. For example, they said, "As for the strike threat at Coastline, we have that one licked. The union is capitulating, and we've won on all the major points. Of course, we may give a little here or there on minor details."

Then it was my turn to speak. I had intended to describe my rationales and practices of intervention, but on the spur of the moment I instead described the current union-management problem. I commented that the critical issue was whether local autonomy in bargaining will be preserved and strengthened at Lakeside. The alternative is that a group of company generals in Atlanta will be conducting warfare with a group of union generals in Chicago, with the front-line trenches manned by lieutenants at Lakeside, Seashore, and so on. They will bear the brunt, but the important strategic and tactical decisions in each unit of the organization will be dictated by the respective generals of EPOCH and the international.

This analogy seemed meaningful and it led to a great deal of discussion. Yet we kept hearing off-key notes of negativism from the headquarters people. For example, when I referred to Lakeside management's inability to provide the union officers with only cursory details about the new benefits program, Jim Hall, from EPOCH, told me, "If we had sent the fine print, we would have had to send three interpreters to help those characters understand it."

All of the Lakeside managers could recognize the win-lose attitude in such remarks. In addition, Quinn, Van, and Wes, whose presentations apparently did not impress the visitors, were already disappointed and gloomy. All in all, the circumstances were far from auspicious as I began my theory and practice lecture.

"In the effort to achieve organizational improvement, the Basic Training Seminar, such as we conducted at Green Acres, is a useful preparatory step. We find that it helps people to listen better and to act more constructively when confronting their daily problems. Another kind of session, the 'leveling conference,' is also involved in the effort. But a series of Basic Training Seminars, though necessary, isn't sufficient in its present state to achieve organization development. Someone with professional competence should be on the scene, available to anyone who seeks consultation. Equally important, he should study the dynamics of the organization and make timely OD interventions and coordinative suggestions. This, roughly, has been my contract with Lakeside since the Green Acres programs were completed.

"How do I work with the organization? My OD Man job is similar to, but more complex than, the job of a clinical psychologist who works with an individual. I work with individuals as well as an entire organization.

"An organization has people, each of whom has his own needs, his own mode of adjustment, and his own desires regarding accomplishment. Sometimes the individual himself is the source of a problem. Under these conditions, my job is to help that person put his problems in perspective, not by revealing deeper lying unconscious motivations, but by examining the here-and-now situation and indicating alternative pathways to legitimate and realistic personal objectives. This can be done best, directly on the job, in the framework of his actual conduct and relationships.

"Having entry into many of the organization's working groups, I have the opportunity to observe behavior which, in repetitive sequence, characterizes an individual pattern of assumptions translated into feelings, thinking, and action. If, in the OD context, a need arises, I confront any individual member of the organization in private to discuss his behavior and its consequences. I have done this, however, only to a limited degree, because there are more significant levels at which to intervene.

"An organization is not only people acting individually and in repetitive behavioral patterns. An organization is composed of groups. Groups have problems, just as individuals do. The problems of the group may be unassociated with the problems of an individual member. They may be dictated by the nature of the task which confronts the group. A group's skill at developing interaction for problem solving may be insufficient. There may be internal communication difficulties between members and the leader, and so on. Here, too, I can intervene and confront a group with the circumstances of its own operation. Sparked by this kind of intervention, group members can examine the effectiveness of their operation and become alert to those leadership inefficiencies causing poor decisions or frustrated individuals, or both.

"At this point, I can combine the interaction of the individual behaviors with group difficulties. One of the most successful group interventions involves members providing insight into one another's behavior. This is done through leveling conferences which are now getting underway at Lakeside.

"Here's how a leveling conference works. One member starts the leveling session simply by presenting the difficulties that he sees himself creating with regard to effective collaboration. He also gives a brief description of the things that he sees himself doing well. Such a thumbnail sketch provides the group a 'can opener' for gaining access to the person. They can give him personal feedback on how each of them reacts to him.

"These sessions are highly valued by the individuals who participate in them. At the content level, they are much better than my personal interventions for aiding individuals to see themselves in perspective. The reason is that rather than an individual being evaluated by someone who sees him only occasionally, he is gaining a perception of how he operates through the eyes of the individual with whom he operates hour by hour and day by day. By *using* such first-hand evaluation, he can improve his skills of teamwork.

"My interventions are *procedural*. They establish conditions of leveling, and later ensure that the way in which the leveling is done continues to be constructive and useful to the individuals involved.

"Another level of intervention involves a group having difficulties with another group and not knowing why. Again, there are two approaches. One is for the intervention to come directly from the behavioral scientist. He might provide feedback of what one or both groups are doing before they make serious mistakes. In the long run, however, the goal is not for the behavioral science interventionist to present one group with a picture of how its behavior might be seen by the other group, but to create conditions under which the two groups can directly confront one another. Direct intergroup interaction is far superior to intervention by the behavioral observer, because a group is provided direct feedback from the thoughts and feelings it has provoked in members of the other group.

"Intervening into an organization is likely to be 'catch-as-catch-can' unless there is a systematic framework in which to work; one which is organically related to a given operating situation. The question that guides me at Lakeside is, 'What are the primary processes that make up an organizational activity?' Identification of these processes, with understanding of how they interrelate in a specific organizational environnent, is a necessary activity for me as Lakeside's OD Man.

"*Climate* is one such major component. Organizations have climates just as places do. The climate is easy to evaluate, particularly by a knowledgeable outsider. In some organizational climates, the interpersonal relationships are very open. For example, people talk within the organization quite freely and without noticeable tension. Other climates are very tight and closed. Lines of command are sharply drawn and violated only with danger of punishment. A result is that people look only at their own problems and rarely communicate with one another about other matters than those of immediate concern.

"Another primary process derives from the *concepts* in terms of which an organization is formed. There are many organizations which are very unclear about their basic aims. The stated objectives may be in some degree unconnected with the true objectives which seem to determine the communication, control, and decision-making activities of those responsible for making the organization 'go.' A frequently voiced concept is 'customer orientation.' In some situations this means that the company relates to the consumer in such a way as to increase the probability that the consumer will return a second time, rather than trying to 'milk' the consumer for a quick gain on a one-shot basis. The goal of such an orientation is to meet the consumer's needs and, by doing so, to increase the prospects of his returning when new needs arise. The potential profit gain from repeat selling is obvious. Another example is market penetration. In exploring new lines of production, one company will only open a product line if estimates indicate that it can capture and maintain a sufficient percent market penetration. This is a different concept, and it produces a much different communication, control, and decision-making system than might be true in another company where the concept is shallow market penetration with high markup.

"A third attribute of an organization is *structure,* which includes levels of supervision, chains of command, spans of control, interdepartmental liaison, and unity for expressing basic concepts in operational terms. Certain features of the structure of any up-to-date company can readily be seen from its table of organization. At least, the way the organization is *supposed* to operate can be seen on the organization chart!

"Another variable can be defined as the *policies* under which the organization operates. Company policies are written to formulate benefit programs and to define age of retirement, to describe how promotions and salary increments should be brought about, and how personnel are to be hired or terminated. There are policies concerning operations, equipment depreciation, and a host of other aspects of an organization. Policies thus provide guidelines for what is to be done. A pertinent question is, 'Are they mutually consistent, and if so, in terms of what?'

"*Procedures* deal with details of the 'how' aspect, rather than with the 'what.' Every organization has routine operating procedures. Indeed, many organizations have an entire section of people concerned with the writing of procedures. In production plants there are procedures for receiving materials from inventory, for cost accounting, for maintenance, for determining overtime, and so on. These are operating 'rules of the game.'

"Another variable is *personnel*. No matter how automated, computerized or mechanical an organization, if there is any complexity at all, it will operate under the judgment of people and from their efforts. There are characteristics of people, both personal and in relation with others, which must be taken into account if their full creative contribution and effort is to be realized.

"*Operations* constitutes another property of an organization, with many issues attached, such as, Are present operations providing an acceptable percent of return on investment? How might operations be improved, streamlined, or simplified to increase profit from them? Would automation or integration of functions facilitate operations?

"The last main variable as I see it, is *environment*. It refers to the profit potential within the consumer's geographical region. Is the profit potential being tapped to the fullest or do additional opportunities exist for market penetration, ones which would result in greater profit?

"Organizational diagnosis and planning for change can be performed by the members of the company with the aid of a behavioral science consultant. The initial challenge arises in leveling conferences, and is further confronted in 'application sessions' where members can utilize the openness and trust gained in basic seminar training to assess the present organization and its systems more objectively and to plot the changes required. These variables—climate, concepts, structure, policy, procedure, personnel, operations, and environment—serve as a checklist to be considered. Not all of them are elaborated upon, but one or several may be singled out for emphasis in any one application laboratory session. Specifically, what is examined is dictated by the situations confronting the organization at a current particular point in its growth and development.

"What is different in this kind of organization diagnosis from the more customary approaches in regular meetings or in times of crisis? There are several differences. Since negative influences stemming from 'politically oriented' interpersonal relationships are reduced, a better analysis of broad and fundamental issues of organization is possible. Another difference is that the examination is less ritualistic. It tends to be more objective and far more creative. A third difference is in the area of achievement. Participants realize that concrete results will stem from their efforts. A fourth is that since participants have worked through the basic organizational issues involved, they uniformly experience greater personal understanding and insight regarding the gains that are possible. Under such circumstances, acceptance of the necessity of change, and commitment to the emerging end product, is greater than when change is engineered by edict or coercion. The major difference is that by direction or edict the top man is rarely able to accomplish as significant a result as might be attained by *collaboration.* True collaboration is only possible against the background of mutual respect and common trust that is generated by laboratory teaching.

"The application session sould not be considered a one-shot affair. Each time new problem situations confront the organization, which require reassessing old conditions, an application session may be indicated."

I summed up, "Behavioral science intervention at the organization level, in other words, involves individuals, groups, relations between groups, and the organization as a whole. The job requires more than simply changing one individual's approach. Here the issues are, How do you aid hundreds or thousands of individuals, interrelatedly, to become more effective? How can you aid groups to interact with other groups to produce better results? Finally, How do you design and modify an organization *in toto?* Beyond these matters are problems of improving relations between the total organization and its headquarters, which is another intergroup relationship problem."

I was ready to field questions, but few were asked by the EPOCH visitors, apart from one or two on operational matters that were not within my province. The wage union was to meet with the headquarters visitors at 11:30, so we closed the session and escorted Hall and the others to the IEW office.

Before receiving them, the union men said they wanted to see Quinn, Van, and Wes in private. Thomas, seemingly in command by virtue of his wrath, said, "We don't want to go forward with this matter until we have something cleared away. I want to ask you in public and in the presence of Dan, Max, and Dick, straight out. Did these three mention bargaining and the general wage increase when you set up this conference with them on Monday?"

Quinn and Wes said, "Yes."

Thomas said, "Repeat that. I want to have it on the record good and sure."

They repeated it, but added that there was no bargaining, only that the three simply expressed a point of view and, in doing so, avoided in any way taking a bargaining position.

Thomas said, "That's all. Now we're prepared to receive the guests."

28

Pickup from the Down Side

At that time those of us waiting outside the union office had no idea of what was occurring within. After a few moments, Dick came out and welcomed the visitors. We went inside, and immediately noticed how spruced up the place was. After the amenities of introduction, Dick made a prepared statement on behalf of the union. Dan, Max, Sol, Thomas, and the others sat behind him facing the guests, their earnest expressions forming a solid backstop of support.

Dick said, "We agree that when labor and management can solve problems together, mutually beneficial objectives can be attained. This we have learned. We realize the advantages available to ourselves, to management, and to the total organization if we can collaborate. But you people have to recognize something. We, as an independent union, are in competition with the international, which is trying to take over representation of the people at Lakeside and other plants. You've always said that you prefer to deal with an independent union. If you still think so, you'd better bear in mind what is needed to keep this one in existence. We must produce more than our adversaries, because if we don't, they will become the bargaining representatives.

"While we're around, we'll always stand up for our people; we'll never be in your pocket. But endless hassling does more harm than good, because no matter who wins, everyone loses. We're not competing with you, like we are with the international or the way Lakeside is with Seashore and outside companies. We need each other, and we should collaborate.

"From our side, we feel we've been collaborating pretty well and this year's profit figures show it. Quinn and these other fellows might be a bunch of wizards, but the job couldn't have been done without us wage plugs pitching in good and hearty. And we accommodated you in a big way a couple of years ago when the consolidation went through.

"Now we're looking for *your* part in the collaboration, gentlemen, and you know what we're referring to. What it all boils down to is that our people are looking to us for results, and we haven't got any yet. The international is telling them to junk us. So the real question is, 'Do you truly want to work with an independent union?' "

The visitors seemed impressed with the pertinence of this question. Although the union has been fighting an internal war for two weeks, nonetheless, when the big wheels from headquarters arrived, the union men closed ranks with management and did a good job of communicating their common goal.

Shepherded by George Hall and Wes, the EPOCH mission then met with the salary union. I went with Quinn and the others back to their offices for a brief pre-lunch check on everyday business. They were broody, with little to say about the morning's events or their expectations for the afternoon.

I wondered why Darrell Granger, the assistant general manager from Seashore, was attending the conference. Mac informed me that Darrell was being transferred to EPOCH and was here today to meet his new boss, Larry Jones, as well as to familiarize himself with Lakeside. During the morning, Darrell exhibited management attitudes that reflected current thinking at Seashore. While he thought that Lakeside might be pushing seminar application sessions too hard, he conceded that Seashore had made the mistake of not following up on the Green Acres learnings and insights. He said it was because, at Seashore, there were many different interpretations of what Green Acres meant. I remarked that this was a kind of chicken-egg enigma since, in the absence of followup, there has been little opportunity to investigate what the Green Acres experience *did* imply for Seashore.

Darrell is to be Larry Jones' technical subordinate. Under Larry, there is also to be a personnel coordinator. I asked Quinn, "Do you know who Larry's new personnel coordinator will be ?"

He replied, "It's not been decided."

I said, "This is a highly critical appointment from the standpoint of what we're trying to accomplish here."

He snapped back, "I have not missed the fact, but rather have given it a great deal of thought." I couldn't surmise from this whether or not he's boosting Wes for the appointment, but I hope he is.

I learned this morning that a week ago, headquarters concluded that it would be "inappropriate" to extend retroactivity back to October 27, because the original offer stipulated that retroactivity would be provided only if the offer was accepted by November 16. Now, on December 26, the offer is two months old, and in default of any announcement that it's been withdrawn, the money is still on the table. They are still unable to shove it down anyone's throat at Lakeside or Seashore.

The retroactivity issue has not become a matter of concern locally, because when it has been mentioned, no one has seriously believed that EPOCH would cancel retroactivity. While EPOCH's recent conclusions would create a hot issue if they were known, the situation stays calm because no one at EPOCH has as yet nerved himself to actually take the money away.

Talking with Jim Hall at lunch provided an excellent opportunity to discover how much backing there was for slicing retroactivity to one half of the time elapsing between the October 27 deadline and the eventual date of union acceptance. Jim said that about ten days ago Neal Young, after talking to Quinn, asked him how he felt about granting full retroactivity.

Jim has been in EPOCH for 35 years, and he's a sharp operator. He immediately took two actions. He first called Seashore to find out what their reaction would be to a full restoration of retroactivity if it unblocked the general wage increase impasse. Seashore management originally thought the wage increase offer was bad, but they have come around to thinking it is good. They now regard the union as very ungrateful for not accepting. Will Grigg said that he was dead set against full retroactivity. Thus, Jim got his clue. He was in trouble between his two largest operating units. Will apparently proposed (as he and Quinn had done, previously, to Neal Young and George Ingle) that it might be too severe to withhold all retroactivity, and suggested that retroactivity be limited to one half the time between the original offer date and that of acceptance. This was only if the situation cleared up quickly.

Jim told Neal who then told Quinn. To cover himself, Jim took the issue to the Board of EPOCH and got their concurrence on the concept of one-half retroactivity. There appears to be no possibility now, short of a board reversal, that the retroactivity feature will be restored in full. As often happens, headquarters may ask plant managements to reverse themselves, but the plants have much greater difficulty in asking reversals of headquarters. The EPOCH executives are in no mood to reverse decisions once taken, even though the general wage increase offer and its consequences already have been the most disturbing influence around the company circuit since 1957. In addition, it may cost the union president at Seashore his position which is important of course, because Abe Baker is seen by most as a good independent-union president.

In spite of these uncertainties, it appears that Jim has himself protected on all sides. With one of the two holdout plants wanting less than one-half, and the other wanting full retroactivity, he has taken the one-half position. Furthermore, he has nailed it down with the board of directors. It is very clear in his attitudes that it is more important to him to be in accordance with EPOCH's board than it is to get the wage issue settled equitably.

I asked what headquarters had in mind when it offered a 5% increase to salary personnel and only 4.2% (14 cents per hour) to the wage earners.

Jim Hall told me, off the record, "Well, if we had it to do again, we would do it differently, even though we still think the present offer is fair." He said that consolidation had brought the wage personnel more rapid pay gains than the salary field. Since salary personnel had not undergone consolidation, there had been relatively less favorable salary increases during the past two years. "So we offered more to the salary people this time to even things up," Jim explained.

I thought his reasoning was rather curious, and the union men, if they'd been there, would have had a pithier term for it. They argue consolidation has brought on larger, more onerous, and more skilled jobs for the remaining workers. Additionally, they do not feel that they have received rewards commensurate with their past efforts. They see the white-collars still having as easy a time as ever and being paid more.

Later during lunch I checked this over with Don Cooper. He considered it a fair wage offer, and was sorry that it did not get accepted. But he knows they are in trouble now, and if the board of directors would tolerate it, he would consider an upward revision. He complained, however, that Lakeside management did not really try to sell the 14 cents, but he had no evidence to support his suspicions. I pointed out to him that speculations of a wage increase were reported from Atlanta headquarters and published in the local newspaper. This caused the union to believe that the offer came directly from headquarters.

So two influential headquarters executives now recognize the invidious salary-wage distinction to have been unfortunate, if not a mistake. Will they do anything to correct it? The answer is probably *no*. EPOCH has some 83 contracts with various unions, and about two-thirds of these are with independents. The general wage increase offer has been accepted by all of the independent unions except those of Lakeside and Seashore. There are only three other non-acceptances, and these are from international units at Coastline. Thus, even though headquarters now regards the initial position as having been wrong—Don remarked that it would have been better to go 4% across-the-board—they nonetheless feel it would be inappropriate to make an adjustment at this time. They probably can get by with the present situation, and therefore they'd rather do nothing than make an equitable correction.

Allen O'Dell, another vice president, gave the board information on what the reactions to this wage offer would be, and he tried to get it adjusted at the time, but without success. No doubt about it, it is a mess. The pathetic feature is that no one can see any correction in the situation from a headquarters point of view.

I found out that Jim Hall is the pressure source for getting wage rates into line. It was he who inspired Quinn and Allen Eastman to hack at the red circle. Then, once Lakeside and Mountainview had applied a common 7-cent cut, the various headquarters executives thought that this is the way to rectify the wage structure all over the system. From what Jim said, and also from remarks by Don Cooper, it appears that headquarters has now adopted Lakeside management's position and fixed it immovably rather than leaving it as locally negotiable.

However, the attitude in Lakeside management toward the red circle issue is, "We will make some adjustments if we have to in order to get an agreement. Since we haven't been told not to, we won't ask. We'll just go ahead, and it will be a *fait accompli*." That is a power tactic which frequently works in this imperfect world. The blame for letting Lakeside management shift its position will fall on subordinates at EPOCH headquarters who were obligated to communicate headquarters' latest thoughts but failed to do so.

The afternoon was spent in "operations review," involving numbers, charts, graphs, and the other pertinent technical data. Only Jim Hall did much questioning, and his queries would be of the following character. "Does this mean that you're going to have a continuing over-capacity? Is that profit before or after taxes?" And so it went. The work part of the day ended by Jim's saying, "Well, it's a quarter of five now and drinks are not being served until five-thirty. What am I supposed to do between now and then?"

All day, Jim, as the EPOCH mission's highest-ranking member, had been scrutinized by the Lakesiders, who were looking for some glimmer of a positive reaction. In a sense, he was the crystal ball of their hopes. By evening though, it was crystal clear that he had not caught the spirit of the occasion. He was leery, cagy, and suspicious. His questions were narrow, detailed, and picayune. The spirit of his reactions was, "I'm from Missouri. What have you got up your sleeve? What's the hidden angle?"

As Jim sat there waiting for "happy hour," Larry Jones turned to Quinn and said, "I've been watching Lakeside daily for a decade. I could see the main outline of what we have been told here taking shape. But this review, and most particularly the constructive attitudes we found when meeting with the two unions this morning, have placed a true perspective on what I was unable to see from a distance during the past decade. The job that's been done here is magnificent. My hat is off to you and your organization."

George Ingle spoke in a similar vein. He said, "You have turned in a performance which is next to unbelievable."

But the other EPOCH visitors did not speak. At five-thirty we had cocktails, followed by dinner, and the visitors departed about nine o'clock. Lakeside management stayed on, for what they called an "Oh!-group." This affair was a real "let your hair down" type of session. It was decompression. People were disappointed, and defeat reactions were noticeable. The theme of this session was, "It was not we who failed to be convincing, it was they who failed to realize."

In retrospect of the day's events, various aspects emerge. Conditions of collaboration were not present because each group was looking at the problems from a different point of view, each incompatible with the other. There are areas of agreement between the two, of course, but presently the areas of disagreement overshadow them.

The basic difference in attitudes can be formulated this way. EPOCH is saying, "We have to formulate positions, make sure they're right, then stick with them and get them bought. Problems with our independent unions are essentially selling problems for local management to resolve."

Lakeside is saying, "We must not take advance positions. We must explore actual problems, find the best pathways to resolution, and move them along under a general mandate from headquarters.

EPOCH is saying, "We can't give free scope to each plant to go about solving its problems in its own unique way, because coordination throughout the system would be lost, and then we would be in a terrible mess."

Lakeside is saying, "We must have leeway in local autonomous problem solving. We are confronted with unique problems and therefore we must find unique solutions that fit our situation."

EPOCH is saying, "There are definite rules of the game which can be applied with equal effectiveness everywhere."

Lakeside is replying, "The situation is organic rather than mechanical. We have to find the best fitting solutions for our own situation."

Three contrasting points of view seem to define two major alternatives. Either the organization views itself as mechanical and follows a uniform, EPOCH policy, or it views itself as organic, allowing each of the plants to find the best solutions in its own decentralized situation. This is where the nub of the conflict exists. Lakeside management is in trouble with Jim Hall and Don Cooper in having gone "too far," in terms of seeking local solutions. But Quinn and his managers are neither enthusiastic nor able to sell to the union mechanical solutions that have little bearing on local problems.

It is interesting to examine the non-leveled attitudes of the two sets of spokesmen toward one another. For example, Jim Hall remarked to me, "We are worried about Quinn. He works too hard. He has no outside interests, no ways of relaxing from the tension. He is going to kill himself."

Don Cooper said during our lunch chat, "We think we could have swung this general wage increase thing had Quinn done a better job of selling for us. As I see it, Quinn didn't carry his responsibility, but laid the blame and passed the buck to us at headquarters. Decentralization is the cornerstone of our company's policy, so he ought to have made the union believe the package he was selling was his own."

I told Don that I'd seldom heard such a pure example of the mind-wrenching "double-binding executive expectation." I reviewed for him some of the crosshatched implications of his statement. Don's relative silence for the rest of the day may be an indication that he was digesting that fundamental piece of feedback.

During the late-evening "Oh!-group," I discovered how Quinn sees EPOCH and Jim Hall in particular. To Quinn, EPOCH is a massive, coldblooded giant which has scant appreciation of the contributions and needs of local plants. He does not think Jim is dedicated to the same principles of human relations and fatherly care of employees as was the old EPIC organization. He called Jim a "golfer," someone who would prefer to play golf rather than work. In addition, he sees Jim as a tailor's dummy and, in truth, Jim's clothes are a little more dashing than those of any Lakeside manager's—even Mac Anthony's.

Cal commented, "I was amazed as I looked at those fellows. They all look alike and act alike. They are not like EPIC vice presidents I remember, each of whom was a distinctive personality—rugged, strong, and essentially human. These fellows seem to have been cut from the same bolt of gray cloth. They are organization men and they have one standard way to react to each situation."

As we left the bar last night, Quinn passed the word, "Let's have a management committee meeting tomorrow morning at ten."

Just before nine-thirty this morning I received an urgent phone call from Quinn. He said, "Can you come over and give me a shot? I need a boost. I am down. I didn't sleep a wink last night."

I said, "OK, Quinn, I'll be right over."

I went to his office. Even though this was Sunday morning, he had broken his weekend custom by putting on a business suit. All that was missing for complete mood-coordination was a black-and-blue necktie. "I've had it," he said. "How can I face this group at ten o'clock? They all know we've had it. We didn't get through to Jim Hall. He doesn't understand. What can we do? How can one plant like ours change the entire system? The whole company is defeated. My years of effort are wasted. Would Hall want me working for him? Of course not. He sees things one way, and I see him the opposite way. He doesn't give a damn about preserving independent unions. He doesn't want bargaining at the local level. He's an operator, playing games out of headquarters when he's not on the links. We're lost. It's hopeless."

I said, "Quinn, it surely is a tough situation, and I agree with you that Lakeside *is* out of step with the rest of the system. Let's not act as though there were no problem. But Lakeside is on a sound footing, and it is making progress. We have all kinds of evidence that you and I and thirty others know how to intervene and collaborate against a background of intergroup conflict. While *you* may think that one small component of a system may have little impact, *I* say that one small component can provide the signals through which the rest of the organization can learn. True, if we were at headquarters, we could alleviate the conditions that are causing so much local conflict, but we are not. We are here. All we have is a justifiable confidence that we're going in the right direction."

A couple of minutes before ten, Wes dropped in, sized up the situation and said, "Quinn, brace up, for God's sake. Don't communicate your dread to the other fellows. People are already far enough down."

Quinn replied, "I'll try not to."

We left and joined the larger group. Quinn, who had changed his mind along the way, said, "I thought we turned in a top-notch performance yesterday. Let's find out how it was received." In the two hours that followed, I saw all the classical behaviors of a group in defeat, and I want to describe these in some detail.

The session began under the theme, "We were not wrong, they failed to comprehend."

Cal said, "Did you look at their faces? They never cracked a smile. Look at the stupid questions they asked. They didn't even know how to get into the factual material we provided them. Did you see Don Cooper? He never looked up. What a bunch. Leadership went down the drain the same time as EPIC."

Then some deeper self-deception and beginnings of self-destruction began to appear. Van said, "I think I dropped the ball. I didn't convince them of what has been going on in the wage bargaining. Maybe they shouldn't be blamed for failing to hear. I guess I failed at the start by not getting through."

Then Quinn spoke up and said, "I feel the same way about myself. I still don't know whether they couldn't follow me, or whether I couldn't make myself understood, but it amounts to the same thing, I goofed. There were several ways I could have made that presentation, and I picked a loser."

Wes chimed in and said, "My speech was too long, but the reason is that as I talked my way through the stuff, I ran into the great stone face of Jim Hall. Then, recognizing that I had not gotten through, I covered the same ground again. I knew damn well I was repeating myself, but I didn't know what to do to get through except to say the same things over and over."

During this speculating phase, a new theme arose. It was introduced by Quinn, who began with, "Maybe we tried too hard to sell them. Maybe we pushed too hard, placed too much emphasis on human relations, employee relations, and labor relations. Maybe we went too fast." This prompted the idea that "Maybe the emphasis we've been placing on improved human relations is out of balance. Maybe we sounded too extreme. What we were saying could even be construed as socialistic and all that kind of thing. We need to get back in line and keep on stressing production. We've been going overboard on labor-management relations." Then I heard the old standby again, "Let's go back to business as usual."

Suddenly there was a fascinating fight discussion between Wes and Cal on some highly technical detail regarding the way the truck drivers are paid in the sales division of EPOCH. It was a highly technical, esoteric and picayune topic which bore no relation to the present problem. Here was an example of two people, who ordinarily get along extremely well, ventilating their tensions over an irrelevant issue. Loaded with tension and frustration, everyone's nerves were on edge and feelings were jagged. All were looking for someone to fight, and so again, we had completed another cycle in the post-defeat washer.

I will predict, in contrast, that had Jim Hall known what was being achieved at Lakeside, and had he shown a sympathetic appreciation for these improvements, the day would have been chalked up as an outstanding success. People would have said, "Well, that was a real boost, it's good to feel appreciated. Let's go all out and finish the job."

But one man, Jim Hall, now hundreds of miles away in Atlanta, Augusta or wherever, was clearly dictating the dimensions of defeat so vividly seen here.

Sitting in, listening and watching, I asked myself, "Should I intervene and stop this internal massacre, or would it be better to stay out and let it continue?" From the findings of many experimental intergroup victory and defeat situations, I concluded that the way to handle the situation was to allow the self-destructive interactions to continue. Why? Because repeatedly it has been seen that one of the fundamental ways in which a group becomes stronger is to work through its own internal examination to an end result. Of course, had I intervened, it possibly would have eased tensions by bringing insight to what these men were currently doing to one another.

But, in my judgment, insight at this time was less important than permitting people to work through their frustrations and to formulate the eventual conclusions themselves. It takes longer this way and is more painful, but there is good reason to presume that it is the better route to travel. The group is stronger for having dealt directly with its feelings of depression and defeat, rather than having examined these feelings analytically from the standpoint of the motivations that supposedly were producing them. Out of defeat and decompression sessions eventually flows some recognition of the true character of the problem; and so it did today. They began to see that their problem was not that a defeat had been suffered, but rather that OD pioneering is much more difficult than anticipated. For Lakeside, the job includes giving headquarters ideas that increase perception of the full performance dimensions of its plants.

Before the end of the meeting, new ideas were floating around. One was, "The next step we have to take is to arrange interviews at EPOCH headquarters for members of our management committee. By this means they can get to know the people in EPOCH who influence policies affecting us. As they do so, they can also communicate our point of view and get a hearing for our efforts." Another idea was, "Let's try to get some of our own personnel transferred into headquarters, so they can influence policy formulation which will be helpful to us." I think we see the good use of a defeat: to take your licks, endure the pain, and then come back with stronger and more creative thoughts for solving your better-identified problems.

Indeed, there was a meeting of the management bargaining team the next morning to explore how solving the red circle issue may uncork the impasse presently existing between management and the union. Almost immediately I could sense the heaviness of defeat lifting as people started thinking constructively again. Once Quinn realized that we had to look for a variety of solutions—not just one package to give the union—then people really went to work. They began to formulate a number of alternative possibilities with which to confront the union early in the week.

29

A New Year Begins

Management Leveling Sessions

The second summit leveling session was completed yesterday, New Year's Eve. It was one of the best leveling sessions that I have seen. By going slower and being more thorough, greater success was achieved in reviewing each participant's relationship with other individuals and with the management committee as a whole.

Sam Allen, of Staple Products, learned that, as a department spokesman, he had problems. Because he listens more to some members of his department than he does to others, his conclusions do not reflect a full range of viewpoints. Sam also learned that many problems of interdepartment cooperation are produced because he tends to be highly loyal to the people for whom he is responsible, and this makes his behavior rigid and inflexible.

Bill Jones, head of Business Services and the newest member of the management committee, questioned his own competence and said that perhaps someone more qualified should be the new department head. The others told Bill that his behavior is open, he doesn't generate conflict, and is skilled at offering a service without being pompous.

However, Bill revealed an important aspect when he said, "It's true that I avoid conflict with others, but this doesn't imply a lack of involvement. Rather, I bide my time and take a flanking approach so that my point of view doesn't draw any flak. I rarely tackle a problem face on."

Wilson Jennings, head of the technical department, was told that he submits too easily to opposition, always looking "up," rather than "across." Rather than seeing a peer, he sees a superior. His competence should earn him respect, but such is not the case because of his aversion to conflict and continuous deference. Another identified aspect of Wilson is that he approaches situations intellectually, devoid of any emotion.

Paul Simpson, head of the medical department, said he sees Wilson, rather than being unemotional, as being unable to cope with his emotions if they are aroused beyond a certain pitch. Because of this, Wilson suppresses his emotional involvement in a situation.

The most dramatic personal feedback of the day concerned Randy Cox, head of supply and distribution. Since he coordinates the inflow of raw materials with the outflow of finished products for the entire EPOCH production system, his job requires great skill in bargaining and diplomacy. He deals with many individuals, each of whom has a vested interest, and he must make decisions which affect Lakeside as well as the entire corporation. Often what is good for the corporation as a whole is not good for Lakeside's profit and loss statements. Occasionally, Randy must tell the department heads they cannot operate at full capacity because the available supply of raw materials is needed elsewhere.

Randy felt his colleagues did not understand his job, that he was unappreciated, and regardless of his effort, he received little recognition. He needs recognition and appreciation. He needs help but receives very little. This confession astonished the rest of the management committee.

They said, in essence, "Randy, that gives us an entirely different perspective of your situation. You appear so self-confident with your usually flip demeanor that we thought you were on top of things." The flip element, which no one really dislikes, nonetheless has had the effect, as Van said, "of making it a pleasure to rough up Randy occasionally." Sometimes, when Lakeside is denied a potentially profitable task because it would be more lucrative to another EPOCH plant, Van tells Randy, "Look, you idiot, can't you do a better job than that?" By doing so, Van unwittingly has chided Randy at his point of greatest weakness, making him feel rejected and unnecessary. This was a significant revelation for the entire group.

The cocktail hour and dinner that followed the session illustrated the relaxed atmosphere which had been achieved. There was no reference to work, no serious chatter, only a series of stories concerning World War II, problems of flying, the Navy, and so on. It was a light, attractive conversation which, according to several members, had never happened at Lakeside before, and probably would never have happened unless tensions had been relieved by the summit conference approach.

A month ago, I wouldn't have believed it possible for a group of engineers to effectively deal with delicate problems of emotions and relationships. I now look forward to further group meetings, possibly for a day every two weeks, in which we can solve the complex problems confronting Lakeside. Perhaps the leveling conferences can achieve the desired results.

Who or What Has Got to Give?

At Seashore, a possible solution to the salary/wage problem has been found. Seashore's union represents salary as well as wage personnel. The proposal is to grant 5% across-the-board to salary personnel, provided it does not exceed twenty-five dollars per month. At the same time, the wage personnel would receive 14½ cents per hour rather than the 14 cents previously offered. I think this proposal would eliminate the invidious discrepancy between salary and wage offers. Since Seashore has no red circle problem, no controversy arises there, but the retroactivity issue remains to be explored.

Would such an offer be acceptable to the union? Disregarding retroactivity, I think it would be acceptable; however, retroactivity could constitute a block. More important, is this offer acceptable to the EPOCH board of directors? From Seashore management's point of view, this new offer would involve the same amount of money as the original one. What they want is permission to distribute it differently. The only indicator I have is that the board has already rejected two such propositions, one of which came from Seashore, and the other from Mountainview.

This morning there are faint glimmerings that the wage increase problem may be resolved at Seashore before the day is over. If so, the formula for Lakeside solution would have taken shape.

With Will Grigg's concurrence, the union at Seashore arranged for negotiators from the Federal Mediation Service to meet on Monday and Tuesday with the bargaining partners. The negotiators separated the two groups, with one negotiator working with the union and the other negotiator with management. The two fedderal officials met periodically and exchanged thoughts, and then each returned to his own group.

By the end of the second day, the union accepted the 5%-14 cents package. I don't understand the logic of the union's capitulation.

The next step involved retroactivity. Will Grigg tried to start from the date of the acceptance as the date to begin payment. This was totally unacceptable. Then he offered retroactivity to November 16. Abe Baker said, "No soap. You've got to do better than that."

Finally, late yesterday, Will met with the union and asked, "Could you fellows accept here and now and sign on the dotted line, if I could meet your requirements on retroactivity?"

The union said it couldn't, but agreed to have a council meeting that night and would return to discuss the matter in the morning.

The labor relations specialist at Seashore has no idea why Will Grigg made that proposition. Incidentally, this specialist is against any retroactivity because the foremen and supervisors are steadfastly resistant to the idea.

It appears to Lakeside people that either Will has influenced the EPOCH board or they have influenced him. In any event, the Lakesiders believe that EPOCH and Will have agreed that the matter needs to be settled now and that the future of the Seashore independent union hangs in the balance. If true, the EPOCH board must have yielded on retroactivity, thus showing its interest in maintaining and strengthening the independent. But it probably also stipulated that, "If we move off the one-half retroactivity position, it is only under the condition that you get a clean acceptance here and now."

Quinn's eagerness to resolve the problem may possibly be interpreted as management's effort to push a non-negotiable package. The plan is to begin bargaining at 8:30 Friday morning. Management will suggest that the union can accept either a 7-cent withholding from the red circle people, or the initial offer of the full 14 cents with an understanding that there will be a half-cent per hour per month reduction until those with red circle rates are earning wages proportionate to their present work rather than their work prior to consolidation.

Rumors indicate that the union is as eager as management to find a resolution. Therefore, the conditions may now be right for final agreement. It is assumed that since full retroactivity apparently is being extended to Seashore, it will be extended here, too. That seems to be no stumbling block. Management is much more flexible with respect to the red circle today than was Quinn in late October when he and I had a fundamental talk. I remember asking him, "Are you taking a bargaining position to move toward a negotiated settlement, or are you taking a position of conviction which prevents such movement?" He said the latter was true. So it goes. Apparently he is now ready and eager to finalize a negotiated settlement.

Dan, Dick and Max returned today from a three-day meeting in Washington where they conferred with officers of other independent unions, and went to the Department of Labor to discuss the fate of their "unfair labor practice" charge. Yesterday when the Seashore union accepted, unamended, the general wage increase offer, it obtained full retroactivity to October 27. But there had been an agreement between the union president at Seashore, Abe Baker, and Dan that neither would accept any final contractual agreement until clearing with the other.

This morning, Mac Anthony, Dan, and Max set up tomorrow's meeting for negotiation on a revised red circle offer. Mac asked Dan what he'd heard about the Seashore agreement, but Dan had no information. So, Abe Baker must have done one of two things. Either he tried to contact Dan at Lakeside or in Washington and could not, or he made no effort to do so. At all events, their agreement broke down at a crucial moment. So much for inter-union alliance.

What's happening *within* IEW? The infighting seems to have stopped, or at least quietened down. Sol Sommers' splinter group, composed of members of the executive board and rank and file men, had said they'd take court action this week and flood the plant with handouts. As of Thursday night, there had been none of this.

After the leveling conference, Quinn, Van, Cal, Wes, Mac, and I discussed the forthcoming meeting with the union about the general wage increase problem. By now, members of management had agreed that the important issue was to establish a progressive attitude toward aligning the red circle rates with prevailing rates. But it still is desirable to eliminate the red circle rates, which are a continual irritant to the people who are doing the same work, but are not getting as much pay.

Of course, there are really two issues here. One is whether or not the union will accept as a bargaining topic the elimination of red circle rates. The other relates to the mechanism by which the adjustment of rates could be accomplished. Up to now, management has held to a fixed position which has been so unacceptable to the union that bargaining has ceased. This fixed position has applied to the principle and the mechanism. At present, management has not changed its standpoint in terms of the principle, but has become flexible about the mechanism which would reduce red circle rates.

When bargaining resumed Friday, management proposals were put on the table. One of these was their previous call for a one-half reduction in the general wage increase for those on red circle. A second proposal, one that Quinn had already broached to Thomas, concerned raising the red circle offer from 7 to 10 cents per hour, but with no general wage increase for the masons. The third alternative proposal was that, initially, the 14 cents would be given to everyone but the red circle problem would be gradually eliminated if the union accepted a monthly half-cent decrease of red circle hourly rates until these rates had reached parity with the regular rates.

Rather than beginning from the standpoint of being prepared to bargain the red circle issue, chairman Van began with the proposition that the red circle issue must be "corrected," and therefore, the issue itself was not bargainable, but the method of correction was entirely bargainable. After about five minutes, Dan threw his springing slip on the table saying, "Sign it, I'm getting out. You don't have a new idea. You're still playing games the way you were last month."

Dan's outburst came just as Van had gone to the board to explain how the monthly reduction would take effect over a year's period. Van stayed at the board. The springing slip lay there for a few moments until Wes signed.

As soon as Van finished his financial lecture, Thomas also got up and announced to everyone, "I didn't want to leave when Dan did because it seemed impolite to interrupt Van, but Dan's remarks express my feelings also," and thereupon had his slip signed and left.

Dick made a few feeble attempts to test whether or not some progress might be possible, but the interaction broke down within fifteen minutes and the meeting closed with Dick's saying, as he had on December 16, "We're ready to start talking whenever there are fresh ideas that you have to discuss with us."

Management is completely discouraged. They feel that although they made a constructive attempt to break the bind, the union has rejected their efforts. But they feel self-righteous rather than defeated. Rather than fighting among themselves, they are closing ranks, because they have an enemy again—the union.

Wes decided on his own initiative to have a personal conference with Dan. They met at nine o'clock and talked about an hour. There were a number of items discussed, but the critical attitudes that Dan expressed seem most pertinent to record here.

"We've suffered one setback after another in the last four months. First it was the reversal on maintenance of membership. Then it was the invidious 14 cents-5%. Then it was the red circle. Then it was the benefits program. We aren't getting anywhere with this management which is under EPOCH's thumb. We've been wasting our time talking about collaboration. It was just a dream, Wes. You're on one side of the hassle and I'm on the other.

"The independent is a hopeless mechanism for getting results with this company. It's time to close things out. I plan to let a judge decide whether or not the old contract is still in force. If he concludes it isn't, then our aim will be to call a new election and let the people choose new representatives. If the court says the old contract's still in force, well, okay, you may try to enforce that red circle proviso you bludgeoned us into signing last time, but let me warn you that kind of blind arrogance will open the gates to a union that carries a big enough stick to defend its people.

"Personally, I'm sick and tired of all this. It's an impossible task for a little independent union to pit its strength against a massive company and come out with meaningful results. What the hell use is this committee? You have no autonomy, and we have no power."

All Dan would say about the latest proposal was, "I can't speak for the union, but the only way I will agree to reduce the red circle rate is if the money squeezed out of it is given to other wage people in some form. That way, at least, you won't profit by taking money from the workers' pockets. You're in the business of trying to help management save money, I'm in the business of trying to help the people."

All of the management committee members are ready, if not eager, to grant a straight 14 cents across-the-board, save for Van Gray and Earl Higgins. Why is it that these two are not willing to remain flexible and get on with bargaining? The reason is that approximately 220 of the 230-odd red circle people are in the Engineering Department, which Earl Higgins heads. Van Gray is its former boss. And the eyes of EPOCH are upon them. Obviously, these two have a vested interest in phasing out the red circle rates.

This morning, before going to Engineering's leveling conference, I attended a session with Van, Quinn, Wes and Carl in which the problem was debated for the hundredth time. There were no fresh ideas. Van said, "We should hold out. Something might change in the next couple of days as a result of the three different offers we made last Friday. There may be some heat building under Dan to accept the offer."

In general, it was a very frustrating type of session. All they could do was put the present trouble in perspective by thinking of a batch of other problems waiting for them down the road. "Well, if we get through this one, it's only a matter of time until we bog down on the next one. There are all those MacArthur items that have been put back on the shelf to be returned to later . . . " Interestingly enough, this point of view was expressed by Wes.

Recognizing a self-fulfilling prophecy I intervened at this point and indicated that the condition which ensures failure is to expect it. What I saw was a group of completely frustrated people realizing that the red circle issue must be resolved before further bargaining can take place, but exaggerating it beyond rational limits.

To me, it seemed that the wrong problem was still being examined. I summed up my alternative viewpoint. "If you look back on the recent past from the union standpoint, starting with the crane crisis, going through work samplings and the unilateral benefits program, and then the invidious 14 cents and the red circle rates, this has been very ineffective win-lose bargaining all the way. On each occasion, the union has been on the losing end of the stick. Now, it is in a position of strength to ensure getting one or two results that are more acceptable to it."

This formulation enabled the management committee to see that it had reacted to the red circle rates as an isolated item, and had labeled the union "unreasonable" for not accepting management's point of view. But they continued to repeat the old axioms. They have a hundred reasons why the union should accept the red circle reduction, but few have formulated what, in the minds of the union, makes that proposition unattractive. It is in this way, through continous reaffirmation of *management's* rationale, and the forgetting of associated matters, that *present circumstances alone* are seen as causative. This indicates how perspectives are lost under conditions of frustration. It is quite difficult to maintain a broad perspective when one is under heavy pressure, and without such perspective, problem solving is very difficult.

In my view, the two things that will promote acceptance are (a) to grant the full 14 cents to red circle people and (b) to make the entire offer retroactive to October 27.

Some Engineers Level

On January 4 the Engineering Department had its first leveling session. In attendance were Earl, Jack Smith, Bob Bell, Stan Wood, Steve Jacobs, and Bill Carter. During the session, each person was discussed except for Earl and Bob.

Engineering is reputed locally to be composed of hard nosed, tough, work-pushing, driving people. It would rarely, if ever, receive the criticism of being soft, kind, or understanding. As Jack, Steve and Bill talked about managing, it was impressive that none of them could sense strong authoritarian tendencies in their own behavior. I think the reason is that their similarity reinforces one another. When two or more people approach problems from the same point of view, they have no basis of contrast which might reveal alternatives. The single non-authoritarian exception to the departmental rule might be Stan, who describes himself as a humanist. I'm not sure how I'd classify Earl presently. In any event, the Engineering Department is somewhat worried about its plant-wide notoriety as being hard nosed. The members ask, "Why do they characterize us this way? Is it really ourselves who are tough, or are all the others soft?" They cite the following evidence to support this belief that they have a sound operational perspective whereas others have gone overboard for human relations.

Hal Harvey agreed with the department heads to invoke certain rules regarding minimum overtime, absenteeism, and discipline. All department heads agreed to do this, but only Engineering carried the program into action. So what is the situation? They are deviants to be sure, but isn't this because the rest of the organization didn't have guts enough to go along with the commitment that it made?

All the same, recognizing that it is in a certain amount of trouble with the rest of the organization, Engineering wants to correct its difficulties. For example, within the department there are frequent complaints that other departments are not pulling their weight. Engineers say, "The others create requirements for heavy overtime due to *their* poor planning of the use of equipment. We get the rap because the overtime shows on our time sheets. If *they* would just perform properly, *we* would have no problem. These days, if Quinn puts the bee on us to push down overtime, we don't respond. We just go ahead and do what's necessary. It's Chemical Products and other production departments that are responsible, not us."

Strong evidence of intergroup competition *within* the Engineering Department showed up today among the representatives of each of its divisions. Jack Smith, head of maintenance, came under heavy criticism for trying to corner the talent. The charge was that he gets the best people locked up in his division where they are unavailable to others who perhaps have even more legitimate needs for their services. The maintenance division enjoys the highest status in the department.

Next in the pecking order comes the construction division, whose head is Steve Jacobs. Accordingly, he gets the next best people. The lowest status division within Engineering is headed by Stan Wood, who operates shop services and equipment sections which provide motor repairs, engine overhauls, and so on, for Engineering's equipment. Consequently, Stan's division is a service agency to the other two, and there is a constant three-way conflict.

Bill Carter, another division head, has a staff function of statistical analysis and work planning, and has no line responsibility except over those who directly report to him.

There is another intense conflict—a "foreign war"—going on between the maintenance division and one of the divisions of Chemical Products. The particular division over there, headed by Andy Stewart, runs a complex and continuous process with batch production.[1] It requires about fifty engineering wage personnel to maintain the process equipment. One of Jack Smith's region supervisors is responsible for these people and their work.

In a recent conversation, Andy mentioned to me privately that it would be better if the maintenance personnel who operate in his division reported directly to him. Chemical Products is a profit center. Andy, who does not have direct control over the Engineering's maintenance workers or their supervisors, pays large engineering service bills which substantially reduce the profitability of his operation. Andy thinks that the engineers and mechanics who service his equipment should report directly to him. Then his own deputies could plan and supervise the maintenance work, and the fifty maintenance workers would feel membership in and owe loyalty to the division for which Andy is responsible. Jack, on the other hand, wants to hold on to "his" engineers and mechanics because they represent a part of Engineering's own work force.

First to describe himself and be discussed at the engineers' leveling session was Jack Smith. He is a tall 35-year-old Irishman, hard driving, dollar-centered, and impulsive. He makes up his own mind, and then asks others if they have any basis for disagreeing. He knows "damn well" the difference between right and wrong, and he judges others with respect to how well they accept his conception of that difference. He is in continuous conflict with the other division heads because they can never achieve equal grounds in an argument with him. Of course, as he says, "Occasionally I make mistakes. But in this kind of an activity, it's the batting average that counts, and mine is pretty good. I'll start to listen when I get more evidence that people are talking sense."

In summary, Jack is the kind of person who leaps to his own conclusion and then acts. If his conclusion runs into trouble, he modifies it. The underlying assumption is that he is right until he is proved wrong. In this sense, he does come toward situations with an open mind.

Next to be described was Bill Carter, who has many times been characterized as the original 1/0 autocrat.[2] I wish I could have made a recording of his own thumbnail sketch of how he operates his division and his family, and what things were like for him as a child.

First of all, how does he operate the division? He feels that no one puts out enough work. He works all the overtime that comes along and considers it a way of life. Others should, too. Since they have the opportunity to work for this company, why should they gripe? He said, "I can see no reason for people not trying to put out more. After all, this is a job; a job is a responsibility; a responsibility is something that requires effort. But I have to keep checking on people, otherwise they won't stay on their toes. How else do you keep people hard at it these days, unless you stand over them?"

He continued, by way of illustration, "Y'know, I have a daughter who also works for EPOCH. Sometimes, when she feels sick, I have to push her to go to work. It's everyone's obligation to go to work regardless of the circumstances. One time I drove my daughter to work in spite of her whining that she wasn't feeling well. I thought she was trying to goof off as usual. It was only when the medical department sent her home with a 104° temperature that I began to feel a little guilty.

"But that's the way most people are these days, goof-offs. Even my own kids. They don't love their jobs or want to work. You have to keep watching them all the time. I guess the generation in which I grew up is the last sound generation. The new generation is one that wants to give as little and get as much as it possibly can."

He went on to say, "It wasn't this way when I was a kid. My father would sit down at the table, and I would sit down immediately on his right, and if I ever opened my mouth, or left any food, I got a good slap on the face. I had to eat exactly what my father ate. He set the standards. I can remember many times when I was sick because I ate every bit that was on my plate. There was no choice, actually. I ate it because I didn't want to be slapped, but sometimes I couldn't digest it, so I'd wait until supper was over and upchuck. There was no question about leaving food. I ate it. The choice I had was whether or not to keep it in my stomach. If I was too full, I could go to the bathroom or sneak out into the yard and throw it up. That was my solution. There are many foods I can't eat because of the attitude I developed toward them when I was a child."

"Well," he said in conclusion, "I know I'm a hard son of a gun, and that a lot of people either hate my guts or are scared silly when I'm around, perhaps both. I can't help it. In many ways, though, I think I have treated my own children a lot better than my father treated me. Occasionally I beat them up, but I always climb the stairs in disgrace and ask them for forgiveness. I may not be entirely consistent, but my old man never climbed the stairs to make amends with me after he'd beaten *me* up."

Bill's reminiscences got the others thinking about their respective childhood experiences and tracing conditions to the present day.[3] I almost intervened to help them refocus their thoughts, but I decided to hold off a bit longer.

Steve Jacobs said, "I don't participate well with you-all, I know. I have strong convictions, but I got punished when I was a kid for expressing my thoughts. Even today, I have a tendency to stay silent in a controversy unless it's a life-or-death matter. But I still have my convictions, and I don't like a lot of what is going on. Someday I'd like to tell you about the many things going on in this department that should never happen anywhere."

Stan Wood, the last person to come up for leveling that day, described himself as being out of step with the group. Stan said that he felt like a second rate citizen in relation to other division heads. He is consulted only on minor issues. He told the others that his natural reaction to being left out is to sulk. Stan immediately received feedback about his sulkiness. Apparently it had been making the others loath to bring him a problem that required a policy formulation.

Having disposed of that misunderstanding, they turned to his positive qualities. Stan, as he says, is a humanist. He takes the human dregs of the other Engineering divisions and finds jobs that are suitable for these persons' limited skills, creating conditions under which they try to give optimal performance. He is well liked, and his division has the highest morale in the department. Bob Bell, personnel coordinator in the department, says that Stan has the broadest perspective in terms of constructive ways of working with the union.

Now, at the end of the day, I have a few general thoughts to record.

Almost inevitably, when several managers operate a component of an organization, they become personally involved in the decisions that must be made. Such involvement develops spontaneously unless the leadership is so autocratic and unilateral that each person has only a restricted area to supervise, with no glimpse of the larger picture. When involvement in decision making does occur, hosts of phenomena are released in the areas of competition, friction, suspicion of one another's motives, relative feelings of strength, weakness, and personal competence.

Out of these attitudes and actions, a pecking order is generated. Internal social structures arise. Normative criteria to guide action begin to appear which are not in the rule book.

A "production" system of relationships can easily turn into a "political" one. Unless the official leader of the group, or its members, are able to discuss the relationship problems of the informal pecking order and the social structure on normative criteria of action (to ensure that the organization continues developing in an *intelligent* manner), it is likely to develop along unsystematic lines of *friendship* influences and unfairly distributed rewards and sanctions. Then, as a spoils system begins to intrude, people start reacting to the political aspects rather than to the production aspects of their relationship. This increases dislocation in the formerly rational production system, and produces discouragement and withdrawal of its members. This is the situation in Quinn's management committee, and also in the Engineering Department.

A group, through interacting, should gain control of itself and align its activities with regard to production requirements rather than interpersonal politics. In a leveling session the goal is to uncover each individual's perception of the situation and his place in it. In addition, each person can see how his operation within a certain social structure influences the behavior of others. Another goal of the leveling session is to explore how the social structure itself came to be formed, and how individuals presently relate to one another within the social structure. The ultimate purpose of this diagnostic work is to rebuild the social structure in order to bring the skills and limitations of those who compose its membership into a relationship compatible with the task at hand.

Let me describe three things that a leveling session should *not* aim for. First of all, a leveling session is *not* a confessional where individuals reveal their past sins and promise to do better in the future. Nonetheless, a leveling session does have aspects which could be misconstrued as being of a confessional nature. From the objective point of view, a confessional would make little contribution to performance because the catharsis-contrition-penance-absolution sequence is not conducive to long-term behavioral modification. It doesn't get at the motivation of the guilty act. Though confession reveals some known or secret peccadilloes, the motivation to repeat them may remain.

A second thing that a leveling session is *not* is a brain-washing program in which a person recounts his misdeeds in the presence of others who then can use these revelations as tools to control him.[4] By comparison, the material discussed in a leveling session is completely work oriented and related to the here-and-now situation. The only components of adjustment that are examined in any detail at all are those which are directly connected with work and the context of social relations under which it must be accomplished. Notwithstanding the possibility that some people, like Bill, may spontaneously bring up details of their personal lives, these sessions need not, and really should not, involve an examination of one's childhood experience or one's performance as a husband, or as a father. Thus, if the concentration can stay focused on diagnosis of the immediate situation and of whatever problems individuals have within the work structure, the brainwashing dynamic is precluded.

And finally, a leveling session is *not* a charm school. The goal is not to aid individuals to speak more softly, more forcefully, or more eloquently, though all of these may result. The heart of the problem which leveling addresses lies deeper. When a person doesn't speak forcefully, it may be because he is fearful; thus the conditions producing this fear must be sought. When a person doesn't make sense, it could be that he is under tension. The most direct way to improve the logic of his discourse is not to send him to a course in speech, but to look for conditions that are making that individual defensive and are prompting him to generate complicated sentences and formulations.

References

1. See: Buffa, E.S. *Modern Production Management* (3rd Ed.). New York: John Wiley & Sons, Inc., 1969, p. 139.

2. The "Power Spectrum" is described in Blake, R.R. and Mouton, J.S. *Group Dynamics—Key to Decision Making*. Houston: Gulf Publishing Company, 1961, Chapter 3. "1/0" denotes a situation where the person in the position of leadership actually controls all of the weight on the decision that is made regarding one or more matters of collaboration between himself and a subordinate.

3. For comparable examples, see Brandon, N. *Breaking Free*. Los Angeles, Nash Publishing Corporation, 1970.

4. Schein, E.H. "The Chinese Indoctrination Program for Prisoners of War: A Study of Attempted Brainwashing." *Psychiatry, 19*, 1956, pp. 149-172.

30

Switchback to a Settlement

The IEW stalwarts were at the gate this morning, January 5, handing out Dan's latest pamphlet. Its theme is that once again management has insulted the workers, this time by first giving 14 cents to red circle people and then reducing it a half cent per hour every month until the red circle rates have been phased out.

As Dan put it, "Nothing short of fair and equal treatment will satisfy us. This is a general wage increase, not a merit adjustment. It is to compensate for rises in the cost of living, and the red circle people are entitled to this just as much as anyone else. We will not settle for less than 14 cents for everyone; and indeed, we want to do better than that. Why should we be treated less favorably than the salary people? That would constitute a violation of union principle." The handout concluded, "Regardless of where your emotions lie—independent, international, or wherever—don't sell out for the glitter of gold. The principle is more important than the pocket book." In my view Dan is right, as he has been since he assumed this position. In his simple way of formulating issues, the problem was clear at that time and it remains clear.

Management initially reacted with, "Maybe we'd better issue our own bulletin to inform the people about the real issues." This reaction was short lived. Management soon concluded that it was profitless to get into another feud. Perhaps the union was inviting an eye-and-tooth fight on this one, but the worst thing that management could do would be to accept. This is what Quinn told all the management personnel today. He did not phrase it in quite this way, but the message expressed his thinking and conviction.

Management is tremendously fearful of submitting, and the question I keep asking is, "Why?" One answer is that if management ceded the 7 cents it would be reprimanded by headquarters for failing to align its wage rates with area standards. This is an important consideration even though Atlanta is not presently applying pressure. Another reason for not wanting to submit is that management has upheld its red circle position for more than two months and feels that to give up now would show weakness. Furthermore, Dan is behaving like a bully, and if you're a real man you don't submit to bullies.

There are, however, pressing reasons for settling the red circle dispute quickly, with submission offering the quickest means. Lakeside recently clinched a lucrative contract for packaging certain materials for other major companies, and it needs to begin a packaging line by Monday. This can only be done with the union's collaboration. When Wes mentioned the matter, Dan replied, "We have told you, we can't discuss anything further until we settle the wage offer. If you try putting people to work on that job, we will find a way to beat it. If you want to take the risk, we will answer the challenge."

A second matter is that a massive and complex new piece of equipment is to go into use next week. It requires one less operator than the equipment which it replaces, and the conditions of this situation have not yet been bargained. A heavy burden of costs and foregone profits is incurred every day the new unit is not in operation.

Mac Anthony told me this Thursday morning that he talked to Quinn last night. Mac said that he felt impelled to advise the general manager of what he, Mac, saw to be the present state of the union-management situation: that Quinn was in trouble now because of the spreading ramifications of the problem, and that, in Mac's opinion, he needed to get it quickly resolved.

Responding to this warning, Quinn, with Cal's assistance, gathered information from those whose opinions were important to his decision. A meeting was held, which consisted of the bargaining team, its backup committee, and myself.

Just prior to the meeting, Mac told me he wanted to create conditions under which management's bargaining team could change its position without losing face. My reaction was that management had gotten into its present predicament by virtue of its own decision and, therefore, it should not search for face-saving measures but should openly and honestly proclaim that it made an apparently unwise decision.

Management Reevaluates

As I arrived at the meeting, the issue being discussed was, "Who should we bargain with at this juncture, with Dan, or with 'the people'?" Earl thought that now was the opportune time to bargain with the people, because it is they who can put pressure on the union officials to settle the dispute. Randy Cox, in rebuttal, said since Green Acres, management has been committed to treating the union officers with dignity and respect. Cal suddenly jumped on Randy, demanding, "Why didn't you tell us back in October what you're telling us now?"

"We *did* tell you! You didn't listen. Everyone was so devoutly committed to eliminating the red circle problem that our voices were simply too small to gain an adequate hearing."

Randy's retort sparked off a confused kind of squabble as various members harked back to October and reconstructed what they thought their understandings and keynote statements had been at that time.

At this point, I made a critical intervention, pointing out two things that I saw and heard going on right nowm "First, a defeat reaction is coming through loud and clear. If you see 'moving off the 7-cents position' as a defeat, that's how you'll feel it. Since you're apparently about to do that, tensions are very high. People are accusing one another of incompetence, of not having listened, and of not having achieved consensus in the first place. While this is an understandable reaction to what's perceived as a defeat, it is not a productive one. It keeps one's thinking focused on yesterday, neglecting to search the environment for a future alternative."

The other point in my intervention was that, with factions in the committee batting back and forth, Quinn must be getting few, if any, glimpses of the present array of options, much less any comparison of their relative merits. Therefore, it might be best to go over the entire matter again with the department heads, and establish some definite plan of action.

At eleven o'clock, the decision was made to do just that. A telephone call went out and the entire group of 13 was assembled in 30 minutes. Quinn put the problem to the group in the following way: "We can't stay where we are, but where do we go? One position is to go with the 14 cents, and the other is to move to a new offer, one which provides a more liberal basis of adjustment, but which preserves the principle of improving the red circle situation."

It was decided to go around the table and have each member indicate what he thought management's action should be.

Wes Stratton led off with, "We've had it. The situation is going to hell in a handbasket. We can't do business with the union either on contract negotiation or on manning the packaging line and new equipment, because they want to settle the wage issue before going on to other matters. We can't move the union off its position. It's time to admit we're licked, give them the 14 cents and start anew."

Carl O'Brien had another viewpoint. "We think we're right, and the union thinks it's right. The way things are, neither side is able to look at the situation objectively. Let's have a mediator sort out what's acceptable to us and to the union."

Earl Higgins' recommendation was, "We tested them last Friday by offering the downward adjustment of a half cent per month. They didn't buy, so let's try something else, say, 10 cents instead of 7 for the red circle.

"Sure," he continued, "Getting back into negotiation with the union is the first goal, but the principles underlying the red circle issue should be discussed because the union doesn't clearly understand them.

"There's a good chance that it will work out in our favor. As of now, it would be a good idea to mention the retroactivity problem as something for them to worry about, but we should improve our offer. I feel we should make another test, and watch the reaction. That will indicate how much support Dan has from his people. Then we'll have a basis for a quick agreement, one way or another."

He summed up explicitly, "Let's hold out, put in another offer, wait a few days and see what happens. That may be enough to dislodge Dan from his obstructive position. If this doesn't work, then maybe we can go all the way to 14 cents."

Van Gray counseled, "There's no rush, time's on our side. The longer people have to wait for their wage increases the more pressure builds up against the union. The wage people are going to force Dan to come to terms. It's a wonder they haven't already. Let's wait a few more days. Then if there's no breakthrough, we could go to 10 cents or something comparable and see if we can't settle below the 14-cent level. Even if we have to go to 12, at least we'll have retained the principle that the red circle problem has to be corrected. But if we just give up and hand over the full 14 cents, those who are not red circle will be hurt and the supervisors will feel that we have sold out."

Wes then commented on Carl's proposal. "Bringing in a mediator would help to save face, because if the mediator said, 'Management has a good position, but the union can't buy it because it violates union principles,' then management could yield without losing the supervisors' confidence. But the disadvantage of Carl's proposal is that the union, which has held so steadfastly to its point, would feel that it hasn't influenced management's thinking one iota, because it took a mediator to do the trick. That would leave a bitter after-taste to carry into the next round of negotiation."

Earl disliked the mediator proposition because this would establish a precedent. When the next bargaining deadlock occurred, the union would say, "Okay, bring in the mediator."

Wilson Jennings said, "I am certainly not ready to recommend going all the way to 14 cents." Then he played the old grind, "We have a responsibility to the *non* red circle people to correct the wage structure. They expect us to be fair, as well as firm. If we fail to get a compromise, it's important that the supervisors and wage people know that we tried."

Quinn remarked, "The way we're set up in union relations prevents us from correcting the inequities that exist in the wage structure."

Burt Porter said that we must remember two related issues: (a) the number of cents in the offer, and (b) retroactivity. To supervisors and foremen, retroactivity is a burning issue. To them, it seems unreasonable for management to offer full retroactivity at this stage of the game, since the union, having been offered the wage increase back in October, has repeatedly refused to accept it. Therefore, the union should suffer the consequences of its refusal. "If we give in on 14 cents and retroactivity, how can these front-line supervisors respect us?" Burt then recommended that the bargaining team certainly shouldn't go all the way to 14 cents plus retroactivity. "If you go all the way on one, hold back on the other. Since we started out with the conviction that red circle rates should be phased out, we should still have that conviction."

Randy Cox harked back to Quinn's initial posing of the problem. "There is an important element here, which is concerned with the question, 'Is the 7-cent issue dead?' If it *is* dead, then we should bury it and pay up. After all, did the October strategy for getting a red circle correction have a logical basis?"

Someone who was substituting for Bill Jones said, "Last October we put the union in an intolerably tough spot; Dan had to choose between either fighting us or dropping dead in the eyes of his members. We all know what's happened since, he's fought well, and he's still gaining points. Our problem today boils down to 'How to get out of the ring and back to the table.' No timekeeper's bell is going to save us, so we'd better induce Dan back into bargaining. My proposal is that we go to 10 or even 14 cents pronto."

Sam Allen remarked that he sensed an inevitableness in the 14 cents, but he thought that the masons, and one or two other skilled-labor grades of people who have disproportionate wages, ought to be focused upon as an area of improvement. "Maybe we could bargain out a non-increase for the masons, et cetera, as *quid pro quo* for the full 14 cents for the rest of the red circle personnel. It's worth a try anyway. If this doesn't work, let them all have their 14 cents."

Paul Simpson commented that while both red circle proposals were intended to take money away from many people, the second offer, the downward adjustment by one-half cent per month, seems to have been much more offensive than the first, judging from the additional union resistance it has generated. He believes, too, that he has heard the first rumbles of an impending strike.

As to particular red circle rates, Paul, like Sam Allen, wanted one or two of the rough ones like the masons bargained out of existence, using the offer of 14 cents for everyone else as an inducement. Paul felt that there should be no retroactivity at all, because he felt the union might have earned a slap on the hand.

Next, I was asked for my opinion. I said, "I'd prefer not to comment on the pros and cons of the issue, but I can comment about the process. Beginning with the red circle offer and continuing through last Friday's modified offer of a rolling adjustment, management has tried to keep its ear to the ground through two listening posts. One listening post tries to pick up wage earner reactions, and the other listening post monitors union affairs. This kind of bargaining involves motivational levers that would cause people to desert their union leaders. In the last few minutes, as well as over the last several months, I have heard management trying to produce desertion dynamics. In this way, management can win its point and teach Dan a lesson at the same time. This is bargaining with the people."

My intervention produced a very hostile reaction from Van, because in the light of Lakeside history, "bargaining with the people" is a dirty phrase. He did not want to be accused of bargaining with the people. Yet the evidence is clear that he and Earl are trying to cause a rift between the union membership and its officers.

When Quinn asked Cal for his opinion, Cal burst out that there were "some characters" who were being two-faced on this issue, saying one thing in public and another thing in private. Wes, who frequently has been accused of doing this, reacted sensitively but had no opportunity to reply because Quinn quickly suggested to Cal, "Let's get together later and discuss this." Evidently Cal had learned of Mac's "night call," in which Mac warned Quinn of impending disaster, and considered this as an instance of Mac working out of channels—an outrageous transgression by someone in a "staff" slot.

Finally, Quinn presented his position, which was the same as one already proposed, "Set up one more meeting with the union, take an intermediate stance between 7 and 14 cents, and if that isn't accepted, go all the way." But having listened to the several points of view expressed, he wondered what they might be risking by dragging their feet. As compared with Van, who considers that time is a pressure on the union, Quinn said that he regards time as an even greater pressure on himself and on Lakeside management. "The pressures from EPOCH headquarters aren't particularly strong at the moment, but they're saying 'You people had better find some basis for resolution quickly. You've made a lot of progress with your union, but this delay represents a failure to make further progress. It indicates a possibly serious deterioration in union-management affairs.'"

"Was that Satan condemning sin, or do I hear Jim Hall?" Wes queried. Quinn said that he'd been giving a composite summary, and quoted directly from some telephone conversations he has had recently with Atlanta and Chicago. Gerry North, one of the EPOCH directors, feels that it's silly to continue this hopeless effort, that Lakeside management ought to wake up, realize its predicament, and begin to bail itself out. Henry Nesbit, a high-ranking officer in superheadquarters, is fully informed of the union-management fracas, and he, too, feels that management is acting absurdly. He has said, "Get with it, and get a solution." But Allen Eastman at Mountainview feels it would be terrible to give up at this time.

"Well, that's awfully sad about Allen's feelings," Wes interjected, "but we're not obliged to keep him happy."

"Well, in a way, we are," Quinn replied, "and Jim Hall's got a stake in it too." Wes and some of the others expressed puzzlement and so eventually Quinn related the whole sad story.

An Unknown Factor is Revealed

Last October, before deciding what to do about the red circle, Quinn called Allen Eastman about his prospective position. At that time, Mountainview had a very minor red circle problem which would have involved a cost increase of only $3,000 per year. When Quinn suggested amending the EPOCH offer as a way of adjusting rates, Allen's reaction was, "We have a good, stable union relationship, and I would hate to disrupt it by making an issue of the red circle."

Quinn rejoined, "Allen, if you don't stand by me on this one, I'll never be able to correct my red circle problem here, because our union will say, 'They were able to get it, so give it to us.'" When Allen still jibbed, Quinn applied more pressure on him to comply. It was subtle pressure like, "Well, if you can't support us, we are sorry. We thought you could, but we understand." Allen did not like the pressure, but found it hard to resist because Quinn, his former boss, had once made the key recommendation that resulted in his becoming general manager of Mountainview.

Eventually Allen agreed to ally himself with Quinn, with the understanding that neither would weaken. Allen liked this situation because, with Quinn's support, he could make modest improvements that would net him a few points from headquarters, and when he took a favorable position, Quinn was very complimentary, and boosted him to John Edwards and Neal Young of headquarters.

With the zeal of the newly converted, Allen at first tried to eliminate Mountainview's red circle rates. He got a strong reaction from the union, but it was just about to give in when headquarters told Allen to trim 7 cents, as Quinn had done, rather than 14. After some more hassling, the union accepted in time to meet the first of EPOCH's retroactivity deadlines. However, Johnny Johnson, the union president, insisted on a rein check proviso that in a better settlement were achieved "elsewhere," Mountainview would receive a corresponding increase.

Quinn told Allen that if Lakeside restored the entire general wage increase to the red circle people, Allen would be informed in advance so that he could offer it to his own plant's union first. After hearing the reaction from Mountainview's union, Quinn could make the appropriate adjustment with the Lakeside union.

It turned the stomachs of everyone, that Allen would try to portray Mountainview as being enlightened enough to reconstitute the red circle, instead of revealing that it was Dan's obdurate resistance which caused the improved offer. While no one in management wanted Dan to win, they surely didn't want Allen to enjoy the blessings of his red circle employees and the union at Mountainview, while Lakeside was being forced to capitulate to its own union, apparently as a result of what had occurred at Mountainview. To quote Wes, "For God's sake, why the pantomime? Why should Allen get an employee-relations bonus at our expense? *He's* not sacrificing anything; he hasn't taken part in the battle we've been through. And he's not losing any brownie points with Jim Hall either. Everyone in Atlanta knows that *we're* having to yield, not Allen."

Quinn replied, "Okay, okay. But I *have* made that commitment, and he's holding me to it."

At this point almost everyone joined in chorus and said, "We've got to put pressure on Allen to free us to move." Rather than scapegoating internally, the group was unifying to face an external threat. Quinn said he'd already approached Allen, who told him it would be at least a week before the Mountainview union would react.

Quinn leaned back in his chair, brows knitted, and paused a moment. Finally he said, "The situation's gotten bad, but it could get worse." Then he hit his punch line. "We took that 7-cents position, which was a mistake. EPOCH's 5% and 14 cents was a wrong offer. It drew an invidious distinction where none was justified. We made things worse by reducing the red circle to 7 cents. The benefits program was bungled too, mostly by headquarters, but partly by ourselves. We've made mistakes, and we continually seem to cause people to be against management.

"All right, then," he said, "I'm going to telephone Allen and turn him around. I think I still have enough clout with him to do that, if necessary. That'll free us to move here, but we'll have to make another offer. To get things moving so we can hammer out a contract, this next offer has to contain a concession on the red circle. Is that agreed?" He glanced around the table; there were a few nods and shrugs.

Wes said, "I think it's the logical thing to do. In this case we're having to buy movement, but there's nothing shameful about that. Hell, if you've an important appointment downtown and you lose your way trying to get there, you take a cab and pay the fare to get where you want to be. What I'm saying is, this is not a defeat or a bribe for Dan or any other such crap. We're buying transportation back to the bargaining table, back to contract negotiation, back from the wilderness where we've been since October."

Wes added, "And it's imperative that we move on this issue right away, because Dan's going OUB tomorrow and will be on vacation after Saturday."

Cal jumped in, "Who told you that? Mac?"

With a hard look and soft voice, Wes replied, "No, Cal, it was my secretary. Dan had just telephoned her."

"That was at least two hours ago!"

"I don't know what you're getting at . . ."

"*Oh*-kay," Quinn interposed, "Now, if we're all agreed, let's get with it. I'm going to put in a call to Allen, which may take awhile. Wes, find Dan and see if we can get a bargaining session between 4:30 and whenever he's leaving. If we have to meet with them at midnight, so be it. Van, would you please tell the rest of the team to stand by while Wes makes the arrangements."

From the look on his face, Van didn't feel that this was the right approach, but he is a good soldier. When "Colonel" Quinn speaks, "Major" Van salutes and obeys.

People were getting up out of their chairs, so I pitched in hurriedly with an intervention I had intended to make in a more apropos context. I said that Quinn, when he makes the new offer, should indicate that management hasn't lost sight of developing an effective, collaborative basis with the union. Quinn resisted taking that position, arguing that it would encourage the union to take a win-lose stance the next time an issue arose. Then he and the others sped out of the room.

So here's more evidence of management's lack of faith in the integrity of union officers. There is no reason to assume that because the union has taken an understandably antagonistic position against what management has now admitted to have been an incorrect move last October, they will, on the next occasion, be pugnacious.

Dan Reveals the Union's Despair

When Wes contacted Dan, Dan suggested that 8:30 tomorrow morning would be an acceptable time for him and the rest of the delegation. He offered to reschedule his other union business, and even postpone his vacation if necessary.

Wes felt a little irritated by what he took to be gloating eagerness on Dan's part. But he thought to himself, as he told me later, "Hell, I've got to admit the man's achieved something. Why should I be unsportsmanlike about it?" He wanted to congratulate Dan on his success, but it would have been scooping Quinn, so he decided not to. Instead, he remarked, "That was a real piledriver of a handout you circulated, Dan."

The union president gave a wry grin. "Yeah, it scared the daylights out of our own people!" Dan said that the union had been hurt by publicizing the "rolling adjustment" offer, because many of the wage people thought it meant that management had the union by the short hairs and was dictating ever more severe terms. Consequently, they think it is hopeless to try for a better settlement; in fact, Dan admitted, there's a general feeling that the union should throw in the sponge. Therefore, he continued, the union would favor any offer that was a bit better than last week's. He did not indicate whether or not the union would come to terms even on the bare 7 cents, but the implication was very strong.

This put Wes into a severe internal conflict, which was worsened by Dan's cooperative mood. Wes now felt that management should move quickly, skip the intermediate positions, and get right to the 14 cents. Up to this moment, he had been convinced that the union had effectively wrestled management into submission. Now Dan was saying, by implication at least, "We've had it, Wes, we're ready to surrender. Buddy, can you spare a dime?—or maybe 7 cents?"

At this point, Wes was tremendously tempted to tell Dan to hold out for the 14 cents and that he would get it. But he couldn't bring himself to be a traitor to Quinn and his colleagues.

"I came damn close to doing it, Bob," he told me later, "and y'know what stopped me? A name popped into my mind, and I thought to myself, 'Aren't you just trying to lash back at Cal, really?' He'd been bugging me all day with his aspersions about Mac. But I still felt that Dan was entitled to the full 14 cents."

Quinn had already dutch-uncled Allen Eastman into meeting with the Mountainview union tomorrow. He and Allen still hadn't agreed on the amount to be offered, but Quinn favored a 10 or 11-cent position which would preserve the "correction" principle but which would be an improvement over previous offers. Thus Quinn's offer would satisfy Dan's expectations, even though it was more than he might have settled for, and less than what he might get if he stood firm. Once again, Wes was in a moral quandary. He decided not to tell Quinn about Dan's unwillingness to take less than 10 cents.

"I was wrung out by this time, Bob. I remembered Van and Earl bragging about how well they could evaluate the union's actions, and that did it!"

A Giant Step is Taken

So today, Friday, January 8, is the critical day for the red circle problem. The office building was dark when I arrived this morning at 7:45. A few minutes later, Quinn arrived nervous and wanting to talk with someone. He was wondering what to do and how to do it; whether to raise the red circle offer from 7 to 10 cents, or whether to go all the way.

The issue was almost already decided, because Mountainview is going all the way. Last night, Allen Eastman told Quinn that he, Allen, didn't want to make a federal case of it; he preferred merely to announce the increase in a matter-of-fact way, and get back to business. This closed out any realistic prospects of Lakeside going for less than 14 cents, even though Quinn still had the idea in his mind. "After all," he rationalized, "Allen won't be getting with *his* union for a few hours yet, and maybe, in the meantime, we could clinch it at 10 cents and then ask Allen to hold it there too." But I think Quinn realized his organizational-fatherly influence on Allen was fading fast.

Wes joined us and advised Quinn to think a straight 14 cents. Quinn attempted to rationalize why management had been right and why the effort had been wrong. This continued when Van and Earl came in at 8:30.

At 8:45, the entire bargaining group had assembled, and they met with the union. Quinn, true to form, went into a long, boring analysis of the red circle problem. He restated that "if our wage rates are out of line it means that we're not competitive enough to attract new capital investment to Lakeside; red circle rate inequities are unjust to the rest of the people," and other items of litany. Finally, the other members of the management team became so itchy that Wes passed Quinn a note suggesting a caucus.

Then, in private, Wes and some of the others urged Quinn to get down to brass tacks. They said, "Dan's got one hand on his springing slip and the others are dozing off. Let's stop yacking and tell them what we've come here to say."

Upon returning to the bargaining table, Quinn said, "As I was saying, our intention has been to correct inequities between various rates. But unfortunately we have gotten into a win-lose fight which has gone on for months. We sincerely want to restore an atmosphere of problem solving and collaboration. In order to resolve the issue that has been separating us, I would like to offer 14 cents across-the-board, retroactive to October 27th, and I hope that you can give us an answer within a week."

Dan went into a sort of deep-breathing exercise, and became dewy-eyed. He replied, "I'll tell you, we're in a difficult position. There've been so few occasions when the management of Lakeside has ever offered anything, that we don't know how to accept. It might take as long as two weeks to book a hall, advertise a meeting with due notice, and then hold a referendum on ratifying the offer."

Quinn said, "Well, it would be awfully good if you could get it ratified within a week."

"Okay, give us five minutes for a powwow." The union took a caucus and came back in no time at all, with Dick as spokesman.

"We've decided in principle to accept the offer. We wish we'd been able to get 5%, and we'll report to our people that we tried for more, but getting the full 14 cents is the best we could accomplish." Dick said they'd try to organize a membership meeting by next week. Meanwhile, they agreed to announce that the new 14-cent offer had been made and that it would be taken to the membership for ratification.

Dan left the bargaining session, and in twenty minutes was phoning back to say that a membership meeting for ratification would be held next Tuesday night.

Meanwhile, there was still an open question as to who, union or management or both, should announce the "agreement in principle"; the *Lakeside Today* newsletter would not be issued until next week. At the close of the meeting, Van indicated that "for reasons of communication" members of the union delegation should break the news at the meeting on Tuesday, and not before.

When Dan returned to the room, he said, "We can't o that. Everyone will want to know, and they'll start asking us questions the moment they spot us. We don't want to be dishonest and say that we have not gotten agreement, especially when you've settled on our terms."

He peered at Van, and went on, "Look, you fellows shouldn't be so down in the mouth about all this. We're back on the track now, and can start fresh. This agreement's restored dignity and respect to us as representatives of the workers. It shows that we're strong, dogged and determined. Maybe, too, we're just a little smart, even though we don't have college degrees and big offices. But the main thing, Van, is that we never would have submitted. I might have carried the union down to destruction with me, but I wouldn't have given in, and neither would any of my brother delegates." Max, Thomas, Sol, and the others voiced their solidarity. Wes, apparently, was the only one present who could recall Dan's mood of yesterday. The union president concluded, "Don't worry, things are bound to go better from now on. As for myself, I feel six tons lighter. I just didn't see our way out of this one, but I knew I had to keep plugging 'til we got some movement."

Van eventually saw that there was no hope of pledging Dan to confidentiality, and discussion ended with the implicit understanding that each group would report separately to its own constituency.

The meeting ended with handshakes on the settlement. As Max was going out, he said to one of the secretaries, "Y'know, I feel better today than I've felt in five years. This is a good day. It's a bright day. It's the beginning of a new era."

By noontime, a feeling of victory was permeating the wage ranks. Workers were table-hopping in the dining room, congratulating one another, shaking hands, and making cracks about various members of management.

In the management committee, however, the mood was quite different. The immediate after-effects were being felt most keenly by those members—Mac, Wes, Carl, and Randy—who had been in favor of the 14-cent resolution all along.

It didn't take long for depression to set in. Nearly three months of intensive and daily analysis, re-analysis, cross-checking, verifying and comparing, and coordinating with other plant managements and headquarters, had produced great strain. Now, the way things had developed, no one could feel completely certain about which of the many positions taken was the most valid one. I think Wes and the other three are depressed because although their point of view prevailed, it never achicved consensus among the hard-nosed members of management who had no alternative but to accept the situation as it turned out. Van, Carl, and Earl still believe that their point of view ultimately would have proven victorious.

On the other hand, those members of the management committee who accepted Quinn's decision without conviction either way, now appear numb.

The issue is gone, and they're glad to be rid of it.

My reactions are interesting as well. I am not depressed, just let down. All afternoon, I paced the floor, unable to lock my attention on any concrete problem. I wanted to escape the situation. Several times I thought I would catch a plane for home. When it was too late to get connections, I began saying to myself, "I'll go to my hotel early and have a nap." Around 5:15, just as I was leaving, Wes came by with his calendar book in his hand. He said, "God, I'm bushed. By the way, what is your hotel phone number?"

I told him.

He went on, "I think I'll need to talk with someone this weekend, and I'm glad you'll be staying around. I feel I'm going to need some help."

I said, "Okay, give me a ring."

31

Pecking and Packaging

Doug Fowler, EPOCH's labor lawyer, visits Lakeside often to counsel management about legal issues between itself and the union. As a result, Doug is intimately acquainted with Lakeside's management and personnel coordinators on both the wage and the salary side, as well as knowing the wage and salary union officers. When he visited the plant today I asked him what changes could he see in attitudes toward the union problems.

He replied instantly, "The most dramatic change is that management, at the top echelon, has grown up. It now has a mature understanding of labor relations that it didn't have three years ago. Management no longer thinks that if it sees a problem, it should immediately go to the union before checking the contract. They've had some trouncings in the past because of that, I can tell you! But these days, the whole atmosphere is different; and it's not because they've learned, grudgingly, from their past humiliations. I think it's a genuine respect for the unions and their officers. This is a much better plant to work with than any other, because these more mature attitudes make problem solving possible between myself, the management, and the union."

He made another point too. "Lakeside attitudes are now different not only from those in other plants that have independent unions, they also are entirely different from those in plants that have an international union. Where there is an independent union, management's attitude is one of callous disrespect. Where there is an international, the attitude is one of unctuousness, of gentlemanly politeness while supping with a long spoon. But Lakeside's attitude is more mature and more realistic."

It's Monday, January 11, and there is no visible trace that a conflict on the red circle problem had been raging here for nearly three months. The social atmosphere is almost completely tranquil, and the only way to stimulate any discussion of the red circle problem is to ask questions about the behavior of a specific union official. Such a question might bring a reaction concerning Dan's uncouth militancy, Max's subtle generalship, and so on; but little about the issues which a few days ago were white-hot controversies. Managers seem glad to be back dealing with technical and operational problems. During

Quinn's staff meeting today, no reference was made to the red circle problem which this group had been debating since October 27.

On Friday, immediately after the union had said it would give the news to its constituents, department heads hastily met with their division heads and told them what the score was. There was no discussion on the pros and cons. The second-level managers simply told their supervisors and foremen and that was that. Over the weekend, management has had an opportunity to lick its wounds and face familiar everyday issues. I sense a parallel here with what happened after the upward influence conference.

On Tuesday night, the union officials took their agreement-in-principle to the wage membership and asked that it be ratified. One hundred and sixty-five members were present at the meeting, this being the biggest turnout of any in the past two years. Usually there are about sixty to seventy members present. The 14 cents across-the-board offer was accepted unanimously.

On Wednesday morning I talked with Cal Carroll about attitudes and how they influence management to take various positions with respect to union and labor issues. During this discussion, Quinn dropped in, and asked me if I would be free this afternoon.

I said, "I have a commitment, but I can cancel it."

"Why don't you, then? About three o'clock would be fine."

"Okay."

I kept the appointment. As he is accustomed to do on the rare occasions when he and I have a private confab, Quinn got up and shut his office door. Soon he was letting his hair down, saying, "You know, that fool Dan Ives hasn't capitalized one iota on getting the full 14 cents. He's made no attempt to boost himself as a leader who can get results for his people. There's been no 'victory' handout. He hasn't had a word to say, hasn't been around. They tell me he's gone on vacation. He doesn't care whether the IEW wins the next election or not.

"Van is depressed because every report he gets indicates that the international is getting stronger and that the independent is going out the window. No one in the plant respects Dan. They call him a big Polak. They're disgusted with him. I don't respect him myself. How can a union bargain with management and fight off the international when it's got that kind of leadership?"

Quinn looked out the window at some of the plant buildings and continued, "What really gripes me is that after a year of hard work, we haven't influenced a single foreman to think constructively about improving union relations."

And so the monologue went. I was struck not so much with the content of Quinn's remarks but more with what his behavior indicated: a post-defeat kind of decompression. Quinn is edgy because he doesn't know if he was right in settling with the union. No one's come in to congratulate him on the 14-cent decision, and he wasn't even told about the wage personnel celebrating in their cafeteria at lunchtime last Friday. He doesn't trust the information he gets from the yard because, as he said, "I talked to the same two people that Van does, and they always say the same things." He is aware that he doesn't know what is going on in the lower reaches of the organization—particularly in regard to the international's signup campaign—and this makes him uneasy.

I told him, "It seems that much of the pertinent evidence hasn't been reviewed yet. Maybe it isn't necessary for Van or yourself to poll seventeen hundred wage-earners, but a sample of *two* isn't a sound base for forming conclusions. If your present two confidants are always saying the same thing, it seems to me you've got two 'yes men.' "

"Okay, okay," he snapped, "I get the point. So what else is new?"

I said, "We decided a long time ago that the best way to foster a strong independent union is for the managers, supervisors, and foremen to have sound relations with their wage people. If the wage people are satisfied by management, then they're hardly likely to seek international affiliation in order to get their problems solved."

"I, too, believe in Motherhood," he interjected waspishly.

"Splendid. Now, let's go back a year or so. My first goal, wage-personnel training, was effectively forestalled. We next tried foreman training, which was initially well received, but because of division level decisions, it was discontinued."

"The problem today," I said, "just as it was last year, is that from the division heads downward, everyone is straining to implement policy actions that produce profit results. 'Labor relations are for the birds,' these middle managers say, because they recognize that they are being judged according to operations results, not according to labor relations results. The reward system dictates the route that people will take."

Our discussion then turned to Lakeside's concurrent dimension, union-management, when Quinn exclaimed, "There aren't many months to go until the next representation election, and things had better start cracking soon!" Van had told Quinn, on the basis of that two-man sample survey, that the international is running strong. This has almost panicked Quinn. He has scheduled a meeting for the department heads at Lincoln Lodge a week from today, at which he will emphasize the importance of creating conditions which ensure a resounding election victory for the independent union. If Dan is reelected, so be it; but I'm sure Quinn would be delighted to see Ted Rogers or Sol Sommers seize the IEW tiller and come out ahead of the international's budding candidate, Morris Jenkins.

Renewed Bargaining

The first bargaining session after the ratification was held on Friday, and it was a tenterhooks meeting. Neither side could attain the objective state of mind necessary for hiring people to work in Receiving, Packaging and Shipping (RP&S)—the area where a new production line is being created to service orders from non-EPOCH companies. I'd surmise that both bargaining partners, from force of habit, were waiting for emotional stimulation, but not finding it. The issue had already been correctly formulated as a problem to be worked out, not as another controversy to be fought to a victory-defeat conclusion. The union has developed criteria for its part in the solution, but can't apply them until management reveals how the line is to be manned. Management seems to be somewhat reticent; partly, perhaps, because of a burned-finger reaction to the wage increase outcome, and also because the intellectually-formulated issue is, as yet, emotionless. The meeting ended with a good exploration of the problem, but without an adequate search for possible alternative solutions.

Departmental and Divisional Conflicts

I spent the rest of Friday with the Chemical Products Department assisting Carl and his men with its internal operation, much as I had done with the Engineering Department two weeks ago. This second departmental leveling session contrasted in several respects with the earlier one, but I also noticed one broad common theme in both departments, which can be described as follows.

In the social structure of a department or division, its formally appointed chief can exert "reward or punishment" control over his subordinates. These conditions may produce very few *manifest* tension problems. Frictions and animosities may exist, but little overt evidence of trouble emerges because the reward and punishment system of hierarchical control is sufficient to squelch them and to remind everyone what the department or division head wants.

So, generally the department head gets from his division head what he expects. If not, he takes corrective measures, either through reprimand, replacement, or some other device in order to ensure that he gets the results which he considers important. And so it is with the division head. If his expectations are not met, he exhibits impatience or tries to find out why. Those beneath him will click their heels and somehow or other come up with the result he wants, either in fact or by appearance. Thus, the intra-department problems, whatever their severity may be, appear to be under relatively good control. Most of the problems are so subtle and deeply ingrained that they are extremely difficult for members of the department or division to examine among themselves.

By comparison, the problems that do produce observable evidence are those that exist *between* departments or divisions. Here, the conflicting groups are at the same level. What brings about open conflict is that one chief has no coercive authority over another chief; at least in the formal sense. Informally, there may be exceptions to that principle, such as when one division head has the ear of the department head, and thereby is able to exert pressure on another division head. However, if the division head is either unable or unwilling to invoke his department head's authority to bring about cooperation, he has no power available to exercise on a peer. His only alternative involves one-on-one confrontation. In these circumstances a division head interacting with another division head succeeds or fails by virtue of his own interpersonal skills of collaboration. Wherever these skills are inadequate, the failure of one or both division heads becomes recognizable in the conflict that is generated.

In the Engineering Department, for example, there is conflict between the maintenance and construction divisions, between maintenance and the equipment section, and so on. In Chemical Products, conflicts exist between the RP&S division, which puts finished products into a transportable form, and the other divisions of the department which convert raw materials into finished products. So, obviously there are fundamental intergroup conflicts, both within and between departments, that no one knows how to deal with. Even the ultimate hierarchical reward-punishment type of control is not being applied, and the problems are becoming worse. I conclude from these two leveling sessions that the general problem confronting this organization is one of inter-departmental and inter-divisional collaboration. It is a problem of obtaining an effective economic result between heads of groups, where no one has the power to coerce a desired result from another.

When such a problem arises within a department, all kinds of power plays can be seen between division heads who attempt to use the department head as judge and arbiter. In Chemical Products, for example, Barry Sims, head of the White Oils division, goes to Carl and says, "We can't reduce our cost because RP&S is not cooperating."

Roy Moore, the head of RP&S, goes to Carl and says, "We can't run our operation according to the whims of White Oils. We have to schedule our activities for the other major divisions that require packaging and shipping also." Thus, Carl is subjected to pressures from both Barry and Roy to intercede in the other's operations. In effect, he's expected to take the role of an arbiter in order to resolve the dispute.

Another typical conflict situation occurs when two divisions report to different department heads. For example, Jack Smith, of Engineering, is responsible for maintenance. In Chemical Products, Barry Sims' division has heavy operational requirements that frequently demand maintenance services. But Jack is responsible not only for the maintenance of White Oils equipment, but also that of the Acetone division, RP&S, and so on. At any tick of the clock, Jack may receive a call from White Oils for maintenance work. From his point of view, he has to apportion the priority of this call against other calls from RP&S, Acetone, and so on; not to mention calls from other operating departments such as Staple Products. He can't respond instantly to any will-o-the-wisp demand. However, Barry loses money every time Jack fails to respond to one of his needs. Open inter-departmental conflict occurs under those circumstances.

Who is to be the arbiter between departments? The two division heads cannot assign priority with respect to one another, nor can their respective department heads. Theoretically, they can go seek arbitration by Van, the operations superintendent, or by Quinn himself. But this would expose the conflict between the two departments to top executives. Van and Quinn become frustrated and indignant when they learn that departments are unable to solve their own problems. To them, it reflects on the managerial competencies of those who have wandered away from "sound business consistent with good human relations." Van and Quinn are Lakeside's most powerful dispensers of rewards and punishment. Department heads know this, and so they generally avoid going to Van, and almost always avoid going to Quinn.

What is the result? The conflicts are driven underground so that Van and Quinn won't notice them. Intergroup hostilities fester, stereotypes emerge, and norms for thinking about the enemy department develop. Then, division heads react to the very thing which they themselves have created—emotionally exaggerated norms for thinking about the other department. Under these circumstances, the easiest personal defense is an attack. You can protect yourself from blame for doing a poor job by putting the responsibility on your adversary, the person who is not giving cooperation. He also can gripe, saying that the problem is not his, but is caused by the refusal of the other department's division head to offer the kind of help which he is, according to the tenets of organization, obligated to offer. Jack, for example, can protect himself against an operational division's criticism of his "unhelpfulness," simply by saying, "They won't let me schedule in advance their maintenance programs; they want to run their equipment red-hot, twenty-four hours a day, and then press the panic button when they have emergencies; they notify us six hours after we can do anything about it," and so on.

In summary, organizational systems, in which direct power relationships exist between supervisors and subordinates, are structured to achieve the results that the supervisor wants. If they don't, the supervisor has many punitive tools available to correct the situation. If they do, he has numerous rewards which express his pleasure and satisfaction. The system may not be perfect in its operation, but at least it effectively suppresses antipathy, acrimony, and animosity. But this system will not work *across* divisional lines, even within departments, much less across divisional lines that are in different departments. In the intra-departmental situation, a division head has no formal authority to exercise on his peer. The informal recourse he has is to play friendly politics with his department head, a dangerous game for any division head to play. What can he do if he is in conflict with a division which is in another department? Either he can accomplish his end result through excellent interpersonal relations that promote working collaboration, or he can go through his department head, who then goes across to the other department head, who goes down to the division head and then forces cooperation. The latter course of action also is a difficult game to play, because a larger-scale intergroup conflict is set up, which, rather than relieving the difficulties between the two departmental divisions, has a tendency to exaggerate it.

Another step is to go to the third layer up to get a judgment. Arrangements of power control within component sub-systems of the total organization provide no basis for interdependency between departments except by geographical arrangement, that is, as materials flow through work-in-progress toward packaging and shipping. Skeletonized organization charts, even when fleshed out with volumes of position descriptions, leave the biggest organizational problems essentially unexamined and unrelieved. They provide few arrangements which resolve the massive needs for cooperation.

Ostensibly, the linked position descriptions may attempt to do this, stitch by stitch; but the multitude of details and contingencies usually defeats the draftsman, so that he settles for a few helpful bromides.[1] In spite of the fact that classical organization theory says that each subordinate can appeal to his own boss, who then is responsible for mediating the problem, the system doesn't work for two reasons. Within a department, unless they feel the pressures of emergency, division heads don't want to appeal to authority in order to pressure their peers. Between departments, department heads don't want to invade one another's jurisdictions in solving problems between their respective memberships. So what they see clearly, and decry and scoff at, in the inter-union disputes, they fail to see in their own case.

The massive issues *within* management, that is, separate from those of labor-management relations, are intergroup in character, with a myriad of interpersonal implications.

At Lakeside, the problems of inter-divisional conflict are under intense discussion in disguised form. Each department and each division is trying to develop an organizational structure that would be optimal for accomplishing its *own* task. Interestingly enough, most of the suggestions recommend that all of the services that they need for autonomy be located *within* themselves. For example, the operational departments are designing organization charts in which maintenance services come directly under their authority. The same type of approach is being taken with respect to inspection and technical services. The identical, though undiscussed, rationale adopted by each chief seems to be, "If I can get control of the services I need, no one can argue with me, because everyone will be my subordinate."

The Packaging Job Slots

A bargaining session on the RP&S problem of how to man the new packaging line took place Monday afternoon. Lakeside hopes to get contracts with non-EPOCH plants in the vicinity, for example, a neighboring company that produces anti-freeze. By receiving the anti-freeze in bulk and packaging it in gallon cans for commercial distribution, Lakeside can make considerable money on the contract. By making near-capacity use of its own equipment and supervisory personnel, there is also an additional return on investment.

The issue is that the new packaging line requires additional operators, but only for the duration of the contract. It would be good to hire extra permanent employees if it was certain that other packaging contracts would be signed, but currently there is no assurance that this will happen. Therefore, if people are hired on a permanent basis, there might be no way of occupying them when the contract expires, and the company would be stuck with the problem of overstaffing. Or again, if permanent employment were granted, the sales staff might feel compelled to obtain contracts in order to keep equipment and personnel employed, even though this activity returned little or nothing to the company. That is not a profitable basis of operation either.

Another way to fill the temporary vacancies created by the packaging contract is to transfer, from other departments and divisions, some of the presently employed people. The problem here is that those transferred would have to be paid at higher rates than RP&S intends to pay on a temporary employment basis. So if the line were to be manned by transferees, much of the anticipated profit from the contract would be lost.

From management's angle, then, the answer is to employ temporary people while the packaging-contract business is being built up, and eventually, when the volume of work requires it, use permanent employees. But the union wants either presently available permanent employees used now, or have those who are recruited from outside hired on a permanent basis.

Nonetheless, I learned that the Monday meeting was much better than the one last Friday. The conversation was open, and the union appeared to be knowledgeable and flexible in its approach to the problem and in its attitude toward management.

Another bargaining session, to nail down the general wage increase, took place on Tuesday afternoon. It was traumatic. Everything went wrong. Open warfare was the spirit of the day.

Now that the union has ratified acceptance of the general wage increase, it is time to sign a legal document. Management, with Doug Fowler's assistance, had prepared a legal draft which carried three motions. One was the 14 cents per hour increase to all wage personnel. Another stated that this agreement would not be connected with the contracts. This second clause made it unnecessary to face the litigable issue as to whether the old contract was still in effect. Neither of these matters provoked any disagreement.

Then the red circle reared its unwelcome head. The legal draft indicated that red circle rates remain in existence, separate and distinct from the regular wage structure, notwithstanding that the general wage increase has been added to all existing rates. The union smelled a rat and accused management of trying to sneak in a clause that had nothing to do with the present transaction, but which allowed future maneuvers against red circle people. Dick was adamant that the document should mention nothing about the red circle; rather, it should simply say that a 14-cent across-the-board increase was being extended to all wage personnel. Dan Ives made some inflammatory statements questioning management's good faith and openness, and management gave him some salvos of verbal shot and shell. Van and Earl led the counterattack, accusing the union of being tricky in trying to remove from the record a factual statement of the existing position. The union men scoffed at this argument, and the meeting ended with the document still unsigned.

At the post-mortem session, Van was fuming. Earl said, "Van, don't let it bug you. He's pathological. It's impossible to get any genuine agreements with this crook. Relax, stay loose, play it cool. There's no way we can change things. The law says we have to sit down and bargain with whichever characters are in office."

Bargaining got underway again on Thursday morning, and the document-signing problem was given priority. The management group held a strategy session beforehand. Word had been going around the yard that management was up to tricky legal shenanigans, trying to cheat the red circle people.

The situation is aggravated by the fact that tomorrow is pay day, and the wage people expect to receive the full retroactive increase at that time. Indeed, the payroll has already been drawn up on that basis. The question confronting management was, should it pay on the strength of the January 6 oral agreement, hoping that it can get a legal draft signed in the future, or should it withhold the increase if the union did not sign today?

Carl O'Brien felt that the increase shouldn't be withheld over a matter of wording, when there was already a handshake agreement that the union's membership had later ratified. Earl took the position, "It's our money, and we have a right to hold it until the document has been signed." Van thought that not paying the retroactive increase tomorrow would be seen by the wage earners as poor faith, and that, therefore, management would have to go ahead, even though from a legal standpoint the action left much to be desired.

During the afternoon, the management lawyer got through by telephone to Fred Henry, the union's attorney, who was on vacation in Canada. The two lawyers talked awhile but were unable to agree about the language of the legal draft that would confirm acceptance of the general wage increase. As of late afternoon, Doug Fowler was trying to formulate a basis for more long-distance discussion if a suitable draft can be agreed upon tonight. If not, the present plan is for management to hand-deliver a "letter of intention" to the union, and to go ahead with the full retroactive payment in the morning.

Packaging

A new complication arose with the union yesterday, when one of Wes' assistants was in a meeting with Don King, president of the salary union, who is a very good personal friend of Dan's. Over coffee, the personnel man had remarked, "It looks as though things are going better with the wage union."

Don replied, "Don't kid yourself. If there were an election today, it would be a landslide. Dan wouldn't stand a chance. It's absolutely hopeless. The international will take over at Lakeside come the next election."

Time ran out, and the group still had no clear strategy when bargaining resumed. Some of them had become more aware that, strong as Dan may be, the independent union itself is viewed as weak and inadequate by a growing number of wage people. It is under attack for being undemocratic, poorly led, and incompetent. The attack is being mounted by the international organizers at Lakeside, who are led by a very clever person, Morris Jenkins.

So some members of management no longer feel comfortable even when bargaining goes well, because collaboration under these circumstances is almost equivalent to complacency. On the other hand, they don't know whether—or who—to fight, because eliminating Morris Jenkins does not strengthen the independent union, nor keep the international out of Lakeside.

When the team arrived at the bargaining table, they found that Dan had left on urgent union business, and that the rest of the union delegation would not settle the agreement until he returned.

The committee then took up the next listed topic—the manning of the new RP&S packaging line. Dick stated the union's requirement and in a few minutes the meeting had gotten into such a hopeless deadlock that management took a caucus and invited me to rejoin them. I did so, and got them to fill me in on some more of the background. It will take twenty people to man the new RP&S line, and the union's initial position was that at least ten of these should be employed on a permanent basis, leaving the other ten to be hired on a temporary replacement basis, subject to release if contract work ran out. This morning's deadlock occurred when the union went further and said, "We can't discuss other matters of the contract until there has been agreement on the hiring of at least these ten as permanent employees. We will not go on until you agree to this."

Earl in particular had seen it as an ultimatum, and as the post-mortem began, he maintained that management should take the diametrically opposite approach. It should say, "We have got to get agreement on these other matters first, and only then are we prepared to talk about permanent or temporary hiring."

I intervened to point out that the union is taking a fixed position as a power device in exactly the same way it had done on the red circle issue. An underlying problem to be discussed with the union might be the way their fixed positions tend to provoke antipathy, polarization, and taking of strong counter-positions.

"But that won't be new to them," I continued, reminding management that it had already been through one such contest, which the union did not provoke. This, of course, was the red circle dispute, where management had taken the first fixed position—on a 7-cent reduction. As soon as the union had discovered the central issue, which would force agreement, it terminated all other bargaining until management had been forced to capitulate. Having learned this strategy and succeeded with it, the union is now reapplying the strategy in a new situation with even greater skill than before.

"Is this because the union is uncooperative or vicious? I would think not. It's just that the union has learned an effective technique for forcing management out of the bushes, so that at least some outstanding issues are resolved."

I concluded by saying that both sides should review the existing areas of agreement as a prelude to discussing the issues of discord. They agreed to do this, and when the meeting reconvened, Carl described the whole problem. His procedural suggestion was well received, and Max summarized what the union understood the areas of agreement to be. Then Earl pointed out the "hopeless" disagreement that he thought Carl and Max had not seen.

It was now lunchtime, and as Dan was still not back, the meeting ended, with another regular session being scheduled for next Tuesday. Outside, the secretary was waiting with messages for Van, Earl, and Wes, and together they added up to a new batch of trouble.

References

1. See, for example: Brech, E.F.L. *Organization: The Framework of Management.* London: Longmans, 1957.

32

Dan on the Carpet

The "hopeless" situation which Earl mentioned was instigated by one Frank Evans. Frank Evans is a region supervisor in the Engineering Department. Frank is very authoritarian and does not compromise with the union officers. He has power, and he knows it. He is also a tough disciplinarian and expects his rules to be obeyed. Some of his rules are that no more than three employees can be away from the job at any one time, and smoking is prohibited on the job because it is too dangerous, although a covered trailer is provided for this and other purposes.

Frank made an inspection tour this Thursday morning and went into the trailer to check up. When he found more than three wage men present, he was enraged and immediately ordered them out, tongue-lashed the foreman, and decreed that there would be no more smoking during the working shift. He had the trailer door locked until such time as the vehicle could be towed away. Since coffee is available there, he automatically eliminated that privilege as well. In this way, all were disciplined for the misbehavior of a few.

When Dan learned of this, he went to Frank to have the privileges reinstated. Frank was adamant, domineering, and impossible to interact with, but polite. Dan pushed harder and became excited. His behavior was inadequate in terms of diplomacy and statesmanship; his accusations were loud and derogatory.

On the issue of smoking, I asked, "Is management under the same restrictions, or is there a double standard?"

Van and Earl did a double take. After a pause, Van said, "Sure, a foreman can smoke in his office and he can be gone as long as the work is proceeding along at a good pace."

Earl said much the same thing, but then chuckled, and continued, "Oh, let's stop kidding. A foreman can step out of the work area and have a smoke if he wants. It's his privilege, so, I suppose there *is* a double standard." He turned grim again. "But that's no excuse for Dan to insult Frank. He's gone too far this time, Van."

Earl reported the gist of what Dan told Frank. Quinn became inflamed. He said that management should never tolerate that kind of behavior, that it was a gross personal insult which is inexcusable from anyone, whether a member of management or president of the union. He was grievously indignant and impressively righteous. He did not inquire into how the dispute between Dan and Frank began, nor did Earl describe the conditions under which Dan had manifested this kind of behavior. So Quinn helped himself to be finagled into not recognizing the real issues that enraged Dan. I'd predict that if he ever does hear the facts he will reprimand Frank rather than to give Earl license to take punitive action against Dan.

Then, for the remainder of Friday, one picayune detail after another was discussed. No one was able to rise above the morass of trivia and focus on the issue. Finally, around noon, I said that further floundering and indecision would be wasteful and profitless. I put a time dimension on the chalk board, indicating that from right now, the available time for bargaining was only through August 12, when the international can file for a representation election, thus automatically ending bargaining with the independent. Thereafter, the months from August through next January, when the election is scheduled, will only be a period of stagnation and failure. Management will have wasted thousands of hours over an incomplete, inoperative bundle of contract drafts which become utterly worthless if the international wins. And from August through January, the independent will be running for reelection under the banner of failure. What a record—six months drafting a contract proposal, another thirteen months of bargaining, and no contract! The time dimension, with its schedule of crises, had an immediate impact. It pointed out to the management committee members that they could get in a terrible bind on bargaining if they proceeded slowly because, as August approaches, their desperation to complete a contract would put them at the union's mercy.

After lunch, an issue was defined. It was, "Should we go to marathon bargaining, or should we continue the next dance waiting for the union to pay its quarter for the next whirl around the floor?" By looking at the pros and cons of marathon bargaining,[1] many different considerations were evaluated. All the evidence points toward the possible advantages if marathon bargaining were initiated.

Then, another question was posed. Should the present management bargaining group continue to do the bargaining or should its composition be altered? This question is very pertinent, because the high ranking people on the bargaining committee can't, simultaneously, bargain and operate the plant. Alternative arrangements are putting subordinates on the team and rotating short-term assignments for the senior men. It soon became apparent that the team should not be altered. Thus, two basic desiderata were outlined.

One was to speed up bargaining and get a contract by August if possible, and the other was that it would be necessary to have full-time bargaining activity as well as full-time management of operations.

A new issue was defined. It concerned the question, "How can the lower-level supervisors and foremen participate more meaningfully in solving labor-management problems?" The issue was debated almost to a standstill and it seemed to me that no one had grasped the essential point. So I intervened in a critical way by asking, "When you reported on the Upward Influence Conference, the one you'd already made to the EPOCH visitors, were the frontline supervisors and foremen invited?" The answer was obvious. They had not been. I asked, "Why?"

The management committee was stymied. Through lack of foresight, professional and hierarchical caste considerations, or whatever other reasons, the very group whose support is now thought to be essential was not even considered as an audience to hear this report. I got the pin in deep and I kept prodding. They knew that here was a recent and crucial incident in which supervisors and foremen had been excluded while the goals, achievements and problems of Lakeside were being explained.

The discussion was long, intense, and disturbing. Every member of the committee knew that he had been tagged. The conclusion they eventually reached was that a meaningful two-way flow of information and problem-solving discussion should be started; but in doing so, it would be necessary to experiment to find answers to the question of "how to deal with a large audience intimately." An intimate situation, in this sense, would be one where each person's queries and suggestions were heard and responded to in a genuine and constructive manner. I indicated I would be willing to help, were a task force to be appointed, and that I would like to have Dick Butler, a consultant who is skilled in designing large audience-type communication programs, as a colleague working with us.

It was 3:30 p.m. when Earl launched into a persuasive speech, saying that he wanted freedom to move in his department in regard to rectifying relationships with wage people, as well as union officers. This topic became the final one of the day. It went on and on with Earl continuously confusing the issue. Ostensibly he was requesting permission to work with his managers in instituting an attitude-improvement program. But somehow, in the content of his words, I caught glimpses of other hidden intentions. He seemed to be seeking authorization for an "open season" in which he and his managers would be free to hunt, trap, corral, and tame some targeted union "mavericks." Earl is so slippery that the management committee was unable to tag him on this now-you-see-it, now-you-don't sleight of mouth. I dogged him to find out what he was really after. I kept pressing the key questions, which were, "What precisely are you seeking authorization for? What *is* the spectrum of actions you'd like to take and in respect to *whom*?" He weaved and wiggled, and never answered these questions, even though we didn't break up until around 6:15.

During Earl's speech, Carl said to me, "I don't want to collaborate with Earl on this one. He wants to put up his dukes and fight the union."

I think the others got the pitch too, but the issue of Earl's precise intentions remained confused. Wes didn't participate. Quinn asked questions in an attempt to expose Earl's real motives, but Earl evaded them.

Van continuously favored Earl's interpretations, recommendations and requests. He engaged in defense, justifications, and rationalization to support a friend, as contrasted with solving the clarification problem—and he knew that I knew. At the end of the day he was frustrated, and said, "I want to get together with you and give you some feedback."

I said, "Okay. When?"

"Soon."

"How about nine o'clock Monday morning?"

"I don't know for sure that I can."

We settled on having lunch together Monday. I look forward eagerly to this.

I'm really picking up the scent of a hidden agenda worked out in detail, and well in advance of the meeting, by Earl and Van, probably with some ground baiting of Quinn included. One point of evidence is that, a few days ago, Quinn remarked to me that he and Van thought Carl was acting "righteous" rather than right. Wes' uncharacteristic silence today may indicate that he also might have known that Van had been working on Quinn. If so, Quinn is being set up. Since this went on under the table none of the other members of the management committee realized what actually was transpiring.

On Monday morning, at Quinn's regular department heads' meeting, Earl, while giving his stewardship report on Engineering Department operations, made allusion to the possibility of warfare. He said the number of grievances for the past three months had dropped to one. He implied that no unfavorable conclusion should be drawn from that one pitiful grievance, for he added, "With the new mandate given us at Lincoln Lodge, we can anticipate a jump in the number of grievances this quarter." No one confronted him in regard to that remark. I pondered it momentarily, but decided that I and others needed to watch for the emergence of the first moves in his game plan, since he'd avoided divulging it.

Over a lunch-for-two table, Van Gray socked it to me. He wanted me to know that he saw my active purpose in the Lincoln Lodge conference as one of pulling strings as the "Invisible Manager." He charged me with ignoring Earl's earnest pleas that he needed to be freed up in order to take appropriate actions in the Engineering Department.

I did a little feedback myself, and asked Van about certain key attitudes he had. I told him I thought he was the intellectual captive of Earl and was being led into a warfare role, notwithstanding his defense of Earl as being legitimate and aboveboard. I said that at least one other line member of Quinn's top team sees Earl as manipulative and destructive, and as searching for freedom to be openly belligerent to the union.

Van took me on, and started naming names. He sees Carl and Sam, among the line department heads, as naïve and misguided in their efforts to improve relationships with the union. As for personnel chief Wes, "naturally" he's in the bleeding-hearts category as well, but he's also cunning, and is somehow connected with the collapse of the red circle campaign. Not one of these three, according to Van, knows the "facts of life." They are acting in a manner which, if unchecked, will lead Lakeside to ruin. On the other hand, Van is a realist, and so is Earl. They know the score on things.

The lunch break was too brief for either of us to turn the other around. Probably he's despaired of me, but I go on wanting to persuade him, somehow, to adopt OD assumptions, and with them, work toward transforming the present unhappy state of affairs into something much better; because, for the life of me, I can't see anyone getting anywhere guided by *his* assumptions. I think that Van revealed his true attitude toward bargaining during the discussion at Lincoln Lodge last Friday. In effect he was saying, "It's hopeless. Why work at it? Let's just go through the routines that it requires, in order to give the impression that an effort toward collaboration and good faith bargaining has been made. But let's not kid ourselves. We won't succeed."

I was away on Monday afternoon, and during my absence, Quinn convened the management committee to assess the Lincoln Lodge session.

One of the first matters they got into was the lack of leadership. The committee members recognized that they had floundered for three and a half hours before I took over the easel and crystallized the issues.

Next, the issue of marathon bargaining was reviewed in detail. They concluded that if the union hastens the pace of bargaining, management should respond. Quinn made it clear that he has strong reservations about segregating the bargaining committee from operations to permit full-time bargaining. Within limits, though, he is ready to go along with a heavier bargaining schedule.

They went on to a third major topic. The Friday confrontation about the information-involvement gap between foremen and the rest of management, produced the Monday conclusion that immediate steps should be taken to close that gap. Now, two separate presentations have been planned, one for this week, and one for the following week; even though this means that it may be impossible to study alternative communication methods in an experimental situation.

The Engineering Department thought it had won a mandate to correct the alleged misbehavior of union officers. This presumption was reviewed on Monday afternoon, and a fundamental decision was made. Rather than declaring open season, the best step would be to ask the three line departments—Engineering, Chemical Products, and Staple Products—to report a week from this coming Friday on what plans each department has made to launch an intensive human relations program. This, of course, eliminates any presumed Lincoln Lodge mandate.

All of these indications suggest to me that the Lincoln Lodge conference though depressing at the time, has had very constructive effects, because it confronted the organization with its basic dilemmas. It threatened complacency and alerted the organization not only to the dangers ahead but also to opportunities available in the situation.

I was heartened by what I heard about all this on Tuesday morning. Also, some information came through that had a bearing on Monday's lunchtime confab. Van Gray and the department heads meet every Monday morning to review labor-relations problems in their respective installations. At yesterday morning's session this group also reviewed the Lincoln Lodge experience, particularly with regard to Earl Higgins' effort to extract an undefined mandate from the management committee. Sam Allen and Carl O'Brien directly confronted Earl with their interpretation of what kind of mandate he was trying to obtain. They said, in effect, "We don't trust your motives. We think you're trying to manipulate Quinn and us into giving you a mandate that would let you engage in whatever kinds of activities you wished, including going to war with the IEW. Are you after revenge for the red circle, Earl?"

Bargaining resumed this Tuesday morning, January 24, and the scheduled topic once again was the issue of employing twenty people to man the new RP&S operation, whether on a permanent career basis, or as temporary hires, or on a mixed temporary-permanent basis.

The union came in waving management's contracting-of-work plans for the coming year. Dick said, and I don't know the validity of this, "There are at least 350 people needed on a permanent employment basis just to cover work which is contracted to other organizations. We can do it better. Surely, in terms of company policy, it's better to provide career employment to Lakeside people to do the work, rather than contract it out on a day-by-day basis. So, as we read it, what you need are 350 new permanent hires to eliminate this unhealthy contracting of work. And here we've been sitting, arguing about whether or not to put twenty people on RP&S employment with only ten of them being permanently hired. . ."

Dan suddenly started quizzing Van. "Don't you have a sense of the broader scheme of things? Are you just an eight-hours-a-day engineer? We get the impression that you don't have the big picture. You get lost in the details. You can't make sound, economic decisions because you simply don't have the breadth and scope."

Van reacted in a "more in sorrow than in anger" manner, indicating that the union obviously did not understand the complexity of contracting. There are periods of peak work and periods of no work. Fluctuating levels of work can be accommodated more cheaply under contracting conditions, and so on and so forth.

Someone on the union side said, "Bosh. Don't give us that stuff."

After the bargaining session, Dan decided to attend a training meeting being held in Frank Evan's section of the Engineering Department. The meeting, on safety practices and similar matters, was being conducted by one of Frank's subordinates. Dan came in around 12:45 and stayed until 1:30. When asked if he'd been authorized to be there, Dan said, in a vague sort of way, "Yes, it's been okayed." He didn't produce a springing slip and wasn't asked for one.

As he sat in at the meeting, Dan acted in a very orderly manner, save for one or two things. When the problem of wearing safety glasses came up, he chipped in, "As far as we're concerned, they don't have to be worn. We haven't even bargained, far less, come to any agreement with management that workers ought to wear glasses. I'm not wearing them and I don't intend to wear them. (By now, in his free-and-easy, spontaneous fashion, Dan had bypassed the chairman and was directly addressing the wage people present.) You can wear them, or sunglasses, or a monocle if you want. Legally speaking, our friend here is only making a recommendation on behalf of management; it's not a contract requirement that's been agreed between the union and the company."

The chairman, with his safety message in tatters, and feeling very put down personally, did a slow burn but couldn't nerve himself to tell the union president to shut up and get out. The meeting continued, and the matter of coffee and smoking at the construction site came up. This time, Dan gave a little lecture to management, as the wage people listened attentively. "You can put a man on a job, but you can't *make* him work. If it takes four blows to pound a nail in, and the man actually takes eight, well, you can't say that it *has* to take four. Who can really measure the number of strokes needed to pound a nail into a board? It's purely a matter between the man, the hammer and the nail. Management isn't entitled to say that he's driving it too slow. As long as a man's working and moving, he's doing his job."

The chairman then closed the meeting and phoned Frank Evans who went into a conniption. When Earl was informed, he rushed back to his office to find out who had authorized Dan to be present at the meeting. No trace of authorization could be found. The engineers were outraged, and they wanted to take punitive disciplinary action quickly. Conferences took place. Earl and his division heads debated the kind of punishment that should be meted out.

Two alternatives were discussed. One was to give Dan a warning letter, and the other was to have him expelled from the plant two days without pay. They concluded that an apology was not sufficient, nor was anything less than a warning letter placed in Dan's file.

Earl took this recommendation to Van, and the penalty of a warning letter (which is hated throughout Lakeside) was further endorsed. This issue was then discussed between Van and Quinn and, according to Earl, it was agreed that Quinn would call Dan on the carpet Thursday morning. Quinn further checked the regulations out with Wes, who went along with the proposition that Dan's action was inappropriate.

At 8:15 on Thursday morning, Dan appeared for this closed-door session with the general manager. Quinn opened up.

Dan's reaction was one of disbelief and surprise. He said, almost in a whisper, "I can't believe that I was heard to say what I'm supposed to have said. I am a man of my word, and I want my word to be understood. I didn't say these things. Will you let me meet with this same group at their next meeting? I want to repeat my words to them, and clear up the misunderstanding. I didn't recommend that people slow down work or violate rules. I only talked about what my personal attitudes would be if someone hassled me rather than consulted me, or punished me for someone else's action. Sure, I did indicate that the ban on smoking and coffee breaks was unfair. The foreman was there, and I thought it worthwhile to let him know that management should think over what it's done, and try to be more fair. But I didn't say the things I'm accused of saying. I would like the opportunity to set the record straight."

This spontaneous and seemingly genuine reaction on the part of Dan caught Quinn completely off guard. He did a retake, thought for a moment, and said, "Fine, that would be a good way to relieve the tension and to correct the situation. Why don't you do that?"

As far as I know, the warning letter was not discussed, nor was disciplinary time off.

At lunch, I asked Earl how the problem was being addressed. He said, "Well, for better or worse, the boss has spoken. Now I have to work this through with my department and it's going to be difficult for me." He would say no more.

Later in the day, the personnel coordinator in the Engineering Department told me that the department feels utterly defeated and that its own values were affronted when the company "sold out" by restoring the full 14 cents to red circle personnel. By this action, the anticipated elimination of a $90,000 budget item, representing the pay increments that go to Engineering's red circle people, did not occur. They see themselves as being continuously under the gun to increase their efficiency, without being able to reduce the cost of labor. Of course, doing the latter, by slicing into the red circle, would make no real contribution to actual efficiency, because it would have produced no more work.

Nonetheless, the so-called "efficiency index," a numerical ratio, would have looked better, at least in the short term. Engineering feels isolated and under attack by the rest of the organization, and is retaliating vigorously on the union-relations front. It is saying, "We need a more cooperative union that will buckle under and give us the $90,000 red circle correction we need to meet the efficiency competition with other divisions around the organization." As a result, there has been increased negative reaction toward Dan. Dan, as we've seen, is responding in kind, and so the struggle escalates. Temporarily, though, Quinn has confused everyone by reversing field and dropping the disciplinary charge against Dan. I'm still puzzled as to whether he took his decision because of being convinced of Dan's innocence, or as a statesmanlike industrial-peace move in spite of being privately convinced of Dan's guilt. Whichever was the case, Engineering reads the message as, "The boss is telling us to be more careful—whatever that may mean."

It is early February and this week, in response to the decision made at the post-Lincoln Lodge meeting, each of the three line departments is putting into words its union-employee relations plans. Interestingly enough, in Chemical Products and Staple Products, the plans point toward nonpolitical, nonmanipulative action. They say, in spirit, "We don't want to get into any more cloak-and-dagger activity. We're aiming for sounder conditions of collaboration." Engineering, however, is going in the opposite direction, thinking up ways in which it can directly influence a desired election outcome, which involves eliminating Dan, Max, and Dick and replacing them by a slate led by Sol Sommers, Ted Roger's heir. This is a rerun of Earl's program last year which became the organization program during the last union election campaign. The program failed then, but present circumstances are markedly different, and Earl and his henchmen want to play it again. This time they have next-to-the-top support.

Van's recent statement to me that, "Sam and Carl are 'babes in the woods,' " indicates that Van already has his defenses up. He already "knows" that Chemical's and Staple's plans will not work, even before he hears them.

Engineering and Van are now convinced that Wes is responsible for the "sellout" that lost them a $90,000 correction. Consequently, a leveling session that Wes and Mac tried to get going between themselves and Earl's group yesterday was a flop.

The bargaining continued today, Friday, but failed to concentrate on the central issue. All kinds of extraneous matters were referred to by management's chairman, in what seemed to be a kind of free-floating search for a topic that would really produce a "knock-down and drag-out" skirmish. The management team's secretary remarked as they came in for a post-mortem session, "Just before the caucus, I thought you were going to club Dan in the face."

It embarrasses Van when that kind of remark is made in my presence. He immediately denied it and placed it in another frame of reference. Then, as the meeting continued, he made token gestures such as, "Did I say that well?

Did they understand what I meant? Did I take a fair point of view?" But it became evident that he had been ill-equipped to enter bargaining today, because he really was unaware of the basic issues requiring debate.

As he talked, I noticed his eyes continuously searching out to catch Earl's. He knew he was floundering, but he didn't want to be caught in a blunder; and Earl is his intellectual mentor.

It came out that Max, who Van sees as the most vicious and dangerous member of the union, said this morning, amidst all the waffling, "We've lost the good relationship we used to have, and it is because of the red circle issue. Now that's behind us, why can't we heal the wound and restore collaboration?"

In post-mortem, Carl said that he'd immediately picked up this remark and had tried to move the conversation in the direction of leveling, but was unable to do so because he received no colleague support.

Earl looked aghast, and said, "Oh, Carl, I did my utmost to support you. I thought we were on the right track and ought to go that way."

Carl said, "No, you didn't."

Then, as though talking out of the other side of his mouth, Earl said, "Dan is a bull. All he knows is how to break the china in the shop. You know his type." Some minutes later, I heard him say, "We can't work with those people because they're acting legalistically. They're not interested in solutions to problems, they only throw up legal barriers to prevent communication. They don't want solutions; they want to fight." Later still, he said, "I did want to get into leveling, to see what the problem beneath the surface is."

Now *I* was almost aghast, although I'm no longer surprised. He is manipulating several members of the bargaining team, and he seems to be behind many of the destructive tanglings which plague management. It is an amazing thing to see a man take a step and then turn around and cover it up so that it appears he was not there, and then to take another step and cover it up so that it, too, is imperceptible. Earl is almost uncannily skillful in covering up the motivations that govern his actions.

Discussion then turned to the tempo of bargaining. Tempo in bargaining relates to a number of complicated factors. One question is, "How fast do you want to go?" Another is, "How much time do you have available to come to a successful resolution?" A third is, "How much does bargaining time intrude into routine operations?" A fourth is, "How well are the individual departments organized so that, if you release management and union personnel to undertake bargaining, operations can proceed in a routine way rather than in terms of an emergency or crisis situation?"

Earl said, "Look, Van, I had a talk with Dan after the meeting, and I told him that we must stop bargaining in this way of an all-day affair."

Van immediately looked at me, and then back at Earl, and asked, "Why?"

"We're bargaining so rapidly that I can't deal with labor-relations problems in my department. I must keep in touch over there, in order to develop positions for making recommendations and bargaining over here."

Van said, "Can't you turn some of these matters over to others?"

"Well, there are a number of outstanding issues that involve union officials who are not on the bargaining delegation. And you know how Jack Smith feels about the union. I can't turn these matters over to him."

Dan, at one time, had refused to meet with Jack Smith because he considered Jack to be absolutely obnoxious. But this episode passed, and was treated partly as a joke, and partly as an initiation rite. One of the membership tests in the Engineering Department, for some years, has been that you have to be a tough guy. One sign that you are tough is that you act in such a belligerent manner that the union refuses to meet with you. Jack had won his spurs.

Later on, it became one of EPOCH's policies that the progress of an engineer in management was partly based on his relations with the union. Jack saw the broader implications of being hated by the union.

I'd surmise that, because the union is such a source of concern and frustration to Jack, he is avoiding contact with it, and that this really constitutes the logjam for Earl. Rather than create managerial growth conditions under which Jack finds it possible to meet and solve problems with the union, Earl is doing Jack's duties. It is Earl's compulsion to manipulate everything, thus elevating himself to the respected status of a "busy, busy" bottleneck.

The first significant ray of hope for successful bargaining shone through very dark clouds today, February 4. Since January 6, when the 14-cent offer was extended and accepted, management's bargaining efforts have been relatively listless.

Today the union put it on the line, regarding the RP&S issue. They said, "For goodness sake, employ the people permanently just like you employ everybody else. Then, if you want to have a further understanding with them that the RP&S project may be only five months in duration, let them know it at the time you hire them. There is an employment procedure for acquiring people, and there is a layoff procedure for discharging people. The seniority rule applies on a last-in, first-out basis. The system's operating day by day, so what's the problem? Let's stop this needless haggling and get down to business."

For some reason this proposal which, according to Dan, was made three weeks ago, finally struck home today. It was accepted, and they were able to move on to other matters with respect to the RP&S project. Then another enlightening phenomenon transpired. When the management team began talking at cross purposes to itself, Dan suggested that management take a caucus to reach an agreement. This is an amazing turn of events, when the president of the union diagnoses that managers have an unrecognized problem, and then, instead of taking partisan advantage of their confusion, proposes that management take a caucus and try to resolve its internal difficulties. What this demonstrates, as I am beginning to see very clearly, is that if a person has a high concern for results and a high concern for the people with whom he is working, and the two concerns are unified in his attitude, he will feel compelled to intervene when he sees people are in trouble. And, Dan, the non-manager, the non-behavioral scientist, the man from a different background altogether, had made a remarkably positive, skillful, and timely process intervention.

Management followed his suggestion, and the caucus was clarifying. They came back and settled down to the relevant issues. This tells me something about the work that Jane and I have been doing in developing two-dimensional theory. If Dan could only stay in that frame of mind, that combination of high concern . . . , if Earl and Van could get there . . . , Carl, Sam, and Wes are already there, most of the time . . .

Early in the afternoon, the union itself began to split on one of the RP&S issues. Dan suggested, "Why don't we take a caucus and see if we can get straightened out?" They did. Its effectiveness will appear in the morning when the next bargaining session occurs. In any event, there is a ray of sunshine through what have been dark and threatening clouds over the past few weeks.

I got some more news afterwards from Wes. Dan told him with deep conviction, in a session prior to bargaining this morning, "We are really going to have to step up bargaining and get to an agreement. We just *have* to have a signed, sealed and deliverable contract by May 1st. If we don't have it by then, vacations will intrude to interrupt our efforts, bargaining will bog down, and our hopes for getting a fair and equitable contract will have been shattered."

Wes interpreted this as a constructive sign. Also, he'd heard, Thomas came up with the same notion in a discussion with Carl outside of the formal bargaining sessions.

It seemed remarkable. The questions I asked myself were, Which group is searching constructively for a good result? Which group is more alert to procedural and process problems? Which group has the better time perspective? Which group is more open? Which group is apparently more genuinely interested in success? My answer to all of these questions has to be, the union!

"Wes, I begin to wonder whether Lakeside is getting its OD money's worth, when the union, with whom I haven't worked, gets itself together in this manner; and management, with whom I've worked for over a year, keeps on falling apart!"

Wes laughed. "Let's not either of us be over-modest. I had a part in all this and more fundamentally, you did too." He traced out the circumstances.

Wes was present at Lincoln Lodge when I confronted the management committee with the time perspective and drew the conclusion that contract bargaining would be impossible after August 12. Up to that moment, management had been proceeding in a relatively demoralized, yet complacent fashion, not really seeking conditions of agreement but, rather, meeting because the union was requesting meetings. It wasn't committed to achieving agreements that would succeed over the long term.

When he got back from Lincoln Lodge, Wes had a one-on-one conference with Dan. He pointed out to Dan the time perspective problem that I'd indicated. Dan turned this one over in his mind, and discussed it with his executive officers, and bargaining delegation. Then, almost as though he failed to recall the source of the stimulus, Dan returned to Wes and told him flatly that the union considered it imperative to achieve a contract by the end of May.

"So you see, Bob, this is too interesting a moment for you to be packing up and leaving us."

"I'll drink to that!"

References

1. "Marathon bargaining" involves a stepped-up schedule of negotiations, including longer sessions than may have been customary.

33

Change Becomes Official

Earlier today, Thursday, the human relations measurements committee reported to the management committee, but the problems of human relations measurement were forgotten and the topic shifted to the problem of the union. Almost everyone thought management should push harder on human relations improvement because it improves organizational health. Van Gray listened to this for one and one-half hours, and finally asked, "But why are people running away from this problem of saving IEW? Why is it that whenever we bring up the internationalization problem, people say that saving the independent is not a primary objective?"

For the first time, Van realized that he was out of step with everyone in the two committees except Earl, who today was silent. Because Van is so respected, his colleagues usually do not vigorously voice their disagreement with him. Today, however, Sam, Carl, Wes, and a number of others told Van, "We're from Missouri. If you cry, 'Save the independent!' you don't really believe in improved human relationships as the basis for improvements throughout the plant. It seems that you're only concerned with using this to get what you think is a tamer union. If that's your reason, it's lousy in terms of foresight and rotten in terms of ethics!"

I don't think Van sufficiently considered what he was being told, so I intervened and said, "Almost everyone here who has spoken has agreed that relationships improvement constitutes a valid objective for improving the total operation of Lakeside. There are some, however, who have not spoken. Is it because they have reservations? We say that human relations improvement can be gained through leveling. If so, do these unexpressed reservations mean we are not leveling with one another? People who have reservations have the obligation to express them." Still Earl kept quiet, in spite of this effort to prod him into exposing his attitudes.

The meeting ended, and I came away feeling that the effort to manipulate management back into warfare is crumbling. This may indicate a culture change—where pressures toward collaboration have gained enough impetus to overcome warfare. Both committees have sufficient definition of the issues to reject Earl's bait. They are doing a good job of diagnosing the dilemma, and are exerting countervailing forces to restrain those who are oriented in the direction of militancy.

The other day I met with about fifteen people in the Staple Products Department. The group was composed of James Young, a division head, Ken Jennings, the personnel coordinator, all of the unit supervisors, and the shift foremen. Here, then, was a group of men who, save for James, were directly implementing policy, applying procedures, rewarding and punishing on the basis of performance, and accounting for actual material output. It is very different from the group composed of top management heads, such as Sam Allen, Van, and Quinn. The latter are concerned with policy, planning, and performance evaluation according to broad statistical categories and gauges, but the lower executives plan tactics and evaluate production on a daily basis.

It is also true that these division managers are in daily contact with the wage people. They communicate upper management's attitudes and guidelines. They are the people who know at first hand the wage earner's attitudes. In effect, they are the critical link. It is their actions which speak louder than words.

The topic of discussion was the problem of achieving "sound business consistent with good human relations" in the sense of improving the relationship with the union. This happened to be the same topic which has been under examination by the higher echelon groups for some time. So I was provided an excellent opportunity to compare the insights of this group with those of the top team.

One reason for believing that I could get a clear comparison between the two groups was that I'd assumed that the Staple Products group possessed the basic information necessary to understand broad managerial strategies and intentions and to interpret these to the wage earners. But this group was so ignorant of the facts, I was astonished. They felt, for example, that management "sold out" by giving 14 cents across-the-board. This illustrates how giving conclusions not only fails to yield true understanding, but does little to explain actions that are consistent with intentions.

I asked, "In what way did management sell out?"

They said, "Management capitulated when the union said that it wouldn't man the new icebreaker unless it had the 14 cents."

I can say from intimate acquaintance with the red circle decision dynamics that the icebreaker was no more involved than was the man in the moon. But all of these people shared a uniformly inaccurate perception. They were worked up about what they thought they saw, saying that they had put in a lot of time and effort explaining the reasons for the 7-cent red circle chop and then, all of a sudden, the rug was pulled out from under them. They asked, "Why did management make this about-face without telling us even one hour in advance? We were humiliated."

So here are indications of two organizational pathologies. One of them is that this level of management has never been informed on the background facts which led to the hurried 14 cents across-the-board decision. Secondly, the "why" bit, they were not informed partly because of ignorance of communication methods, and partly because of a lack of trust that they can keep presently sensitive information confidential.

In addition, every member of this group places the "blame" on the representative of the out group. Their attitude is, "Dan is an agent of the international, there can be no doubt about that. By exploiting grievances and by continuous rabble-rousing, he builds up a following among the impressionable employees. He makes militant, grandiose demands which thrill his audience but which management can't possibly meet. This way, he is making himself look strong and the IEW look weak. This process is working so well that, unless management is able to expose his cunning plans and get him rejected by the people, he will smoothly deliver their votes to the international at the next election."

This is almost a carbon copy of upper management's party line of more than a year ago. It bears no resemblance whatsoever to their perceptions, since last July, that Dan can be statesmanlike and constructive; not only in leading and uniting the union in its contract negotiations, but also in trying to help management deal with its problems.

So I've discovered two things: (a) that lower-ranked members of management are uninformed as to why top management entered into an important bargaining agreement, thus drawing erroneous conclusions; and (b) they are just as poorly informed and self-deluded about the realities of present-day relations and collaboration between the union and management bargaining delegations, not to mention the Green Acres principles.

Perception of this discrepancy inspired me to give these people a hastily conceived verbal true-false test of fourteen items concerned with reasons for upper management's recent decisions. My questions were of this nature, "Do you know the role that Mountainview played in the 7-14 cent offer?" Everyone replied, "No."

"Do you know about the mediation that took place at Seashore?" Another chorus of "No."

"Did you know that out of the 83 contracts affected by EPOCH's general wage offer, the Lakeside-IEW one was the very last in terms of settlement?" The uniform answer was "No."

"Do you know whether Lakeside's initial position on the red circle matter was imposed by EPOCH or was locally produced?" Some, without great certainty, said "Yes," and others, with more conviction, said "No." I asked the "yes" people to explain their understandings. The answers were varied and mutually inconsistent.

And so it went through fourteen questions.

Since then, I have been administering the same test to managers at several levels, and I completed this pilot experiment today with a division in another department, Chemical Products.

What I have learned is relatively straightforward, but very disturbing. Department heads have all passed the 14-item test, mostly with complete accuracy. Division heads have flunked it with about 30% accuracy, and unit supervisors and foremen made a score of zero or slightly above. This means that the foremen are in a position of ignorance from which they must give to the wage man an interpretation of the bargaining issues and of management's position with respect to each.

In this context, I have found that upper management, in its efforts to communicate with lower management, customarily provides "a summary of the facts." A typical management communication to foremen about the progress of contract bargaining goes this way. "Management said the agreement on Clause X should be *this*. The union refused to accept this. The meeting broke up."

Under these circumstances, what does the foreman know? He doesn't know *why* the management bargainers were pressing for *this,* nor does he know why the union wouldn't buy *this;* but, rather, he gets the impression that the union is belligerent, always saying "Nyet," and making unreasonable use of the veto.

Another complication is that people at the department-head level, like Earl Higgins, sometimes formulate questions and poll the lower ranks of management in order, as Earl says, "to keep in touch with what's happening down there, so as to be able to take sound positions when bargaining." But from the questions that I've seen, it appears that many of them are biased in ways that coax out the answers that reinforce Earl's standpoint. It is this knowledge-communications mix that causes management to take very inappropriate and inconsistent positions which repulses the union and angers the wage man.

It is now becoming apparent why it is difficult for the top of the Lakeside organization to make policy decisions which are acceptable to the wage man. It remains to be diagnosed why the upper components of management fail to keep the lower components adequately informed of matters that are very germane to their everyday work and industrial relations. The best hypothesis is that upper management is still acting under old traditions, precedents, and past practices. The routine way is to *tell*. But as you go lower in the organization, the need for people to think through the issues rather than "salute" greatly increases. They need to be educated, not told.

Apart from the reproductive aspect, union and management are somewhat like husband and wife. They are legally joined, and have one another whether they want to live together or not. The ideal matrimonial circumstance is one of mutual support, collaboration and constructive problem solving. Things go wrong occasionally, and one partner or the other storms out for awhile.

Sometimes one partner decides that the situation's become impossible, and then files for divorce. But, unlike marriage, it is very difficult for a management and a union to divorce. One way of avoiding any future divorce problems is not to get married at all. However, in a company that already has a union, or in an unsatisfying marriage, secret steps are sometimes taken to acquire a new partner, with the intention that when the tactical situation is ripe, the present partner will be eased or thrown out of the house.

Since Dan was carpeted by Quinn, and in spite of Quinn's reversal, sending Dan off in peace and amity, the union president has been carrying a burden, and today it began smoldering with a hint of flame. Dan feels he has been insulted. How did this happen? Most managers describe Dan as crude, rough, gruff, and always ready to be nasty and use his boots in a fight. Yet, as he talked to Carl today, Dan said in a very hurt manner, "Quinn called me a troublemaker."

At the time, Carl was trying to clear an RP&S matter with him. Dan, with a queasy expression, shrugged and said, "I'm not up to discussing it, Carl, honestly; I feel I'm coming apart. Why did he call me a troublemaker?"

Nothing could have been said to disturb Dan more. His belief is, "I'm doing what's right for the people, what they've asked me to do. I'm doing my best for them. It's hard sledding all the way, but I go home with a good conscience, and I can sleep." This is a self-image which he portrays to others as he has to me.

When someone of Quinn's prestige rejects him by saying, "You're *not* doing what's best for your people, you're just a troublemaker," it hurts him. He feels a sense of personal rejection and injustice.

During a coffee break in the bargaining today, Dan asked Wes for authorization to attend the upcoming meeting in the Frank Evans section of the Engineering Department. He wanted Wes to take care of it, rather than having to approach Frank or Earl directly.

Frank told Wes that Dan's second coming to the safety meeting was certainly anticipated, but that he, Frank, had some reservations about Dan's attitudes. Frank wanted to know if Dan would be wearing a safety helmet and safety glasses. If not, it would be impossible for him to attend the meeting. It seems that Frank wants to rub Dan's nose into those earlier uninvited comments.

There is another clue to the strategy as well. After the bargaining session today, Earl had a private talk with Dan. He said, "Dan, I don't want you coming into my part of the yard without a safety helmet on, or for you to be seen by my people without safety glasses on."

Dan said, "Well, I have a safety hat, but I don't have safety glasses."

"You'd better get them before you come to that meeting."

Earl went on to sketch out the kind of apology that Dan should make. In a very casual way, Dan said, "Okay."

Dan has no legitimate beef regarding management's enforcement of safety precautions that are consistent with the risk factor on the construction site. However, the question remains as to whether management could find a somewhat less provocative way of handling the issue. Engineering is ready to tar and feather Dan. They are just waiting for him to enter. I guess that Frank and his cohorts will chuckle and jeer at Dan when he comes into the meeting wearing a safety helmet and glasses. Presumably he will do it. But, on the other hand, he is just stubborn enough to buck and kick in response to these degrading pressures.

At about noon the following day, Dan went to the meeting in Frank Evans' section of the Engineering Department. Frank had gotten his people there fifteen minutes earlier than usual so that when Dan turned up exactly on time, Frank and the others were sitting there in a room located hundreds of yards from the remotest perils of construction, uniformly wearing their safety hats and glasses.

As he entered, Dan was wearing his safety helmet but was without glasses. He saw Frank Evans staring at him, and he gave a polite nod. Frank penciled a note on the yellow pad he was holding, and then resumed staring. Dan, staring back, raised his hand to the brim of his safety helmet. He might have been saluting or he might have been about to take off his helmet; it was difficult to figure which. Dan held this posture for about five seconds as the group sat in total silence. Finally he gave the helmet a rakish tilt toward the back of his head. His hand left the brim and went into the top pocket of his coveralls. Out popped a monocle, which he smartly jammed into position over his right eye.

The meeting broke up with laughter. Even Frank couldn't prevent himself from smiling, though he quickly got his lips moving into a comment that went unheard.

The formal meeting began, and Dan said, "Look, the boss has had me on the carpet, but I want to set the record straight. I didn't suggest that a man shouldn't wear safety glasses, I only meant to point out that there was a recent proviso by management which had not been mentioned to us at the bargaining table. Okay, so we all want to keep our eyes; I guess that wearing these glasses is the safe thing to do. I haven't got mine yet, but I intend to. Likewise, I'm sure I didn't say a man should violate company rules by not wearing his safety helmet."

I talked with Earl before quitting time and asked him if he was satisfied with Dan's retraction. Earl said that Dan's not wearing safety glasses indicated that he was still unregenerate. In fact, with his monocle act, Dan had "mocked" Frank Evans. In an even more damning fashion, according to Earl, Dan had failed to retract his earlier recommendation that if management did such-and-such, the wage men should slow down.

I asked Earl, "Are these matters still keeping the issue open?"

"Well, of course, it's Quinn who should be most interested in seeing that these malicious recommendations aren't broadcast around the yard. I don't know what his reaction will be when he gets back tonight. As far as I'm concerned, we've made our point and Dan knows it'll be even riskier next time he tries to push his luck. But Quinn just might want to pursue the matter further."

Three weeks have passed since the Lincoln Lodge conference on January 22. It seemed imperative to me to intervene at Quinn's staff meeting today, even though Van Gray was absent. After various items of good news had been reported and discussed, I plunged in saying, "It's now three weeks since you all took some vows at Lincoln Lodge. There has been little accomplishment in terms of bargaining a contract, save for the specialized discussions on the RP&S manning issue. Unless there is faster action, another three weeks will pass with little progress. This is a very dangerous period. One can be complacent when there is no emergency under debate. But it seems to me that the contract completion deadline, and progress in relation to it, ought to be on the agenda of all your review meetings through next August. After all, Dan says he wants a contract by the end of *May*, and from what I hear of the bargaining sessions, *he's* not dragging his feet."

Quinn really pricked up his ears. He felt stabbed, and I'd intended that he should be confronted on this issue. Given the rate at which they're presently progressing, one day between now and August there will be so many items that remain unresolved, and so little time within which to get through the piled-up details, that some member of the management bargaining committee will say, "It's hopeless, let's quit."

It's now Tuesday, February 14. A tough problem arose the other day in Chemical Products Department. Two men are found sleeping when they should have been working. Under ordinary conditions, the punishment for such an infraction of rules is a warning letter and a two-day unpaid suspension. The case sped up through channels until Van Gray contacted Dan. Dan said he would like to investigate it and would be back soon to check his own findings against Van's.

Dan assumed that Van would reserve judgment until Dan had completed his investigation. Van claims that he merely said something like, "Okay, Dan, come and see us if you have any disagreement with the way we handle this," and that, very definitely, he didn't invite Dan to sit beside him as fellow judge. At all events, Van went right ahead and meted out the warning letters and the two-day suspensions.

Dan was furious. On hearing the news, he immediately responded by saying, "Van, all bargaining is off. We're not meeting with you or your delegation until you've come to your senses and stopped breaking promises!" He hung up before Van could react. Van gave his desk an awful slap, then phoned Wes to tell him the story.

Wes called Dan and said, "What in the world are you doing? So many times you've said that if things ever went wrong around here, you'd always be ready to help if we could see the need. But you also said that sometimes when we needed help and didn't realize it, you'd step in and show us how we might get back on the track. Now somethin's gone wrong, but rather than talking things over with Van, you threatened him and so we're all in considerable difficulty."

Dan rubbed his chin bristles for a moment, while staring into the distance. "Well if that's the way you feel about it, I'll meet with Van in the morning and settle this thing. There's no connection, of course, between this matter and what we're bargaining about. Bargaining will proceed as planned."

Wes had done a good job in calming the situation. How was Van reacting? First, he'd gone to talk with Quinn about it, thereby turning it into a federal case. Now the word is going around that Dan is making trouble again. Again, top management is going off its rocker because it is confronted with a minor problem. Again Quinn is discouraged and is saying, "What this union calls 'cooperation' is nothing but 'Give, give, give.'"

After each of the last five bargaining sessions, there have been the usual post-mortem meetings at which the management bargaining team discusses the various process interactions that took place during the meeting. Earl Higgins was absent from all five post-mortems. Earl has not explained the reasons for his absences; either he had made a brief apology while heading out of the bargaining meeting or Van has remarked that Earl's unable to attend.

I haven't yet asked him why he's staying away, but I think I should, and soon. The last time I talked with him was a few evenings ago, when he and some other engineers were unwinding with a few drinks. Earl remarked that lately Van has been telling him. "Earl, it's fine to give the union the business as long as you have the facts to support your position. It's legitimate for you to snap back when accusations are made against you, as long as you have the *facts* to support you. However, to make a blanket statement without access to the facts is no good at all."

Evidently, Van was advising Earl to examine his behavior. This implies that, since our recent lunchtime mutual feedback session, Van has considered my remarks and is now working on the premise that Earl might benefit from being *Van's* intellectual disciple, rather than vice versa.

Even so, this still does not answer the question of why Earl is not coming to post-mortem meetings. In management meetings Earl usually comes through as pleasant and friendly, and he can be very eloquent and persuasive. However, if others start hassling with him, he soon shuts up, sometimes for long periods. Probably he feels uncomfortable and threatened in such situations.

I speculate that Earl privately "knows things" which he is unable or unwilling to put across convincingly in open debate. He "knows" that the management bargaining team is all wet, "knows" that the approach developed over the past year is wrong, and "knows" that the union is evil. Therefore, in order to avoid wasting his time in losing debates and getting lectures from Van, the best way to stay out of trouble is to be absent and off on maneuvers.

I had a little chat with Wes today regarding a problem that is very salient to him. Wes is seen by Van and by Engineering's managers as having a direct pipeline to Quinn. They feel, therefore, that he sometimes frustrates their recommendations and proposals. I queried, "Rather than dealing so frequently and directly with Quinn, why don't you try to have a leveling session with Van?" His retort was interesting. "You can talk with some men one way and some men another way. Some men respond in terms of the big picture, the interconnection of facts, the time perspective and the requirements of achieving one's goals. Others respond to each issue as an item to be considered independently of every other issue. They are case method boys.

"When I talk with Quinn, I speak in terms of a broad framework of ideas, and then paint in the details of the picture with respect to issues and actions. When I talk to other people, including Van, all they can do is talk issues, 'this particular point, that particular point.' I can't get behind the issues to some organizing framework which provides a basis for interconnecting the issues."

"Do you think Earl's in that category too?"

"No. He has his *own* framework. He's organized, believe me, but not for anyone else's benefit. Earl came back from the first Green Acres session, and concluded in his own mind that they shouldn't continue. He built up a resistance movement among his people so that they gave hostile feedback toward the whole effort, and effectively took the wind out of its sails. It was Earl who almost singlehandedly scuttled the Green Acres effort and prevented it from getting down to the foreman and worker levels." Others had alluded to this in the past, but it never was so clearly put as by Wes.

The rumor mill started grinding this Wednesday morning, February 16. The routine schedule of the day had called for the general manager's staff group to meet at 2:00 p.m. when a specialist from the Personnel Department was to review the ranking and rating system. At 9:00 a.m., however, this session was cancelled and replaced with a meeting of department heads. Wes had already received a call from Quinn at about 8:30, and they vanished until 10:00 when a thirty-year award ceremony was scheduled.

As soon as the 9:00 announcement got batted around a bit, rumors started flying. This kind of move, when there was no visible emergency and no announcement of an agenda, could mean only one thing: a high level personnel replacement. The issue of "Who is it?" began to be debated. Some thought it could involve Quinn; others thought it must be Wes. There was a sprinkling of people who thought it might be Cal or Van or Hal.

About 1:00, a new element was added to the mystery. It was requested that the two union presidents be in attendance in the department heads' meeting. This put an entirely different color on the conjectured situation. It is only in matters of high state affairs that Dan Ives and Don King ever meet simultaneously with the management committee. Indeed, it would be the first time in the past year and a half that this had happened. The arena of contestants for personnel replacement narrowed to Quinn or Wes. In spite of rumors that had drifted around sporadically for months that Quinn might be going, no one could see any presently vacant slot for him to move into. On the other hand, if Wes was about to go, it would be appropriate to invite both union presidents because he, in a sense, is a liaison man between the line organization and the unions. Another line of speculation pointed in the direction of Quinn, but this was a potentially tragic one. It is known that he had had some medical condition of late, and that over the weekend he had some tests. Perhaps his medical report has forced him to step down.

All the department heads, plus Dan, Don, and myself, were present at 2:00. Quinn made a bit of a late entry. He sat down, and said, "I have an announcement that involves a personnel change." Pause. "I'm leaving Lakeside, effective April 1. ERA is creating a division to coordinate its operations in the eastern hemisphere, and I have accepted a job as its manufacturing coordinator."

Fending off congratulations, Quinn began his lecture with the "golden oldie" about running a sound business consistent with good human relations. To have solid security you must have sound business arrangements consistent with good human relations. As he went on and on, the union presidents sat, I sensed, with some impatience, listening to the old record they'd heard a thousand times before.

Finally, Quinn announced that his replacement here at Lakeside would be Travis Apley, presently the general manager at Plainfield. The general manager of another plant would transfer to Plainfield, and further transfers were imminent. Eventually, all major production centers will have had new general managers, save for Seashore.

As the department heads began buzzing in muted conversations, Dan chipped in to say that both Don and he were sorry that Quinn was going because, finally, they were getting to the place where the unions and the management could see eye to eye on significant matters.

Quinn thanked them, and remarked, "Travis looks at things very much as I do, and the good relationship we have should continue. Indeed, things should improve because we are on a sound financial base. But as of now, our greatest area of possible improvement is human relationships." This wonderful self-contradiction was spoken with great sincerity.

More small talk occurred, and then people got up and one by one, all present shook hands with Quinn as they left the room.

I got to know Travis Apley some time ago when I conducted a pilot seminar at Plainfield, in which he participated. He is 38 years old, prematurely gray, handsome and extremely well liked. He has not fused his personal destiny so completely with EPOCH's as has Quinn, but nonetheless, he is very dedicated and is moving rapidly toward the top. Before going to Plainfield, he was at Lakeside as department head of Staple Products.

It is amazing to see how quickly Lakeside turns its eyes from its departing leader toward its future mentor. Even the headline in Friday's edition of *Lakeside Today* emphasized the return of Travis rather than the departure of Quinn.

The following Monday, management gave the union its final position on rate improvements in the RP&S contract package. They had been debating the issues for six weeks, giving the RP&S matter priority over other items on the bargaining agenda. All other outstanding aspects of the problem had been solved save for the rate structure.

The union said the present offer was unacceptable and offered a counterproposal which paid slightly less to one rate, and slightly more to another. This counterproposal involved an additional two thousand dollars a year, which is a very small percent of the total wage cost. Management sought EPOCH headquarters' approval to accept this RP&S package.

EPOCH's reaction was predictable, because Lakeside has the highest rate structure in the entire industry. Allen O'Dell immediately said, "No go. I wouldn't have the courage to take this request to the Board." Quinn didn't press the point any further.

At the Thursday bargaining session, management announced, sadly but firmly, that "our" final offer could not be improved. The union rejected it.

Then Dick said, "Anyway, we'll take this package to the people for their decision. In the light of our recommendations they probably won't want to accept it. You are all welcome to come to our RP&S members' meeting and have your day in court. You've been unable to convince us, perhaps with them you can do better."

"We'll take you up on that," said Van, in the belief, I suppose, that the case would be won when management told the people what a good offer it really was.

The meeting took place the following Tuesday after work, with eighteen union members of RP&S present. The management team presented and described the offer, and the union delegation gave its evaluation. Members asked questions of both sides. The tone of the meeting was serious and unemotional. After two hours of intensive high-quality debate, the eighteen members unanimously voted not to accept the offer.

34

Transition and OD Theory

Two or three weeks ago, I suggested to Carl, Sam, and Earl that it might be productive for their department and division heads to have a leveling session with the wage union. I said I would like to attend if such conferences were to be convened. Next Tuesday, March 7, the Chemical Products and Staple Products departments are going to have a combined meeting of their department and division heads with the union, to which I've been invited. As for Engineering, nothing more was heard about this suggestion until yesterday.

Earl told me that he had been with Dan and had made arrangements for a leveling session Friday afternoon of this week. According to Earl, Dan intimated that the union did not feel secure enough with its Engineering membership section to let an outsider attend. I responded that, in any event, I would like to discuss leveling session procedures with Earl and his division heads in advance of the actual meeting. He agreed, and we held a session this afternoon.

Earl kicked off. "As we've seen recently, Dan's riding high and is apt to get insolent if he senses weakness on our part. If they don't need discipline, no problem will arise, but if they do need discipline, we must be fully prepared to exert it."

I said, "From the standpoint of this meeting, the union is an equal-status group. They have just the same right to discipline you as you have to discipline them; and neither right, such as it may be, has any connection with formal hierarchy, far less, a master-servant relationship." This remark went unnoticed.

I next brought up the subject of constructive reactions to the other leveling party's frankness. I cautioned them by describing other intergroup leveling sessions in which one group was always meeting the other's complaints by explaining "Why we did what we did," and not hearing the emotional undercurrent. I said that the defensive reaction itself is an emotional response which meets a complaint with a counter complaint, or with an intellectualized explanation why the other person's complaint is invalid. The appropriate response would be to search out the emotion that motivates the complaint and to react to the emotion *per se*. This recommendation might have been understood by one or two of those present.

Earl then listed the issues that he thought the union might bring up. There is one that the union has complained about frequently. Due to Earl's membership on the bargaining committee, he is frequently unavailable for meetings with the department's IEW representatives. They complain that there are many outstanding problems that need to be relieved but cannot be because of Earl's unavailability.

My reaction to all of this was that a discrepancy existed between what I thought the union would want to discuss and what Earl thought they would want to discuss.

I waited in vain for any one of his division chiefs to say something like, "Don't worry, Earl, we'll resolve these problems in our divisions without needing to refer everything to you." So I launched out and said, "Earl, I think that the issues the union will wish to talk about, if provided the opportunity, involve your participation in the last union election. They may want to explore what your role was in the supporting of an opposition candidate. Were you, as the story goes, responsible for writing the literature which was distributed in Ted's name? Did you have your foremen telling the employees how to vote and so on? These may be the kinds of issues, whether "valid" or "inappropriate" is irrelevant, that the union may wish to discuss in this upcoming session. How can an honest relationship be established if these unknowns or uncertainties exist in the background?"

Hal Harvey, who is still convalescing from his operation and has not yet resumed command, said, "Why in the world would they want to talk about those kinds of problems? They are past and gone. What the union should want to talk about is how to do a better job. We have plenty of answers for them. Why should they want to bring up topics like this?"

I kept on the track of the problem like a bloodhound after a killer. First I had to deal with Hal. I said, "Hal, from your standpoint, Engineering's participation in the political activities of the last election may be unimportant, but that does not imply that it is unimportant to people who won in spite of management's effort to unseat them. There is considerable reason to believe that these matters are of supreme importance to them, because they are the very kinds of past actions which have generated these problems of distrust and disrespect. The department's critical problem is how to establish a more constructive relationship than the one that presently exists."

I turned back to Earl, saying, "Earl, how prepared are you to review the details of your participation in the last election?"

Earl answered quickly, "I say now, and I've always said, that I am for an independent union. I don't mind telling anyone that I have always advised and guided people to vote in the independent direction."

While he was saying this, Earl kept his eyes glued on me. In a sense, I was the image of the union, so I took him up on it.

"Earl, imagine I'm Dan. What you've just said doesn't satisfy me. I know, and have documents to back it up, that your participation was more extensive than you're admitting. You are blurring the issue in saying that you are "for" an independent. I know that. The question is, Were you against *me* during the election? Did you do things to defeat me? This is what I want to know. And if you did, have you changed any since then? Can I trust you in the future or are you playing a game?"

The others were listening intently. Earl looked into space and said, "I repeat, I am *for* an independent, and I always have been."

In spite of my best effort to confront Earl with a direct examination of his values, my intervention had failed. I dropped the effort and the conversation turned in other directions.

Union-Management Leveling

On Tuesday afternoon, March 7, the union executive officers and the union's departmental representatives got together with the managements of Chemical Products and Staple Products for a leveling session. There were several minor irritations that precipitated this session. Many problems of mutual concern were explored in full openness and trust. Along the way, management explored with the union its lack of communication with its people. Dan said, "Well, we try to have membership meetings, but during a period of tranquility, these are always poorly attended. Certainly we're not looking for new crises as a means of getting people into big solidarity meetings. We prefer the present gentleman's agreement basis that neither of us will use sources such as *Lakeside Today* or union handouts to incite people to riot. Let me say, too, in passing, that there's been excellent communication on the part of management, of major activities for which the union has been responsible. Everyone knows about the $14,000 settlement case with the mason, the Cramer case, the 14 cents and so on."

Dan concluded, "When the time is ripe, we'll communicate, don't worry. We'll point out how much money we've brought to the union membership. We'll point out the number of agreements that have been settled favorably and the few that have been settled unfavorably. We'll point out the number of injustices that have been redressed, and so on. We're aware of the need for communication. We're not dropping a little item here and a little puff of mist there. We are saving what we want to communicate until the appropriate time, and then we'll burst forward."

Responding to further questions, Dan, Max, and Dick said that sure, there'd been times when they felt depressed enough to consider affiliating with the international. Nonetheless, they had been elected under a mandate to support the independent, and they wanted the independent to continue if it could accomplish its objectives of protecting the people's welfare, security, and dignity. "No fooling about it," they said, "if the independent can't work, then we want an international. But we're trying to make the independent work, and we want to see it perpetuated."

The same day, during his staff meeting, Quinn asked Van, "What must we do to get bargaining completed by the end of June?"

Van surprised me by replying, "It's relatively simple. If the people responsible for bargaining are separated from operations, then we'll have time to do it."

Quinn turned to me and said, "What do you think?"

I immediately burst forth with, "Van, your words could not sound sweeter to me if they were made of molasses."

This broke the tension, but it also told Van that I, like others, have seen him blocking the kind of action that is needed so as to move ahead.

Last week Quinn asked who should be the new Personnel Department manager when Wes leaves to take a post in headquarters. He already had Mac Anthony in mind for a line position elsewhere in Lakeside.

I didn't want to help select this or that person, for I felt that to do so would draw me across the line from being an OD Man to being a company executive. Yet, in the OD sense, there was an issue that surely needed raising. So I said, "This Personnel Department vacancy is not the key problem of the organization. The key problem, as I see it, is one of building an OD orientation into the line departments themselves, and most particularly into that line department which is having the greatest difficulty in shedding the old industrial-warfare approach: namely, the Engineering Department."

During the next few days, Quinn said to Van, "We have some organizational improvement to do in terms of selection and placement of people, and I want to discuss with you the matter of placing Earl in a new post."

Van hit the ceiling. He insisted, with an infuriated attitude, that Quinn was moving in the wrong direction. He was taking away one of Lakeside's strongest men from the critical spot where he can offer constructive contributions. Then, he voiced his suspicion.

"Quinn, who have you been talking to? Is Wes feeding you this stuff?"

"I haven't said a word to Wes. He knows nothing about my thinking."

Last Thursday and Friday, Travis Apley was here. Quinn first went over the matter of replacing Earl. Travis, from the background of his previous tenure here over two years ago, soon comprehended the dynamics of the situation. He gave his full support to the idea that Earl should be replaced and that the action should be taken before Quinn takes off his sneakers and goes to the shower.

Quinn met with Randy Cox and said, "I am thinking about making a move, and I have the feeling that Earl represents a bottle-neck. He is the focal point of conflict within Lakeside and has been for a number of years.

Furthermore, Randy, I am thinking about moving him into *your* operation. Before you react, let me tell you why I am thinking of this.

"Earl knows nothing but manipulative labor relations. In spite of all the coaching and opportunities he's been given, he hasn't taken a more constructive approach so I think we have to give up on him in that area. There are a few technical areas he hasn't been exposed to, but supply and distribution is probably about as remote, in terms of Earl's personal comprehension and its distance from labor relations, as any activity that you can name." Quinn continued, "I'm not really prepared to dictate to you on this, but how would you react if Earl were to be assigned to you as a division head?"

Randy immediately said, "I have two spontaneous reactions, but I know they're right, so let me tell you. My first reaction is, Thank God! It's taken you a long time, but you now see the real problem confronting the organization.

"My second reaction is that even though Earl knows absolutely nothing about supply and distribution, I'll gladly make the effort to integrate him into a job where there are no human factors involved."

Today Van is still "dead against it." He thinks this would be the most regressive and inappropriate move that the organization could possibly make. He sees Earl as sound, hardboiled, and realistic. Van recognizes, as does Earl, that workers are lazy. They have to be pushed. He concludes that any soft person who tried to manage Engineering would be run over.

Quinn continues to tell me of his moves. "Last Thursday and Friday in my conferences with Travis I went in the right direction. I'm not so dumb, I've learned several things from human relations training. One thing is not to debate these matters with each person on a one-by-one basis, but to bring the primary protagonists together and lay the cards on the table. Therefore, last Friday I had a conference in which I, Travis, and Van all confronted the issue together.

"I reeled out my plan. First I would move Andy Stewart, presently assistant head of Staple Products, to be in charge of Engineering. I'd hate to do this because it's almost too tough a test of any man to see if he can bring about the necessary kind of constructive collaboration in that bull-of-the-woods department, but Andy is without doubt one of the strongest men we have. I'd make him assistant department head of Engineering, rather than department head, because there's no other place to put Hal. But for all practical purposes, Andy would be the boss of Engineering. It would be a make-or-break situation for him.

"Everyone except Van agreed that this would be a sound move. Van agreed that Andy is a strong man. Van's reaction was that this was not an unsound decision in relation to Andy, it was only an unsound decision with regard to Earl. In the end, we had Van over the barrel."

As Quinn detailed several more of the intended promotions and transfers, it became apparent that an extremely critical thing is happening in Lakeside.

The reward system has changed very dramatically and with great consistency. Every appointment is one in which the person selected has already demonstrated his ability to integrate production and human relations within his operation.

To me, this is evidence that the culture has changed at Lakeside. The old norms have shifted and actions are being taken consistent with sound behavioral science principles. Furthermore, the new norms have been internalized because managers themselves are considering the issues, making the decisions, and ensuring implementation in line with the theory of integrating people and production. At last it seems as if I have accomplished the impossible!

On Friday, March 10, Quinn took the bull by the horns and made a number of important personnel changes he'd mulled over and cleared with Travis. It is rumored that Wes will be off to Atlanta soon, but there was no formal announcement.

Thus, in one fell swoop, a series of critical promotions, transfers and stay-puts have occurred. The move of Earl is ostensibly lateral, but truly downward. Jack Smith, also of Engineering, thinks he should have moved up. He didn't move at all. So it is with the others.

There has been no movement now for some time in Engineering, but a lot of action in Chemical Products and Staple Products. Careerwise, the Engineering Department is becoming a dead-end street. The signal from upper management is, "The kind of behavior we see in Engineering is not what we prefer. Until some leadership appears which integrates human values with production values, there will be no promotions."

Apparently there are mixed feelings in the organization, but I have not been able to track them all down. Some feel that the lateral move of Earl was a good one; others think it was bad.

Earl was satisfied with his transfer. I don't know in detail what Quinn told him, but one thing I am sure he did say is that, "Earl, you know nothing but manipulative labor relations. You don't know anything about supply and distribution, and here is a chance for you to learn."

That night Earl got plastered, and phoned several people, including Dan Ives.

Earl said, "Dan, have you been putting the skids under me in your private confabs with Quinn?"

Dan said, "No, I haven't."

Hal Harvey will be returning to the bargaining table in place of Earl. Andy Stewart thus will be given full time in which to take the helm of Engineering and try to turn the department around.

Hopefully, Earl will overcome his depression and snap into his new job. In the long haul, it could represent a new line of progress in his career. It is up to him to measure up to the new challenge, and to eradicate the unfavorable assessments of his past performance.

Now, a few days later, the whole of management is trying to guess why Earl was moved. It is fascinating to hear the various arguments and explantions which center around relatively few things. One view is that it was a move to get Earl out of the way. Another is that this was a move to expand Earl's managerial experience in order to aid him to become more effective.

On the side of the first argument are two feelings. Some argue that Earl had Van in harness, and that there was no way to break Van out of harness, save to transfer the person who was holding the reins. The other explanation is that since Earl has been in the thick of union-management controversy for several years, upper management felt that the only way to relieve the tension points created by him would be to send him far away.

A third explanation is related to the decree by the government which has voided the last union election and scheduled a new one within seventy-five days. According to Wes, the determination took place last week, and he heard about it on Thursday. It was on the same day, also according to Wes, that Quinn made the decision to transfer Earl. Some see a contagious connection between these two events. They conclude that Quinn made the decision to get Earl out of the situation, because he knew that a new election was to be scheduled.

This is not so.

The timing, however, is perfect. Now we have an election coming up which will provide an excellent opportunity to observe how the organization works when, for the first time in perhaps fifteen years, the arch manipulator of union elections is unavailable to wheel and deal.

But the weirdest explanation of why Earl was moved is that in his new job, about which he knows absolutely nothing, he won't have any work to do. Therefore, runs the argument, this indicates that Quinn has decided to free Earl to influence wage-earner attitudes from an inconspicuous background. That's a beautiful example of how the organization seeks to fabricate explanations in the absence of accurate, overt information.

Integrated OD Theory Takes Shape

The recent round of promotions, transfers, and stay-puts, indicates a significant realignment of Lakeside's reward system, which favors those individuals who have integrated high production with improved human relations. It has penalized those individuals with good relations and mediocre performance, and those with acceptable performance but bad human relations. But most of the managers, engineers, and others around the plant, as yet, have been unable to "see it."

A new conceptual schema is needed to depict this shift in the evaluation of managerial personnel. The Power Spectrum (cf. Chapter 29, Reference 2) scale of competence, which evaluates people's "cooperative skills" and which was used in the Basic Training Seminars, is inadequate. A more efficient evaluation method is needed.

In our weekly conferences, Jane and I have created a two-scale evaluative system. A horizontal axis could represent competence in production, with the rightward direction being increasingly "positive." A vertical axis could represent human relations skills, with increasingly good human relations in the upward direction. Therefore, a person qualifying for placement at the lower left-hand corner, where the two scales meet, would be one with poor production and inadequate human relations. In the upper left corner (if you drew two further lines to complete the quadrilateral) would be persons who have wonderful human relations and hopelessly bad production. The lower right corner, in turn, would denote managerial people who had achieved high production coupled with poor human relations and in the upper right corner would be those with exemplary production *and* human relations.

However, Jane and I soon discovered that this method required some refinements. The question arose, Are the states of production and human relations, at any given evaluational moment, truly direct functions of a particular manager's efforts? Also, to what extent do "perceiver variables" enter into the assessments and might distort the accuracy of the evaluation? Such a situation might occur when a manager evaluates his subordinate's performance. It is easy to imagine how differently Hal Harvey and Carl O'Brien, for example, might evaluate the same person from their *own* markedly contrasting positions on the quadrilateral. Again, even though many aspects of *production* are precisely measurable by engineers, there are a myriad of unmeasured contextual variables that would prohibit an equitable comparison of one manager's so-called "production competence" against that of another department's manager. Each man, perhaps, is managing a different set of several hundred individuals. Could Andy Stewart, newly promoted to take charge of the Engineering can of worms, make such a good "measured" result during a year spent there, as he could at Chemical Products? Hardly; and this is not the intention of his Engineering mission.

Furthermore, since managerial activity is a day-by-day and hour-by-hour process, the two dimensions themselves need to relate to aspects of managing which are continually observable from the outside as well as, hopefully, by the individual manager via self-awareness. Periodic performance evaluations are, at best, assessments of history; what is needed is a system by which the individual can monitor his own behavior along two principal dimensions of managerial behavior, and exchange feedback with others who share a similar situation.

Presently, within EPOCH or anywhere else, there is no opportunity for people to appraise their own and others' behavior in relation to overall effectiveness. For example, the standard EPOCH performance-appraisal document instructs each evaluator to "Rank-order the people responsible to you in terms of their overall value to the company." However, EPOCH provides no answer to the question of what is "value." Consequently, the criterion used is a function of whoever is making the evaluation. One man's boss may evaluate according to what he sees as his subordinate's long-term growth potential; another person's boss might appraise him in terms of metered production; another's on the basis of what he sees as the man's human relations; and so on. Any system that creates and tolerates so much ambiguity is bound to be unsatisfactory.

The new system makes use of a two-dimensional grid. Its horizontal dimension signifies *concern for production;* and the vertical one, *concern for people.*

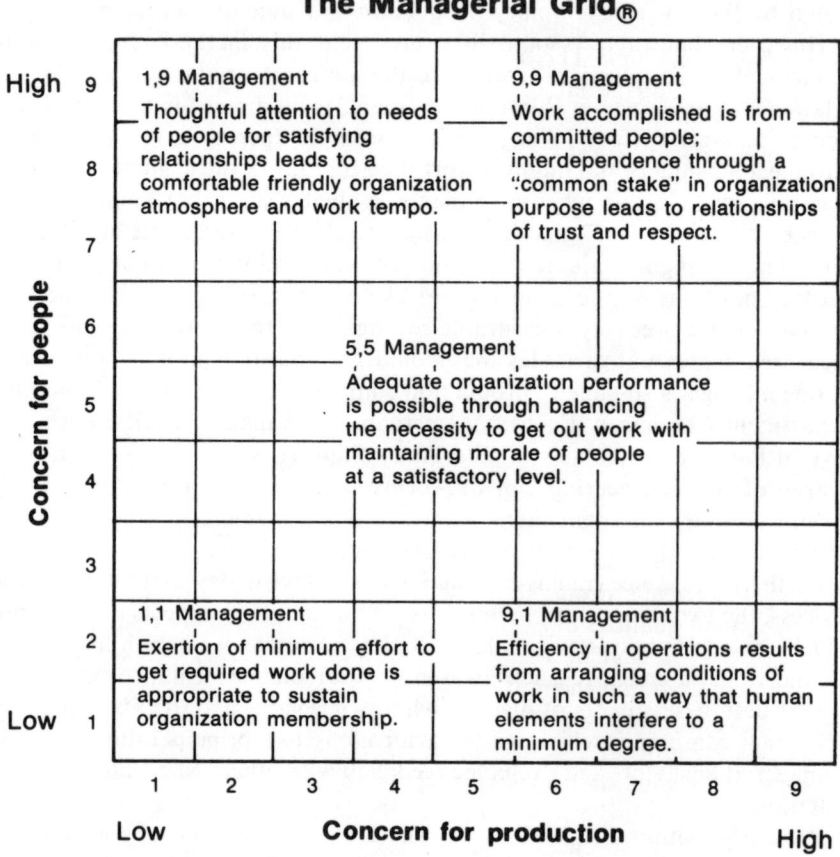

(Reprinted by permission from *The Managerial Grid,* by Robert R. Blake and Jane Srygley Mouton, Houston: Gulf Publishing Co., Copyright © 1964, page 10.)

On either axis, "concern" does not equal mere intentions. It must relate to qualities of personal behavior that are observable by others or, at the very least, are clearly evident from his characteristic behavior. For example, day in and day out, as long as anyone's known him, Frank Evans has been radiating a tremendous concern for production, but little if any concern for people.

However, the other methodological extreme of trying to "measure" concern must be avoided. One could guess that Carl O'Brien has more concern for people than Frank; and this would reveal a sense of your comparative appraisal. But even if one could define such "concern" in a way that covered its every manifestation, the associated problems of measurement are presently unsolvable even by scientists, and far less so by practicing managers.

The numbering of the Grid is rightward and upward from *1*, which signifies the lowest observable degree of concern, to *9*, which signifies the highest. The remaining numbers represent successively increasing degrees of concern from *low* through *high*. The two ends of either scale, of course, are the easiest to discern in managerial behavior. Frank Evans, with high concern for results, and minimal concern for people, presently is in the lower right "9,1" corner of the Grid. Carl O'Brien, who consistently embodies and unites high concerns both for production *and* people, is in the top right corner at 9,9.

By comparing Frank's and Carl's managerial styles, you can immediately see that the *qualities* of their respective high concerns for production are quite different. This difference has a lot to do with the basic *assumptions* each manager relies on for obtaining production through people. Just about every note of Frank's style rings true to the assumption that "people who are provided to accomplish a job are factors of production, *things* in the sense that their feelings don't merit consideration. After all, they're getting paid to do as they're told." However, to Carl, people are as "whole" on the job as they are anywhere else. He understands that people go on thinking and feeling, whether paid to do so or not, and that people at all organizational levels are entitled to be treated with respect because each one of them is an actual or potential resource whose positive feelings and knowledge about his job can enhance Chemical's production. Some assumptions are more reliable than others, and the qualities of Frank's are reflected in the harvest of hostility and negative-thinking that he has fostered among his subordinates.

It was expected that the most frequently observable and clearly contrasting styles of management would be located in its four corners. The two "types" previously mentioned, 9,1 and 9,9, differ significantly from 1,9, where low concern for production coexists with high concern for people. This attitude exists among ordained ministers who are industrial chaplains and with the occasional personnel specialist who views himself as lay confessor, counselor, and comforter to employees who come to him for emotional first-aid. As for 1,1, I continue to see a few managers, who are essentially unconcerned on either dimension, still occupying their offices while their operations and people "run themselves" for better or worse. But away from these corners and in the middle of the Grid there is an increasingly prevalent style of management: 5,5, where there is moderate concern both for production and for people under the general doctrine of "not going to extremes" along either dimension.

35

The End of an Era

This morning I walked into the supply and distribution offices, and found Earl studying some technical documents. In the two years I've known him, this was the first time I'd seen him read a piece of paper.

He stood up. We shook hands. I said, "Congratulations. What are you doing?"

"I'm reading a supply contract; I'm trying to understand what in the world it means. I don't have the slightest idea about what I have to do on this job yet. In fact, I haven't even gotten my people together. But this new job is fascinating. I believe it'll be a lot of fun. This is where you really have to maneuver, manipulate, and manhandle."

It was the same Earl, but I could tell that he didn't like the job *in toto*. He must be confused about his transfer. He might not fully understand yet, but probably realizes that his transfer is the result of disapproval of his overall performance. He's out of things now, away from everything he knows and used to enjoy doing.

I also went to see Quinn this morning, at his request. Again he made it one of those closed-door sessions that are embarrassing to me. As we were talking, Van dropped in and reported on progress in this morning's bargaining.

"You couldn't ask for a more brilliant character than Dan has been in the past three weeks. Understand, he's an international. He's got a game plan to affiliate the independent with Wilson's outfit, but he's a wonderful character; he's working beautifully."

Quinn chipped in. "Dan *was* an international, but he's declared himself independent now."

Van said, "I'm from Missouri on that one."

It should be noted that Dan occasionally says, "Let's give the independent a chance. Let's see if it can solve Lakeside's problems. If it can, well and good. If it can't, then there's always the international." My comment on this viewpoint is that there never was a man more willing than Dan, who would change his opinion in the face of sound logic, effective action, and meaningful results.

The conversation then turned to the prospects facing Andy Stewart, Earl's replacement. Quinn said he had told him in no uncertain terms, "Look, Andy, the finger points at you. You're the one person we see who can pick up the present situation and change it into an effective, constructive department that has good human relations coupled with fine production results."

Van left, and I asked Quinn about the timing of Earl's replacement, "Is there a connection between Earl's transfer Thursday and the government's stipulation of a new election?"

"No connection at all," he said. "It came from my insides. I decided that this thing had to be brought to fruition so I phoned Travis and told him I was ready to move. He said, 'Go!' I moved."

"What was it *inside* you that brought this thing to a head?"

"I don't know. I've been sitting on it, sleeping on it, and thinking about it for almost two weeks, and I was getting sick of it. Either I had to move, or it would never be done, I decided Thursday afternoon, and did it." Our interview ended soon afterwards, but here are two more explanations I've heard so far today for the lateral transfer of Earl.

The first one has it that since Hal continues to be semi-incapacitated, there needs to be a subordinate groomed and ready to take over as department head. Earl just happened to be the next senior man in Engineering who would be acceptable to his colleagues as pinch-hitter for Hal during the latter's absence. If he were still in the post when it became critical to move Hal to a less strenuous job, then he could claim seniority and "I've been doing Hal's job all these months" and even "reasonable production amid difficulties" as reasons for succeeding to Hal's throne. Therefore, rather than waiting until the time when a promotion from assistant department head to department head would be required, it is better to move Andy Stewart into that slot now, groom him, and have him available to move up when the time comes.

The other explanation goes in a different direction. Chemical Products, Staple Products, and the Technical Department all are moving in a human relations, problem-solving direction. All of them have problems with the Engineering Department. Earl is a smart aleck and hard to change. This made it very difficult for many of the interdepartmental problems to be relieved. Thus, according to this second argument, the other departments have won the power struggle. With the replacement of Earl, improved interdepartmental collaboration can now take place.

Some time ago, efforts were made to transfer Earl to EPOCH headquarters and to Mountainview, but neither would have him. Perhaps in supply and distribution, Earl has found a "home."

Hal and Engineering's Predicament

Last November, it will be recalled, Hal let the bargaining committee know that he would be away on a leave of absence because of his illness. He went through a very risky operation and about a month later, he was back on the job. Hal is an Annapolis graduate, six feet two, handsome, tough, hard on the outside, and much softer inside. He is a man of real character.

Despite the evident progress that has been made in union-management relations at the bargaining table, Hal was against the effort the day it started and has been that way since he returned to Lakeside. Only last week he told me, "It was wrong, I knew it would fail. Quinn's responsible for the rot starting, but he's not going to be around when everything collapses."

Hal believes that unions are no good. If you're in a bargaining situation, the only alternative to being adamant is to give, give, give. These convictions are traditional Lakeside managerial attitudes which some members of the top team have changed, but Hal has not. In addition, Hal has been unable to adapt to his illness. He is not himself anymore. He is no more the upbeat, blustering, rough, hit-them-hard, hit-them-low, hit-them-steady character of the past. He is disillusioned, disheartened, and bitter. He is blocking every constructive step the organization wishes to take.

Those beneath him in Engineering know two things. One is that they were defeated during the titular administration of Hal. However, they also feel that the defeat might not have occurred had it not been for his illness. Had he remained strong, vigorous, and adequate, he may have turned the tide with his leadership. The combination of circumstances has been too much. First, Engineering's position has been reactionary and unpopular relative to everything going on in Lakeside for the past two years. Second, they have had no one to represent and lead them for the past six months save for Earl, who was such a well-known manipulator that he wasn't regarded as trustworthy. Thus, the Engineering Department stands today defeated, impoverished, unable to get promotions, unable to move forward or back, unable to strike a resonant chord with the rest of the organization, unable to do anything just yet. It might be said that their present condition is due fundamentally to a shift of orientation by the rest of the organization which they did not make. More important is that the shift took place during a time when they had no adequate leadership. They still don't. It is a pathetic situation.

Union-Management Leveling: Two Different Techniques

Over the past few weeks there have been two union-management leveling sessions. One was between the IEW and the Engineering Department. The other was between the union and the combined Chemical and Staple Products departments.

Both sessions took place at the same location. The Engineering session was a flop; the Chemicals and Staples session was a success. What made the difference? The first clue is that while essentially the same union people attended both sessions, different members of management took part in each. Departmental personnel coordinators have determined what they regard to be the critical variables that account for the failure in one case and a success in the other. Their answer is elegantly simple. In the Engineering leveling session, management reacted to complaints by defending past actions and rationalizing their own negative attitudes. In the Chemicals/Staples session, they did not seek to defend. Rather, they attempted to get a functional awareness of what was causing members of either group to have negative attitudes.

The Engineering managers considered the post leveling session a gripe session. They say the union picked on picayune matters and really did not understand. So they, the anointed engineers, did a teaching job.

The reactions of Chemicals and Staples managers were that union members had made good points, clarified issues that had not been understood, and generally had given them a perspective which would reduce tension. They said, "We don't think the union was out to make trouble. We do think that they were sincerely trying to determine the extent to which we, members of management, are interested in how things look from a union point of view."

Paul Lee, assistant department head in Chemical Products, said, "It certainly is a lot better to hear these kinds of attitudes expressed directly to you by the union than by word of mouth through one manager talking to another."

How do the two sessions look from the standpoint of the union officers? I have talked with Dan and Max, and they were easily able to draw two main distinctions between the two sessions. These are in close parallel with the managerial findings as interpreted by personnel coordinators.

The union officers say, "We were unable to get through to the Engineers. They didn't hear us. All they wanted to do was to explain to us that they think we are a bunch of stupid troublemakers. The other departments' managers, on the other hand, listened. Because they wanted to hear, we were able to tell them things which were quite similar to what we wanted to communicate to the Engineering Department but couldn't. We feel that the session with Engineering may have worsened the situation.

"What are your next steps?" I queried.

Dan said, "Well, with the new leadership in the Engineering Department, it may be worthwhile to try again. I am not sure, but I think perhaps we will."

I said, "By the way, Dan, how do you react to the new moves that have been made in Engineering?"

"Well, Bob, I have a mixed reaction because I hate to see anybody pushed around. I think Earl has been pushed out because of the problems he's given us. I disagree with him heartily and despise the way he works, but every man has a right to operate as he sees fit. I pity him really. He got on the phone to me that night, drunk as a skunk and sobbing his heart out like a kid who'd lost his yo-yo. So that's why I feel bad about Earl's being moved."

He continued, "But this new setup could be exactly what Lakeside needs to solve some of the problems that have been gnawing at us for years in the Engineering Department. And you know who asked for that leveling session? That wasn't management's idea. That was my idea."

Constructive Bargaining and Destructive Ideas

Bargaining is now proceeding in a constructive atmosphere, with most members of management responding positively to the statesmanlike behavior of the union president and his fellow delegates. Dan's leadership has been outstanding.

During the past week, union and management have referred several technical contract issues to a subcommittee which will attempt to resolve them. The subcommittee is composed of equal numbers of management bargaining team members and union delegates. It would appear that the essential pre-conditions of mutual respect and understanding have been met. Management, in addition to addressing its own goals, is also giving a lot of scrutiny to the unique goals of the union.

Over the past two months my work has shifted in a rather dramatic manner. I am spending most of my time with management groups in functional departments, facilitating leveling activities. Chemical Products is now involved with organizational restructuring, personnel review, and reassignments.

I am also being invited to other EPOCH units. Recently, at a meeting of the Research and Engineering departments, Sid Stevens, a former division head at Lakeside who has returned after a brief absence, said, "If you study the history of Lakeside, it is clear that the organizational development activities were instigated by the problems of human relationships. The many improvements in resolving these problems indicate the effectiveness of the training." Perhaps his comment was premature because today, back in Lakeside's Engineering Department, a new maelstrom is swirling around regional supervisor Frank Evans.

A few days ago the IEW union made a side agreement with management that the dismantling and replacement of a large unit of process equipment would be accomplished by company employees working through two twelve-hour shifts. The agreement was reached in broad principle without going into the "legal-beagle" details of the two shifts, such as provisions for coffee breaks, wash-up time, transportation from the job to the cafeteria, and so on. These are routine arrangements that Dan did not think were important enough to consider. Part of the general arrangement was that the entire project (or "turnaround," as it's called here) would be manned by volunteers if a sufficient number made themselves available. This, indeed, was the case because enough people did volunteer.

Frank Evans was put in charge of the turnaround project, and after only two days, complaints began to reach Dan and other officers. They in turn requested a conference in the Engineering Department to discuss the courses of the complaints. It took place yesterday. On the union side of the table were Dan and the union's departmental representatives, and on the management side was Frank Evans. As the union aired its complaints, Frank got progressively madder. He accused the union of welshing and said he regarded their criticisms and complaints as nitpicking trivialities.

Once again the union characterized Frank as a lord and master, an absolute ruler. He made sweeping statements such as, "There'll be no wash-up time whatsoever for anyone." Furthermore, according to the union, Frank had sent his foremen into the cafeteria as prison guards, to "shake people out" and get them back to the job on time. "He'll be fitting leg-irons on us next!" one of the wage-earner delegates fumed. Supposedly, some of the foremen under Frank are as disgusted and disgruntled as the union members are.

This morning the union confronted management's bargaining team with the following stipulation. "The contract allows us to cancel any side agreement after twelve hours' prior notice. Do you want us to start timing? We're now prepared to apply the same rigid, arbitrary, mechanistic standards to you as Frank Evans is applying to our membership. Just watch it, or we'll cancel our side agreement and the turnaround will be stopped. We hereby give you notice."

Then the meeting broke up.

The management team quickly concluded that something had to be done, and in a hurry. Management was over a barrel, because stopping the turnaround would cost many profit dollars. Some adjustment of the situation, therefore, was urgently required. It was decided to invite Steve Jacobs, division head responsible for the turnaround, to meet with the bargaining committe. He did, and they filled him in regarding the quandary.

Steve's first comments were things like, "Oh, this doesn't mean anything. Dan has been after Frank Evans for a decade. Frank gets a little hot at times, but he cools down. He can give a straight answer that the union may not like, but that doesn't mean he's wrong."

He was asked, "Has Frank told you anything about yesterday's meeting?"

"Yes," Steve answered, "The union people were loud and disrespectful." Then he said, "Rather than discussing this in full committee I'd like to discuss it with the union officials." Before the rationale for this proposal could be explored, he added, "In fact, I'd like a chance to talk privately with Dan first."

The rationale for both requests seems to be identical. Steve's theory reads out as, "If I can handle this on a man-to-man basis without exposing myself to the actual complaints one by one, I can get Dan off my back. A private meeting would keep it in the family, and free me to do a little side bargaining."

Steve also proposed to invite "a couple of people like Van and Hal" to accompany him to a meeting with the union. These two, of course, are the present boss and a distinguished alumnus of the Engineering Department.

Carl and Wes were sitting there, but they were not mentioned. It is the same kind of strategy, "If we keep this thing private, then we don't expose ourselves to public examination, not to mention pressures to change."

This is an old Engineering strategy and Carl O'Brien immediately recognized it. He said, "Hold on, Steve, let's not forget that it's a Chemical Products installation that's being endangered by this squabble. Moreover, it's a personnel matter too. I would like to go to the meeting and have Wes along also. Then as the discussion gets moving, if it turns out that it's inappropriate for us to be there, we'll leave."

Van said, "Okay, let's go."

Since then I've not heard what actually occurred during the meeting, except that Dan concluded it by saying, "I've been making a strenuous effort to train my group to work as an effective team with your group. I think I've done a much better job in getting my outfit geared to collaboration than you've done."

This really hit management hard. Nonetheless, Hal came out of this meeting in essentially the same mood as he went in. His attitudes, evinced by some remarks he let drop, were: (1) The union has us over a barrel, so maybe we'll have to ride with this situation until we can get the upper hand again; and (2) Frank Evans is right.

For the record, it should be pointed out that Frank, in recent months and past years, has almost continuously been in conflict with the union. It was Frank who had the problem on the coffee breaks. It was Frank who started the struggle over Dan coming to a meeting without safety glasses. It was Frank who led the effort to have Quinn discipline Dan. It is also Frank who has threatened his own foremen that unless they carry out his edicts in detail he will put disciplinary warning letters in their files.

Farewell Party for Quinn

Last night at the Brass Horn, the union and management members of the bargaining committee had a farewell party for Quinn. A cocktail party was followed by dinner. The whole evening was a huge success. Members of management were thrilled with the results and so was the union. Almost eight months to the day after a period of intense warfare the two groups were sitting down, putting away their differences, and enjoying the social activity. If you had tried to tell anyone a year ago that the management bargaining team and the union officers would be partying together, your interlocutor would have said, "You have a hole in your head."

My Stay at Lakeside

The transfer of power always creates a problem with respect to commitments made by the prior regime. Some time ago I told Quinn that whatever service-contract commitments he had made on behalf of the organization with regard to me were viewed by me as commitments that ended with his tenure.

This morning, March 19, I had a chat with Travis Apley. He formally assumed the general managership of Lakeside from Quinn yesterday. He mentioned that he planned to continue the program of activities in organization development without alteration.

He said, "With respect to participation and communication and trying to get a condition in which individual, group, and organizational goals are one and the same, I can make a comparison between myself and Quinn. I think I am either more deeply committed to this way of life than Quinn was; or if not more deeply committed, at least more consistently so. In this context, the development of organizational functioning is confined only within the limits of coordinated human performance."

He told me that Van said last night, "Travis, I think it is important that you get into the wage bargaining situation to demonstrate your support of what we are trying to accomplish. You can be formal and invite the bargaining committee into your office, but it might be better for you to come into our usual meeting room, say a few words, be a part of things for awhile, and then leave."

Travis then commented, "I used to know Van back in the old, rough, tough, never-give-an-inch days. Way back then he was something else. But last night it was obvious that Van realized my problem and also the union's problem. His perception of the situation impressed me. Van told me, 'The *process* of what's going on is as important as the issues. We are working very hard to build a good, sound, basic relationship that can help us in problem solving in the future.'"

Then Travis spoke in a way which revealed to me the depth of his perceptiveness. "The sorry thing about that meeting was that Van didn't feel he had gotten through to me. He kept repeating the same point. I felt an impulse to say, 'Van, I understand what you're gettting at and I agree with it. This is the way I want to go, too.' But somehow I couldn't. Van must have felt that I had some shallow comprehension of what he was saying, but couldn't experience his direct concerns with the issues involved. That was unfortunate. But otherwise," Travis concluded, "things are moving in the right direction."

The impending transfer and promotion of Wes from Lakeside to EPOCH is connected with the departure of Quinn and the induction of Travis. Quinn remarked to me before he left, "I would like to make the announcement about Wes before my departure, but Travis prefers to have it withheld awhile. I don't understand, but it's his prerogative."

Today I gained clearer insight into the reason for this postponement. Travis wants to be the person who is clearly responsible for his replacement. If Wes had been transferred to EPOCH under the sponsorship of Quinn, with his replacement being announced by Quinn, then Wes' successor would feel personally indebted to Quinn, who is gone, not to Travis, who is present.

I learned today that the transfer and replacement will only be made when Travis has gotten his feet firmly planted on the Lakeside turf. This reveals excellent insight into the dynamics of loyalty and its cultivation. Travis wants to be known as the man who has a hand in things and who makes appointments according to his own concepts of what is right. By withholding the announcement until it would be clearly his own, he runs the risk of making an unpopular choice but gains an important advantage: making a valid decision in terms of his own selection criteria. These criteria usually are discernible in a top executive's selection of one particular candidate; they are signals by which the organization can learn what he regards to be important, valuable, and significant.

36

The End is a New Beginning

It is now late April, and I have just returned to Lakeside after a few weeks' absence. I have missed very little by being away. The contract bargaining recessed on April 9 because the discussions essentially involved a joint review of the union's proposal.

On many issues there was still deep disagreement, and many "MacArthurs" remained unresolved. Finally, on April 22, management gained headquarters' approval for a counterproposal which was to be presented to the union the next day.

At that meeting, management described the document and answered questions. It was a mature discussion in every sense of the word; no acrimony, emotions, or anything else to poison interpersonal relations. At the end of the day, the union requested two or more days to caucus.

They reconvened on April 28, and the session was said to have been the calmest which has yet taken place. The union asked for clarification of certain proposed clauses. Management agreed to return with these clarifications Friday morning.

Top Team Review

The Lakeside management committee and I assembled at Lincoln Lodge on April 30 for our first developmental effort under the regime of Travis Apley. Wes Stratton was absent because of a trip to EPOCH headquarters, and Hal Harvey was on vacation. Andy Stewart substituted for Hal; Brian Wallace stood in for Wes.

Since Travis was unacquainted with the structure-free format of these sessions, he immediately took his place at the head of the table, thereby assuming the role of procedural technician. Fortunately, rather than selling his viewpoints to the group, he participated in a constructive manner. He began, however, by announcing that Wes is leaving Lakeside almost immediately to become EPOCH's coordinator of labor relations.

I attach great significance to this appointment. Wes has been the most dedicated participant in behavioral science activities of anyone in the entire company. Furthermore, he has been both an applied practitioner in shaping events and an observer of results. He has witnessed the transformation of relationships from warfare collaboration. He is committed to bringing about a higher level of integration between organizational and personal objectives. His concerns encompass individual wage-earners, foremen and managers; each of whom he considers as potentially constructive members of the organization. In that sense, he can make a sharp appraisal of an unresponsive person such as Earl Higgins, without completely giving up on him. He is both fearless and experimental in his approach to problems, whether they involve labor-management or organization development.

Wes' replacement is George Jackson, former personnel chief at Mountainview, who was present at this Lincoln Lodge meeting. Wilson Jennings, the former head of the Technical Department, has also left Lakeside. His replacement is Con Irwin, previously a division head in the department. Con, incidentally, appears to be highly interested in moving Technical toward a much better problem-solving integration.

Then Travis confronted the group with the issues he foresaw arising from the representation election which is likely to occur within the next eight months. The election will be a crucial one. The international union is said to be gaining strength daily, and the IEW independent, in spite of its effective bargaining, is said to be losing strength daily. These appraisals are very difficult to evaluate, because many people are basing their opinion on anxiety rather than objectivity.

The discussion centered on the present state of union-management bargaining as one of the tests that might indicate future developments. This gave excellent opportunities for gauging conviction, direction, and changes in approach as they were needed at the present time. In a variety of ways, I asked the group if the present direction appeared to be sound and, if not, in what direction they thought it should be changed. They all agreed that union-management bargaining is in better shape than it has been in the past decade.

I then reminded them that last July there was a strong managerial opinion which said, "What we have to do is tighten up on the union officers and force them to treat us with proper respect. You can't possibly expect (so the argument went) these scoundrels to behave responsibly. So let's tell them to remember who's in charge here."

I pointed out that, following Green Acres, the opposite approach to the union had been taken. Rather than trying to make the union "responsible," management listened to the union, tried to understand its problems, and tried to communicate management's own problems, In spite of the red circle hassle, which was at least partly attributable to external factors and influences, a productive situation has been established. In a tentative way, at least, wasn't this some kind of proof of the approach that had been pursued?

"The only way that responsibility becomes genuine, it would appear, is when it is offered and earned. Only when management acted responsibly by treating the union with dignity and respect rather than forcing its own wishes on the union or playing politics with it, did the bargaining team earn a return of respect and continue collaborative negotiation.

"To discipline the union into acting subservient never succeeded here and has failed elsewhere. By according the union genuine dignity, respect and concern for its legitimate welfare, the very thing that management wanted, it got; namely, a union which treats management with dignity and respect, and which acts responsibly according to its own obligations."

This point was well taken. I think many members of Lakeside management, and a growing nucleus in EPOCH, now recognize that the key to union-management affairs is to arouse responsible and positively committed behavior in echelons of management which previously had acted as puppets.

This, then, seemed a singularly good moment to attack new problems of management which hitherto have been insoluble by traditional managerial techniques. I said, "In my observation of the organization, the Achilles heel of Lakeside is the foreman. While the foreman is in constant contact with wage people and therefore should communicate legitimate managerial concern, at Lakeside he hardly knows of upper management's current policy aims, not to mention the broader industrial relations picture."

The voice of long experience, Calvert Carroll's, was heard. "For twenty-five years we've been saying that the weak point is in the bottom rung of supervision, but we've never been able to solve the problem. Is there any reason to believe we can accomplish today what we've been unable to accomplish for twenty-five years?"

I responded by offering a summary of what I'd observed over the past two years. "There are few times when foremen are involved in managerial activity beyond the routine conduct of day-to-day affairs. One time is when management has rolled some spit balls and needs someone to throw them at the plant workers. Then management invites the foremen, puts the spit balls in their hands, and sends them out to pepper the wage people. As a result, foremen know damn well that they are tools rather than responsible agents of management."

So the question was revised again. It became, "Would it be possible to involve the foreman in problem solving, to become as integral to organization development as is anyone else?"

I thought it pertinent to describe the recent leveling session of a Chemical Products division at Lincoln Lodge, which unit supervisors and foremen attended. The division head, Tom Morgan, presented a package plan for reorganizing the division. The foremen blinked. Although they would be expected to implement operations in the rejiggered structure, they had not been involved in its reformation. Unit supervisors had been involved, but minimal-

The End is a New Beginning 349

ly. So a situation developed where Tom, with the well-intentioned but message-scrambling support of his unit supervisors, kept explaining to the foremen why the revamped organizational structure would work. The foremen, in very subtle and indirect ways, were reacting point by point, demonstrating why it would *not* work.

At this juncture, I had proposed that the foremen leave and debate among themselves their reactions to the proposed restructuring. Simultaneously the unit supervisors would meet in another room to explore their own reactions. As each group set off to do this, I cornered Tom and suggested that neither of us should participate in the subgroups.

Later, the foreman and supervisor groups rejoined us in general session, all fired up to present their respective findings. The results were astounding. The foremen had been able to spot and define in detail all kinds of artificiality and infirmities in the reorganizational plan. The unit supervisors began to express concerns which had never previously been verbalized, at least in Tom's presence.

Then Tom Morgan took a critical next step. A committee composed of two foremen and two unit supervisors was formed to explore with all division members what would be the ideal organizational structure. For the first time ever, foremen were being involved in integrating planning and doing. The rest of that divisional leveling session was characterized by high involvement and participation.

Travis and the others picked up from here to debate "What caused the foremen and unit supervisors to participate in this mature and responsible manner?" They discovered that the leveling sessions created an open and secure attitude among the foremen which allowed them to speak up and take responsibility for their opinions. The foremen had decided to overcome their weakness by uniting and speaking with a single voice.

By extension, therefore, it was adopted as a working hypothesis that similar results were possible if foremen throughout Lakeside were given similar opportunities. The management committee has begun plans to increase the number of leveling sessions to accomplish this.

Today, May 3, a new series of Lincoln Lodge conferences is now on the drawing boards. "Lincoln Lodge leveling" bids to become as well known at Lakeside for improving organizational effectiveness as is the Green Acres type of conference for bringing about the first stages of managerial integration.

After the management committee's Lincoln Lodge session, I stayed and matched drink-for-drink with Van Gray. During the evening, Van turned to the topic of Earl, and provided me with a significant insight. He said, "Earl is sorry that he participated in those earlier leveling conferences we had, because he believes they caused his downfall."

"Is that how you'd see it, Van?"

"I didn't comment at the time, I wanted to think it over. In a way, he seemed to have a point, people do evaluate one another at these sessions; his opinions were against the grain of most everyone else's; and if he'd kept his mouth shut, perhaps he wouldn't have been banished to supply and distribution's back office. Besides, I've always respected Earl for what he's accomplished. Did you know he started here as a messenger boy and put himself through engineering school?"

I nodded. Van went on, "Besides, he was expressing a lot of what I felt. Since then, particularly after these Frank Evans cut-ups, not to mention a few good tackles from Dan, yourself, and others, I've changed my viewpoint a bit. And for better or worse, I'm still in the same job."

He was looking very troubled as he put down his drink. "Look, Bob, I can't go on staring at a hypocrite in the mirror. Tomorrow morning I'm calling Frank Evans on the carpet for his handling of that turnaround business. One part of my head is full of good ideas about how he ought to change his approach. The other part knows that in my time I've pulled some good ones too. As an engineer, Frank ranks with the best; I wouldn't want to transfer him out of construction, even though the Earl business has set a precedent for that. But that's not a good precedent in my opinion, and I don't want to use it. In fact, I'd like to turn it around someday and bring Earl back on board. I'd like to have him back here with a new set of constructive attitudes. Maybe Randy can work some magic on him over there. Tomorrow, I've got a job to do on Frank Evans. Yet I already feel defeated. Sure, he'll take what I have to say, bow his head and promise to do better in the future. But how can anything I say, really, help him to turn himself around completely? If he could, he'd do better in his career, and everything around him would go a lot better, but he's got to *see* it first, somehow, and so has Earl."

Among its other outcomes, the latest Lincoln Lodge conference has produced a commitment that each component of the organization will step up its human relations effort over the next three months.

Andy Stewart, the new assistant department head of Engineering, was given a clear edict by Quinn that it was his career-critical responsibility to shape up the department. Travis is briefed and ready to hold him to it. Andy is confronted with a demoralized group of managerial reactionaries and with an incumbent chief who is an ailing shadow of his former self. Yet Andy is obligated to bring about change. On Thursday morning there is to be a meeting of the Engineering Department at the community center to set the broad strategy lines for organization development.

One question that needs to be faced, and it will surprise me if they can, is "How can a department develop its effectiveness when its top man is barely able to function, and, in addition, is so negative that he can't see the broad sweep of things?" It's a question that many are revolving in their minds but are wary of posing in open meeting. In such circumstances, surely the kindest thing to do both for Hal's and the department's future well-being would be for Travis and Van to have a heart-to-heart talk with him in the next day or so, and get him to consider passing the reins to Andy and taking retirement.

Exit

I spent the entire morning of May 3rd with Chet Jameson, who has come from EPOCH headquarters on a fact-finding mission for Allen O'Dell, the vice president of manufacturing. Allen apparently wants to check Lakeside out before assenting to the provisions of the new labor contract.

Chet said it would be helpful from his standpoint to get a background picture from my perspective. I began by describing the situation I'd entered about two years ago when management had conducted a "warfare training program" in which the goal had been to oust the incumbent IEW officers. These same officers are now regarded as statesmen. I reviewed our Green Acres series of conferences and emphasized the new consensus that had been achieved there, namely that "The best way to resolve our difficulties with the union is to treat the union officers with dignity and respect."

Then I briefly described last year's bargaining sequence which began in January when management's effort to start was rebuffed by the newly re-elected union officers, who were determined to prepare a proposal according to their own wishes and to use that as the bargaining document. I then skipped to last July and the union's presentation of its own proposal to management. I told him about the August "orbit session' when the members of management's bargaining team were almost unanimously determined to throw the union proposal back in the delegates' faces. I pointed out the extremely tense and momentous discussions that followed this session in which I'd intervened.

Despite the "orbit session," bargaining got off to a promising start from the beginning of August with a shift from the previous "fight" orientation to a problem-solving orientation. This new basis of collaboration suffered a fracture when win-lose provocation came from headquarters wrapped in the guise of a general wage increase. Management took a fight posture on the red circle rate, and the union responded in kind. Much of what had been accomplished earlier abraded away during the fall and winter. Finally, management "lost," by having to settle on the principle which the union maintained all along. Since then, a slow return to bargaining in a mutually respectful and collaborative climate has been achieved.

My final point was that although the union had never accepted our invitation to join in the leveling conferences and other development activities, it had made remarkable progress in knitting itself together as a valued service organization for its members. Dan Ives, in particular, has kept an eye on management as it experimented with what last year were novel approaches.

He has grasped the general outlines of leadership and promotes constructive collaboration.

Chet, who had been silent up to now, said, "This is the very first time I've had any conception of what has been going on in Lakeside over the past two years. If one-half of what you say is true, it's unbelievable. I am dumbfounded and embarrassed that such important efforts could be under way for so long and yet Allen, Neal, Larry, and the rest of us really have known nothing about it."

Later this morning I saw Wes. I said, "I was astounded by Chet's remarks."

"Don't tell me, I know what you're referring to. He was in to see me just now, claiming that if what you say is true, a miracle has been wrought. I said, 'Chet, I've tried to tell you this at least a half dozen times. I know Quinn's told the EPOCH people about the changes here, too. We tried to get it across when Jim Hall and the rest were here for the Headquarters Report conferences. Apparently, you EPOCH people's biases and preconceptions prevented you from hearing us until you spoke with Blake today.' "

Chet said, according to Wes, "From our standpoint, when we received your draft counterproposal to the union and saw the many liberalizations contained in it, we could only ask ourselves 'What's wrong with these people at Lakeside? Why are they giving in like this?' We didn't know that Dan was no longer a dedicated organizer for the international. All the evidence indicated that you were acting foolishly. Now everything is understandable. I'm very worried about the way communication and rapport between EPOCH and the field seems to have broken down, that is, if it's ever existed since the reorganization. All through this we could have been helping, had we understood you. But instead, we've been reacting with shock and horror to an approach which was incomprehensible to us."

Since our interview, and over the past few days, Chet has talked intensively with fifteen or twenty people and casually with perhaps a hundred and twenty-five. Apparently he found detailed confirmation of what I had said. He met with the wage and salary unions, interviewed department and division heads, foremen and workers, and so on.

His findings, which he reported to the management committee before returning to Atlanta, were numerous. First, he found there had been dramatic changes in attitudes and personal approaches within the organization, including better working relationships, better interdivisional and interdepartmental collaboration, better attitudes toward the union, better attitudes between supervisors and subordinates. Everything is better. Nothing is worse.

He said, "In my conferences, no one has said to me, 'It's not like the good old days.' Rather, they got to talking about the many aspects of progress they were seeing, feeling, and participating in."

He also said that he had found some bitterly hostile attitudes toward headquarters. In spite of what people here seem to think, EPOCH *is* genuinely interested in maintaining and strengthening an independent union. Nonetheless, he saw the deep-seated mutual problems of communication and respect between Atlanta and Lakeside, and he thought that these would have to be corrected in the near future. I agree.

However, my strong impression is that EPOCH headquarters still does not realize the ways it needs to change if it is to improve in supervising and supporting the field. I do think that the obligation to change rests primarily upon the EPOCH group and only to a minor degree upon Lakeside management.

Chet's final point dealt with the new concepts' depths of penetration into the organization. The farther down the hierarchy he went, the less awareness and understanding he had found regarding the intentions and efforts of the organization and the union-management bargaining committee. This diagnosis comes as no surprise. The most recent Lincoln Lodge meeting addressed itself to this very point.

Up to now, both in EPOCH headquarters and in the organizational formats of its far-flung plants, the worlds of "production" men, such as Allen, Chet, Neal and Van; and of the "people" men, such as Larry Jones and Wes, have usually been separate. Now that Lakeside has become a demonstration project, I think the situation is well prepared for Wes as the new labor-relations coordinator of EPOCH to really start planning with Chet and others for critical next steps that are needed if longer-term, wider organizational improvement is to be brought about.

Union Results

Last Friday, May 21, under government supervision, the votes were counted for the second-time-around union election. The result proves once and for all which group the wage men of Lakeside want to represent them.

All incumbent IEW officers, Dan, Dick, Max and the rest, were returned to office. The number of votes cast was 657. Dan Ives had the largest plurality of 56%, followed by others, some of whom just squeaked in.

I have learned, informally, that the union is shooting for the date of July 1 to have a contract signed, sealed, and delivered. IEW officers feel their best defense against the international will be a strong contract bargained in good faith, demonstrating that Lakeside's union is fully capable of dealing productively with the present management.

Dan said, before election day, "I think we'll win because we've done a good job but if you want a landslide vote in our favor, let management put its mitts in, *not* on our side, but to help Sol Sommers. All I ask is, don't support us."

He was indicating, of course, that management intervention in strictly union matters is a "kiss of death." The best way to ensure that some union officer you want elected will be defeated is to support him, that is, if you're a manager.

I can't be sure that it's valid to generalize from the momentary Lakeside situation to a broader issue. But it does seem to turn out rather consistently that when the United States is on a "managerial" kick and intervenes in the Caribbean, South America, and elsewhere, in favor of one political candidate or another, its favorite is seldom if ever helped.

At Lakeside, the "manifest destiny" doctrine under which the legitimate managers of one organizational community thought they were entitled to tinker in the affairs of a *different* organization, has demonstrated its consequences and is being replaced by a different world view. I suppose the tentative conclusion in both cases might be that symbiosis by no means necessarily implies satellite status for the smaller member. Rather, a relationship in which mutual problems can be solved to the satisfaction of both parties seems to require, as a *sine qua non,* an ethic under which both organisms respect each other's autonomy and internal sovereignty. Hopefully, in the future, our Lakeside findings will have wider significance.

Afterword

Some time has passed since this undertaking suggested OD as a way for people and organizations to handle their affairs in a more intelligent way. Reading it in the perspective of changes since it took place, the basic approach that was applied at the time was sound and constructive. Yet much has been learned that has resulted in new and innovative advancements in OD. OD carried out by these more recently emerging strategies has been shown to have greater impact than was achieved in this initial project.

In comparison with *then* we now see the following as imperative.
1. As a foundation for change, all who manage and work within the same organization must gain deeper and more systematic insight into behavioral science concepts themselves before trying to apply them.
2. Once learned, these theories and concepts are brought into everyday use through a series of steps of planned change.
3. Primary reliance for intervention is placed on written learning and change instruments, with secondary reliance on man-based consultation.

These three modifications enable managers to convert concepts of sound behavior into valid human practices more effectively than was possible in the beginning.

Soc
HD
8072
B53